Shadowplay

Shadowplay

THE HIDDEN BELIEFS AND CODED POLITICS
OF WILLIAM SHAKESPEARE

Clare Asquith

PublicAffairs
NEW YORK

BOOK DESIGN AND COMPOSITION BY JENNY DOSSIN. TEXT SET IN JANSON TEXT.

Library of Congress-Cataloging-in Publication Data
Asquith, Clare.
Shadowplay : the hidden beliefs and coded politics of William Shakespeare / Clare Asquith.
—1st ed.
p. cm.
Includes bibliographical references (p.) and index.
ISBN 1-58648-316-1
1. Shakespeare, William, 1564–1616—Political and social views. 2. Politics and literature—Great Britain—History—16th century. 3. Literature and history—Great Britain—History—16th century. 4. Christianity and literature—England—History—16th century. 5. Shakespeare, William, 1564–1616—Knowledge—History. 6. Historical drama, English—History and criticism. 7. Political plays, English—History and criticism. 8. Catholics—England—History—16th century. 9. Shakespeare, William, 1564–1616—Religion. 10. Catholics—England—Intellectual Life. I. Title.
PR3017.A75 2005
822.3'3—dc22   2005043160

FIRST EDITION
10 9 8 7 6 5 4 3 2 1

CONTENTS

TO

ANNE OXFORD

Solver of puzzles

Lover of Shakespeare

As an unperfect actor on the stage,
Who with his fear is put besides his part,
Or some fierce thing replete with too much rage,
Whose strength's abundance weakens his own heart;
So I for fear of trust forget to say
The perfect ceremony of love's right [rite],
And in mine own love's strength seem to decay,
O'ercharged with burden of mine own love's might:
O let my books be then the eloquence,
And dumb presagers of my speaking breast,
Who plead for love, and look for recompense,
More than that love which [M]ore hath more expressed.
O learn to read what silent love hath writ,
To hear with eyes belongs to love's fine wit.

WILLIAM SHAKESPEARE, Sonnet 23

ACKNOWLEDGMENTS

Shadowplay owes its existence to four people: Robert Gray, whose eloquent arguments against Shakespeare's Catholicism ended with a proposal that I write a book supporting it, and whose passionate engagement in the subject has been a stimulus ever since; the inspirational Richard Cohen, who turned the idea of a book into reality; my agent Kathy Robbins, whose steady hand guided the whole project from concept to final publication; and Clive Priddle, the book's clear-sighted and level-headed editor. Essential, too, has been the influence and consistent support of Peter Osnos and PublicAffairs. Crucial to my research has been the generosity of a wide range of scholars, chief among them John Finnis, Gerard Kilroy and Michael Questier, while others who have provided invaluable scholarly help include Michael Alexander, Aidan Bellenger, James Carley, Peter Donaldson, Lukas Erne, Penny McCarthy, Thomas Merriam, Peter Milward, Daniel Rees and Geoffrey Scott. I owe a great deal to the encouragement and practical assistance of Simon Fordham, Philip Jebb, Alan Jenkins, Tony Jennings, Nicholas King, John Mahon, Thomas McCoog, Julian Oxford, Francis Petre, Piers Paul Read, William Rees-Mogg, Therese Sidmouth, Philip Stevens, Michael Suarez and Dennis Taylor. Kind advice has been given by a number of experts, including Juliet Dusinberre, Susan Hitch, Henry Hobhouse, Ernst Honigmann, Margaret Jones-Davis, Francis Edwards, Patrick Kelly, Joseph Kerman, Neil MacGregor, Robert McFall, and Alison Shell; and I am very grateful for the expertise and patience of librarians and archivists at the Bodleian Library, the Devon Record Office, the British Library, Downside Abbey Library, the Guildhall Library, Lambeth Palace Library, Oxford County Library, and lastly my local library in Frome, Somerset, who supplied me with otherwise unobtainable material from university libraries around the country. I owe a particular debt to the eagle eye and excellent advice of those who made time to read the book in manuscript and correct its errors, including John Waterfield, Kate Rizzo, Ernst Honigmann, John Finnis and Michael Alexander. I was lucky to have Michele Wynn as an outstanding copy-editor. Finally, I must thank my family for their help and endless patience, and in particular my husband Raymond, whose acumen and classical knowledge have been of crucial importance to the writing of this book.

INTRODUCTION

M Y INTEREST in the coded writing of William Shakespeare's era began in the winter of 1983, towards the end of the Cold War, when I found myself in a shabby theatre in a crumbling, stuccoed building near the centre of Moscow, watching a dramatisation of Chekhov's short stories. The venue was a long room with a podium at one end. It was packed. A group of KGB operatives hung about the door; our two minders slipped into the back row. It was immediately obvious that my husband and I were the only Westerners in the audience.

At first the performance seemed blandly innocuous, an unadventurous subject typical of Soviet theatre. But before long we noticed that the actors were slipping in occasional allusions that gave a risky contemporary angle to the otherwise familiar stories. The hints were too fleeting to alert the watchers in the doorway, but they were enough for an educated audience to realise that the hidden setting was not nineteenth-century tsarism; it was twentieth-century communism. At one point my husband was hauled onto the stage and hustled into the walk-on role of a banker. To the audience's appreciative laughter, he was linked not simply with '*dengi*', which means money, but with '*valuta*'—foreign currency. The KGB men smiled at what they took to be a standard dig at Western capitalism. But they missed the covert meaning. Those following the story would have known that Chekhov's banker was a benefactor and that the scene carried the prophetic message that Russia's only hope lay in openness to the West. It was my first experience of the subtleties of political drama under a repressive regime.

There were two striking similarities between Shakespeare's work and the performance I had witnessed in the Moscow theatre. Both omitted any mention of contemporary politics, and both avoided original plots, dramatising instead classic stories likely to pass the scrutiny of the government censor. I began to wonder if there was a third similarity: a series of puns, hints and allusions linking the 'safe' narrative to the forbidden subject of current events. Ever since his death, Shakespeare's universal plays have been adapted to a wide spectrum of topical and political messages: it could be that the one message we had overlooked was his own.

As the wife of a British diplomat in Moscow during the Cold War, I became fascinated by the artful double language and hidden identities used in Russian dissident writing. At the same time, I was reading the works of historians who emphasise the repressive aspect of late Tudor England and highlight the forgotten extent of the country's resistance to the Protestant reformation. I read slowly through Shakespeare's works, alert, as a Soviet audience might have been, for obliquely topical indications of political doublespeak. After returning to England, I read the works of his contemporaries and predecessors and explored the little-known writings of Elizabethan and Jacobean exiles, preserved in the nearby library of the Benedictine abbey at Downside in Somerset. The trail led further: to the British Library, the Bodleian, the Jesuit library at Farm Street; to Lambeth Palace, the Guildhall, Southwark Cathedral, to the conferences and papers of Reformation scholars. Finally, I returned to Shakespeare and I became convinced. This book is the result.

————

Its starting point is an account of the history of Shakespeare's times, based not on the traditional version of England's past but on the work of a new generation of Reformation scholars who paint a picture of widespread resistance, surveillance, coercion and persecution in sixteenth-century England. It goes on to trace the growth of a coded, dissident language in the repressive years following the Reformation, years of censorship and propaganda during which the subjects of religion and politics were forbidden to dramatists. And it reveals that Shakespeare developed this hidden code into a sophisticated art form, integrating it into his more familiar work with dazzling skill.

The essence of this coded method of writing, of course, was that it be 'deniable'—in other words, incapable of proof. Only a detailed demonstration of the strikingly precise parallels between the momentous events of the sixteenth century and the references concealed in the censored literature of the time will persuade modern Shakespeare lovers, accustomed to centuries of resolutely universalist readings of his work, that there is now a case for re-examining his writing in the light of its revised historical context. For many, this will come as a shock. Unlike the great classical authors, Shakespeare is usually seen as a writer so outstanding that the politics of his time are irrelevant, even distracting. But increasingly, historians and literature scholars are unearthing conscious echoes of the times in the literature of the day, echoes so subtle and allusive that they amount to a hidden language.

Once accepted, the new history and the forgotten code, outlined in Part 1, provide the tools for the reader to investigate one of the most anguished periods of England's history, seen through the eyes of the country's greatest creative genius. This approach demonstrates that Shakespeare was a man passionately involved in the upheavals of his day, increasingly concerned that the truth about what was happening to his country would never be recorded. Instead of diminishing Shakespeare's work, awareness of the shadowed language deepens it, adding a cutting edge of contemporary reference to the famously universal plays and giving them an often acutely poignant hidden context. The pleasure of experiencing his work on this dual level can be compared to the discovery of a hidden optical illusion that gives a new perspective to a familiar masterpiece. Once the standpoint for 'seeing' the hidden dimension is found, readers and spectators can explore for themselves the full range of Shakespeare's topical insight and ceaseless, in places obsessive, cryptic ingenuity.

Among the revelations thrown up by this approach to Shakespeare's work is the significance of his obscurities, digressions and 'problem' plays. It emerges that these are the areas where the hidden language is at its most intense; often, where Shakespeare has the most difficulty containing the urgency of his covert message. The same is true of characters who act incongruously or indulge in irrelevant flights of fancy: the reason can be found in the allegorical demands of their secondary, hidden role.

Another revelation is the extent to which Shakespeare, a court dramatist, had specific audiences in mind and demonstrated extraordinary psychological insight in his approach to his various patrons. Three plays appeal personally to Queen Elizabeth; four to King James; and three of his last plays to James's young heir, Prince Henry. The hidden level of the 'Roman' plays is directed primarily at England's Catholic subjects. Apart from one painful period of enforced conformity, the concealed narrative reveals that Shakespeare pursued his own spiritual and political objectives with unwavering determination, protected and supported by powerful members of the aristocracy. Finally, the forgotten history of the times, highlighted in his own subtext, answers a number of the puzzles about Shakespeare's education and upbringing that have led many to propose that someone else wrote the plays.

The Glossary at the end of the book illustrates the way Shakespeare and his contemporaries used apparently innocuous words and phrases to develop their common dissident language.

Authority for the prevalence of coded writing among Shakespeare's contemporaries comes from Christian humanist writers of the time, for whom civilised literature was coded by its very nature, and from the many allusions by Elizabethan poets and dramatists to the way they exploited this allegorical tradition in order to dodge political censorship. But the real key to the code lies in the rediscovery of the 'forgotten' history of early modern England. So precise are the parallels between this suppressed history and the covert literature of the day that in many cases it is now impossible to miss them: Curtis Breight is one historian who uses Shakespeare's 'hidden' plays to illustrate his thesis.[1]

This book relies heavily on the long tradition of specialists in the 'recusant' history of English Catholicism, who over the centuries have preserved, transcribed and published the little-known works of Catholic exiles and dissidents: they include J. H. Pollen, Philip Caraman, David Rogers, Thomas McCoog, Gerard Kilroy. The importance of their work has become more widely recognised as mainstream historians, working on a new range of neglected sources, have begun to question the traditional 'Whig' version of the English Reformation. The first was the authoritative John Lingard, whose twelve-volume *History of England* was published in the early nineteenth century. Later scholars include Jack Scarisbrick, Christopher Haigh, John Bossy, Michael Questier, Edwin Jones, Pierre Janelle, Patrick Collinson, Eamon Duffy and Diarmaid MacCulloch; there has been further research by popular historians of the period, among them Antonia Fraser, John Carey and Charles Nicholl. A new school of Shakespearean biographers has begun to present ordinary readers with the full story of Shakespeare's Catholic background: Park Honan's lead in 1998 was followed by Anthony Holden, Michael Wood, and Stephen Greenblatt.

But the full implications of this new history have made little impact on the study of the literature of the period. The many specialists in sixteenth-century literature who have uncovered seams of suggestive dissident reference remain cautious about what their findings mean. As Shakespeare's work in particular has never 'fitted' the traditional history of the times, there has always been an implicit veto on setting his plays and poems in a political or religious context: most attempts to do so have resulted in unsustainable, often ludicrous, theories. Set against the background of the revised history, however, his works and those of his contemporaries begin to take on a significant new dimension, highlighted by a few unusually bold scholars, among them Richard Wilson and Peter Milward. Milward, an acknowledged expert on Shakespeare's religious context, has been for many years a lone voice, claiming that Shakespeare consistently used allegory to communicate with an oppressed and persecuted England. The exact nature of that coded allegory is gradually emerging through the work of more guarded scholars, among them Alison Shell, Velma Richmond, Gary Hamilton, Lucas Erne, John Klause, Richard Dutton and Gary Taylor.

This book builds on their findings and those of recent historians in order to reclaim Shakespeare for his febrile, revolutionary times. We now know that England's most brilliant writer lived and worked during the country's most turbulent era. It is impossible to believe he had nothing to say about the drama of his day. In fact, it infuses everything he wrote: England's crisis was Shakespeare's passion.

I

BACKGROUND:

THE ENDING OF THE OLD ORDER

I

THE SILENCE OF JOHN NOBODY

In Act Thy Bed-Vow Broke[1]

O N 15 NOVEMBER 1539, a procession wound its way up Glastonbury Tor, a steep conical hill overlooking the peatlands of Somerset in the south-west of England. The journey over the windy
ridges was arduous, for the crowd struggled to drag with them three men
tied to sledge-like wooden frames. On the top of the hill stood a newly
constructed gallows; near it was a fire, knives and a cauldron.

Though some of the spectators may have been jeering, many would
have been aghast, not only at the barbarity but at the sacrilege of what
they were witnessing. Glastonbury was the most ancient and sacred Christian site in Britain. Long ago, when it was still surrounded by sea, it was
called Yniswitren, the Island of Glass, where Joseph of Arimathea and his
eleven companions were believed to have arrived by boat from the Holy
Land, bearing with them the Holy Grail containing the blood of Christ.
On top of the island they built a small church of willow reeds in honour of
the Virgin, a church that would be preserved for centuries. In time the
place became known as Avalon, the Isle of Apples, where King Arthur was
said to be buried with Guinevere sixteen feet deep under a great stone
slab. The first missionaries from Rome came to Glastonbury, repaired the
church and settled there; St Patrick, returning from Ireland, became their
abbot and was buried under the church. The learned St Dunstan established a great Benedictine monastery around the Tor, and until the Reformation, the ancient Celtic site remained one of England's greatest centres
of pilgrimage—the burial place of saints and a direct, mysterious link with
Christ himself.

The old man standing under the shadow of the gallows in 1539 taking his final look at the wide stretch of Glastonbury lands spread out below him was Richard Whiting, the monastery's last abbot, a humanist scholar and respected administrator, condemned to death on the orders of a government determined to appropriate the wealth of the great abbey. Along with his two fellow monks he uttered a final prayer, asking forgiveness of God and his captors; the cart beneath him jerked and for a moment he dangled from the gallows. Then he was cut down, his chest sliced open, his bowels removed and tossed into the cauldron, and his heart, still beating, torn out and held aloft by the hangman who proclaimed it 'the heart of a traitor'. Finally, his body was dismembered and boiled, the head fastened up over the gate of the deserted abbey and the quartered limbs exposed in the cities of Wells, Bath, Ilchester and Bridgewater, a terrible warning to the West Country of the price of resistance to the King's new regime. Meanwhile, the monastery went the way of all the other religious houses in England. The monks were evicted, their possessions auctioned, their lands, treasures and buildings seized by the Crown, which sold them off to the highest bidder. The abbey itself was dismantled and used for building stone.

No laments survive for the passing of the abbot and his monastery or for the destruction of Avalon, the spiritual heart of England. Yet the assault on shrines like Glastonbury were acts of cultural vandalism as shocking and irrevocable as any in human history. Searching for suitable words, the usually restrained historian David Knowles ends his account of the destruction of Glastonbury by quoting Shakespeare's description of the death of Duncan in *Macbeth*. 'Sacrilegious murder' has broken open 'the Lord's anointed temple' and stolen thence 'the life of the building'.[2]

For centuries, English children have been taught that their country gained from the Reformation, that sixteenth-century England watched with indifference as the vast and intricate fabric of late medieval Christianity was gradually dismantled by a powerful group of politicians and religious reformers. People were released from an age of superstition to one of enlightenment; the transfer of wealth created an industrious middle class, energised by a new sense of national pride. The Protestant Reformation, according to generations of Protestant historians, was welcomed by the English.

But this rendition of history overlooks one all-important fact: England was not a free society. The precarious Tudor regime made sophisticated use of propaganda and exercised tight control over the country's small number of licensed printing presses. We read only what they wanted us to read—histories that reflect the vested interest of the new property owners in the official version of the Reformation. Henry VIII's chief minister, Thomas Cromwell, was 'the first man in England who consciously worked as a minister of propaganda';[3] his was a regime that 'manufactured history on an unprecedented scale'.[4] A contemporary ballad survives lamenting 'little John Nobody, that durst not speak'—the silenced voice of the Catholic opposition.[5]

Since the mid-twentieth century, however, things have changed. England's Protestant identity has been called into question, and historians have begun to take an interest in John Nobody's forgotten story. Recent 'revisionist' historians, among them John Bossy, Eamon Duffy, Jack Scarisbrick, Edwin Jones and Christopher Haigh, have resurrected evidence neglected since the sixteenth century: churchwardens' accounts, local wills, family histories, private manuscripts, the writings of exiled dissidents and foreign diplomats; and they have looked again at the pioneering research of the nineteenth-century historian John Lingard. As this testimony has been painstakingly pieced together, the full extent of the Tudor government's propaganda drive has been revealed; it now emerges that the repression of John Nobody was crucial to its survival.

The first surprise is the size of the Catholic opposition to the new Protestant order. It was in a majority right up to the end of the sixteenth century. A powerful group, it was easily capable of removing the regime that oppressed it. Yet there was no organised opposition: most religious dissidents chose the path of passive resistance. Even at the time, the extent of John Nobody's silence was puzzling. Edward de Vere, Earl of Oxford, himself an uncertain and vacillating Catholic, observed caustically that instead of saving their heads by rebellion, Catholics chose to wear 'Ave Maria cockscombs'—the haloes of martyrdom. Elizabeth I was repeatedly warned about her 'strong, factious' Catholic subjects.[6] All over the country, Protestants fretted constantly about the hidden Catholic threat. Very few at the time made the mistake of assuming that John Nobody's silence denoted consent.

The story of his quiet surrender begins in 1533, the year in which Henry VIII divorced his dull, popular wife, Catherine of Aragon, to marry Anne Boleyn. Henry's motive was simple. He needed a male heir and was prepared to defy the Pope in order to get one. As a good Catholic, the King had done his best to make his case to Rome, but he had failed: the Pope refused to permit the divorce.

Instantly, the King found himself surrounded by members of his new wife's entourage, urging him to widen the breach with the papacy. Anne Boleyn and her circle were followers of Martin Luther, the first great Protestant reformer, a German ex-monk who portrayed the Pope as Antichrist and the Catholic Church as a monstrously bloated edifice, a barrier to true religion. A country's beliefs, according to Luther, should be decided by its prince, not by the Pope. To the Lutherans gathering at the English court, Henry's quarrel with Rome was a gift: it offered them the chance of winning England over to the new religion. And to Henry, the Lutheran arguments were a godsend. He could end the long-running wrangle with the Pope by taking over the English church himself. There was a further bonus. For some time now, he had been enviously eyeing the vast wealth of England's religious houses. 'Would to God they were all dissolved', Luther had said, denouncing such institutions as hopelessly corrupt. Henry could not wait. Royal commissioners were dispatched to investigate the state of the country's monasteries; and he himself was proclaimed Supreme Head of the Church in England. England was cut loose from Western Christendom, having played a leading role in it for centuries.

The reformers moved in with a speed and thoroughness that occasionally alarmed the King, who had recommended acting in 'secrete silence'. In 1538, the cult of saints was abolished, along with their feast days and holidays. Pilgrimages were banned and shrines wrecked. The statue of Our Lady of Walsingham was carted to Chelsea and publicly burned; Canterbury, one of the greatest European centres of pilgrimage, was ransacked, its treasures seized by the Crown. Henry's supporters rushed out books, sermons and plays that stressed a new theology of obedience, identifying God's will with submission to the King. New laws passed by Parliament required subjects to consent on oath to the Royal Supremacy. According to the terms of the oath, the monarch was Supreme Head of the English Church, the Pope merely a foreign bishop with no authority within the realm. To swear to such terms was impossible to a Catholic. Yet to refuse it was to deny the King—in other words, to commit treason. Over the next seventy-five years, this key device for enforcing loyalty was repeatedly portrayed by Catholics as the wedge that divided the country's soul from its body.[7] When the Lord Chancellor, England's most senior legal authority, Sir Thomas More, refused the oath in 1534, Henry had him executed, to international outrage—More was famous among humanist scholars for his wit, learning and personal holiness. Within five years, 9,000 men and women had been turned out of the country's monasteries and pensioned off, while their buildings, tenancies, common lands, schools, hospitals, almshouses and libraries were dismantled and privatised. Tracts and woodcuts poured from the presses, portraying the monks as idle, ignorant and corrupt. Gradually it was forgotten that places like Glastonbury and Evesham had been enlightened centres of scholarship, fostering literate lay students and university scholars enthusiastic for the new learning of Catholic reformers such as Desiderius Erasmus, the great Dutch theologian and close friend of More.

This sudden development was so unexpected that it was widely believed the King had been bewitched by his new Queen. A few years earlier, Henry had been in the forefront of the international condemnation of Luther, earning the title 'Defender of the Faith' from a grateful papacy for his learned theological work denouncing Luther's teachings. Moreover, though parts of Europe had been quick to attack the Catholic clergy and embrace Protestantism, England had not. There were many who recognised the need for change, in particular the need for an English translation of the Bible. Its provision, scandalously opposed by the clergy, was one of the major attractions of the new religion. But the University of Oxford had provided a beacon for the international humanist movement for reform within the church, not outside it. On a humbler level, parish records indicate a people deeply and contentedly committed to their own flourishing brand of Catholicism. On the eve of the Reformation in England, the time-honoured certainties and beauties of English Catholicism still penetrated every aspect of ordinary life. Distances were judged by the length of time it took to say familiar prayers, time was measured by feast days, and seasons were marked by great communal events like the Corpus Christi plays or the liturgical drama of Holy Week. As one historian, Diarmaid MacCulloch, puts it, the old liturgy was 'not only good for the soul, it was fun':[8] he quotes the 'cosmic hooliganism' contained in religious drama and sees the apparent irreverence as the ebullient reaction of a people comfortable with their system of belief.

At the heart of the life of every parish lay the essential Catholic doctrine of the Mass, which transported the Christian into the presence of the divine sacrifice. The 'Real Presence' of God was the object of profound devotion: the bread, or 'host', consecrated by the priest, hung richly ornamented above the altar in every church, representing the spiritual core of England before the Reformation. Merely to set eyes on the host at the moment of consecration was a channel of grace, the reason Catholics were often dubbed 'gazers' by Protestants. To Protestants, devotion to the saints and the Virgin distracted from the relationship between God and the soul—but well into the 1530s, parishes continued to produce a wealth of devotional imagery in stone, alabaster, and glass, accompanied by verbal equivalents in drama, poetry and song, all of which gave vigorous expression to England's spirituality.

Especially precious to Catholics was the concept of the 'communion of saints'—the idea of a web of spiritual relationships linking living and dead. They believed that those who died in a state of sin were condemned to a period of 'purgatorial' suffering that could be shortened by the prayers and actions of the living. These devotions, which ranged from funeral rites to commemorative masses, endowments, chapels, tombs and chantries (chapels for private devotions for the dead), were an essential part of pre-Reformation culture, along with the belief that those who had died could still help and care for the living.

England in 1535 was a country that by and large embodied the ideal of Erasmus—a place where the two complementary spirits of contemporary Christianity could coexist, 'the spirit of free and critical enquiry stemming from the Renaissance, and the spirit of respectful, trusting adherence to dogma that formed the traditional strength and unity of the Church'.[9] Henry's destruction of this balance had nothing to do with popular demand or with his own theological convictions—it was an act of expediency, which before long he would regret.

At first the schism appeared to be just one more blip in England's scratchy relationship with the papacy. In fact, it had triggered events that would alter the identity of the country forever. The royal sale of monastic property amounted to the biggest peacetime land transaction ever seen in England. It attracted a new, pragmatic breed of landowner—those among the nobility, courtiers and gentry who were prepared to set spiritual matters aside for the sake of a share in the bonanza. Privately, many were out of sympathy with the reformers; but they and their descendants became supporters of the new order, well aware that a national return to Catholicism could mean the loss of their lands and manor houses. These *nouveau riche* formed the first and most decisive element in the make-up of John Nobody. No matter what their personal beliefs, if they were to keep their new wealth they 'durst not speak'.

In 1536, the country erupted in protest at what had happened. Demanding the restoration of their native religion and the reinstatement of the monasteries, 30,000 commoners, priests, and gentry, the largest rebellion in England's history, gathered in the North and marched on

London under a banner of the Five Wounds of Christ, one of the popular devotions banned by the new order. Henry agreed to consider their demands, and, taking him at his word, the 'Pilgrimage of Grace' dispersed. As soon as it was safe to act, the royal promises were broken and the leaders of the protest executed. But the scale of the revolt had shaken the King. In 1538, he began to reverse the religious changes, affirming orthodox Catholic teaching, but he was too late.[10] On his death in 1547, they were reinforced by Henry's radical archbishop, Thomas Cranmer, under the King's nine-year old son, Edward, a fervent reformer reared by radical Protestant refugees from France and Italy. Within the short space of six years, much of the country's spiritual heritage was swept away in the name of fundamentalist doctrines Luther himself found extreme. Altars were stripped and smashed, the Mass was replaced by a simple communion service, thousands of illuminated religious books were burned, and royal instructions stipulated the removal of every trace of imagery from England's richly decorated parish churches. Chantries were destroyed and 'idolatrous' graves obliterated. There were severe penalties for the many who attempted to hide their parish treasures from the commissioners. Most insidious of all was the assault on the network of religious guilds and fraternities that for centuries had offered material support and stability to crafts, professions and civic communities across the country. Catholicism was now variously branded 'Spanish', 'Romish', or 'Papist'. The names were especially galling to English Catholics, to whom Protestantism was alien: 'I would to God Germany might have kept thee still so England had never been troubled with thee', wrote one miserably of the new religion.[11] In 1549, a series of riots culminated in the Prayer Book rebellion, beginning in the south-west of the country. Again there was a bloody repression, this time accomplished with the help of Italian mercenaries. There are records of sword fights in churchyards. Priests were executed and hanged from church towers and steeples along with their 'Popish trash', while the decapitated heads of recalcitrant laymen were impaled on town walls and gates.

New Faith Torn

BUT THE PROTESTANTS suffered a huge setback when Edward, only fifteen, died in 1553. His administration tried to cling to power, boldly diverting the succession from his Catholic sister,

Mary, to Jane Grey, daughter-in-law of Edward's chief adviser. But within days a huge wave of support for Mary had brought her to the throne and, with her, a return to Catholicism. Many of the reformers fled abroad; others, among them a rising civil servant named William Cecil, retained office by strategically conforming. But some met a terrible fate. The resentments built up over the previous decade found an outlet in a series of barbaric executions. During Mary's reign, 273 Protestants were burned as heretics.[12] This atrocity is all that people now remember of 'Bloody' Mary. It is forgotten that in the short period of her reign, England began to enjoy a brief taste of the fruits of a new movement for reform that was convulsing Catholic Europe and that incorporated the artistic, educational and spiritual riches of the Renaissance—the initiative known as the Counter-Reformation.

Spearheaded by a church council gathered at Trent in northern Italy, the Counter-Reformation brought new life to European Catholicism. It reinvigorated the religious orders, particularly the Franciscans, stressing personal asceticism and the importance of good works. It encouraged the translation of the scriptures into the vernacular, and it promoted the new Order of the Society of Jesus—the Jesuits—which combined a disciplined spirituality with an organised and highly influential system of schools and colleges. Unlike England's rigorous Protestantism, the Counter-Reformation was not the exclusive domain of the godly. It took art seriously as a method of raising and educating spiritual awareness, and quickly became the avant-garde intellectual and artistic movement of the day. The Counter-Reformation supported such painters as Caravaggio and El Greco, and encouraged popular drama. Jesuit plays were ground-breaking: they combined classical, burlesque, morality and mystery traditions in a sophisticated school of theatre that was soon in demand in towns throughout Catholic and Protestant Europe.[13]

It all looked hopeful for Catholic England. A Yorkshire priest voiced the general sense of relief: 'This realm is united and knit again to the Catholic faith as all other Christian realms be, whereof our holy father the pope is the supreme head'.[14] Mary's husband, the powerful Philip II, King of Spain, proved a retiring consort, and she had a distinguished Catholic reformer at her side, the English cardinal Reginald Pole, newly returned from the deliberations at Trent. Local communities enthusiastically restored their parish churches and shrines. But Cardinal Pole was cautious. He introduced reform slowly. He was especially wary of the Jesuits, keeping them at a distance and depriving the country of their galvanic educational impact. And not all of the changes were popular. The Protestant regime had allowed priests to marry; now their marriages had to be dissolved. As for the monastic lands, though the Queen herself did her best to return what her father and brother had seized for the Crown, very few others followed her example. But what suffocated the prospects for the Counter-Reformation in England was another premature royal death—Mary's, in 1558. Winter that year brought several disasters to English Catholics. The Queen's death was swiftly followed by Cardinal Pole's. Mary's army was forced to surrender Calais, England's last and oldest French stronghold. When a flu epidemic decimated the country, it was as if a national malaise had taken hold.

Vowing New Hate After New Love Bearing

T HIS MALAISE HELPS to explain why Elizabeth was able to assume her Catholic sister's throne unopposed. But there was another reason. Throughout Mary's reign, the upwardly mobile William Cecil had been secretly grooming Elizabeth for a possible Protestant succession. One of the most brilliant political operators of the age, Cecil was to remain Elizabeth's closest adviser and confidant for forty of the nearly forty-five years of her reign. The country's smooth transition to Protestantism on Elizabeth's accession was typical of his backstage methods.[15] Bribery, coercion and imprisonment disabled the opposition in a House of Lords already depleted by illness. One man who dared to speak out, voicing the silent opinions of his peers, was Anthony Browne, 1st Viscount Montague, one of the few who returned some of his monastic gains under Mary. He objected, not to the doctrine of Protestantism but to its enforcement. 'To force subjects of this realm to receive and believe the religion of the Protestants upon pain of death' was 'contrary and repugnant unto all laws of men, natural and civil'. He proposed instead that all should 'remain in unity with Christ's Church and our neighbours'. Even in Germany, he pointed out, there was a degree of toleration: but in England 'the Mass was abrogated, the sacrifice of the Church rejected, the Sacraments prophaned, the holy altars destroyed, temples violated'. He was indignant at the treatment of 'the religion which I professed in my baptism, when I was made a member of Christ's Mystical Body, and vowed to believe in the holy Catholic Church, as the spouse and only beloved of Christ', a religion over which no temporal governor could preside. A seasoned ambassador, he foresaw the dangerous isolation of England abroad, rightly predicting excommunication and the threat of invasion. He prophesied weakness and poverty at home, foreseeing 'men's minds discontented, great sums of money due and more of necessity demanded', and, given a religion that permitted every man 'to follow his own way', he reckoned 'the peril of the realm almost inevitable'.[16]

The 1559 law re-imposing a uniform state religion headed by the Queen was passed by a narrow margin of twenty-one votes to eighteen. There were desperate attempts to get the result vetoed, but it was too late. An era had begun which was to be known abroad as the 'Regnum Cecilianum', when for fifty-two years William Cecil and his son Robert effectively governed England. In the process, they created a dynasty so powerful that members of the Cecil family have remained a periodic force in British politics ever since. '*Sero sed serio*' was the family motto—slowly but surely. They were content to wait for years, even decades, for a policy to come to fruition. Under the Cecils, a spy service grew up that became an invaluable tool of intimidation and suppression throughout Elizabeth's reign. William Cecil has been hailed since then as a selfless public servant, but contemporaries were in no doubt of his motivation: 'So did he good to none, to many ill, / So did he all the kingdom rob and pill, / Yet none durst speak, no none durst of him plain, / So great he was in grace and rich in gain'.[17]

William Cecil was a trained lawyer with long experience of the secret workings of government. Well aware that the law was the most effective means of subduing a traditionally law-abiding country, his first step was to frame a series of parliamentary acts designed to revive the religious reforms brought in by Edward and to exclude Catholics from public life.[18] His approach was surreptitious, and at first, the acts remained dormant. Most English men and women were unaware that the changes in religion were now being driven by hard-line exiles returned from Geneva, where they had been sitting at the feet of John Calvin, a far more radical reformer than Luther. Instead, the public tone was set by the Queen's own moderate Lutheranism, a compromise that later came to be known as Anglicanism. She had a fondness for vestments and ceremony; she loved church music; her prayer book contained pictures, her chapel had a crucifix. But no such licence was extended to her subjects: possession of a crucifix or a rosary was now illegal.

A few lone voices were raised against the new laws. Radical Protestants objected to the oath: they had always wanted a religion entirely separate from the state. And in 1563, Viscount Montague was on his feet again.

'What man is there', he demanded, 'so without courage and stomach, or void of all honour, that can consent . . . to receive an opinion and new religion by force and compulsion?' But lack of courage was by now a major element in the silence of John Nobody. Bewildered by yet another change in religion, sickened by decades of mutual persecution, many stood by mutely while thugs and religious fanatics took to the streets once more, gleefully jumping on chalices and pyxes, defacing statues and burning 'al ancient Church relics and new made Images in Queen Mary's time'. By now, too, the Protestant information campaign was beginning to have its effect. Distributed to every parish along with the English Bible was a propaganda work that was to prove one of the most influential English books ever written. Known popularly as '*Foxe's Book of Martyrs*', it demonstrated that England was God's chosen instrument for the restoration of his church and featured a series of horrifyingly graphic woodcuts depicting the burnings of the Protestant martyrs under Mary. For generations of English men and women, these pictures would be the only images permitted in their local church. Reproached at the obligatory monthly service with the record of their crimes under Mary and with the promotion of the long-awaited English Bible banned by the church until the Reformation, many Catholics maintained a guilty silence.

Besides, onlookers at home and abroad were certain that before long the country would revert to the popular Catholicism of the previous reign. The imminent prospect of a return to the old religion was the chief reason they refrained from open rebellion. Encouraging Catholic hopes, the Queen entertained one Catholic suitor after another—a Catholic marriage, perhaps to a Hapsburg, perhaps to one of her Catholic courtiers, seemed inevitable. Moreover, Elizabeth's health was frail: she almost died of smallpox in 1562. Catholic successors were waiting in the wings. It would pay to keep quiet, especially as in the early days of the reign both Catholic leaders and the government turned a blind eye to 'church papists'—Catholics who attended the obligatory Protestant communion service in public and Mass in private.

In 1564, during this long period of suspense and uncertainty, William Shakespeare was born in Warwickshire, a county that remained defiantly Catholic until the next century. It was a year when one exile, John Rastell, was beginning to despair. 'They have so crossed the ways', he wrote sadly, 'and broken down so many hedges, and trodden down so much good corn, and so many fair pastures of all pietie and devotion . . . that they can never come to good end'. But life in Stratford-on-Avon still revolved around its town guild, a threatened organisation of which it was intensely proud, and in which Shakespeare's father, John, a well-to-do glover, took a leading role. Biographers find echoes of a happy provincial childhood in Shakespeare's work: his close observation of nature, his colloquial Warwickshire terms for places, trades and flowers, his retention of Stratford surnames for his rustics and minor characters, his affection for country ways, and detailed knowledge of them. Reluctant schoolboys in the plays parrot the syllabus taught at Stratford Grammar School; there may even be a parody of the Welsh Stratford schoolmaster, Thomas Jenkins, in the ignorant Hugh Evans who catechises a long-suffering 'William' in *The Merry Wives of Windsor*.

Another bright schoolboy, Lucius in *Titus Andronicus*, undergoes a more chilling ordeal. Clutching his textbooks in a state of panic, he is pursued by a nightmare allegorical figure: a beloved aunt, who now bears the gruesome marks of the religious vandalism of the day. Deprived of speech, she begs the boy's help, pointing to his copy of Ovid's *Metamorphoses*, which proves to be the key to her hidden story. It is a scene that may owe something to Shakespeare's darker memories. There were Catholics on both sides of his family; as he grew up, relatives and acquaintances suffered, at times appallingly, for their beliefs. The pressure on him could have been considerable: it was a family that may have expected great, perhaps heroic, things of a brilliant son. Shakespeare's early years would have echoed to angry discussions of the impact of fines and imprisonments, the liberties taken by the Queen's commissioners, the wreckage under Edward and the wicked errors of the old King. Monastic lands around Stratford now belonged to the Earl of Leicester and followers such as Sir Thomas Lucy, brutal and unpopular men who were beginning to turn on Catholics. For thousands of small, thriving towns like Stratford, the civic and spiritual were inextricably entwined; to such citizens, an England without the old religion was an England that had lost its identity.

Thou Art Twice Forsworn

I T TOOK TEN YEARS for the frustration to come to a head, a decade during which William Cecil had been busy making alliances and exploiting rivalries among England's leading families in order to build up a small but crucial power base in the court and in the south of England. At last, in November 1569, chafing at the long delay in the return of

Catholicism, indignant at the increasing network of legal restrictions and deprivations, the North of England rose under the leadership of the earls of Northumberland and Westmorland. The banner of the Five Wounds was raised again, Protestant prayer books were torn up and great crowds attended Mass in Durham Cathedral. The five-year-old Shakespeare would have been swept up in the tide of excitement that ripped through the Midlands. But, like similar violent demonstrations against the new religion under Elizabeth's brother, Edward, the rebellion was short-lived. The Catholic leadership was divided, and as they debated and hesitated, the uprising evaporated. Stratford's vicar and schoolmaster were both sacked for sympathising with the rebels. Hundreds were killed in the savage reprisals. Some leaders escaped and fled abroad: the powerful earls of Northumberland and Norfolk were imprisoned and executed. Commoners and gentry began to realise that although most of the nobility were Catholic in sympathy, none was a match for Cecil and his Privy Council.

The next turn of the screw came from an unexpected quarter—the papacy. In February 1570, the Pope offered belated support to the Rebellion of the Northern Earls by excommunicating the Queen in his *Regnans in Excelsis*, a bull that absolved English Catholics of their duty to their sovereign. The consequences were disastrous. Catholics were now portrayed as traitors who had been authorised by the head of their banned church to assassinate their monarch. Their situation was made still worse by the St Bartholomew's Day atrocity in 1572, in which vengeful Catholics all over France turned on their neighbours, massacring some 10,000 Protestants. For English Protestants, the images in *Foxe's Book of Martyrs* took on a horrible immediacy. Catholics now began to experience the full impact of Cecil's stealthy legal inroads on their status as native subjects in their own country. A new law, the 1571 Treasons Act, associated Catholics unequivocally with treachery. By insisting that all members of Parliament swear to uphold the Oath of Supremacy, Elizabeth ensured that Catholics were disbarred from the legislative chamber. The oath also banned them from government service and university teaching positions. Increasingly, they were being denied access to power, influence and, thanks to the severe fines, wealth. The penalties quietly introduced earlier for 'recusants' who refused to attend the state communion service were now enforced. Those who informed the state authorities on recusants received one-third of the fine, a colossal £20 a month, the annual salary of a grammar school teacher. Those unable to pay risked imprisonment and forfeited two-thirds of their property. Freedom of speech was further curtailed: access to the few printing presses was permitted only to literature written 'in the spirit of the prayer book'. A boy like William Shakespeare would have been particularly affected by the loss of the 'mystery cycles', a series of plays staged around the feast of Corpus Christi; these were lively, inventive productions staged by local guilds and 'masteries', and they dramatised the fall and redemption of man in a tradition popular all over Europe. The scope of these sophisticated expressions of civic pride was awe-inspiring, many of them conveying profound theological truths in memorably entertaining form. The York cycle included 300 speaking parts in its fifty plays, each of which was performed by an appropriate craft guild: *The Flood*, for instance, was traditionally staged by the Fishers and Mariners. In the course of the 1570s, these cycles ceased in England as a ban on unlicensed drama came into force. They were succeeded by a different spectacle—terror executions of priests and their accomplices, more frequent now that Catholicism was associated with treachery.

During the long years of inconclusive negotiation between the Catholic powers and breakaway Protestant England, English Catholics began to feel as ill-used by their supporters abroad as by their own country. A distant papacy had worsened the dilemma of double loyalty. Now Philip II of Spain, head of the superpower of the day, was preparing to use military force to return England to the Catholic fold—but Spain's military build-up was painfully slow and the promised rescue seemed as distant as ever. English exiles in their turn felt let down by fellow countrymen who were increasingly reluctant to be associated with the Spanish. Quick to detect the friction between domestic and exiled Catholics, William Cecil moved to deepen the rift by means of disinformation and double agents. The 1570s was one of the lowest points in the morale of the beleaguered Catholic dissidents. There is a reminder of the lonely lives of those who found the strain impossible in an inscription in the church of San Gregorio in Rome:

> Here lies Robert Peckham, Englishman and Catholic, who, after England's break with the Church, left England because he could not live in his country without the Faith, and, having come to Rome, died there because he could not live apart from his country.[19]

It looked as if this was the end of the road for English Catholicism. By 1587, Elizabeth felt secure enough to execute her imprisoned Catholic successor, Mary, Queen of Scots, hunting down suspected supporters in a series of raids characterised, according to one observer, by 'wild fury and savagery beyond human endurance'. And the following year provided Protestants with conclusive proof that God was on their side. Philip II's long-awaited invasion force, an 'Armada' of ships reported by awed onlookers to be invincible, was sunk and scattered by storms as it sailed majestically up the channel, pursued by the smaller British fleet. National exhilaration knew no bounds: even exiles in the English College in Rome leaped to their feet and cheered at the news. As patriotic bonfires were lit across the country, William Cecil should at last have been able to relax about the insidious Catholic threat.

The Phoenix

INSTEAD, HIS HEAD must have been in his hands. Against all expectation, the persecution was backfiring. Throughout the 1580s, a steady revival had been taking place in the Catholic underground. Its emblem was now the phoenix, the bird reborn in the ashes of its funeral pyre.[20] The revivalist identity was so distinct that there were some who questioned its continuity with the old religion, blaming new missionaries for dividing the Catholic community.[21]

The revival was pioneered by two undercover Jesuits, Edmund Campion and Robert Persons. Among the most distinguished of the many Oxford scholars who had left the country during the 1570s, they returned to England in 1580 hoping for a public debate with their Protestant opponents. Campion's charisma was legendary: when he was at Oxford, his university followers had imitated his rhetorical manner, his gestures, even his walk, and the Queen had singled him out for preferment. Upon their return to England, these two men brought with them the long-delayed spirit of the Counter-Reformation. They created a revived identity for wilting English Catholicism—a new image of personal holiness refined through suffering. Denouncing the double standards of 'church papists', they advocated instead a policy of heroic passivity. Catholics were not to attend Protestant services, yet they were to offer no resistance to persecution, waiting patiently instead for the promised invasion, led by their exiled leaders.

Many of Campion's co-religionists resented this uncompromising stance. But in the course of their journeys across the country, during which they were welcomed in secret by thousands, the two Jesuits stayed frequently in Stratford with friends of the Shakespeare family. It is highly likely that the sixteen-year-old Shakespeare met the two celebrated scholars and missionaries who were the focus of the Catholic underground. Hundreds of years later, a document was found hidden in the rafters of the Shakespeare home signed by John Shakespeare, affirming his Catholicism. It was eventually identified as one of the spiritual 'testaments' distributed by Campion to those facing death without the Catholic Church's last rites.

Within a year, Campion was arrested, racked and executed, to international protest. Persons escaped abroad, where, together with Cardinal William Allen, another Oxford exile, he oversaw the growing influx of missionaries into England from the new colleges in Douai, Rome and Valladolid. 'We have made a league cheerfully to carry the cross you shall lay upon us, and never to despair your recovery', Campion had written. 'The expense is reckoned, the enterprise is begun: it is of God, it cannot be withstood'.[22]

Two of the missionaries were men Shakespeare almost certainly knew. The new Jesuit Superior who arrived in 1586 was a plump, retiring mathematician, Henry Garnet. A keen musician who became a close friend of the recusant composer William Byrd, Garnet survived a number of narrow escapes to lead the underground mission for the next nineteen years. With him came Robert Southwell, a boyish idealist fired by Campion's example and determined to right the wrongs done by his grandfather, one of Henry VIII's most unscrupulous henchmen. Southwell was not only a talented poet; like Persons, he was one of the finest English prose writers of his day. He countered the impact of the government printing presses by launching a literary crusade in the late 1580s that was to have considerable influence on his fellow writers in London.

Garnet's meticulous reports to his superiors abroad paint a picture of a deeply divided country.[23] Thousands of Catholics had 'converted' during the backlash following the Armada; many others had been ruined. In the course of the reign, an estimated 30,000 Catholics left the country or were imprisoned, out of a national population of under 5 million.[24] Garnet describes people driven to desperate extremes to escape the government 'pursuivants'. Some were 'compelled to desert their homes and live in the woods and fields' while others subsisted for weeks in caves or 'in ancient ruins underground, with all their household'. There were thousands of unrecorded deaths in prison. All over the country, finding space to incarcerate recusants was an administrative headache.[25] New jails had to be built; churches were used to hold suspects during the frequent raids. 'A slaughterhouse of Catholics', Robert Southwell called Bridewell prison in London, where prisoners died of disease and starvation in dark, sodden cells lapped by the waters of the Thames. During his time in the Tower of London, Thomas Cottam, a priest whose brother had taught at Stratford grammar school, was bent double in a hoop of iron known as the Scavenger's Daughter, an instrument that was tightened until blood burst from the victim's nose and his bones cracked. The rack on which prisoners were hung or stretched for hours was a favourite device, as it left no marks. Asked at his trial to show signs of torture, Robert Southwell answered bitterly, 'Ask a woman to show her throes'.

It was Southwell, in his *Humble Supplication to Her Majesty*, who gave the most eloquent summary of how it felt to be a Catholic in England in the late 1580s and early 1590s, when Shakespeare, by now in his late twenties, began to write: 'We are generally accounted men whom it is a credit to pursue, a disgrace to protect, a commodity to spoil, a gain to torture, a glory to kill . . . no tongue so forsworn but it is of credit against us; none so true but it is thought false in our defence'.[26] Only those who were prepared to die for their beliefs could afford to write so openly: even then, copies of the *Humble Supplication* were immediately confiscated. Southwell's kinsman, Sir Richard Shelley, died in prison for handing the Queen a similar petition on behalf of Catholics.

But though Southwell rejected them, there were ways of criticizing the regime and surviving. Over the long decades of oppression and censorship, John Nobody had not stayed entirely silent. A hidden language had developed, a coded vehicle for expressing the hopes, pleas, frustrations and repressed anger of England's dissidents. Over the centuries, as John Nobody's story faded from memory, the idea that Elizabeth's Protestant England had any need for a shadowed, dissident language became unthinkable, and its very existence was forgotten. Nonetheless, it has survived, ingeniously preserved in print by writers who became expert at dodging censorship. Once the key has been rediscovered, much of Elizabethan literature begins to look very different. Here, ingeniously submerged, lies the one ingredient missing from the copious literature of the day—an arena for the arguments, protests and appeals of a disinherited England.

CHAPTER

2

SECRET VOICES

LATE SIXTEENTH-CENTURY England was a country that provided a ready audience for dissident code: its people were addicted to hidden meanings. Codes, devices and punning allusions were everywhere—in street songs and ballads, conversation, poems, plays, woodcuts, portraits, jewellery, costumes. Entire buildings were constructed in the form of riddles. The architect John Thorpe designed one house around his own initials; another curious building, the triangular Rushton Lodge in Northamptonshire was created by a Catholic nobleman, Sir Thomas Tresham, as a symbol of the Mass and the Holy Trinity. Emblem books were immensely popular. Heraldry was another medium for witty devices 'obscure to be perceived at the first' whose cunning workmanship, once discovered, 'may greater delight the beholder'.[1] Those applying for a new coat of arms worked hard at puns on their own name: Shakespeare's device was a brandished spear. Queen Elizabeth herself delighted in word-play, setting the emblematic tone at court with teasing nicknames for her courtiers: the ubiquitous William Cecil was her 'Spirit'; his diminutive son Robert, her 'Pygmy'; the Earl of Leicester, her 'Eyes'; the French Duke of Alençon, her 'Frog'. Sir Walter Raleigh was 'Water'; he responded with a wealth of poetry in which Elizabeth as Cynthia, the moon goddess, held sway over Sir Walter, the Ocean. The vast extent of the classical and religious imagery applied to Elizabeth herself survives in contemporary portraits and literature; every year, splendidly mounted courtiers attended her obligatory Accession Day tournament under the guise of mythical figures accompanied by heralds who delivered elaborate poems explaining the various ways their devices honoured the Queen.[2]

There were literary codes, too, accessible only to a sophisticated elite. Sir Philip Sidney, the most admired poet of the age, who died just as Shakespeare was beginning to write, confirms that he and his contemporaries were using a shadowed language that, so they believed, was the essence of good writing. Sidney explains the theory in his influential *Defence of Poetry*, published in 1595. Though love poems like his own sonnets may seem trivial, they acted as cover for mysterious deeper meanings—he calls them 'wanton shows of better hidden matters'. He chooses the popular classical tale of the rape of Lucrece as an example—however decorative and sensuous such stories may be, their real function, Sidney maintains, was to represent deeper philosophical and spiritual truths.[3]

Readers delighted in decoding. For centuries, allegory had been an essential part of all artistic and literary appreciation, and in the late sixteenth century the humanists of the Italian Renaissance were taking it to new heights. Its ultimate source was the great Western philosophical allegory dating back through the fathers of the church to ancient classical and Jewish teaching, based on the theory that all creation, rightly interpreted, could be seen as an image of the divine.[4] This concept became a central, though not always obvious, part of Christian teaching from the fourth century through to the sixteenth.

An essential humanist theme, elaborated by famous writers such as Dante, Petrarch and Chaucer as well as countless anonymous medieval poets and song writers, was that of an unrequited human love that turns out to be an image of the soul's yearning for God. To humanists, Cupid and Venus both had dual identity—they could represent either human or divine love. Accepted symbols indicated which role they were playing. 'Little' Cupid suggested physical love; 'blind' Cupid was spiritual love, dazzled by the mystical vision. Shakespeare introduces a teasing variant—'Saint' Cupid. This allegorical tradition was one of the casualties of the English Reformation. Doctrinaire theologians at Oxford and Cambridge disapproved of image making, calling instead for a return to 'Scripture alone'. But broadminded scholars refused to abandon the humanist system of thought that had so deepened and enriched medieval spiritual life. They continued to write tales interweaving the divine and the secular. But they wrote them cautiously and 'darkly'. Like many other works, Sidney's books, full of borderline 'hidden matter', circulated only in manuscript during his lifetime.

For most modern readers, the writings of sixteenth-century poets often remain an impenetrable allegorical jungle. Not many of Shakespeare's contemporaries are read today.[5] Without any insight into the 'better hidden matters' behind their work, many seem simply verbose and long-winded. But the newly researched history of John Nobody throws a shaft of light on a number of these neglected English writers. To dissidents, the allegorical tradition provided an ideal vehicle for smuggling forbidden political and spiritual material into print. And they plainly made the most of it. Read with the fate of John Nobody in mind, certain obscure poetic passages take on new life. Lengthy and difficult sections emerge as devices to deflect official attention from passages of dangerous topical significance. One court dramatist describes his play as a Trojan horse: an elaborate gift concealing an unpalatable message.[6]

The minor poet Robert Chester has often been derided for his long, rambling poem *Love's Martyr*, published in 1601. But to contemporary Catholics, Chester's line 'love is a holy, holy, holy thing' would not have been ridiculous. It flagged up the message that his poem was really about spiritual love—and spiritual love of a particular kind. The most sacred section of the Mass begins 'Sanctus, sanctus, sanctus'—holy, holy, holy. These words, carefully inscribed by Sir Thomas Tresham on the walls of Rushton Lodge, evoke the heart of Catholic belief. Once 'love' is understood as the spirituality expressed by the banned Catholic Mass, the poem yields up a rich political subtext, celebrating forbidden hopes, practices and emblems. At points Chester drops his guard completely, extolling 'the image of Our Lady with her Son held in her arms' and praising the crucifix as 'a great triumphant sign, a sign of joy' before which 'the righteous man bows down his head'. His awkward style unwittingly lays bare a clear seam of code terms for the underground church—terms shared by many of his fellow writers.[7]

His famous contemporary, Edmund Spenser, author of the greatest epic poem of the period, *The Faerie Queene*, is usually portrayed as a pillar of the Elizabethan establishment. But he turns out to be equally subversive. His work is full of sleights of hand, including deliberate obfuscation. He is at his most bewildering in the elaborate footnotes to his often dangerously political poem, *The Shepherd's Calendar*. At one point Spenser went too far and was exiled to Ireland for mocking William Cecil as a power-hungry fox in an animal fable.[8] His technique was clearly studied by Shakespeare's rival playwright, Ben Jonson, whose learned footnotes to *Sejanus* are designed to divert attention from the play's seditious content.

The poets and playwrights Michael Drayton and Samuel Daniel reveal their Catholic sympathies in their contributions to a popular genre of poems known as 'complaints'. These were lugubrious monologues delivered by the ghosts of illustrious sinners who return from the grave to entertain the reader with accounts of their earthly crimes. Like the Catholic Church, Drayton's and Daniel's unlaid ghosts are the victims of the lust of kings. They mourn the destruction of their own tombs, once sited in the chantries of the vanished abbeys of Godstow, Dunmow and Langley. They hope that their poems will replace their gravestones, reminding the reader of their continuing need for banned prayers for the dead. Two other leading poets, Thomas Lodge and Henry Constable, authors of love poetry that uses suspiciously religious language, eventually admitted their Catholicism and went into exile, where Constable wrote more openly spiritual works. It is clear that they consistently used the word 'love' in a double sense, at once secular and spiritual. Philip Sidney's first version of *Arcadia*, which remained unpublished until 1926, contains a number of densely allegorical romantic passages critical of the effects of the Reformation.[9]

Little by little a picture emerges of a self-consciously artful community of intellectual writers engaged in an exhilarating and often risky cat-and-mouse game with the state authorities.[10] Robert Chester describes his fellow poets, Shakespeare among them, as men who possessed 'an invention freer than the time'. Even at the time, however, only an educated few would have been able to appreciate dissident meanings concealed within elaborate poems. Disaffected writers who wanted to reach a wider audience turned to a medium that was at once more accessible and more hazardous—the popular theatre.

The Chroniclers of the Time

I RONICALLY, IT WAS the reformers themselves who had opened up the subversive possibilities of the English stage. In 1535, John Bale, an ex-friar bitterly critical of the old religion, was commissioned by the government to write new versions of traditional morality plays, replacing the figure of Everyman with England, Lucifer with the Pope, and the seven deadly sins with cardinals, monks and friars, while the reformers were represented by the heavenly virtues. His efforts were greeted with violent hostility from indignant theatre-goers opposed to Henry's assault on the traditional church. The disturbances were so serious that Henry introduced new laws in 1543 that forbade actors to interpret scripture or to dramatise matters of doctrine. Censorship of the stage had arrived for the first time in England.

But Henry's move initiated a covert form of drama that gave a new dimension to the great sixteenth-century game of witty concealment. Like romance literature and poetry, popular drama in Shakespeare's day was an allegorical medium ideally suited to subversive writing. Based on complex medieval methods of interpreting scripture, the banned mystery plays had always been rich in secondary meanings. But dissident playwrights, particularly those who lacked patrons, ran serious dangers. The biographies of Shakespeare's fellow dramatists make sobering reading. Almost all of them underwent some form of government pressure, ranging from interrogation by the Privy Council to imprisonment, exile, even death. Ben Jonson, Shakespeare's ebullient rival, characterised a playwright as a man under threat—he 'takes private beatings and begins again'.[11] One poignant example is Thomas Kyd, of whom little is known beyond the fact that he died, broken and destitute, after a period of torture in murky circumstances. Yet Kyd was the author of the most popular drama of the age, *The Spanish Tragedy*. The play's immense popularity, lasting well into the next century, has always been a mystery; but read from a Catholic dissident viewpoint it is a deeply moving work, giving full expression to the frustrations of a patient people driven to the brink by intolerable impositions. The details surrounding the death of the suffering hero's son, found hanged in an orchard, recall both contemporary martyrdoms and the crucifixion scenes from the mystery plays, evoking a handkerchief 'besmeared with blood', Judas, bleeding wounds, a fair son 'not conquered but betrayed', and the apple tree in the Garden of Eden, which traditionally provided the wood for Christ's cross. Safety for playwrights like Kyd depended on the protection of aristocrats who patronised the few licensed acting companies. Kyd was a humble 'noverint', or clerk, all too vulnerable to intimidation.[12]

Writers concerned for their well-being gravitated towards the country's most powerful patrons, such as William Cecil and Sir Francis Walsingham, Elizabeth's dour spymaster. They turned out stridently Protestant plays, some with heroes like 'New Custom', who did battle with 'Idolatry', and 'Superstition', and others in a subtler style. But good government playwrights were few, and always liable to defect to the smarter dissident set. The career of Shakespeare's exact contemporary, Christopher Marlowe, was typical of a writer who became embroiled in the underworld of the state intelligence services. Recruited while he was still at Cambridge by Walsingham, Marlowe worked as an *agent provocateur* secretly bound for the seminary at Rheims. He reported back to the government on the activities of the Catholic underground before turning his pen to propaganda plays like *The Massacre at Paris*, full of crude digs at Catholicism. But Marlowe turned out to be a writer of extraordinary calibre. Aware that such a line was unpopular with audiences, and in particular with the intellectual circles he aspired to, he took to undercutting his primary political message with a second, subversive one. *The Jew of Malta* contains a strand of bitter self-parody, and finally in *Doctor Faustus* he shows dangerous signs of allegiance to the religion he was paid to undermine. *Doctor Faustus* includes the usual attacks on the Pope and the clergy. But in two of the most powerful theatrical scenes of the age, Marlowe gave terrifying expression to the fear that made worldly men go to great lengths to die as Catholics: Faustus perjures his soul and is damned. The manner in which the play dwells on every detail of Faustus's suicidal oath, signed in his own blood, followed by his descent into Hell, created havoc among frightened playgoers—for many believed that, like Faustus, they too had incurred damnation when they had taken the Oath of Supremacy to avoid the penal laws, and, worse, abandoned the Mass.

Marlowe ultimately made the same mistake as Spenser. In *Edward II*, the corrupt advisers bore a perilously close resemblance to Elizabeth's political architects, William and Robert Cecil. Marlowe was no doubt relying on the Cecils' powerful enemies to protect him. But the evidence is that in spite of his dazzling brilliance—or perhaps because of it—they mistrusted Marlowe. He died, murdered by intelligence agents in 1593 at the age of twenty-nine.

Given the unreliability of their own propagandists and the ease with which dissidents were using code to elude censorship, the clear solution for the regime was to ban drama altogether. By 1581, it very nearly succeeded, drafting a series of laws that achieved the total suppression of local community drama. The 400-year-old Corpus Christi mystery plays ceased: Shakespeare's was the last generation of English children to witness them. Only a handful of companies under the patronage of the nobility were allowed to continue performing, and though they regularly toured the country, their base was in London, the heartland of Protestantism, under the watchful eye of the civic authorities and the government censor. During times of plague, the authorities extended the closure of playhouses for as long as they could—in 1564, Grindal, the Bishop of London, had prohibited all plays within three miles of the city 'for one whole year', adding impatiently 'and if it were forever, it were not amiss'.

But at this point the reformers came up against an unexpected and immovable obstacle—the Queen herself. She provided the loophole that allowed a handful of acting companies to continue to perform in city inn-yards and theatres, for they were able to argue that they needed to perfect their productions for eventual presentation at court. Elizabeth's personal fondness for poetry, drama and music was largely responsible for the flowering of all three art forms in England towards the end of the sixteenth century. A famous example of her toleration of Catholicism in talented artists is her patronage of the great composer William Byrd, who but for her would have been unable to continue writing—and writing not only music for the court but, encouraged by the Jesuits, an ambitious re-setting of the old Catholic liturgy to suit an underground church that now needed masses not for choirs, but for three, four or five voices. The Queen was well aware that certain court plays carried covert political appeals, and, provided they were cunningly concealed, she tolerated the practice. One of her own cousins, Thomas Sackville, presented her with a dark allegory of the dangers of a divided England in his tragedy, *Gorboduc*. Another court dramatist expert at offering delicate and highly ornamented advice to Elizabeth was the Earl of Oxford's secretary, John Lyly.

The result of this royal patronage was that street performance flourished. If the reformers had hoped that their crackdown on amateur drama would discourage England's deep-rooted love of theatre, they were wrong. A satirical play written at the turn of the century, *The Return from Parnassus*, portrays an exhausted censor overwhelmed by the task of combing through the texts on his desk. London could hardly keep pace with the demand for plays, while the book-sellers in St Paul's Churchyard did a roaring trade in printed texts. Professional actors, previously classed as vagrants and despised as 'a very superfluous sort of men', flourished and some grew rich; university wits competed to write plays for professional companies and their aristocratic patrons. Entrepreneurs built theatres around London's walls and along the south bank of the River Thames. By 1600, there were seven of them, including the Globe, the Rose, the Swan, the Curtain and the Fortune, some capable of holding up to 3,000 spectators.

The protests of the establishment repeatedly stress not simply the licentiousness of performances at these theatres but the way they appeared to challenge—even replace—the new Protestant religion. Performances were timed to coincide with religious services and were so popular that they emptied the churches. 'The devil's service', they were called by some Puritans, who attacked 'the continual profaning of the Sabbath which in the country is their play day'. Plays were acted in 'suspicious dark and inconvenient places', often on the sites of priories and abbeys known as 'liberties', because they were legally outside the city's jurisdiction. The Holywell Theatre in Shoreditch, in North London, was built between two holy wells, still places of pilgrimage and healing. The ubiquitous government spy and playwright Anthony Munday reported that priests came to say Mass in the late 1580s at the theatre and travelled the country with the players, disguised in their livery. It was during this turbulent period and at this suspect playhouse that Shakespeare's plays were first performed.

The Noted Weed

WHAT BROUGHT Shakespeare to London? Apart from anecdotal evidence, information about his early life is notoriously scarce. The seventeenth-century gossip John Aubrey records that he was 'a well-shaped man', 'very good company and of a very ready and pleasant smooth wit' who 'did act exceedingly well'; Aubrey believes he spent some of his youth as a country school-master.[13] But Shakespeare's name is not registered at either university, and apart from the assumption that he attended Stratford Grammar School as a young boy, nothing is known of his education or of his occupation before he appears on the London literary scene in his late twenties. Recent biographers speculate that in 1581, at the age of sixteen, he joined Edmund Campion as the Jesuit travelled north via Stratford to Hoghton Tower in Lancashire, which under Alexander Hoghton was a centre of recusancy, where priests were trained, children educated and religious drama enacted. When Campion was arrested, Alexander Hoghton made his will, naming a 'William Shakeshafte' as one of his servants and recommending him to his neighbour, Sir Thomas Hesketh, a patron of actors; the theory is that it may have been through Hesketh's contacts that Shakespeare found work in London.[14]

There is another possibility. His writing breathes exactly the kind of Christian humanist training students received at Oxford, while his early plays in particular reveal a precise knowledge of current theological disputes and a close acquaintance with Italy. Many have wondered whether a more educated man wrote the plays, a nobleman perhaps, rich enough to tour the Continent, who later adopted the Stratford actor's name as cover. But a more obvious explanation lies in the forgotten predicament of English Catholics, excluded from all forms of education in their own country.

Oxford and Cambridge were the seedbeds for the country's governing class, in particular its clergy. In the years following the Reformation, these ancient institutions, once bastions of humanist learning, had become intensely politicised, Cambridge inclining to the new religion, Oxford clinging obstinately to the old. One expedient for those who wanted to gain a university education while ducking the Oath of Supremacy and avoiding obligatory Protestant services and catechism classes was to attend one of the halls at Oxford still sympathetic to the old religion, either by taking an alias or without registering at the university at all. Shakespeare could have done the same. Like others, too, some of them from Stratford, he could have been forced to complete his education in Italy, for by the mid-1570s dissident colleges were under increasing pressure to conform, and many Catholics left Oxford to finish their studies abroad, a number of them in the English College in Rome.[15] Two biographical details support this possibility: for unknown reasons, his father began to lose money in the late 1570s, perhaps as a result of this expensive course of education. And Shakespeare reappears in the Stratford records in 1582, a year after the government had recalled all those studying abroad on pain of ruinous fines.[16]

What is known for certain is in that year, he married a local Stratford woman, Anne Hathaway; that their first child, Susannah, was born in 1583, and their twins, Hamnet and Judith, in 1585. Within five years, he had left his family behind in Stratford and was making his living as an actor and playwright in London, where he was associated with a dissident acting company, Lord Strange's Men.

Robert Greene, a talented, heavy-drinking writer who worked for a rival, government-sponsored company, the Queen's Men, resented his arrival. 'There is an upstart Crow, beautified with our feathers', he wrote in 1592, who 'supposes he is as well able to bombast out a blank verse as the best of you . . . in his own conceit the only Shake-scene in a country . . . .'[17] Professional jealousy may have been one reason for the attack. But there could have been a second motive. The pair were writing for different sides in the great stage debate. Had Shakespeare, like the schoolboy Lucius, decided in the end to use his wits to fight for the persecuted cause? If, as most biographies imply, he had indeed turned his back on the ideological battle raging in the London theatres, he would have been exceptional.

Contemporary comments suggest he was one of the crowd, a member of the group who prided themselves on being 'freer than the times', one of the same 'witty' dissident company as Daniel, Drayton, Spenser, Lodge and Sidney, among 'the most passionate among us to bemoan and bewail the perplexities of love', according to an observer, Francis Meres. *The Return from Parnassus* portrays him as a literary model for excitable young noblemen who dabbled in suspiciously spiritual love poetry.

Shakespeare was the one sixteenth-century writer who, it appears, never fell foul of the authorities. Yet in a strangely insistent passage, the editors of the First Folio of his work, published in 1623, urge us to look beneath the surface of the great universal plays to something hidden below. Though they are sure that his wit can 'no more lie hid than it could be lost', they press us to 'Read him therefore, and again, and again'. We must seek help from his friends if we miss his 'hidden wit', and we should act as guides to others if we find it. The insistence on readers acting as guides is striking and unusual.

A similar plea for close attention occurs in one of Shakespeare's sonnets. Sonnet 23, 'As an unperfect actor on the stage', describes the anguish of enforced silence—an anguish with which all those in England who 'durst not speak' would have had immediate sympathy. 'For fear of trust' he does not dare to say 'the perfect ceremony of love's rite'. Here, beneath the mock-religious terminology common to courtly love poetry, Catholics would have detected a precise description of the Mass. In deliberately dense language, he laments an irony highlighted by exiled writers: the fact that the faith of England's Catholics was approaching breaking point because of their own church's insistence on a heroic profession of that faith. He has not been totally silenced: his writings are his 'eloquence'. But he begs the reader to study them carefully. 'O learn to read what silent love hath writ' he says, 'To hear with eyes belongs to love's fine wit'. The phrase 'to hear with eyes' accurately defines a pun. And the poem supplies a demonstration of the kind of pun he is talking about. At first the line looks like a misprint. His 'books', says Shakespeare, 'plead for love and look for recompense / *More than that love which more hath more expressed*'. But a pun makes sense of the phrase: 'More than that love which *More* hath more expressed'. The reference is to Henry VIII's martyred chancellor, Thomas More, whose writings were now proscribed but who wrote the last openly Catholic works before the Reformation, pleading the cause of a faith for which Shakespeare pleads with even more intensity.[18]

Both the preface and the sonnet alert the reader to an exceptionally discreet form of secret writing that requires effort in order to be understood. Both express the fear that the technique may prove almost too successful. In one sense the anxiety was justified. Whatever its impact at the time, Shakespeare's cautious artistry was so great that his hidden language remained undetectable to succeeding generations that accepted the official version of England's Reformation. Yet the subterfuge was essential if he and his work were to survive. He was writing in a climate more dangerous and oppressive than anything experienced by his predecessors. By the 1580s, the censorship laws, regularly tightened under Elizabeth, were strictly enforced. Yet he could not remain silent. He was driven to write by a different fear, to which he returns throughout his work. This was the growing concern, shared by many contemporaries, that the true history of the age would never be told. Walter Raleigh refused to include the story of his own time in his *History of the World*, observing wryly that 'whosoever in writing a modern history shall follow Truth too near the heels, it may haply strike out his teeth'. Objective historians such as John Stow were being bullied into revising their work, while in the hands of industrious writers such as William Camden and Raphael Holinshed, the Protestant version of England's 'island story' was proving to be widely popular. Memories of the true nature of the old religion were fading, to be overlaid by images of lustful friars and heretic bonfires. Shakespeare not only needed to write; he needed to find a new method of writing, one capable of recording the whole unhappy story of the country's political and spiritual collapse against the background of a regime for whom the slightest topical reference was justification enough to imprison a playwright.

In his comprehensive work on Shakespeare's plays, *Shakespeare—The Invention of the Human*, Harold Bloom isolates intelligence as the single outstanding quality that separates Shakespeare from his contemporaries, a judgement endorsed by his latest biographers.[19] We know that he was also strikingly self-confident. It was the characteristic that Robert Greene stressed in his famous portrait of the upstart newcomer as a jack-of-all-trades—'a regular Johannes factotum'—'in his own conceit the only Shake-scene in a country'.[20] These two qualities of intelligence and self-confidence are the hallmarks of the way Shakespeare set himself the task of encoding and perpetuating the true story of England.

He decided against Spenser's method of slipping brief passages of topical reference into otherwise innocent material. It was inelegant, and the passages stood out too clearly. Nor would he adopt Lyly's shadowy parallels—they were too vague and imprecise for his purpose. The references in

Sidney's *Arcadia* were too obscure, whereas Marlowe and Kyd were dangerously obvious. Instead he set himself an almost impossible task. His plays would be seamlessly organic: every detail of the plot material, from first to last, would serve a dual purpose. Seen from the right angle, they would act in the same way as a pun—perfectly clear, yet perfectly deniable. This plan involved a decision breathtaking to modern readers, accustomed to regarding Shakespeare as literature's most profound and subtle psychologist. All his plots and characters, however complex, would have equally complex shadow identities.

There was of course nothing new in the idea of shadow characters. When they heard Shakespeare's line in *The Two Gentlemen of Verona*, 'Who is Silvia? What is she' (4.2.40), listeners at the time would not have thought the phrasing was a slip of the tongue. They were used to the multiple identities of the mystery plays, and would have taken the question seriously—Silvia might indeed be something, as well as someone. Medieval writers and Renaissance humanists liked personifying qualities as women. Erasmus gave Folly an endearingly comic character in his best-selling present to Thomas More, *In Praise of Folly*. In a daring passage in *Arcadia*, Sidney casts the old religion as a blowsy Venus and the new as a bad-tempered Diana, goddess of the moon; between them stands the elusive spiritual ideal, the humble, beautiful Mira. Shakespeare's great successor, the poet John Donne, still a boy in the 1580s, went further still, caricaturing England's religions as three women in a satirical passage he could only afford to publish many years later.[21] The first, banished Catholicism, flees to Rome where her rags are adored like robes of state; the second, at Geneva, is 'plain, simple, sullen, young, contemptuous yet unhandsome'—an equally clear picture of Calvin's Protestantism. The third, who remains at home, is the English reformed religion, portrayed contemptuously as a sluttish bride forced on a ward by his greedy guardian.[22]

Vivid though they are, there is a huge gulf between these crude figures and characters like Lear, Cleopatra, Viola and Hamlet. But Shakespeare had his sights set on dramas far more complex than the simple choice between three religions. He intended to chronicle every twist and turn of the aberrations that led his country into the moral wasteland of the 1590s. He wanted to portray the long, wrangling relationship between an exhausted, once noble England and a fickle Spain. He wanted to evoke the exact nature of the spirituality England had lost and to make his audience long for its recovery. He needed to confront London's courtly intelligentsia with a searching analysis of their own inertia in the face of the

Cecil takeover. For the endlessly complex situation he wanted to dramatise, only endlessly complex characters would do.[23]

In these dramas, there would be no room for asides or explanations.
Instead, Shakespeare worked out a set of simple markers, basic call-signs
that would alert his audience to the entry point they needed to access the
hidden story. Unlike Erasmus, Sidney and Donne, who were poets and
essayists, he was a seasoned actor addressing restless spectators, so he kept
his signals simple and consistent. But he was also one of a brotherhood of
dissident writers, and to them his pointers would have been as readily—
even wittily—recognisable as they became baffling to later readers.

The master key to the hidden level is so simple that it is easy to miss. It
takes the form of twin terms that identify the polar opposites in Elizabeth's England. They are not Shakespeare's only terms, and he uses them
sparingly, but with pinpoint accuracy. They are the terms 'high' and 'fair',
which always indicate Catholicism, and 'low' and 'dark', which always suggest Protestantism. Shakespeare's treatment of these words is sufficiently
remarkable for critics to have wondered whether he was writing for a tall
blond actor and a short dark one—but the theory is untenable. Shakespeare was not a dramatist who would have deliberately created casting
problems, and the references span a ten-year period.

The opposition of high and low, representing the two opposing sides in
the Reformation, was commonplace at the time. The modern Christian
distinction between high and low church goes back to pre-Reformation
days, when High Mass, high days and high altars involved full liturgical
ceremony—Low Mass and low altars were for every day.

The opposition of dark and fair was equally recognisable. The glittering, skin-deep attractions of the scarlet woman were constantly under fire
from Protestant plays, sermons and literature: the sober reformers wore
plain black, and the new Prayer Book was shorn of illuminated initials
and, as far as possible, red print. A Protestant poem published in 1573
entitled 'A sonnet written in praise of the brown beauty' praises a dark
woman in clearly sectarian terms—she is contrasted with a fair, 'pam-
pered' beauty, whose 'glittering' clothes and 'too much red' complexion
'in thralldom binds the foolish gazing eyes'—'thralldom' a common thrust
at the authoritarian Catholic Church and 'gazing' a hit at credulous Mass-
goers.[24] Shakespeare adds a qualification to his dark-fair marker, a typical
instance of the reliable detail of his hidden plays. Unlike his contemporaries, who used the terms loosely, Shakespeare applies the opposition
scrupulously, and in the end with an element of irony, to hair colour.[25]

His markers are morally neutral. Fair, tall characters can be corrupt, while dark, low ones are often noble—the words merely identify the religious allegiance of one or two characters, providing a key compass-bearing from which alert readers and spectators can work out the rest of the shadowed plot. In the process an enjoyable trail of punning wordplay emerges, deepening and confirming the discovery.

The call-sign appears throughout the plays, becoming more oblique and infrequent as his audience became familiar with his technique. The fullest example occurs in *A Midsummer Night's Dream* (1595), enabling Shakespeare to orchestrate one section of a complex hidden drama about England's political impasse. In an absurd quarrel, short, dark Hermia feels slighted by tall, fair Helena:

> HERMIA: Puppet! why, so: ay, that way goes the game.
>   Now I perceive that she hath made compare
>   Between our statures: she hath urged her height;
>   And with her personage, her tall personage,
>   Her, height forsooth, she hath prevail'd with him.
>   And are you grown so high in his esteem,
>   Because I am so dwarfish and so low?
>   How low am I, thou painted maypole? Speak . . .
>   *(3.2.289–296)*

The 'maypole', centerpiece of the banned May Day festivities that were once an essential part of parish life, underlines Helena's Catholic identity. The squabble between Helena and Hermia over their height continues for the next thirty-five lines and ends with Lysander's final thrust at the distraught Hermia:

> Get you gone, you dwarf
> You minimus, of hindering knot-grass made;
> You bead, you acorn!
> *(3.2.327–329[26])*

Hermia is also 'a tawny Tartar' (3.2.264), 'an Ethiope' (3.2.256); the audience would have been alerted to her prudish, fractious nature, a common stereotype of 'puritan' Protestants.

In *Much Ado About Nothing*, the demure Hero, like Hermia, is dark and short. In contrast to her exuberant opposite, Beatrice, she is 'Too low for a high praise, too brown for a fair praise' (1.1.177). Again, in *As You Like It*, quiet Celia is dark and low, playful Rosalind tall and fair. In both plays, an educated audience would have realised that Shakespeare was covertly dramatising England's persecution and banishment of both aspects of true spirituality, Catholic and Puritan.

The high-low opposition does not always refer to stature. There are witty variations. Here is exiled Julia, already connected with banned Whitsun holidays, studying her rival's portrait in *The Two Gentlemen of Verona* and wondering what her unreliable lover, Proteus, sees in Silvia:

> Her hair is auburn, mine is perfect yellow
> If that be all the difference in his love
> I'll get me such a coloured periwig ...
> Ay, but her forehead's low, and mine's as high ...
>
> (4.4.185–189)

Antony and Cleopatra uses the same distinguishing terms as the earlier plays. Cleopatra is relieved to find her rival is 'dwarfish' and has 'brown' hair. In the domestic quarrel in *The Taming of the Shrew*, the shrew is 'brown in hue', her sister Bianca's name means 'white'. In *Troilus and Cressida*, Cressida is darker than Helen. Marina and her stepsister in *Pericles, Prince of Tyre* are as different as dove and crow. Berowne in *Love's Labour's Lost* claims his dark Rosaline outshines her fair rivals.

The most condensed version of the high-low, dark-fair image comes in *Hamlet*, when the furious prince forces his mother to compare the portraits of her first and second husband. Old Hamlet is like the sun god, or 'like the herald Mercury / New lighted on a heaven-kissing hill' (3.4.58–59), and he demands, 'Could you on this fair mountain leave to feed, / And batten on this moor?' (3.4.66–67)—'moor' a pun on the dark looks of Claudius and low-lying land, the opposite to the fair mountain.

Almost as central as these two binary terms is an image Shakespeare uses consistently for the Reformation: that of a storm or tempest. 'Tempest' was a common term for the Reformation upheaval in England, used not only by the Jesuits in their 'Merchant' code (see Glossary) but by writers of all persuasions. Shakespeare's many tempests—there are at least ten in his plays—always embody at least one of the two central Catholic criticisms of the Reformation: they defy the heavens, and they destroy a natural unity. Once unpacked, his dense use of language often sharpens the image, bringing out a particular aspect of the Reformation. A typical line like 'The chidden billow seems to pelt the clouds . . .' conveys simple defiance of heaven. 'The watery kingdom spits in the face of heaven' goes further, locating the defiance in England (the 'watery kingdom') and relating the English iconoclasm to the blasphemy of those who spat in Christ's face after his trial—a scene familiar to onlookers who remembered the mystery plays or parish images of the Passion. Hidden, concentrated lines such as these work like religious miniatures, drawing on the tradition of imaginative English spiritual literature cut short by the reformers. The description of Desdemona's survival of the storm in *Othello* represents Shakespeare's *tour de force* of this kind of writing, associating Desdemona's escape with the way true spirituality came through the first stages of the Reformation unscathed. The twins in *The Comedy of Errors* are parted in the 'unjust divorce' of a storm—the unjust divorce still preoccupying many, as we have seen, was Henry's divorce from Catherine, the origin of England's schism. The terms in which reformers and traditionalists argued about the Reformation are ingeniously mirrored in the argument about the storm between Casca and Cassius in *Julius Caesar*. The seas in *Pericles* 'wash both heaven and hell': a literal reference to the whitewashing of religious paintings in parish churches. From *The Comedy of Errors* to *The Winter's Tale*, families and friendships are severed in storms—which, in an image of England's forgotten Counter-Reformation, simultaneously give birth to new life. Innocent, rejuvenating characters such as Marina, Perdita, Miranda, Sebastian, Viola and Antipholus all emerge almost miraculously from storms and tempests. The tempest is a fundamental term in the grammar of Shakespeare's hidden plays.

Other equally consistent markers turn up on the journey through the plays and are listed in the Glossary at the end of this book: they include everyday words such as 'Time' and 'Moon', allusions to the old liturgy and more arcane classical and theological terms for the elite among his audience, many of them familiar from the poetry of the day. Together they comprise a set of precision tools that allow Shakespeare to fashion hidden dramas of unprecedented complexity, invisibly fused to the master plays.

But if he were to write like this and avoid the fate of Marlowe and Kyd, Shakespeare would need a great deal more than a sophisticated allegorical tool-kit. Before long, his subversive slant would come to the attention of the authorities. He needed to attract powerful patronage from the ranks of the aristocratic opposition—a rapidly diminishing resource in William Cecil's England.

3

THE PROTECTORS

A FORGOTTEN CAST of characters steps out from recent researches into the neglected Catholic records of the sixteenth century. In order to rediscover one of the most vivid, an elderly woman related to Shakespeare's two known patrons, we need to preface our chronological journey through his professional life with a short detour, for she is the subject of an extraordinary tribute in one of his last and greatest plays, *The Winter's Tale*, written shortly after her death in 1608. The tribute is closely linked to a coded level that had by then become highly sophisticated. But it also stands on its own: anyone familiar with her distinctive character would have recognised her at once. She was Magdalen Browne, Viscountess Montague, second wife of the Viscount Montague who had spoken out against the Oath of Supremacy at the beginning of Elizabeth's reign; by 1608, she had been a widow for sixteen years. Her great-nephew Ferdinando Stanley, Lord Strange, was Shakespeare's first patron; her grandson Henry Wriothesley, Earl of Southampton, was his second.[1] The tribute implies that she meant a great deal to Shakespeare: a close look at her remarkable character and the way he celebrated it reveals why.

Lady Magdalen's public Catholicism remained resolutely unaltered from her early years spent in the pious household of Anne, Countess of Bedford, until her death, three reigns later at the age of seventy-two. Her intimidating personality evidently made a deep impression on everyone who knew her. An account dating from the days when she was a young Lady of Honour at the court of Queen Mary records her reaction when Philip II of Spain incautiously made a pass at her. As Philip reached lecherously in through an open window, she 'took a staff lying by and strongly struck the king on the arm'.[2] Elizabeth herself was plainly awed by her. Almost alone among prominent Catholics, she was permitted to practise, and indeed to flaunt, her religion unmolested. A tall, majestic figure, ever conscious of her descent from the earls of Shrewsbury, she would 'pace abroad' in black, her face devoid of make-up (her conscience, she said, was her mirror), the forbidden rosary and crucifix in full view. If anyone dared object, then 'with a certain pious indignation she so rejected them that they durst not twice attempt the same'. One reason for her charmed life may have been that Magdalen Montague clearly inspired affection as well as respect in Elizabeth. The Queen overlooked the fact that the three Montague houses were not only storehouses where statues, chalices, relics and altar stones awaited the restoration to England of the old religion (there is a story of one precariously balanced altar stone falling on a visitor) but were well-known centres of refuge for priests where Mass was celebrated openly and with ceremony. In their house at Cowdray, known as 'Little Rome', Magdalen built a large new chapel, complete with high altar, choir and pulpit. In 1591, the aging Queen Elizabeth stayed for a week at Battle, telling Magdalen afterwards that 'she fareth much better for your prayers, and therefore desireth you ever hereafter to be mindful of her'.

She was, it appears, solidly built and unusually tall, 'her very body being erected by her upright mind'. Her gait was 'upright, sober and full of majesty'. Her head was 'round', but seemed little in proportion to her body. She had a strong chin, and short, sharp nose; her face was 'beautiful and long'. This description forms part of a memoir written by her confessor, Richard Smith, which he based on the address he gave to a 'large audience' at her funeral. As many in the audience must have known her personally, he begins by admitting disarmingly that she was no saint. Nonetheless, he goes on, in many ways Lady Magdalen resembled—or tried to resemble—St Jerome's handmaid, another noble widow called St Paula. In his role as confessor, Smith had clearly proposed to Lady Magdalen that she take St Paula as her model, for 'as she did equal St Paula in nobility, so she did imitate her virtues'—a parallel he returns to several times throughout the memoir. The success of this imitation, not always complete, he assesses under the headings of the various virtues, beginning with Humility. 'She was humble but amongst the humble, for among the potent and proud she seemed more lofty and potent'. Chastity—here her eight children, her many grandchildren, and of course her memorable repulse of King Philip made her 'an example to all matrons'. Patience: though 'sweet and mild to servants' she herself was the first to admit that she was full of "choler"'. Obedience: 'Often she said she left her will at St James' where she married'—a catchphrase that implies that wifely meekness might have been something of a struggle. Generosity—here she was exemplary, maintaining large Catholic households and assisting and feeding the poor, often, in those difficult times, one and the same thing. She was constant to her husband, devoting herself to his memory after his death—in this connection Richard Smith recalls another saying that might have raised a smile among those who had known her: 'Most frequently when she took her repast, and often at other times, even to the last day of her life, she was most gratefully mindful of him, using these or like words: 'God be merciful to his soul who left me this'. Above all, she was pious, praying 'day and night' like St Paula, observing the divine office and attending daily Mass. In spite of her faith, however, she did at one point despair of God's providence, as the penal laws tightened and the fortunes even of the privileged Montague family began to decay. At her funeral in 1608, when the Oath of Allegiance had just been re-imposed in even more stringent form, this might well have been the point in the address where the audience identified most closely with Magdalen Montague: it seemed that even she, byword for unflinching courage though she was, 'became melancholy at the ruin of her family'. In the end her faith was revived by a dream, and her life was subsequently devoted entirely to prayer, piety and good works.

The family immunity continued into King James's reign, by which time, Magdalen Montague, now a widow, had become a byword for Catholic recusancy: 'So manifest was her religion that scarce any in England had heard her name who knew her not also to be a Catholic' wrote her biographer; and 'the priests in England did everywhere extol her as the worthy patroness of the holy faith and the singular ornament of the religion in England'. In 1604, her grandson, Anthony Browne, 2nd Viscount Montague, made a speech in the Lords even more daring than that of her husband, condemning the new acts against recusants. In what amounted to an indictment of the whole process of the English Reformation, he 'inveighed', according to the *Journal of the House of Lords*, 'against the whole state of religion now established in this realm, pretending the great antiquity of their[s] and the novelty of this; saying that we had been misled to forsake the religion of our fathers, and to follow some light persons, of late time sprung up, that were of unsound doctrine, evil life or to that effect'. His outspokenness earned him a mere four days in the Fleet prison.

Towards the end of Magdalen Montague's life, it looked as if the Montagues might founder at last, for Guy Fawkes, a member of the 1605 Catholic conspiracy to blow up the Houses of Parliament known as the Gunpowder Plot, had once served as a retainer in their household. 'Let us say the litany and commit the matter to God' was Lady Magdalen's response—and sure enough, when the expected message arrived, it was to inform her that her house was indeed to be searched, but only by four people, and those to be nominated by herself. In 1607, the King's Council commanded that no sentence should proceed against her, in spite of her flagrant disregard for the law 'in regard that she is a noblewoman, aged, and by reason of her fidelity in the time of Queen Elizabeth was never called into question, it pleaseth the King's majesty that in her old years she be free from molestation'. This sounds, as it is meant to, like a magnanimous gesture on the part of the King, but in fact her position by this time was virtually unassailable. In the absence of any Catholic figurehead, Magdalen Montague had come to symbolise the Catholic cause to a large proportion of the population increasingly angry at having been cornered into a position in which their religion was synonymous with treachery.

Some time over the two years that followed her death in 1608, *The Winter's Tale* was first performed at the Globe Theatre. Based on Robert Greene's novel *Pandosto*, it has two important variations that make it less an adaptation of the original than a riposte to it. As Greene's novel enjoyed enormous popularity, Shakespeare's riposte would have drawn immediate attention. In both tales, a king is seized by a fit of jealousy and accuses his wife of adultery with his friend. Although the Delphic oracle vindicates the queen, she is punished, and the friend banished. Years later the king's long-lost daughter and the friend's son marry, healing the original rift.[3] Greene's, however, is fundamentally a grim story, whereas Shakespeare's, thanks to the introduction of a single new character, is one of redemption and joy. In Greene's version, the slandered wife dies, whereas the final act of *The Winter's Tale* reveals—all the more sensationally to those who knew *Pandosto* and expected the plot to be the same—that she has in fact been spirited away and preserved, to reappear lovingly united with her daughter and husband. The second variation is that Greene's jealous king compounds his original crime by unwittingly falling in love with his own daughter—when he discovers her identity, he commits suicide. The audience of *The Winter's Tale* are teased with this expected ending—but in

Shakespeare's version, the king's unhealthy interest in his dazzling daughter is cut short by sharp reminders of his vow to be constant to the memory of his dead wife. The agent in both cases, the catalyst that transforms a tale of death and despair to one of pure happiness where 'dear life from death redeems you' (5.3.102), is an entirely new character whose name and personality are Shakespeare's own invention—Paulina.

Paulina is a wholly unexpected creation. Instead of being a servant—which is all the plot requires—Shakespeare has made her a formidable *grande dame* with a retinue of her own who lives independently and in impressive style. The last scene opens on a guided tour of her house with its 'many singularities' (5.3.12), among them a chapel. At this point in the story, Paulina has been a widow for many years; when the story opens, however, she is still married to one of the king's trusted servants, Antigonus, a man who struggles to reconcile the dictates of his own conscience with the immorality of what he is required to do under his oath of allegiance—an oath brutally enforced by his sovereign. His outspoken wife's independent mind protects him to some extent—under his breath he encourages her in the bold stand he cannot afford to take himself. The king repeatedly derides Antigonus for this cowardly subversiveness—he calls him a dotard, woman-tired, unroosted, incapable of controlling his wife, a traitor. The blustering threats of fire, treachery and heresy establish a religious context. To a contemporary audience, this would not have been a loose digression but a reminder of the way the Protestant authorities constantly condemned outwardly conforming Catholics, government officials among them, for giving covert support and allegiance to the old religion through the activities of their wives, 'pernicious' female recusants over whom the law had less control. King James himself irritably contrasted Catholic wives, whose consciences were 'overruled by their Romish gods' with others whose vows were 'ever subject to the controlment of their husband'. The Montagues, of course, were one of the most conspicuous examples of just such a Catholic marriage.

Indeed, Paulina's whole background—her role in protecting the divided loyalties of a husband at court, her social status, her successful stand against the sovereign, her upright widowhood set in a great house with a chapel—mirrors that of Magdalen Montague. Furthermore, in a completely unnecessary digression, Antigonus mentions that they have three daughters—as did the Montagues. Antigonus even goes to the length of calling them 'co-heirs'—a ludicrously irrelevant detail, except as a form of covert identification. For the three Montague daughters were indeed co-heirs—Montague's son pre-deceased him, and the title passed instead to his grandson, Anthony Browne. Paulina's name, too, recalls Paula, the model Magdalen Montague took for her widowhood. Her rank is also suggested when Leontes sarcastically calls her 'Dame Partlet', and then 'Lady Margery'—the second a distinct reminder of the name 'Lady Magdalen'.

It is not only Paulina's family and social position that are defined well beyond the requirements of the plot and strongly recall the family and social position of Magdalen Montague. Her highly idiosyncratic character is one of the richest in the play. It combines near contradictory qualities: 'red-looked anger' (2.2.34), upright, rigorous principles, a strong sense of her own status, grandmotherly tenderness, awesome spiritual authority, brisk and fearless common sense. Her diction is distinct, exclamatory, imperative; her presence formidable, quelling not only the servants who attempt to remove her—she threatens to tear out their eyes—but also the king himself. 'Godlike indignation' was how the Victorian poet Algernon Swinburne described her manner, an almost exact echo of Richard Smith's description of Magdalen Montague's 'pious indignation'. Altogether, Paulina's character evokes that of Magdalen Montague, who was also choleric, physically and morally formidable, a model of integrity, a matriarch who saw herself as the guardian of threatened sacramental life, a fearless scourge of the court, 'lofty and potent' among the 'potent and proud'. A further Montague characteristic is suggested towards the end of the play: although the king and Paulina are reconciled, she tries his patience almost to the limit by constantly, at times maddeningly, recalling the virtues of the dead, a habit of Lady Montague's stressed, as we have seen, by Richard Smith. Paulina repeatedly recalls the dead queen and her own dead husband. This characteristic is, however, central to the play, for it is this nagging, this prompting to be constant to the memory of the old that prevents Leontes from abusing the new.

The great climax of *The Winter's Tale*, the statue scene, is the fundamental reason for the allusions, suggestions and parallels designed so far to encourage the audience to connect Paulina, 'that audacious lady' (2.3.43), with Magdalen Montague in the earlier parts of the play. By this time, Paulina's household has a secret. For sixteen years it has concealed what Paulina calls 'honesty and honour' (2.2.10), personified in the living presence of the true, beautiful and slandered Hermione. In just the same way, Magdalen Montague preserved in her houses not merely the treasures and altar stones of the old religion, but what to Catholics was the living, misrepresented reality—the sacraments and the Mass. Paulina's chapel becomes the setting for the most dramatic and mystical episode of the play—indeed, of all Shakespeare's plays. In a scene fraught with the sacramental and the numinous, Paulina reveals her role as the preserver of what was lost. She draws aside a curtain to reveal an extraordinarily lifelike statue of Hermione. The onlookers marvel at the sculptor's skill; to music, the statue stirs, steps down and embraces her long-lost husband. The religious dimension of this scene is heralded by the arrival, incognito, of the king's long-lost daughter, Perdita, embodiment of the new spirituality of Catholic underground England. But thanks to Paulina, the king is prevented from idolising Perdita purely for her own sake—instead, by following Paulina's advice to renew his faith and revive his love for the old, for the rejected and lost Hermione, he is brought to see the true relationship of new to old, that of child to mother. The language surrounding this profound recognition scene is resonant with the idiom of the old faith, so that one is invited to see it as a union of old and new on a spiritual level, as well as a human one. All those present are aware that the ceremony could be seen as 'superstition', 'magic', 'unlawful business', 'assisted / By wicked powers' (5.3.43–96)—precisely the objections levelled at the Mass. Those who decide to stay at a ceremony through which only Paulina can guide them are required to 'awake their faith' (5.3.95). To the sound of music they instinctively kneel; they realise that what is happening is not just mystical but natural—'holy . . . lawful as eating' (5.3.104–110). The great line 'dear life redeems you' (5.3.103) is thus set in the context of an event that for 1,500 years of Christianity had been seen as the deepest of all religious mysteries. The prolonged, dreamlike intensity of this happy ending arises from the intensity with which many longed for such a real-life ending, in which the old is revived by the homecoming of the new, and the new confirmed in the embrace of the old.

The Winter's Tale embodies in Paulina not only the flavour of Magdalen Montague's personality but her symbolic significance as custodian of the old religion, which many of Shakespeare's audience still believed was the soul of England and fervently hoped would one day revive again. Paulina is a rounded, unmistakable tribute to the life of Magdalen Montague made more poignant by the knowledge that she was both a moral example and, through her great-nephew and grandson, a practical patron to Shakespeare.

With this vivid character in mind, other symbolic vignettes begin to emerge from Shakespeare's earliest plays, the point at which he would have been most aware of Lady Magdalen's patronage. The manner and the role of the Abbess in *The Comedy of Errors* strongly resemble Magdalen Montague; and she also figures as Alice Montague, the Countess in *Edward III*, an early drama only recently restored to the canon that contains a barely disguised compendium of Catholic resistance language and incident.[4] Indignantly, she repels the adulterous advances of the king and sets him on the path of virtue. The chastened king praises her in terms that highlight the courageous behaviour of an earlier England, embodied in Alice Montague. The countess is given extended poetic treatment in language often identical to the language of the sonnets, and she bears a string of familiar allegorical marks of the English Catholic Church. She stresses the union of her soul and her body in terms of the indissoluble union between the spiritual church and its visible buildings:

> As easy may my intellectual soul
> Be lent away and yet my body live
> As lend my body, palace to my soul,
> Away from her and yet retain my soul.
> My body is her bower her court her abbey
> And she an angel pure divine unspotted
> If I should leave her house my lord to thee
> I kill my poor soul and my poor soul me.
> *(590–597)*

Like Macduff's exclamation in *Macbeth* that King Donald's 'sacrilegious' murderer has 'stolen thence the life of the building' (2.3.65–67), the Countess's image of her body as an abbey threatened by the King with the loss of its soul recalls the dissolution of the monasteries and chantries under Henry VIII. A little later, she uses the term itself: 'resolute to be *dissolved . . .*' (3.2.994). In highly specific language, she recalls, like Catholic polemicists, the conditions of the coronation oath, and the different forms of homage required by God and Caesar.[5]

Thanks to the constancy of Alice Montague, Edward retires, his virtue intact. The rest of the play presents him in the way the England of Shakespeare's day saw him—the archetype of the ideal English king. The drama is an image of the way things might have been if the monarch had acted with restraint, and the old church with discipline.

The Montagues were unusual in taking a courageous public stand on the subject of the oath; and *Edward III* contains one of the earliest and

fullest of Shakespeare's many treatments of this painful subject. Like the
king in *The Winter's Tale*, Edward uses every possible legal argument to
coerce Alice Montague's father, the Earl of Warwick, into persuading his
daughter to submit to the royal embrace. He begins by forcing him to
swear unconditional loyalty, ensuring that his subject's personal honour
will not stand in the way of his oath to his sovereign; next he demands, on
the word of honour he has just given, that he betray his deepest principles.

KING: Thinkst that thou can'st unswear thy oath again?
WARWICK: I cannot nor I would not if I could.
KING: But if thou dost what shall I say to thee?
WARWICK: What may be said to any perjured villain
    That breaks the sacred warrant of an oath.
KING: What wilt thou say to one that breaks an oath?
WARWICK: That he hath broke his faith with God and man
    And from them both stands excommunicate.
KING: What office were it to suggest a man
    To break a lawful and religious vow?
WARWICK: An office for the devil, not for man.
KING: The devil's office must thou do for me.
   (682–693)

And he leaves poor Warwick to soliloquise mournfully on the moral
dilemma so familiar to those in the audience, radical Protestants and
Catholics alike, 'sworn . . . by the name of God to break a vow made by the
name of God' (2.1.705–706).[6]

Contrasting the manly courage of old Catholic England with the
humiliating years of female rule that followed the Reformation was a
favourite ploy of resistance writers, stung by accusations of treachery and
collaboration with the Spanish. It looks as if one of Shakespeare's concerns
was to remind the country of one honourable pedigree in particular, for
his history plays not only go out of their way to dramatise instances of
divided loyalty, they repeatedly alter events in order to highlight the patriotic bravery of the Montague-Stanley forebears. In this aim, he was triumphantly successful. His early *Henry VI* plays were a tremendous hit; and
their undoubted hero was not the weak, saintly king, but Magdalen Montague's great-great-grandfather, Talbot, Earl of Shrewsbury. In the words
of Shakespeare's ebullient contemporary, the satirist and playwright
Thomas Nashe:

How would it have joyed brave Talbot, the terror of the French, to think that after he had lain two hundred years in his tomb, he should triumph again on the stage and have his bones new embalmed with the tears of ten thousand spectators at least (at several times), who, in the tragedian that represents his person, imagine they behold him fresh bleeding![7]

Ten thousand spectators several times—the surviving playhouse accounts bear out Nashe's testimony to the box-office success of Shakespeare's portrayal of Magdalen's ancestor. Even more gratifying to the Montague family, it was a portrayal designed to correct any misconceptions the public might have about the patriotism of his descendants. In the first place, he is the 'Terror of the French', trouncing decadent Catholic forces led by Joan of Arc. For the audience, there was a strong parallel with their own times. At the moment when *Henry VI* was at the height of its popularity, English forces were fighting alongside Henry of Navarre against the army of the Catholic League in France. On the surface, this emphasised the Montagues' strongest card, noted as we have seen by Elizabeth—they did everything they could to demonstrate that their religion was no bar to loyalty to their country. But here again Shakespeare shows himself the master of double meanings. His Joan of Arc is no saint; in fact she has strong parallels with crude contemporary representations of Luther. She acts from direct inspiration, which she claims comes from God, though in fact her prayers are answered by fiends. She is the object of a slavish personality cult. Shakespeare allows the parallels to grow on his audience before inserting some decisive markers at the end—the Lutheran doctrine of salvation by grace is mentioned, and finally, when Joan is found to be pregnant, he gives her the label 'precise', a word virtually synonymous with 'Puritan', evoking rigorous moral observance: 'Is all your strict preciseness come to this?' (5.4.67). So Talbot dies fighting not only the duplicitous French, but—with a more hidden topicality—a false foreign idol who believes in personal revelation.

Talbot's deathscene was the highlight of the play at the time, according to Nashe; and it suggests that Shakespeare was already hoping to gain the ear of the Queen herself. From the hero's ashes, he predicts, 'shall be rear'd / A *phoenix* that shall make all France afear'd' (4.7.93). The play points to Talbot's descendants: Montague thoughts would have turned at once to cherished hopes that one of the scions of the family—Henry Wriothesley, Anthony Browne, or Lord Strange—would one day help to return England to its pre-Reformation position in Christendom. But it also points to England's peerless, virginal phoenix, Elizabeth I, whose forces were currently fighting in France on behalf of her beleaguered fellow Protestants.

Shakespeare's plays compliment the noble family acting as his patrons; but more than that, they dramatise the political and religious ideals they stood for, elegantly pleading the Catholic cause in the halls of great houses, in the new London theatres, and, before long, in front of the Queen and the court. There were those who resented his good fortune. The bitterness of Robert Greene's attack on the cocky young playwright arises not simply from the fact that Shakespeare was an upstart actor who conceals a dangerous 'tiger's heart' under his 'player's hide'. Greene was jealous. While Greene is dying in poverty, 'Shake-scene' has found himself a comfortable billet with grand protectors. Greene describes him as a maddeningly thrifty ant, who, thanks to his prudence and industry, is now sheltered from the storm and being 'fed with cates' (good meals). Worse, the 'waspish little worm' refuses to help out his old friend Greene, a starving grasshopper, whom he coldly bids 'pack hence . . . my house doth harbor no unthrifty mates'.[8] Another contemporary, Thomas Edwards, is kinder. In 1595, he describes 'Adon'—widely assumed to mean Shakespeare—holed up, 'I have heard say', somewhere in London, 'the Centre of our clime', hidden by the 'purple robes' of the aristocracy and 'tilting under Friaries'. The 'friaries' evoke Holywell, Blackfriars and the dissolved priory that was Montague Close.[9]

His shadowy patrons evidently set an unusually high value on their protégé. A year after Greene's attack appeared, its publisher, Henry Chettle, was forced to issue a grovelling apology. He realizes the attack was 'offensively taken' and regrets his own lack of judgment. An interview with a number of personages 'of worship' has changed his mind. Shakespeare was not, after all, an upstart crow. On the contrary, he was civil, upright, honest and talented, with a 'facetious grace in writing that approves his art'. Chettle's cringing volte-face confirms the reason for Shakespeare's surprisingly long run of covertly dissident drama. His passion for his cause was shared by dedicated, influential people prepared to go to great lengths to protect him.

II

Passive Resistance,
1588–1594

4

RECONCILIATION, 1588–1592

England's Divided Family

B Y THE YEAR 1588, as far back as most people in England could remember, the country had been governed by two women and a boy. At court, all talk of the succession was forbidden; but to Elizabeth's grumbling subjects, the solution to the country's dangerous instability was obvious—it needed a strong, masculine ruler. A divided, unhappy family tearing itself apart had become a favourite resistance image for what one of the Montague family called 'this miserable country of ours'.[1] It was an image that would become one of the primary themes in Shakespeare's earliest coded plays.

Robert Persons, Campion's fellow Jesuit who managed to escape from England after his arrest, paints a graphic picture of the family quarrel between the country's temporal mother and spiritual father. 'In a great and noble house, where there are many children of the self-same parents, if those same parents come to breach and fall out among themselves, what can the children be but sorrowful and silent and sigh at such contentions, without taking willingly any part, for that they love, fear and reverence both . . . Her Majesty being our Queen is thereby also our mother, and nourisheth us her subjects as a careful parent . . . the Bishop of Rome to all Catholic men of the world is their spiritual father . . . but now our said two parents are fallen at debate'.[2] At his most persuasive, he envisages the quarrel's resolution. The English would at last 'laugh and sing together' and, 'united in defence of the realm', all would 'pray to God most heartily for Her Majesty's health, wealth, and prosperous long continuance'. In this ideal England all would be 'friends and familiar together, as in Germany and other places, notwithstanding the differences of religion'; it would be a place where each man could 'show his reason without fear and hear another man's arguments without suspicion of fraud or violence'.[3]

Persons's plea for national reconciliation was repeated even more eloquently by the Jesuits' most effective man on the ground in England: by 1588, the charismatic young Robert Southwell had set up one of the country's few illegal printing presses somewhere in Spitalfields, just north of the City of London's walls. The books he managed to print and distribute argue passionately for toleration, contrasting what he termed the natural 'obedience' of Catholics with the divisiveness of Protestant sects. But he went deeper, identifying spiritual apathy as the root cause of the country's family quarrel. England was a land where 'the variety of religion hath abolished almost all religion'.[4] His goal was to use all possible literary means to convert the country's influential ruling class. Well acquainted with this often cynical elite, he stressed the humanist aspect of Catholicism, portraying all creation, however profane, as a ladder to God. He urges a return to the religious life; without God, human beings are 'wandering strangers in this far and foreign country . . . drudges in the miry farm of this world'. He describes the neglected soul as 'a forlorn and left widow, deprived of her spouse's fellowship'.[5] Southwell's language is youthfully romantic—but it is vividly illustrated with everyday images; his love of England and his chivalric view of spiritual life are carefully targeted at the country's nobility. Before long he began to produce openly Catholic religious poetry, adapting the language of romance to divine subjects and calling for similar boldness from his fellow writers. His literary offensive was successful—there were conversions among unlikely London authors; by the early 1590s, even such hardened hacks as Robert Greene were writing of 'repentance' and exhorting others to live better lives.

Just up the road from the hidden press at Spitalfields, even further from the vigilant authorities within London's walls, was the Holywell Theatre, notorious resort of priests and papists, arena for the first run of Shakespeare's apprentice plays. A gibbet stood outside the theatre, a grisly warning to dissident companies like Lord Strange's Men: two priests had been executed there in the wake of the Armada.[6] Robert Southwell must have watched the dense crowds thoughtfully and reflected on the influence of the nearby playhouse, a more effective media channel than his own hunted press. He had wide experience of drama in the schoolrooms, the streets and the theatres in Rome. It had been his principal teaching tool: theatre, it was widely acknowledged abroad, was what the Jesuits did best.

And back in London it seems that he, or someone like him, made an inspired approach to William Shakespeare.

It seems likely that Shakespeare, who may well have met Campion and Persons years earlier, was already in sympathy with their cause. Or perhaps, like many of his contemporaries, he had been affected by an encounter with one of London's underground missionaries. Whatever the reason, the forgotten, coded purpose of Shakespeare's earliest plays coincides strikingly with the aim of Persons's and Southwell's 'publishing apostolate'. These light comedies address the same message of spiritual revival and political reunion to the same target audiences; their plots revolve round the same image of a divided family; the most polished of them attempts to plead the cause of toleration with the Queen. And a small detail, suggesting a coded signature, hints at a discreet link with Southwell's mission. This is Shakespeare's apparent fixation with the name 'Luke'. St Luke's feast day had a profound significance for Robert Southwell. It was the day on which he joined the Jesuit order, a feast day shared by St Faith, whose priory his unscrupulous grandfather had robbed to build the family home. He and Garnet adopted Luke as the patron of their dangerous enterprise; the pair attributed one of the most dramatic escapes of the Jesuit missionaries to his protection.[7] Shakespeare's coded drama repeatedly gives variations of the name 'Luke' to Catholic figures and places.

In the late 1580s, Shakespeare was a member of the acting company Lord Strange's Men, and Ferdinando Stanley, Lord Strange, was a man as enigmatic and intriguing as his name suggests. The great-nephew of the outspoken Magdalen Montague, he was strongly suspected of Catholicism. 'All the Stanleys are traitors' growled one of the hit men of the regime, Richard Topcliffe. But most of the Stanleys were also cautious characters who played their cards close to their chest. Strange's understated portrait gives little away, yet he was clearly an attractive and highly intelligent man. The future Earl of Derby, he was the unwilling focus of hopes for a Catholic succession, and he kept his religious and political allegiance carefully secret, adopting instead the harmless role of a scholarly dilettante. Of the same generation as Shakespeare and Southwell, he was the leading light of a group of intellectual noblemen that included the equally suspect Henry Percy, a scientist and necromancer known as the 'Wizard Earl' of Northumberland. Strange's own plays and poetry were widely admired, and his patronage was courted on all sides. Many of the leading writers of the day were on his payroll—among them Kyd, Marlowe, Lodge and Nashe. Unlike their rivals, the Queen's Men, who could be trusted to stage patriotic propaganda while touring the country, Lord Strange's Men were a seditious group, sailing perilously close to the wind with daringly subversive plays and responding in 'very Contemptuous manner' to an order to cease playing in 1589.[8]

A number of Shakespeare's sonnets, read 'with eyes' in the way he himself recommends, contain wordplay on Strange's name and situation revealing that during this early period, these two clever, circumspect young men became unusually close in spite of their difference in rank. Passages throughout Shakespeare's work suggest that this golden period was one of the most profound and formative experiences of his life. A comic digression in *Edward III* portrays an impatient patron giving his secretary a tutorial in the double-edged art of writing his 'love' poetry for him. The scene appears to be a witty tribute to the man who drew Shakespeare into the centre of the dissident Catholic entourage that revolved around the Montagues, initiating what one of the sonnets calls a 'pupil pen' into the craft of coded literature.

The spiritual drive and idealism of Southwell, the sophisticated humanism of Strange and their shared concern for the future of England's feuding family—these are the staple ingredients of the hidden material of Shakespeare's earliest comedies: *The Taming of the Shrew*, *The Comedy of Errors* and *The Two Gentlemen of Verona*. The first stop on our journey through the turbulent years between 1590 and 1612, during which Shakespeare wrote his greatest plays, these imperfect early dramas reward close examination, for like the first productions of many other great artists, they give an invaluable glimpse of the master in his workshop.

These plays sparkle with wit, pace and optimism. Greene was right: William Shakespeare was an ebullient young author in no doubt of his own powers. Quite how new to the job he was in the late 1580s is revealed by the naive style of *Edward III*, the single play he did not revise for later publication. Gradually increasing in political insight and artistic subtlety, these comedies draw on the resistance image of the divided family in order to propose the reunion of the various strands of post-Reformation England under the firm spiritual leadership associated with the old order.

The simplest of these dramas is *The Taming of the Shrew*, the most accessible entry point to Shakespeare's hidden writing. It features a notorious instance of the way the code can mislead and even repel modern spectators. A shrewish wife is brought to heel by a forceful husband, and exits with a meek speech recommending female submission. Feminists are horrified: Shakespeare is normally more sensitive about relations between the sexes. The best excuse has been that he was attempting to appeal to the Holywell groundlings. But as so often in the early plays, the topical meaning distorts the universal one. The young Shakespeare is still struggling with the demanding task of sustaining two detailed plots within a single story line. The oddly political language used at the end by the chastened shrew is meant to alert us to the play's secondary level. A good wife should not be a 'rebel' or a 'graceless traitor' to her 'sovereign'; she should observe 'such duty as the subject owes the prince' (5.2.155). Audiences remembering the many levels of the mystery plays would have been on to it at once: and the comic context would have made it doubly entertaining to English spectators suffering exactly the conditions Shakespeare describes.

This is the parallel story they would have enjoyed alongside the now famous tale of a comic domestic squabble in Padua. England is torn apart by two quarrelling factions. A weak ruler despairs of controlling the dominant Puritans, who, from a mixture of motives—partly envy, partly revenge for their own sufferings during the previous reign—persecute the passive but more appealing and beautiful old religion. Papal authority is flouted, Catholics are imprisoned, whipped and impoverished and the beauties of the old religion are destroyed. In its place, the Puritans attempt to enforce an unpopular new form of worship. The play ends with a proposal as familiar to London's streets and taverns as it was to great houses and foreign embassies: a return to a lost social order under the rule of an idealised pre-Reformation monarch—a straightforward, full-blooded and above all masculine authority. He quells the upstart Puritan faction, stands well clear of devious Catholic plots and disputes, and teaches both of them civil obedience within the unquestioned authority of Catholic Christendom.

The key to this hidden story lies in a set of coded markers, clustered around the identity tags of dark and fair; they include a Catholic 'Luke' figure and, in the background, a 'St Luke's' chapel. (The Glossary at the end of the book explains a number of terms more fully.)

The setting is a household in chaos. Two sisters caricature the country's warring factions, the dark and shrewish Katherine, 'brown in hue as a hazel nut', representing the new religion—Protestantism—and Bianca, a name that means 'white' in Italian,[9] representing the old. When Bianca refuses to reveal the name of her lover, Katherine ties her up and beats her, forcing her to strip off her pretty clothes, while repeatedly threatening, for no clear reason, to be revenged.[10] In a parody of the crackdown on freedom of worship, Katherine's weak father is forced to bow to her demands that no one should 'worship' Bianca until she, Kate, is married even though, unlike her, Bianca is surrounded by admirers. In true Puritan fashion, the volatile Katherine smashes a lute over her tutor's head, calling him, in the Puritan slang of the day, a 'twangling jack'.[11] Bianca is passive and self-pitying, a natural victim, but sanctified in religious terms by her suitors—one of them a foolish old man and another, Lucentio, disguised as a student of Greek and Latin from Rheims, the scholastic centre for Catholic exiles. The suitors are portraits of typical old and new Catholics, passionately idealising the sacramental religion, the younger ones ardent activists who become hopelessly entangled in their own plots and disguises. The helpless father is given a name that is oddly feminine—'Baptista'—and has overtones of the reformed religion, in which baptism was one of the two remaining sacraments.

Enter the swaggering Petruchio—an equally suggestive name, diminutive of Peter. He is a personification of all that is most vigorous and irreverent in an idealised pre-Protestant England. He accepts the task of taming Kate so that the suitors can attain the sacramental Bianca but discusses the job in pragmatic, political terms. His marriage will be a reign; he talks not of love but of law and covenants. In the simplified landscape of the play, he represents the kind of ruler able to check the chief obstacle to religious co-existence—vengeful Protestant extremists.

He sets about the task with pre-Reformation relish, wrecking his solemn Protestant wedding service with rude and riotous behaviour, ridiculous clothes and a smacking kiss.[12] He woos Kate 'in her own humour' by giving her a prolonged and varied taste of her own medicine—subjecting her to the same joyless regime that the Puritans proposed for England. This passage must have given particular amusement, for a common accusation against many Puritans was hypocrisy—they prescribed austerity while enjoying all the benefits of wealth and high office.

First, he re-christens Kate, reversing this common Puritan practice so that she is no longer 'precise'[13] and solemn 'Katherine', but domestic 'Kate'. In case we have still missed her Lutheran credentials, Petruchio announces at the wedding 'Here she stands'. This echo of the catchphrase for which Luther became famous, 'Here I stand', is another ironic reversal of the Reformation stance, for he is in fact overriding Kate's Lutheran defiance.[14] He next subjects her to sermons and to moralising, tantalises her with extravagant clothes that he then slashes to pieces, railing against her hat as 'lewd and filthy', and makes her fast. All this was standard Puritan practice, imposed by the government and deeply resented. Most tellingly of all, Petruchio commands Kate to call the sun the moon. This has always been seen as a crazy whim to enforce ultimate obedience—and in the outer play, it is just that. But covertly, it is a reminder to the almanac-conscious audience that the man who prevented England from signing on to the international agreement on the Gregorian calendar was Grindal, the Archbishop of Canterbury, a Puritan sympathiser, backed by the dominant Puritan faction in Parliament. As Voltaire later observed: 'The English mob preferred their calendar to disagree with the sun than to agree with the Pope'.[15] In the play, the happy ending begins when Kate's views on the sun at last agree with Petruchio's.

Down to the last detail, then, Shakespeare associates Katherine with the Puritan faction. With equal accuracy, Petruchio's household is made to embody an idealised picture of pre-Reformation life—earthy, rumbustious, full of servants with exaggerated names of banned saints—one of them is called Gregory, recalling the calendar Pope—yet all merrily obedient to their unpredictable master. The same is true of Bianca, who is as typical of the oppressed Catholic faction as Kate is of the Puritans. She defines herself as clearly as a character in a morality play: 'Old fashions please me best' (3.1.78). Kate may be married by a vicar, but Bianca, at St Luke's, has a priest. She is surrounded by admirers in disguise who call her sacred, sweet, patroness of heavenly harmony—phrases common to coded madrigals and lyrics. Suspecting by the end that she may also prove a handful once Kate is out of the way, one suitor secretly attends Petruchio's taming school.

Shakespeare never revisited the Punch-and-Judy simplicity of *The Taming of the Shrew*, a cartoon world of upstart Puritans and furtive Catholics not so very different from the picture most modern readers have of Reformation England. *The Comedy of Errors*, written at around the same time, is a complete contrast. Hilariously entertaining, it is also one of Shakespeare's most ambitious coded works, intended for spectators like the clever young lawyers and clerks of London's Inns of Court before whom it was performed in 1594. Again, family division is the central image; but this time the story digs far deeper into the national psyche. It downplays the sectarian issue, restating the rift in fresh terms that would have broader appeal. England's religious divisions become part of a wider drama, one that traces the relationship between a forlorn, secular England and its exiled spiritual inheritance. A Catholic contemporary, Thomas Lodge, develops the concept in his poem 'Truth's Complaint over England': 'disdained' Truth takes flight with the words 'You Islanders adieu, /

You banished me, before I fled from you'.[16] But Shakespeare enriches the image. In order to highlight the full spiritual significance that Catholics read into this theme of Reformation loss, Shakespeare borrows profound religious language from scriptural and humanist teachings on man's dual nature. He gives the age-old theological theme a novel political twist by applying it to the dual nature of his own country, whose material and spiritual elements had been torn apart some forty years earlier.

To stage such abstractions in a London playhouse was an almost impossible challenge—but Shakespeare hit on a graphic image from his own family life that precisely conveyed the idea of a divided psychic entity, longing for reunion. He was by now the father of young twins aged around five, Judith and Hamnet, and had clearly pondered the phenomenon of two distinct individuals who resembled complementary aspects of a single being. Twins were the ideal metaphor for the divided halves of an organic unity.

In *The Comedy of Errors*, loosely based on a farce by the Roman dramatist Plautus, twins part at birth in the 'unjust divorce' of a Reformation storm. Shakespeare calls them both Antipholus, suggestive of the Greek word meaning 'Lover of the other', though he distinguishes them by naming one Antipholus of Ephesus and the other, Antipholus of Syracuse. One settles down in Ephesus, where he becomes a distracted businessman with a nagging wife and grasping mistress. He is the image of soulless, mercantile England. The other twin, dreamy, melancholy and religious, wanders the world looking for his lost brother—he represents the spirituality missing from England since the Reformation and matches Southwell's description of the exiled soul, a 'wandering stranger' in a 'far and foreign country'. When he chances on Ephesus, his behaviour becomes very like that of the hunted underground missionaries. He eventually finds an answering spiritual spark waiting to be rekindled in his brother's household in the person of Luciana, his brother's quiet sister-in-law.

But errors multiply. England's soul and body are unable to reunite unaided. They are entangled in political problems that can only be resolved within the firm universal framework of Catholic Christendom, represented here by a no-nonsense abbess, who is in fact the twins' long-lost mother. She prescribes a return to a life of discipline and virtue. The unrecognised father of the twins, condemned to death at the beginning of the play, is reprieved in the joyful denouement, in which the whole family join together in a long-delayed christening feast in the abbey. A united, reconsecrated England emerges from the chaos.

Other writers might have introduced this theme as a shadowy parallel to the intricate plot. But accuracy and consistency were two of the defining tools of Shakespeare's coded technique, and a closer look at the skein of references will reveal just how ingenious he could be when he was addressing passionately held views to an intellectual audience.

The first indication that the setting is Elizabeth's London comes in a reference that pays elegant tribute to the underground Jesuit code, a simple cipher that used the motif of 'merchant' priests, braving the 'tempest' to trade in souls.[17] An innocent 'merchant' is about to be hanged. The site of his execution is located later in the play in 'the melancholy vale . . . / Behind the ditches of the abbey here' (5.1.120–122). Shakespeare is careful to identify this particular abbey as a priory, linking it to Holywell itself, once a priory for Benedictine nuns. No one could miss the allusion to the recent execution in the ruins of the priory outside the theatre. Like all Shakespeare's coded references, it is scrupulously precise. The explanation that 'well-dealing'[18] Syracusan merchants are executed in Ephesus purely because Ephesan merchants have been executed in Syracuse recalls the revenge for the Marian burnings that lay behind Elizabethan martyrdoms. For good measure, Shakespeare adds that the deaths are the result of 'rigorous statutes' (1.1.9) brought in by clerical-sounding 'synods' in both cities.

The calendar marker confirms that the background is Protestant England, not Ephesus. One of the repeated errors in the play is the visiting twin's inability to catch on to the right time. His experience is the familiar one of a traveller who unexpectedly finds himself in the wrong time zone. The visiting twin is an hour out when we first meet him: and by Act 4 the confusion has deepened: 'It was two ere I left him, and now the clock strikes one' says his servant: 'The hours come back!' comes the answer 'As if Time were in debt!' (4.2.54-6).

The aspects of Ephesus that Shakespeare adopts from his sources also point to a city like his own London, a swarming, noisy trade centre, bewildering and hostile to foreigners. The play's Ephesus is a city where commerce rules. Everything has its price; everyone, it seems, is hurrying to a business meeting: even the resident twin's relations with his mistress revolve around a ring and a chain worth forty ducats. Poems and sermons at the time regularly condemned the way England had replaced religion with commerce. Another replacement for religion was superstition and magic, which also flourish in Ephesus.

Unusually, Shakespeare avoids the high-low, fair-dark markers in this play; the earliest version may have predated his first use of them. He falls back on more obvious identifying tags, attaching them surreptitiously to the servant of the 'spiritual', exiled Antipholus. The 'spiritual' servant is familiar with mystery plays and morality plays; he crosses himself and calls for his beads—markers that evoke the lost practices of popular piety. Shakespeare also experiments with the relatively crude device of inn signs. The spiritual twin stays at an inn called the Centaur, associated in medieval imagery with man's dual nature—another nudge towards the play's hidden theme of the soul dissociated from the body. Though the twin arrives in a spiritual mood, the animal aspect of Ephesus soon over-whelms him—he gradually loses his composure, beats his servant, becomes entangled in ridiculous disputes, then is tied up, harangued as a madman by an ignorant 'Dr Pinch' and thrown into prison—where, reduced to the level of a raging beast, he chews through his cords and makes for the abbey. These experiences mirror the disorientation and perse-cution of many of the returned exiles and suggest that some of these idealists, overwhelmed by the problems of the country they had come to evangelise, became frustrated and confused victims rather than missionaries.[19]

This twin's meeting with Luciana is one of the first instances of Shake-speare's most characteristic allegorical moment, one that was to become central to his work.[20] These exquisite passages of mystical union illuminate the encounter between the isolated, persecuted, apparently dormant spiri-tuality of England and the exiles who had spent impoverished and lonely years of education abroad in order to bring the Mass back to their country. The reunion of these long-divided Catholics, often in dangerous sur-roundings, aroused profound emotions. The journals and letters of under-cover priests repeatedly stress their awe at the self-sacrifice and courage of men and women who had struggled to continue their religion against all the odds—some secretly, some in prison or destitution—and who now risked their lives to harbour priests for the sake of the Mass. Conversely, not only for Catholics but for many in England, the returning priests embodied everything the Reformation had hoped for when it attacked the worldliness and corruption of the old church.[21] These of course were the elite—among the many who crossed the English Channel there must have been a number who fell short of the ideal. But the surviving profiles of those who were eventually imprisoned or executed or who for years eluded capture as they continued to celebrate the Mass make impressive reading. Shakespeare is not always flattering about these people: his alle-gorical layer reveals a detailed knowledge of their varied natures, goals and motives. But for their returning encounter with the country for which they gave up so much, and the moment of mutual recognition with their suffering co-religionists in England, he reserves some of his most transcendent writing. Luciana's home, the house of the worldly brother, has a telltale inn sign—it is called the Phoenix. The sign hanging outside the house prepares the audience for the moment when the latent spirituality of England will burst into new life.

But the Phoenix is also an emblem of the end of an old existence. Shakespeare includes in the Phoenix not only the English Catholic revival but the rejection and decline of old Catholic England. It is the home of an unhappy marriage. Bored with his reproachful wife, Adriana, the resident twin has taken to spending time with his business colleagues and a local courtesan. Adriana harangues her more docile sister, Luciana, about her absent husband's faithlessness, and the pair engage in the kind of veiled debate familiar to audiences from the plays of John Lyly. The two women clearly identify themselves: Luciana is the patient, passively resistant new Catholicism of Shakespeare's own day, which recommended a difficult obedience. The scorned Adriana represents old Catholicism, whose slackness drove the country into the arms of the reformers and which, too late, regrets the consequences.[22] Adriana has some of the best lines. She angrily rejects Luciana's 'fool-begged patience' (2.1.41): her love for her lost husband is expressed in language that often mirrors the words of his spiritual brother—for all her faults, she too represents the traditional channel to the divine. The speeches of both these severed lovers, Adriana and the exiled twin, eloquently convey a sense of longing for the re-integration of a damaged unity—'undividable, incorporate . . . better than thy dear self's better part' (2.2.121–122). On the spiritual level, this hope of reintegration is Shakespeare's central preoccupation from first to last.

Shakespeare cannot resist giving Adriana's rival, the unnamed courtesan, a third inn sign—the Porcupine. The ingenuity of the allegory at this point must have amused courtly spectators, and it foreshadows the minute political references and jokes in later plays. From 1589 onwards, England was indeed engaged in a relationship with a 'porcupine', for it was the heraldic device of their one ally against the European Catholic powers, Henry of Navarre. Navarre had star quality for many in England at the time—his liberal-minded court was a place of refuge for exiles from all quarters, he opposed the corrupt Catholic Guise faction, he was Calvinist without being fanatical, and there was the great hope for the beleaguered English government that he would bring Protestantism to France. Above all, he was an ally against Spain. His claim to the French throne was enthusiastically supported by English money and troops, led, before long, by Elizabeth's young favourite, the Earl of Essex. Elizabeth meanwhile embroidered Henry a scarf and flirted with his ambassadors. But the campaign dragged on inconclusively for the next five years and the relationship soured as the pair squabbled over money. For educated observers there would have been a subtle interest in each twist and turn of the twin's negotiations with the grasping hostess of the 'Porcupine', particularly lines such as the twin's rueful comment, '[T]his jest shall cause me some expense' (3.1.123).

The abbess personifies in her practical wisdom much that was lost in the dissolution of the monasteries, along with their hospitals, herb gardens and dispensaries. At her hands, the distraught twin is healed with rest and herbs, not the hysterical exorcisms and confinements of the quack, Dr Pinch. She counsels the reproachful wife, the personification of the old, rejected English church. Adriana should have acted decisively and at once, scolds the abbess: she should have shamed her erring husband, not worn him down by nagging. This is sensible advice on a personal level, and politically the line taken by many modern historians, who pinpoint the weakness of the hand-wringing old order in failing to take a firm stand against the Protestant takeover. Through the abbess, the play ends in the spiritual embrace of the abbey, symbol of the hope that England would one day heal all divisions, and both 'tendencies'—high and low—would return to the fold of the universal church. The final lines have a distinctly ecumenical ring as the servants of the two twins enter the abbey like 'brother and brother', not 'one before another' (5.1.423–424).

This foray into Shakespeare's hidden language gives a snapshot of his political standpoint at the outset of his career. England is presented as a secularised country with a hidden vein of spirituality waiting to be recovered by the influx of priests from abroad. But he depicts these men as vulnerable— they are isolated and lonely; no sooner have they arrived than they are liable to be misrepresented, persecuted and imprisoned, even executed. He ridicules the exorcisms that were practised by a number of churchmen at the time. He analyses acutely the weaknesses of the country's old religious order, which allowed the state takeover, and suggests that the continuing rumbling insubordination of old Catholicism—the nagging wife—only serves to drive the regime further into the arms of Protestant allies like Henry of Navarre—the Porcupine. He recalls the true native strength of English Catholicism in the person of the abbess—it is here, he proposes, in reviving all that was best in the old religion, that England's ideal future lies.[23]

England the Cruel Lover

SHAKESPEARE's first plays develop a second and more specifically Catholic analogy for the condition of England. It makes a brief appearance in *The Comedy of Errors* and later becomes a central theme in six major plays. This was the story of an unstable character who leaves his partner to pursue a new and unresponsive love; he is in turn pursued by his faithful lover, who resorts to disguise and to extremes of self-abasement to recover him. In Shakespeare's work this staple of old fairy tales becomes an emotionally charged emblematic episode: fickle England attempts to pursue and appropriate an essentially foreign faith, rejecting and abusing its true partner, traditional English spirituality. Like the heroines of such tales, those who are constant to 'true' old England will brave danger, impoverishment, disguise and humiliation to remain close to their beloved, believing the infatuation will pass. It is given its fullest treatment in *All's Well That Ends Well*, one of Shakespeare's least watchable plays largely because the polemical luggage and emotional charge of the tale's inner meaning threaten to swamp the surface plot. Helena, the mystical figure who pursues her lover, is given unreal, saintly status, while the worthless Bertram, representing fickle England, acts from motives quite incomprehensible to a modern audience.[24]

The story forms the basis of *The Two Gentlemen of Verona*, another early play directed at Lord Strange's sophisticated circle, though, just as in *The Comedy of Errors*, Shakespeare keeps popular audiences in mind, giving the more rarefied main characters comic servants who provide a simpler version of the debate, with canny old Launce outwitting the literate, gullible young Speed. Though in dramatic terms this is one of his less successful plays, the work that goes into it gives him the final pieces he needs to complete the basic allegorical equipment that, with running adjustments and refinements, will underpin the rest of his work.[25]

One major advance lies in the portrayal of Protestantism. Instead of caricature, Shakespeare for the first time gives a thoughtful portrait of a crucial element in English politics that until now he has overlooked—the original reforming impulse and the ideal that inspired it. *Two Gentlemen* also marks the first attempt to characterise the hapless villain of the piece—not upstart Puritans or furtive Catholics but fickle England. As a country, England will take various personified forms as Shakespeare's work develops—sometimes as a figure of pathos, sometimes senile, sometimes gullible, sometimes desperate and deluded—but, though his analysis of the causes deepens, he never forgets the country's original crime, the desertion and mistreatment of its proper spiritual heritage for the sake of an alien faith.

Proteus ('changeable') is England, and his turbulent relationship with Julia, the traditional English religion, is portrayed with historical precision throughout the play, from the early attempts at reform before England's split with Rome to the inconclusive situation in the 1590s.[26] His close friend Valentine represents the English idealists inspired in the early years of the Reformation by Calvin's Geneva. Mocking his lazy friend for being 'tied by the "chains" of affection', Valentine travels abroad and discovers the new religion in its proper, continental setting, embodied in the beautiful Silvia. Throughout, his actions are upright and honourable. A string of Protestant markers accompanies their courtship. A reference to which Shakespeare will often return is Hallowmass. This was 1 November, the feast of All Saints' Day, the date on which the Protestant Reformation began. According to popular belief, it was on that day in 1517 that Luther nailed his ninety-five theses to the church door at Wittenberg. Valentine is 'a beggar at Hallowmass' (2.1.27). There is a second reference here to the reforming Dutch 'Beggars', who at the time were establishing a relatively tolerant religious regime in Amsterdam. Valentine's defiant passion is that of a reformer defying the Pope rather than a lover—'Wilt thou aspire to guide the heavenly car / And with thy daring folly burn the world? (3.1.154)' thunders Silvia's father—his imperial rank a reminder that Luther's adversary was the Holy Roman Emperor. Silvia 'makes other worthies nothing . . . She is alone' (2.4.166–167), an echo of the Lutheran manifesto 'Faith alone' and 'Scripture alone'. The catchphrase 'Here she stands' (5.4.129) makes another appearance.

Proteus brings chaos. Leaving his temperamental Julia, he also travels overseas and falls for Silvia himself. From here on, the unlikely plot follows the unhappy results of the English attempts to hijack Genevan Protestantism and impose it on their own country, a policy resisted by radical Protestants as well as Catholics. Scholars are mystified by Valentine's behaviour at the end of the drama. When Proteus attempts to rape Silvia, Valentine offers to 'share' her with Proteus. This is another of the awkward points in the early plays where the allegory distorts the literal level.

Valentine is forced out of character—an indication of how determined Shakespeare was that his plays should retain an accurate portrait of England's struggle for its religious and political identity.

Meanwhile, almost unnoticed, Julia has disciplined herself through suffering, pursuing her lover in disguise and selflessly wooing Silvia for him. It is here in the rejected and persecuted underground, Shakespeare will remind his audience repeatedly, that the true English Reformation has taken place.

The sisterly bond that develops between Julia and Silvia—one woman representing English Catholicism, the other German Protestantism—mirrors another of Shakespeare's insistent themes: the ideal, complementary relationship between 'high' and 'low' faiths. Throughout his work, he argues not for union of Catholic and Protestant, nor for the ascendancy of one over the other—but for reconciliation and mutual respect. The pair are sharply individualized. The Protestant Silvia's forehead is 'low', her hair dark; she is not a 'heavenly saint' but an 'earthly paragon' (2.4.146), with claims to earthly sovereignty over Julia. She dislikes the 'idolatry' of portraiture; in an echo of the key transubstantiation debate, she is associated with shadow, not substance.[27] Her attitude towards her disguised and rejected rival is one of indignant sympathy.

Julia, Silvia's Catholic opposite, has fair hair and a high forehead and gossips with a confidante named Lucetta. She begins as a capricious lover, mirroring the confused state of the English Church on the eve of the Reformation. As she tears up, then reassembles Proteus's love letter, she recalls its ill-judged mistreatment of moderate humanist reformers like Erasmus, whose writings were briefly banned by the church, and its equivocal attitude to the English Bible. She becomes a sympathetic character once she leaves Verona in disguise, her careful disposal of her goods, like her servant Launce's ludicrous family farewell, echoing classic accounts of the departures of Elizabethan exiles.[28] In conversation with Silvia, she associates herself with banned practices: she acted in a play 'at Pentecost, / When all our pageants of delight were play'd' (4.4.163). Julia has other idiosyncratic features that characterise Shakespeare's Catholic figures. Like the damaged English Church, she has lost her old beauty: 'She hath been fairer, madam, than she is . . .' (4.4.154);[29] and her trials have exposed her to the sun—Julia's skin is 'black' since she 'threw her sun-expelling mask away' (4.4.158).[30] Lamenting her position as go-between for Proteus and Silvia, Julia elaborates the classic Catholic theme of divided loyalty. This particular passage would have resonated with all those leading

Catholics like the 1st Viscount Montague, deliberately positioned in roles or diplomatic missions that demanded conspicuous loyalty—negotiating with Spain, for instance, or taking part in the trial of Mary, Queen of Scots. Julia expresses what must have been the inner feelings of many:

> And now am I, unhappy messenger,
> To plead for that which I would not obtain,
> To carry that which I would have refused,
> To praise his faith, which I would have dispraised.
> I am my master's true confirmed love
> But cannot be true servant to my master
> Unless I prove false traitor to myself.
> (4.4.89–101)

The play brims with language that makes full sense only on the allegorical level. Here is Silvia advising the besotted Proteus to return to Julia, his

> ... first best love,
> For whose dear sake thou didst then rend thy faith
> Into a thousand oaths; and all those oaths
> Descended into perjury, to love me.
> Thou hadst no faith left now unless thou'dst two
> And that's far worse than none; better have none
> Than plural faith, which is too much by one ...
> (5.4.46–52)

The wit and the allusions are undeniable. England's subjects had been asked in their thousands to rend their faith into the oaths demanded by the conflicting religions. Few at the time would have missed the Reformation context or made the later mistake of thinking Silvia was simply using religious terminology to discuss one man's unfaithfulness. The whole movement of the play is too close to the raw and painful issues of the day, the parallels too minutely, almost obsessively, precise.

The happy ending of *The Two Gentlemen of Verona* is so unconvincing that it must have been deliberate, an echo of the growing despondency among those who hoped for toleration. How could England, the cruel lover, ever be reconciled with subjects treated so callously for so long? In Persons's despairing words, 'Enough time has been given, enough hope has been spent, hope given by others of that woman coming to her senses . . .'.[31]

The most highly worked of Shakespeare's early plays, *Love's Labour's Lost*, deepens the sense that England had reached a political impasse. The first of a handful of plays Shakespeare wrote for the Queen, its most likely setting is the University of Oxford, where she was entertained in 1592 and which she treated to an angry tongue-lashing for its obstinate failure to enforce the new religion. The many puzzles in this conspicuously humanist play were designed for the Queen to solve; the hope was evidently that she would smile on the plea for freedom of conscience cleverly concealed within the plot, which develops a passionate argument against the Oath of Supremacy in the best Oxford rhetorical style. Four young men light-heartedly embark on a three-year course of study. As at Oxford, certain 'statutes' must be observed, including an oath to forswear love. The word 'statutes' was a reminder of the Statutes of Matriculation, which had recently been altered to include the Oath of Supremacy on arrival at the university. Entertaining though it is, the opening scenes echo the terms in which the morality of taking the Oath of Supremacy was exhaustively analysed by Catholic apologists in their attempts to justify outward conformity as the persecution tightened.

Love's Labour's Lost goes on to investigate from all angles the morality of taking and renouncing an unbearably restrictive oath. No sooner have the four students vowed to give up the love of women for three years than practical reasons force them to break their promise: 'Necessity will make us all forsworn' (1.1.150). Like *The Two Gentlemen of Verona*, the play is carefully inclusive, pleading the cause of all those unable to take the oath, Catholics and radical Protestants alike. The charming Princess, graceful centerpiece of a hunting scene, is clearly a portrait of the Queen, who enjoyed an elaborate court hunt as well as a series of plays and pageants during her visit to Oxford. Elizabeth may have been flattered—but she would not have missed the fact that the unsatisfied lovers are sent into penitential exile at the end of the play. The final scenes suggest, not Persons's rosy vision of a political solution that would allow the English to 'laugh and sing together', but Robert Southwell's more practical response to a darkening future—the cultivation of austere and heroic personal virtue.[32]

In political terms, these plays are judiciously balanced: though a return to the fold of universal Christendom is seen as England's best hope, Shakespeare avoids demonising Protestants or elevating Catholics. Both sides are equally faulty; the casualty is the whole world of English spirituality, tragically banished by the Reformation quarrel.

One of the most intriguing revelations of these plays is stylistic. Shakespeare clearly worked from the topical to the universal, not the other way round. Given a choice, he advances the coded plot at the expense of the literal one. This is why *The Taming of the Shrew* is so uncharacteristically chauvinistic, why *The Comedy of Errors* is so discursive and why the end of *The Two Gentlemen of Verona* is so absurdly improbable. Shakespeare's eye is firmly on the hidden message. But in the course of the difficult job of disguising and dramatising a detailed version of the politics of his day, he has already hit, almost by accident, on the mixture of elements that will make him a writer 'not of an age, but for all time'.[33]

The first of these elements is realism. Shakespeare combined the observational powers of a professional actor with penetrating insight into human personality and motive. In his writings, these qualities animate the complex character and tortured relationships of sixteenth- and seventeenth-century England with such startling naturalism that they evolve into something of far greater interest to later audiences than Reformation politics: they become the complex characters and tortured relationships of living people. Where the political narrative can only be paralleled by bizarre human situations, such as the 'sharing' of Silvia, other authors might briefly abandon the topical level. But Shakespeare is the most uncompromising of allegorists. He sticks to his guns and continues to realise developments as naturalistically as he can. Occasionally the result is ridiculous. But, with increasing frequency, he finds himself drawn into uncharted depths of the human psyche. *Comedy of Errors* provides an example. The painstaking fidelity with which he traces the relationship between the unreformed church and erring England sets up a delicate psychological cameo: the contradictory and therefore convincing reactions of Adriana to her erring husband.

The second element is a deep personal engagement in the thought, language and imagery of Christian humanism. Shakespeare's writing is immersed in the mystical and theological inheritance threatened by the state religion. He hits his most profound and distinctive note in such phrases as 'love, a word that loves all men' (4.3.354). When he introduces this unique spiritual charge to the language of his animated figures, they are no longer simply lifelike personalities. What started out as masked political drama now becomes a drama of the soul; its protagonists, following the hidden script of England's unpredictable and chaotic post-Reformation vicissitudes, become unknowable and multi-faceted, universalising their inner struggles in resonant language distilled from centuries of humanist Christian thought.

Realism and spiritual depth grafted onto the demands of a highly circumstantial political allegory: these were the elements that led to the literary breakthrough hailed by some scholars as the invention of 'the human' in literature. The hidden level, it turns out, has a greater significance than at first appears. Irrelevant and transitory though some of its material may seem now, it emerges as the crucible in which the greatest works of English literature were born.

It would take a year or two for Shakespeare to achieve simultaneous control of both the universal and the topical dimensions. In the meantime, another element began to surface, further intensifying the drama: an increasingly passionate and indignant commitment to the resistance cause.

PERSECUTION, 1592–1594

Enforced Love

THE CHEERFUL, almost detached approach of Shakespeare's plays altered after 1592. The confident appeal to common sense, the assumption that the country could be laughed out of its troubles faded as the Cecil hold on power tightened, and Elizabeth's increasingly oppressive reign began to seem interminable. Shakespeare's works now begin to reflect the concerns of the active opposition: a group of impatient young aristocrats chafing under the restrictions of Elizabeth's regime.

So long as France's Protestant King was their ally, Elizabeth's government could afford to relax about the Spanish threat. But in 1592, with the famous words 'Paris is worth a Mass', Henry IV of France converted to Catholicism in order to secure the throne. There was consternation at the English court. England was now surrounded by hostile Catholic powers. To their dismay, English Catholics discovered that the resulting backlash against suspects at home was in expert hands. The new Act Against Recusants confined Catholics to a radius of five miles from their own homes, while those who failed to attend church services were punished with banishment. Catholics now lived in constant fear of raids and summary executions. Swithin Wells, the elderly Catholic tutor of Lord Strange's cousin, the Earl of Southampton, was hanged outside his London house because Mass had been said there in his absence.

Catholics laid the blame for the new wave of persecution at the door of Shakespeare's brilliant contemporary, William Cecil's son, Robert. Coached ever since he was a boy in a type of statecraft that his father had refined to an art form over three Tudor reigns, Robert Cecil is usually portrayed by later historians as an industrious and able contrast to his political rival, the impulsive, militaristic Earl of Essex. Essex was well-born and handsome, the privileged step-son of the Earl of Leichester, a man of dazzling presence and charm, whereas Cecil, just over five feet tall, was hunchbacked and a commoner. 'Wry neck, crooked back, splay foot', according to one contemporary: an isolated, hard-working man, who, unlike his father, was fond of music but who curiously had 'faint sympathy with learning'. An intelligent and interesting face looks out at us from his many portraits, but while Essex was the Queen's darling, Cecil was merely her 'Pygmy' or later, her 'Elf'.[1]

In 1590, at the early age of twenty-seven, Robert Cecil quietly and unofficially took over the job left behind by Sir Francis Walsingham on his death—that of the Queen's Secretary, subordinate only to the post of Lord Treasurer, still occupied by his father, William. In 1596, the appointment was made official, to the fury of Essex, who had been promised the post. Robert Cecil's promotion was followed by a further series of shrewd appointments as hard-headed and often fanatically anti-Catholic men, long ago selected and promoted by his father, were moved inexorably into key political positions: the able, bigoted Edward Coke became Attorney-General; the brutal John Popham, Chief Justice; the sycophantic Walter Cope, Recorder. In terms of wealth as well as power and influence, the Cecils were now becoming pre-eminent. Huge sums were spent on building: between them, William and Robert constructed four houses in London as well as Cranborne House in Dorset, and the great 'Prodigy Houses', Burghley, Theobalds and later, Hatfield. William Cecil worked hard to secure high-ranking marriages for his family, targeting the grandest earldoms in the country, among them Oxford, Pembroke, Southampton and Derby. The spy network was now theirs, for as well as acting as the link between the Queen and her Privy Council, Robert took over the running of the intelligence services, the essential bulwark of Elizabeth's regime and a byword abroad, where it was rumoured that Elizabeth had known more about the Armada fleet than Philip of Spain himself. The pride both Cecil and the Queen took in the achievements of the government spy network is evident in the 'Rainbow Portrait' of Elizabeth that still hangs in Hatfield House. This is a magnificent but disconcerting portrayal of Elizabeth in her late sixties, for her gown is decorated with realistic human ears and eyes, and her sleeve with a huge snake, all a coded message that the nation's splendour and security depended on its ubiquitous secret service.

Cecil's backstairs rise to power was accompanied by the advancement of the most bizarre of all of Elizabeth's favourites, the obsessive priest-hunter Richard Topcliffe, an aging psychopath answerable not to the Privy Council but to the Queen herself, with whom he liked to boast he had sexual relations. As the Queen became increasingly nervous about the threat of assassination, she personally licensed Topcliffe to operate outside the law in order to protect her. And in 1592, Topcliffe was able to announce to his mistress that he had achieved a brilliant coup: the arrest of the most wanted man in England, the country's 'chief dealer for Papists', Robert Southwell.

Topcliffe accomplished his triumph in typical fashion, by blackmailing a girl he had raped, the pregnant Anne Bellamy, daughter of the family then sheltering the hunted priest. The state's subsequent treatment of Southwell was one of the scandals of the decade. For the next thirty-six months he was kept in solitary confinement in the Tower of London. Frustrated by the restrictions on torture there, Topcliffe periodically removed him to his private house, where he used his own methods to interrogate him. Robert Cecil was an occasional witness and coolly described one of these sessions to a friend: 'We have a new torture which it is not possible to bear. And yet I have seen Robert Southwell hanging by it, still as a tree-trunk, and no-one able to drag one word from his mouth'.[2]

Ferdinando Stanley, Lord Strange, was well aware that he himself was now equally vulnerable. His father was ill, and once he assumed the title of Earl of Derby, his dangerous claim to the throne would be in the spotlight. He began to take precautionary measures to reassure the regime of his loyalty, severing all links with his Catholic contacts and ostentatiously cracking down on recusants in the North.

Strange's new stance directly affected Shakespeare. References in Sonnet 89 ('Say that thou didst forsake me for some fault') suggest that he cut off relations with his subversive playwright. More wounding still for Shakespeare, the political reason for the rift had to be concealed under a more personal excuse. Using the wordplay Strange appreciated, Shakespeare vows that 'I will acquaintance *strangle* and look *strange*'. Whatever Strange's explanation for dropping him, Shakespeare himself agrees to play along with it in order to preserve Strange's impartiality as the future Earl of Derby. He will help him to 'set a form upon *desired* change'. The phrase refers neatly to Strange's changed status on his father's death when he would literally be *de-sired*. The puns continue throughout Sonnet 89.[3]

Though distanced from Lord Strange, Shakespeare could still evidently rely on the great Montague clan. In 1593, he dedicated a poem to a very different member of the family: a younger, more flamboyant patron, Magdalen Montague's grandson, Henry Wriothesley, 3rd Earl of Southampton.

In 1593, Wriothesley was just twenty years old, renowned both for his beauty and his generosity to poets and men of letters. Generally characterised as effete and temperamental, he is the subject of unflattering anecdotes in Shakespearean biographies: attributed to him are fits of pique at court, homosexual liaisons while on military campaigns in Ireland, an incongruous concern with his appearance on the battlefield in Flanders, and a foolish affair with one of the Queen's ladies-in-waiting, resulting in pregnancy and enforced marriage. If all this is true, then he cannot have been Magdalen Montague's favourite grandson. His many portraits reveal him following extremes of fashion—make-up, ribbons, coral bracelets, elaborately decorated armour, hair either girlishly long and loose or trained to fall over one shoulder in his trademark lovelock.

Yet there is another side to Southampton, implied by his biographer when he remarks that at times he has 'the sense of dealing not with one man but two'.[4] His firm handwriting, his happy marriage, his successful political career under James I and the dignity of his later portraits all convey the impression of an able and determined personality. There is a revealing comment by a friend, Arthur Wilson: 'He carried his business closely and slily'.[5] His family was staunchly Catholic, and his childhood was spent at Cowdray Castle, Magdalen Montague's Sussex base. Southampton's father, the figurehead for Catholics in the South of England, died when Henry was a boy, imprisoned in the Tower for his religion. Given his background, the role of a vain, frivolous young man was one Southampton would certainly have been well advised to play.

His dangerous ancestry made him representative of many of the younger generation whose parents had suffered for the cause of the old religion. The hearts and minds of these young men, many of whom did their best to keep their true allegiance secret, were the target of an unremitting campaign of persuasion and coercion by a cabal aware that the regime depended on their support, a regime whose image was badly in need of a touch of glamour. As a fatherless eight-year-old boy, Southampton had passed into the care of William Cecil, Lord Burghley, who was making a fortune out of his influential position as Master of the Court of Wards—other fatherless young noblemen included the earls of Rutland, Essex, Oxford and Pembroke.[6] In a characteristic move, William Cecil proposed a marriage between Southampton and his granddaughter, Elizabeth Vere, his favourite tactic for drawing suspect and wealthy young aristocrats into the new establishment, and in particular into his own family circle. Southampton refused—and continued to refuse until he reached the age of twenty-one, when he was forced to sell much of his land in order to pay his guardian the ruinous sum of £5,000 for rejecting his choice of partner. Biographers often suggest that the boy's obstinacy was wilful—an indication perhaps of homosexuality. However, Southampton went on to marry Essex's cousin. His stand was a principled one.

The resistance of Southampton to the blandishments of Elizabeth's regime symbolised to many the mute refusal of a resentful younger generation to sign up to the new order. His quiet reluctance to conform is the hidden subject of *Venus and Adonis*—a poem Shakespeare addressed to the earl in 1593 that turned out to be one of the best-sellers of the age and made his name among contemporary writers. But it is not a simple panegyric to his new patron. Delicately framed advice forms a consistent thread in all Shakespeare's covert work. Here he suggests that mere passive resistance, particularly passive resistance to female oppression, is unmanly. A parallel best-seller, Robert Southwell's poem *St Peter's Complaint*, makes the same point. Peter blames himself bitterly for betraying his master with an oath sworn out of fear of a woman—the servant in the High Priest's courtyard. Rarely read today, the popularity of both poems was due to the way they addressed one of the hottest political issues of the day—the problem of how to resist the increasingly invasive pressure on the national conscience by England's Virgin Queen.

Humour takes the sting out of Shakespeare's critique. He describes the ludicrous seduction of a lovely, helpless Adonis by an outsize Venus, who lifts him from his horse and tucks him under one arm before pinning him to the ground and subjecting him to passionate wooing in terms that in places deliberately parody *Narcissus*, a poem Burghley commissioned to encourage Southampton to consider marriage.[7] The terms in which Adonis resists are reminiscent of not only Southampton's own situation but that of many of his peers. At first, he refuses to speak or respond; he is 'forced to consent, but never to obey' (61); next, he pleads his youth: 'before I know myself, seek not to know me' (525); and in the end he accuses Venus of insincerity, cynicism and promiscuity—unfair to the smitten goddess of the poem, but typical of criticisms of the calculating advances made by Burghley. At last he manages to tear himself away.

The poem goes on to paint a dark picture of the fate awaiting this relatively courteous form of resistance. While Adonis equivocates, his horse bolts, so that when he finally leaves, it is on foot. To her anguish, Venus—

Elizabeth—realises that her advances have driven her frustrated, isolated Adonis into the path of the boar—a boar that bristles with pikes and destroys sepulchres, an image of the thugs of her own regime. In a brilliant touch, she even equates her own loving assault with the vicious attack of the boar: 'Had I been tooth'd like him, I must confess, With kissing him I should have killed him first . . .' (1117). Venus pursues Adonis, hindered by the 'strict embrace' (874) of brambles—a neat echo of the constraints imposed on her by her own 'strict' churchmen. His death is the death of more than one man—'his face seems twain, each several limb is doubled' (1067)—and recalls the quartered bodies of rebels and martyrs. At this point Venus's affronted eyes become the subject of a curiously strained and extended figure of speech—but replace her 'eyes' with Shakespeare's frequent pun on eyes as intellectual leaders,[8] and the whole passage gains focus and sense—lines 1030 to 1050 convey graphically the complex reactions of leading Elizabethan civil servants and politicians to the murders and executions of some of the most distinguished and promising young scholars, writers and courtiers of their day.[9]

Meanwhile, in one of Shakespeare's most anthologised passages of poetry, the impassioned horse has vanished after a mare—'What cares he now for curb, or pricking spur? . . . He sees his love, and nothing else he sees' (285). Adonis's careless loss of his horse is a warning; Southampton's potential support would not wait forever. The indecisiveness of the younger generation of English nobility stretched to breaking point the patience of those ordinary English Catholics who stuck obstinately to their beliefs, desperately awaiting leadership while England's rightful heirs dallied with the regime.

Southampton was aware of the danger. Along with the Earl of Essex, he was already canvassing aristocratic opposition to the Cecil ascendancy.[10] By the mid-1590s his disaffection was becoming obvious and he was risking the disfavour of the Queen as well as her advisers: his name was beginning to be linked with the petite, passionate Elizabeth Vernon, one of the more impoverished of the Queen's ladies-in-waiting. Elizabeth Vernon was an excellent dynastic match, cousin of the Earl of Essex and a descendant, like Magdalen Montague, of the gallant Talbot, Earl of Shrewsbury. Now, however, she had become doubly unsuitable as a marriage prospect. Already driven to selling off some of his estates, Southampton needed to marry money; worse, anyone who paid court to the Queen's ladies-in-waiting without her permission risked disgrace. Yet Southampton persisted. The pair were to marry secretly three years later, incurring the wrath of the Queen and a spell in the Fleet Prison for Southampton; from the letters that survive, the imprudent love match developed into a devoted marriage.

The likelihood that *Romeo and Juliet* was originally written on the occasion of Southampton's secret betrothal is strengthened by the fact that the Italian story of the Montague and Capulet love affair had already been adopted as a 'Montague' family play. Back in 1575, the dramatist George Gascoigne also chose the tale of Romeo and Juliet to celebrate the second marriage of Southampton's mother, daughter of the 1st Viscount Montague, basing his narrative, as Shakespeare did, on Arthur Brooke's 1562 translation. Six lines in *Romeo and Juliet* would have held a personal meaning for Southampton and the covertly dissident circles in which he moved, and they would certainly have been omitted in any court performance, for taken allegorically they were extraordinarily risky. Romeo addresses them to Juliet in the balcony scene.

> Arise, fair sun, and kill the envious moon
> Who is already sick and pale with grief
> That thou her maid art far more fair than she.
> Be not her maid, since she is envious
> Her vestal livery is but pale and green
> And none but fools do wear it; cast it off.
> (2.2.4–9)

These lines precisely evoke Southampton's courtship of the Queen's lady-in-waiting, picking up the conventional association of the moon with Elizabeth I, surrounded, like Diana the moon goddess, by 'vestal virgins'— ladies-in-waiting wearing white and green livery, the Tudor colours. But Romeo's words 'pale and green' were changed in the second edition of the play to the less obvious 'sick and green'—and for good reason. The words of the foolhardy, ardent Romeo echo the rallying cry of the more uncompromising members of the resistance, young men such as Anthony Babington and John Somerville who were ready to assassinate Elizabeth in order to replace the 'usurping' religion with the true one. In addressing Southampton and his coterie, Shakespeare was to repeatedly dramatise the tragic consequences of this kind of extremism. But he would consistently encourage responsible leadership of England's Catholics, not rash individual action, and least of all regicide—a crime against England itself. *Venus and Adonis* and *Romeo and Juliet* give full credit to the integrity of

Southampton's stand in both his political and his private life; both contrast true passion with the grotesqueness of enforced love. But both works also paint a graphic picture of the dangers that await a vulnerable member of the resistance driven to a sudden, desperate move.

Hidden within the text of this richly ornamented play are two coded cameos portraying famous Elizabethan examples of exactly this form of suicidal resistance: one of them a martyrdom, the other a sudden murder. Again, Shakespeare strikes a delicate balance between caution and reverence. If you play a lone hand, he warns Southampton, death will be the consequence.

The first cameo is concealed within the speeches of Juliet's nurse, a usefully garrulous character invented by Shakespeare. Some of her rambling memories are cut by modern directors: but it is precisely these apparently irrelevant details that would have made a dissident audience sit up and listen, suddenly aware that hidden at the heart of this play about love and death was a memorial to the martyred Jesuit Edmund Campion.

The Campion affair was one of the great unmentionable subjects in Shakespeare's England. Guarded references turn up in marginalia; but it was treason merely to possess the poem about his death, 'Why do I use my paper, ink and pen',[11] written by another Jesuit missionary, Henry Walpole, and still little known in spite of its outstanding quality. Recent research has revealed cautious efforts by a wide spectrum of English intellectuals to keep Campion's memory alive through coded reference and manuscript annotation: Shakespeare, it now emerges, was one of them.

The nurse first reminds spectators familiar with the tale of Romeo and Juliet that Shakespeare has transposed the action of the play to the month of July—in previous versions, it took place between Christmas and Easter. Juliet, says the nurse, was born on 31 July ('Lammas Eve'). As her birthday is 'a fortnight and odd days' off, the play must begin in mid-July. The nurse stresses a pun on the word 'July', repeating three times that as a child Juliet fell over and was told: 'Thou wilt fall backwards when thou comest to age; Wilt thou not, *Jule*? It stinted and said *"Ay"*' (1.3.57–58). July was the month in which Campion was arrested; 31 July, the feast day of St Ignatius, founder of the Jesuit order, was the day of his first interrogation after being racked.

Entwined with these 'July' pointers are reminders of the year Campion arrived in England and the house where he was arrested. The nurse remembers that she weaned Juliet just as the 'earthquake' struck. The baby rejected the breast, smeared with bitter wormwood, as they sat 'in the sun under the dove-house wall' (1.3.28). The nurse ran when a tremor shook the dove-house. Again, the details are repeated twice. They would have caused a frisson. The year 1580, the same that Campion and Persons arrived in England, was marked by a violent earthquake; and the dove-house recalls the narrative of Campion's arrest published by his captor just after his death, which stated that it was the discovery of three men hiding in the dove-house at Lyford Grange near Oxford that gave away Campion's presence in a priest-hole there.[12] The nurse's superficially digressive words prove to be an example of the invisible coded method at its most economical and elegant.

An activist member of the Montague family, Francis Browne, a cousin of Strange and Southampton, would have had especially painful memories of these events. Along with William Hartley, one of the priests executed at Holywell, he narrowly escaped with his life after a raid on Campion's press in Stonor Park in Oxfordshire.[13] He would have appreciated the link between Campion and the play's resonant motif of feud and sacrifice. And he would not have missed the spiritual symbolism that also underlies the nurse's comic speech: the idyllic sunlit scene cut short by a bitter weaning; the word 'rood', meaning cross, the repeated image of a figure standing high up and alone before falling backwards, a reminder of the drop as the steps were removed from the gallows. Typical of the depth of Shakespeare's religious allusions, there are echoes here of Peter's triple betrayal of Christ, marked by a cockcrow, and Christ's triple request, after his resurrection, for Peter's love, a request associated with a prediction of Peter's martyrdom.[14] Like Peter, the infant Juliet 'wept bitterly' at a 'perilous knock' associated with a 'cock'rel' (1.3.55). Like Peter, she responds three times with the word 'Ay' to a request for the ultimate act of love, concealed under one of the nurse's bawdy puns: a promise to 'fall backwards when thou comest to age'. As always, Shakespeare associates the martyrdoms of Catholics under Elizabeth with expiation for the church's earlier failings. The 1597 and 1599 editions of this play print this remarkable passage in italics—perhaps to indicate that it is conveniently detachable.

Romeo and Juliet contains a further reminder of the fate of unprotected individual activists. There had been mixed reactions to Christopher Marlowe's murder in 1593. 'One of the wittiest knaves that ever God made', said Thomas Nashe, 'his life he contemned in comparison of the liberty of speech'.[15] It was put about that his was a wicked death: 'He even cursed and blasphemed to his last gasp, and together with his breath an oath flew out of his mouth'.[16] According to Gabriel Harvey, he thought 'hell but a scarecrow and heaven but a wonder-clout'.[17] He was involved in at least one duel before the fight that led to his death. He dabbled in necromancy, attending séances with John Dee's shady circle. A homosexual, his work reveals a bawdy aversion to women. At the same time, he was an acknowledged literary genius who transformed the medium of blank verse. He was also a master of the vivid image, the resonant line and the melodious cadence, as well as the originator of larger-than-life anti-heroes admirably suited to the declamation of his 'mighty line'.

This assortment of contradictory elements is present in the second of Shakespeare's cameos in *Romeo and Juliet*—the cynical, dazzling Mercutio, another original character who barely figures in earlier versions. Unable to find Romeo, Mercutio attempts to 'raise' him as the necromancers raised spirits, 'conjuring' him in the name of love. Like the spy Marlowe, he plays with the idea of watchful disguise—'a visor for a visor' (1.4.30), and is taken up by Romeo for his odd use of the word 'counterfeit', a reminder that in the course of his espionage work abroad Marlowe was arrested for counterfeiting coins.[18] Mercutio's sneering list of heroines includes three from Marlowe's own work, Dido, Helen and Hero. When the nurse asks who his friend is, Romeo replies—'one . . . that God hath made himself to mar' (2.4.111). Like all the key markers in the play, this hint at Marlowe's name is repeated for emphasis: '"For himself to mar" quoth 'a!' (2.4.112), exclaims the nurse in reply, allowing listeners to catch up with the first part of the pun—the answer to the clue 'God hath made himself' being the 'Christ' of Christopher. In the end Mercutio is caught in the crossfire between Montague and Capulet: he belongs, like the disaffected Marlowe, to neither faction. On the Capulet guest-list, he nonetheless defends his Montague friend and consorts with the Montague gang, but dies, as Marlowe was alleged to have done, with a curse on his lips, repeated three times: 'A plague a both your houses' (3.1.88–103). At the beginning of Act 3, Mercutio outlines precisely the circumstances of the sword fight that led to Marlowe's death.

Mercutio's tour de force, a fantastical speech about a tiny, malevolent fairy, Queen Mab, mimics Marlowe. The only difference is that Marlowe wrote about grand, not microscopic beings. Mercutio's 'She plats the manes of horses in the night' (1.4.89) is Marlowe's 'mighty line' applied to a microscopic being. Mercutio's rant is full of Marlowe's resonant lists and cascades of dependent clauses. In spite of its imaginative force, the speech is nihilistic—and in the end, just as with Tamburlaine's magnificent rhetoric, we share Romeo's verdict: 'Peace, peace Mercutio, peace! Thou talkst of nothing' (1.4.95). Mercutio's answer could be Marlowe's own epitaph. 'More inconstant that the wind, who woos / Even now the frozen bosom of the north, and, being angered, puffs away from thence, / Turning his side to the dew-dropping south' (1.4.100–103), Mercutio embodies Marlowe's vacillation between northern Protestantism and southern Catholicism. He is the victim of the 'inconstant' Reformation wind that, Benvolio answers, 'blows us from ourselves' (1.4.104).[19]

The Elizabeth Vernon affair; Campion's execution; the murder of Marlowe. The richness of the writing in *Romeo and Juliet* arises from the brilliance with which Shakespeare combines these underlying dramas of true and enforced love played out against a backdrop of death. His idiom is the mystical tradition of humanist love poetry that drew on the metaphor of night and the sun in its exploration of the journey of the soul. The phenomenal skill and boldness of this play, along with its richly decorative Renaissance imagery, must have been breathtaking at the time. *The Return from Parnassus* quotes it, implying that it is one of the works that made Shakespeare the darling of the various anti-Cecil circles in London—the Catholic underground, the Inns of Court, the Essex and Southampton coteries. Shakespeare had clearly become the recognised master when it came to orchestrating the 'perplexities of love' suffered by Elizabeth's oppressed subjects.

Quarrelling by the Book

ALONGSIDE THESE revolutionary romantic comedies, Shakespeare continued to engage the opposition in the game of giving old histories 'a new face'. The opposition in this case was the rival company, the Queen's Men, set up by Sir Francis Walsingham in 1583 specifically to spread the Protestant message across the country; Robert Greene, Shakespeare's resentful rival, was one of their dramatists. They specialised in propaganda histories, a number of which are so similar to Shakespeare's famous history plays that many critics have assumed that Shakespeare was drawing on memories of a repertoire he knew first-hand as an actor with the Queen's Men. In fact Shakespeare's crowd-pulling adaptations of the reigns of King John, Henry VI and Richard III are not simply improved versions of their predecessors: they 'answer' the Protestant bias of the Queen's Men, restating the historical narrative in dissident terms. It was a game Shakespeare excelled at. Cunning use of language gives a Reformation dimension to the most innocent episode. When Jack Cade leads a peasant rebellion in *Henry VI*, his manifesto exactly mirrors that of the 'Levellers', the most extreme of the early reformers. In Shakespeare's hands King John is no longer an anti-papal hero; he is a duplicitous, uneasy usurper, and his story highlights a wide range of forbidden subjects: the difficulties of taking the oath, the unreasonable demands of both the papacy and the sovereign, the problems of loyalty to an excommunicated tyrant, the motive behind the dissolution of the monasteries, the intimidation of those of the country's intelligentsia ('eyes') who uphold the rightful heir.

As time goes by, his line of attack becomes more pointed. *Richard III*, a play about the hunchbacked fifteenth-century King notorious for murdering two princes in the Tower, dates from the early 1590s and is a startling portrait, not merely of the general style of the 'Regnum Cecilianum' but of the unpopular public persona of Robert Cecil in particular. A popular ballad circulating at his death sums up his image:

Little bossive [hunchbacked] Robin that was so great . . .
Who seemed as sent from Ugly Fate
To spoil the prince and rot the State.
Owing a mind of dismal ends
As trap for foes and tricks for friends

The play must originally have been written to be performed before Essex, Southampton and the growing opposition, Catholic and radical Protestant, that gathered in Essex House to nurse grievances and plot their enemies' downfall. They evidently provided their playwright with invaluable inside material. Cecil is recorded as saying, 'God knows I labour like a packhorse'; the 'pack' one of his joking references to his own deformity. The only play in which Shakespeare uses the word 'packhorse' is when the hunchback Richard describes the services he did for his brother, the King, in the role the Cecils so often adopted—that of the selfless public servant: 'I was a pack-horse in his great affairs, / A weeder-out of his proud adversaries' (1.3.121). This small detail suggests that a number of Richard's mannerisms may have originated in aristocratic mockery of the diminutive Queen's Secretary. The famous speech that opens the play suggests Robert Cecil as much as Richard III (1.1.1–41). The 'clouds' of war, buried in the 'deep bosom of the ocean' recall the drowned sails of the

Armada; during the ensuing peace, while others chafed at the inaction or danced with the Queen, the lame Robert Cecil became known, like his father, for a different activity: 'plots have I laid, inductions dangerous, / By drunken prophecies, libels and dreams . . .'. Richard's spectacular success in seducing the widow of one of his victims over her husband's corpse recalls another Cecil characteristic—his unlikely prowess as a womaniser. Though, unlike Essex, Cecil did not 'caper nimbly in a lady's chamber / To the lascivious pleasing of a lute', his name was linked with those of a number of great ladies, including Lady Suffolk, Lady Derby and Anne Clifford, while his enemies claimed that he was a father at fourteen. 'A man who is all mystery' is how the French Ambassador described him, another echo of Shakespeare's dissimulating Richard. He was 'Robertus Diabolus' to the Essex circle, and Richard is called a 'devil' throughout the play. Both Richard and Robert were called 'Toad'; 'Here lies the Toad' was scrawled on the door of his house.²⁰ Robert was an 'Elf' to Queen Elizabeth; Richard is called 'elvish-marked' (1.3.227) in the play; he is also 'hell's black intelligencer' (4.4.71), a term that, like the apparently innocuous word 'spy' in his opening speech, recalls his best-known role, as the mastermind behind the secret services. Richard's rise to power echoes that of the Cecil regime—a man is killed because 'his fault was thought' (2.1.104); the church and the laws of sanctuary are blasphemously overruled; the people are too cowed to expose his fictitious plots: 'Who is so gross / That cannot see this palpable device? / Yet who's so bold but says he sees it not?' (3.6.11). There is a glance at a type of media spin familiar to modern audiences: 'Look you get a prayer book in your hand', advises Richard's aide, 'And stand between two churchmen, good my lord' (3.7.47–48).²¹

Even allowing for Essex and Montague protection, how did Shakespeare get away with all this? In the first place, he kept unusually close to his source, Thomas More's account of the reign of Richard III, and could claim that in many respects his play was simply a dramatisation of this famous classic. Like Hamlet, who defends his political court play by claiming it is a harmless translation from the Italian, he can point to an innocent precedent. And he reminds his audience of a still older precedent. His Richard compares himself at one point to 'the Vice' of the old morality plays, who lives on in English Christmas pantomimes as the Demon King, entertaining, wicked, master of the sly aside, a figure who like Richard both horrified and delighted his audience. It would be difficult for a censor to ban the play on the grounds that a character so obviously rooted in two well-known stock villains was also a dead ringer for the Queen's Secretary. As we shall see, however, there is evidence that the suspicious resemblance did not escape Robert Cecil.

Shakespeare's history plays return continually to the question of the succession—the burning topic of the day, an issue vital to the ambitious Earl of Essex and his chief supporter, the Earl of Southampton. But even Essex had to be careful. He could not have welcomed being recipient of the dedication in one of the most scandalous books of the decade. Written by the irrepressible Robert Persons and published pseudonymously in 1594, the author openly proclaimed the dread words banned by the Queen, who forbade anyone to turn their eyes 'from the setting to the rising sun'. Persons titled his book: '*A Conference about the Next Succession to the crown of England*'.

The most inflammatory aspect of the *Conference* is the way it traces the lines of descent from John of Gaunt to the rival claimants of the 1590s, actually naming them and concluding that Lord Strange was one of the leading contenders. In modern terms this is an intelligently objective book, 'arguably the best political work written by an Englishman between More's *Utopia* and Hobbes's *Leviathon*',[22] proposing that the idea of divine right is misplaced: a sovereign must earn his right to rule. But in 1594 it was a sensationally seditious tract. Persons illustrates the thesis by recounting the history of the families of York and Lancaster, and in passing proposes the reign of Richard II as a test case for justified deposition. He demonstrates that Richard was a weak and arrogant king who broke his coronation oath to his subjects by milking the country for his own benefit and that of his favourites. His complacent belief that he was divinely appointed led to his downfall at the hands of the popular pragmatist, Henry IV. No wonder the book was rapidly suppressed. Merely to possess it was treasonable. If there was one subject more objectionable to the Queen than the succession, it was the spectre of deposition.

Yet a year later, Shakespeare managed to stage Persons's arguments so adroitly that the Queen herself could have watched it without offence. *Richard II* was an extraordinarily bold venture, nonetheless, and contained political dynamite: a deposition scene, which was not printed in the first three editions of the play. It was clearly valued very highly by the Earl of Essex, who later commissioned a London performance in order to rally the city to his cause on the eve of his rebellion, when he finally challenged Elizabeth's regime. It was after the rebellion that Elizabeth revealed to the embarrassed scholar, Sir William Lambarde, that she was under no illusion as to the real meaning of such plays: 'I am Richard II, know ye not that?'

Robert Persons's moral lies at the heart of *Richard II*—a power that acts arrogantly, presuming on a God-given right to do so, deserves deposition. But Shakespeare is more cautious than Persons. He applies the moral to more than one power. There is the historical Richard; there is the unreformed medieval church; and there is Elizabeth I. Shakespeare manipulates his hologram brilliantly. Just as the suspicion that the play is really about Elizabeth becomes a certainty, the angle tilts slightly—and suddenly the focus becomes the excesses of the old princes of the church. As camouflage, this is a technique he begins to use repeatedly, a subtle defence against censorship and editorial pressure: he changes the allegorical perspective, usually in the third act, and gives his audience the choice of a second covert meaning.

The poetry of the opening conjures up the historical Richard. It starts with scenes as stiff and iconic as the famous medieval portrait of Richard that Shakespeare may have seen: the Wilton Diptych.[23] Once under way, however, the stylised couplets are scrapped for the sinewy blank verse of dirty politics, and the parallels with Elizabeth begin to mount up. There is the suggestive alignment of political coincidences, the familiar staple of history plays: expensive wars in Ireland; illegal seizure of land; a rebellion led, like that of the Northern Earls, by the Percy family; the suppression of free speech; the country leased out. But there is also the more subtle alignment of Richard's character with Elizabeth's. He is raised above all the political scheming by the splendid diction and command of gesture that were such a dramatic part of Elizabeth's presence, the subject of awed reports by foreign ambassadors, and one of the chief instruments of her authority. They also recorded her moody unpredictability, her histrionics, her duplicity, her occasional flashes of cold pragmatism—all central to Shakespeare's study of Richard. But the affinity that really interests Shakespeare, the *raison d'être* of the play, is the conviction of both sovereigns, not simply that they act with divine authority but that they themselves border on the divine. Richard portrays himself as the eye of Heaven, rebuking the sinner; in his fall he takes on the persona of Christ, betrayed by Judas, judged by Pilate. In the same way, the Tudor propaganda machine had long since elevated Elizabeth to the level of a religious icon—blasphemous presumption, in the view of her Catholic subjects. Her speeches, particularly after the providential destruction of the Armada, had become increasingly papal in tone: she was a weak and unworthy instrument, Parliament was told repeatedly, but an instrument chosen by God—'God that gave me here to sit and set me over you'.[24] She was also given to lamenting the heavy burden of such an office, a weariness with 'the hollow crown' that Shakespeare portrays sympathetically in the play—and, as time went on, she was haunted like Richard by a fearful awareness of her possible downfall.

Would the Elizabeth of 1595 have tolerated such a morality lesson? There were precedents that suggest she was not always averse to elegantly concealed advice. *Damon and Pithias*, a 1571 court play by Richard Edwards, Master of the Chapel Royal, dwelt on a guilty tyrant who sheds his burden when he replaces flatterers with honest counsellors. Such shafts had to be directed over the heads of her advisers, cast as the real villains. In their subtle, jewelled form, Edwards' plays and Shakespeare's *Richard II* might have done Elizabeth the service of the court fool she had dispensed with—they sugared the disagreeable but necessary pill of being kept aware of true popular feeling.

And as soon as the contemporary parallels have been driven home, Shakespeare's *Richard II* deftly switches tracks; instead of a horribly pointed spectacle of her own downfall, the queen's attention is tactfully directed towards a more palatable second allegory—the downfall of Catholicism at the hands of reformers. The change is heralded by a heavily political exchange among a group of gardeners who use the language of Puritan pamphlets and sermons to compare their overgrown garden to England, choked with prodigals and profitless weeds. Like the radical cant of the thinly disguised 'Levellers' led by Jack Cade in *Henry VI*, they condemn those who are too 'lofty' in their 'commonwealth'. 'Cut off the heads of too fast growing sprays . . . All must be even in our government' (3.4.34–35); and they make familiar criticisms of the unreformed church: 'O what pity is it / That he had not so trimmed and dressed his land / As we this garden!'(3.4.54–56). From now on, Richard carries the nostalgic aura of 'that sweet lovely rose'—the flawed but legitimate and beautiful king later recalled in *Henry IV, Part 1* (1.3.175). As the play descends towards Richard's death, souls are 'torn' from him, a 'new world' has begun; he connects the separation from his wife, leaving for a nunnery in France, with the familiar Reformation marker of Hallowmass (5.1.80).

Richard II is not a conventional history play: it is a many-sided morality tale, urging royal prudence, just as *Romeo and Juliet* is, on the hidden level, not a romance but a cautionary tale for the resistance. The closest Shakespeare came at this point to straightforward historical drama occurs, paradoxically, not in a play but in a second poem.

Bringing Truth to Light

URING A SINISTER interchange between one of the little princes and his wicked uncle, Richard III, the prince wonders how truth is passed down the ages—whether through the written or the spoken word (3.1.75–83). The prince believes, he says innocently, that the history of the Tower of London—a choice of subject never far from the minds of English Catholics—would survive simply by word of mouth, even if it were never written down. The little prince has stepped into dangerous territory. He is not only defending the role of tradition against scripture—a central Catholic Reformation stance—but he also suggests that the grisly truth about England's persecutions will survive irrespective of what appears in history books. Like any tyrant threatened with exposure, Richard decides on the spot to kill him.

The episode raised a growing and well-placed concern at the time: with such a ruthless and efficient propaganda machine in place, and with a regime adept at ensuring and commissioning politically correct versions of national history from men like Camden and Stow, who would transmit a truthful version of events to succeeding generations? What if the old religion never returned? What happens to the annals of the defeated? Though Shakespeare's history plays do their best to counter state propaganda, their scope is necessarily limited and episodic. In the mid-1590s, he began to consider new ways of recording for posterity a truthful account of what had happened to England as a result of the Reformation. In 1594, again invoking the powerful patronage of the Essex-Montague opposition in the person of the Earl of Southampton, he published another long poem. Like *Venus and Adonis, The Rape of Lucrece* takes enforced love as its subject, but this time, to use his own words, it is a 'graver labour'.[25] Unlike the narrative demands of historical drama, the bare outlines of this classical story allow him the space to embark on a thorough survey of the destruction dealt to England over the previous seventy years. It proved to be another best-seller, running to six editions in Shakespeare's lifetime.

Action is minimal—the effect is that of a tableau or emblem, demonstrating the fatal repercussions of an act of royal lust. In this Roman tale, Lucrece's husband, Collatine, makes the mistake of overpraising his wife's virtue to his fellow soldiers; inflamed, Tarquin, son of the Roman king, seeks her out and rapes her; Lucrece sends a despairing message to her husband; when he arrives, she kills herself out of shame; noble Brutus, symbol of government change to come, vows revenge. We find it difficult to enjoy this slow-motion narrative, full of apparently pointless digressions and elaborate figures of speech. But the tale of Lucrece was not the story that interested so many contemporary readers. What gripped them was the masterly allegory of Henry VIII's lustful passion for Anne Boleyn, and the way it triggered his equally lustful and sacrilegious seizure of the English church.

Shakespeare's great poem was the last word in this particular genre. One vivid image after another compresses into a single line whole pages of laborious argument from the Catholic polemicists of the time. It is as if here, unhindered by the demands of drama, Shakespeare at last felt free to devote all his intellectual energy to the burning issue that provided the underlying spur to his work: the spiritual damage inflicted on his country by the Reformation. It was frequently quoted, not least by Shakespeare himself, who referred to his narrative poems in his later plays as a shortcut to the inner meaning of key episodes. Macbeth's reference to 'Tarquin's ravishing strides' (2.1.55) recalls not only the rapist himself but the steady remorseless pace of the whole poem, its seven-line stanzas a contrast to the epigrammatic neatness of *Venus and Adonis*. Only a careful reading with the revised history of his times in mind will reveal its true status as a masterpiece of contemporary political commentary.

Lucrece is the soul of England. At the beginning she has the familiar markers of old England—she bears the once harmonious 'heraldry' of 'beauty's red' and 'virtue's white' (65–66),[26] she is the white hind, the object of 'high-pitched praise' (41). But soon, 'martyred with disgrace' (802), her store 'rifled', the 'perfection' of her 'summer' 'robbed and ransacked by injurious theft' (838), she is pleading 'in a wilderness where are no laws' (544). Assaulted, despoiled and desecrated, she becomes 'a late-sacked island . . . bare and unpeopled' (1740–1741); some 'pure and red' blood remained, but some, stained by Tarquin 'looked black' (1742–1743)—an evocation of the scarlet-black division between scarlet Rome and black-robed Protestant reformers. During the long wait for her husband, she consoles herself much as despoiled England did, waiting for rescue: she denounces every aspect of the assault, and—like many of Shakespeare's audience—manages briefly to forget her own troubles, absorbed instead in an allegorical representation of them. She finds her story mirrored in a tapestry depicting the siege of Troy and its betrayal by a white-bearded, garrulous Sinon who recalls William Cecil.[27] When her husband at last arrives, they debate the morality of her position in terms that would have reminded readers of the great question of the day—the morality of enforced conformity: 'What is the quality of my offence, / Being constrained with dreadful circumstance? / May my pure mind with the foul act dispense?' (1702–1704). A strange image recalls the exiled landscape in which this anguished argument frequently took place: husband and wife meet 'like old acquaintance in a trance, / Met far from home, wond'ring each other's chance' (1595–1596). In spite of assurances of her innocence, she dies, the syntax artfully transforming the suicide to a murder or even, as her soul flees its 'polluted prison' (1726), an execution.

Tarquin himself is minutely associated with the new regime, and with Henry VIII in particular. Though he is in fact a prince, the kingship of the rapist is repeatedly stressed: the most shocking part of his action is the example it sets: the 'sovereign king' gives 'authority for sin', is now 'the school where Lust shall learn' (617). The pause before the terrible act is fraught with the same theological arguments Henry deployed before the split with Rome, and with significant phrases—should he, 'unhallowed', 'impious', assault 'so pure a shrine' (194), 'a virtuous monument?' (391) His sin involves 'dispensation' (248) and 'dissolution' (355). More consistently than Venus, he is associated with Anne Boleyn's predatory emblem, a falcon.

Tarquin, like Henry, is repeatedly misled by his traitor 'eyes'—here again, they double as 'I's', or advisers—and the persistent idea that his act constitutes treason is one of the revelations of the poem. To Shakespeare, Lucrece is not the Catholic religion—she is the essence of England, from which Catholicism is seen to be indissoluble. Again and again the poem represents the assault on the church as a fatal assault on the 'sleeping soul' of the country, over which the monarch has no rights—it is, therefore, an act of 'high treason'.[28] The rape is described in terms of the full-scale political takeover of the country—Tarquin briefly becomes a mutinous mob pillaging, terrorising and ultimately subduing a capital city, 'the heart of all her land' (398). London, the reformer's stronghold, had witnessed similar scenes on Elizabeth's accession, when a wave of iconoclasm was accompanied 'with such shouting, and applause of the vulgar sort, as if it had been the sacking of some hostile city'.[29] Not just politically, but psychically, the blow to England is seen as profoundly self-destructive: 'Mud not the fountain that gave drink to thee', begs Lucrece, pleading 'holy human law, and common troth'; 'Mar not the thing that cannot be amended' (570–581). The central objection to the English Reformation—

that in the name of reforming spirituality, it destroyed spirituality—is spelt out literally at the start of the poem:

> . . . so then we do neglect
> The thing we have and, all for want of wit,
> Make something nothing by augmenting it.
>   *(148–154)*

The second half of the poem analyses the effects of a Reformation that made 'something nothing'. Lucrece laments her submission to 'wrack-threatening' (590) Tarquin, but she also deplores the whole squad of enforcers and carpetbaggers that follow in his wake, forces of destruction grouped together under the three loose headings of Time, Night and Opportunity. Of little relevance to a rape, the passage amounts to a devastating analysis of the new political order that resulted from Henry's, rather than Tarquin's, crime. One has the rare sense here of Shakespeare going on and on, unable to stop, as he savagely catalogues its crimes, bearing out a contemporary view of him as 'the most passionate among us to bewail and bemoan the perplexities of love', a man repeatedly associated with 'rage'—a 'clear' rage according to another contemporary, Drayton—one who 'seems to shake a lance / As brandished at the eyes of Ignorance'. Read in the light of the Reformation, rather than the rambling complaint of an abused woman, this becomes an intense and powerful indictment of the new order.

The section on Time confirms the impression that for Shakespeare and others Time and the Cecils were synonymous. The link may have begun with William Cecil's passion for clocks, a relatively new invention, which he not only collected but incorporated in the towers of his prodigy houses. Also, in its sectarian refusal to subscribe to the new calendar, the Cecil regime could be said to have assumed autonomy over time in England. The parallel was a gift to dissident writers, for it enabled them to harness one of the oldest literary themes, that of *tempus edax*, devouring time, to their topical treatment of sixteenth-century England. They stressed the ever-present parallel between the impact of the regime and the devastating effects of time—the destruction of buildings and monuments, the obliteration of memories, the alteration and erasure of written history. Just as time drew lines on the human brow, so iconoclasts scored lines in the faces of sacred statues and paintings. Particular details in this poem emphasize the parallel—Time is introduced as 'Mis-shapen Time' (925); the hunchbacks

Richard III and Cecil have both been described as packhorses—here, Time is 'sin's packhorse' (928). Renowned as the tireless servant of an 'immortal' Queen, Cecil would have been recognised in the witty reference to Time as 'the ceaseless lackey to Eternity' (968).

In the course of his examination of the momentous takeover, Shakespeare repeats the pressing question of the little prince in *Richard III*— how will the truth survive? Pre-Reformation England, in the person of Lucrece, correctly foresees that her reputation will go down in history as corrupt and unreformed, 'the story of sweet chastity's decay' (808). The extent of the iconoclasts' destruction will be used as evidence of her guilt. Shakespeare predicts—again correctly—that the written word alone will not be enough to counter the official version of what happened to England during the Reformation: 'Yea, the illiterate, that know not how / To cipher what is writ in learned books / Will quote my loathsome trespass in my looks' (811). The word 'cipher' has a clever double meaning—to read and understand doctrinal debate, but also to decipher coded literature. There remains only one channel for transmitting the truth—artists who were masters of the telling emphasis, the *ad hoc* improvisation, and who were therefore impossible to regulate: 'O be remembered no outrageous thing / From vassal *actors* can be wiped away; / Then kings' misdeeds cannot be hid in clay' (607–609). It is from this point that Shakespeare begins to take on the mantle of chronicler of his era, aware that the native culture and religion in which he had been reared was now threatened with complete extinction: a real possibility, in an age of tight censorship without photographs, film or digital images. Key passages in his greatest plays will pick up the note of savage indignation and lament first sounded in *The Rape of Lucrece*, while the sonnets will dwell repeatedly on his attempts to preserve a doomed beauty in the 'black lines' of print.[30] But at the same time he reveals a chronic awareness of the vulnerability of his chosen means of resistance, the 'helpless smoke of words' (1027). In the next few years, he would become increasingly involved in a more active and dangerous venture.

At the end of the poem a minor character, Junius Brutus, makes a brief but dramatic appearance. He has survived the dangers of Tarquin's court by concealing his true nature under a politic disguise of shallowness and folly. His 'long-hid wits' make an unexpected appearance when he finally steps forward to rally the demoralized group lamenting the death of Lucrece, and he becomes in time the first consul of Rome (1816). *The Rape of Lucrece* was published in the year the Earl of Southampton came of age; and Shakespeare offers him the virile role of Junius Brutus, the single hero of the poem and a favourite role model for sixteenth-century dissidents. The poem suggests that the endangered aristocrat biding his time behind the mask was not an unstable youth like Adonis or Romeo: he was a potential leader, a formidable opponent to the forces of Time, Night and Opportunity; and the preface—'my worth . . . is bound to your Lordship'—makes it clear that Shakespeare was his man.

CHAPTER
6

RAGE, 1594

I n 1594, Ferdinando Stanley, Lord Strange died: and all the evidence suggested poisoning. Word was put about that the Jesuits were the culprits; but those who gained most from the murder were the Cecils. Strange had not only been a threat to the regime, one of the few men with the authority to lead a Catholic rebellion; his death, as events would show, greatly enriched the Cecil family. It appeared to be a chilling indication of how helpless even the great Earl of Derby was; and, along with the continuing ordeal of Robert Southwell at the hands of Topcliffe, it may have prompted Shakespeare to produce his most disconcerting piece of work. Along with his two narrative poems, it made his name among his contemporaries; but it has shocked and mystified readers ever since.

Denial is the word that best sums up the later critical reaction to *Titus Andronicus*. How could Shakespeare have written such a terrible play? Terrible in every sense: not only do its many digressions make it appear, in the words of one seventeenth-century critic, 'rather a heap of Rubbish than a Structure', but it is embarrassingly tasteless, alternating obscure debates with bouts of sadistic violence—hands are lopped off, tongues torn out, severed heads exchanged, a mother is fed her own sons in a pie. Worst of all, scholars believe that the plot is one of the very few Shakespeare invented himself. Nonetheless, along with Kyd's *The Spanish Tragedy*, *Titus Andronicus* was one of the most successful plays of the age: something about it appealed to the popular imagination at the time. Critics have assumed that it was a commercial pot-boiler, exploiting the blood lust of an audience that crowded in to watch revenge tragedies in much the same spirit as they watched executions and bear-baiting. For these critics the play is merely a symptom of a contemporary craze. Curiously, however, these two plays predate a fashion for revenge tragedies that only came in some fifteen years later with Jacobean dramatists such as Thomas Middleton, John Webster and John Marston. Kyd and Shakespeare, in other words, were not part of a trend. And compared with Kyd's play, *Titus* stands alone in the extent and the horror of its violence.

Many scholars have tried to prove that Shakespeare was not the author: but the consensus is that the play is unmistakably his, foreshadowing the themes of later dramas and closely related to the poems he wrote at the time. The current approach is that it was an experimental early work, and much ingenuity has gone into proving that it must have been written in the late 1580s or very early 1590s. However, the playhouse records mark it as 'new' in 1594, when Shakespeare was producing his most sophisticated work; and indeed there is a puzzling sophistication within the brutal framework of *Titus Andronicus*.

One of the revelations of the coded readings is that Shakespeare's 'bad' work always has a purpose, albeit a purpose that relates to a topical context we no longer recognize. Of all his plays, *Titus* depends the most completely for an appreciation of its high degree of artistry on an awareness of the forgotten history of the times. It is the first of Shakespeare's 'Roman' plays, all of which are directed primarily at the Catholic community.[1] Like *The Rape of Lucrece*, though in more sensational style, it dramatises the sufferings of England up to the year 1594; and the strange plot has clearly been devised around the hidden message—a passionate plea to the country's dissidents to refrain from violent rebellion in spite of the now intolerable pressure, and to await instead the promised invasion. This message is identical to the instructions from Catholic leaders abroad, who repeatedly promised that diplomacy or invasion would one day bring rescue.

The play also develops the new, sombre approach to England's Reformation heralded in *The Rape of Lucrece*. There, the rapist was not the only man guilty of the death of Lucrece: her husband, 'proud' Collatine, precipitated the tragedy by foolishly boasting about his wife's beauty. Increasingly, Shakespeare will focus on the folly of England in bringing the Reformation catastrophe on itself, accompanying the indictment with an exposure of the forces that exploited the nation's moment of weakness.

In *Titus*, just as in the later *King Lear*, an aging leader naively abdicates power, allowing it to fall into the hands of a group he fails to recognize as his enemies. They are led by Tamora, the wicked queen of the Goths; her husband, Saturnine; and her adviser, a Moor named Aaron. This was certainly not a play intended for the court: the names are extraordinarily daring. 'Saturnus' was one of the nicknames for William Cecil; Walsingham was Elizabeth's 'Moor'.[2] They subject Titus and his family to appalling indignities, driving him to madness and raping and mutilating his daughter, Lavinia.[3] His only surviving son Lucius (Luke) flees the country to gather an army abroad; his grandson, also named Lucius, devises coded messages attacking the regime. The play portrays these as effective forms of resistance. The literary activities of the younger Lucius unsettle the regime, and in the last scene Lucius senior returns at the head of an army and reclaims power. But in his madness Titus takes the suicidal course Shakespeare has already discouraged in his work for Southampton. By exacting bloody revenge on the wicked queen, Titus brings about the utter destruction of everything he loves.

The play rivals *The Two Gentlemen of Verona* in the precision of its string of coded historical allusions, many of them as dramatically inappropriate as the 'sharing' of Silvia. An instance is the birth of a dark-skinned bastard child, Tamora's son by Aaron. Aaron flees to bring up the baby among the Goths but is discovered by a soldier in Lucius's invading army, cradling his son in the ruins of an anachronistic monastery. Aaron bargains for the life of his child, extorting an oath from Lucius to preserve it, for 'thou art religious, / And hast a thing within thee called conscience, / With twenty popish tricks and ceremonies / Which I have seen thee careful to observe, / Therefore I urge thy oath' (5.1.74–78). On a literal level, all this is irrelevant to the action of the play—'rubbish' and not 'structure'. To an Elizabethan audience, however, the emblem of Aaron and his child by the ruined monastery, featuring the extraction of an oath from a 'popish' believer to ensure its survival, clearly identified the half-caste baby as the new compromise religion—to them, though not to us, its fate in the play would have been of primary importance. The two familiar opposed forces of fair and dark meet in this small allegorical creature; and in a newly polarised form, they run through a hidden topical play so crammed with allegorical detail and political comment that it almost swamps the story designed to conceal it.[4]

Fair and dark again stand as markers for the two opposing sides in the English Reformation. Here, for the first time, the dark side contains unequivocal evil in the form of the black Moor, Aaron. The heartless Saturnine and duplicitous Queen Tamora are also associated with darkness. The fair side—the Andronicus family—includes figures who range from the transcendent to the virtuous to the dangerously fanatical.[5]

Their figurehead is Titus's daughter Lavinia, raped, dumb and helpless—

the horrific primary image of the play. It is difficult to get beyond the ghastly impact of the spectacle, constantly present on the stage and yet unconvincing as a character. But to a contemporary audience, there were other overtones. The faces, arms and attributes of thousands of images of the Madonna and the saints were still being mutilated in exactly this way all over England; some of them, faces slashed and hands removed, still remain in English parish churches. At least one such image was to become the centre of prayers for the reconversion of England: the 'Madonna Vulnerata', a statue of the Virgin damaged in the sacking of Cadiz in 1596 by English soldiers. The statue was not repaired but removed to Valladolid, where it is still venerated as an image of the sufferings of the English Church, ransacked and rendered powerless by the Protestant takeover.[6] It was the focus of an annual ceremony on the feast of the Virgin's nativity, 7 September—a day that had been 'razed out' of the English calendar by 'faithless heretics' who 'instead thereof ridiculously placed in red letters' the official birthday of Queen Elizabeth I on the following day.[7] Many of the damaged images in England were hidden and treasured in the same way.

Other attributes make Lavinia, like Lucrece, a clear personification of England's despoiled soul. Like all Shakespeare's personifications of sanctity, Lavinia's attributes make her the cynosure of the play—the good characters are drawn to her, the evil ones long to possess her. But in *Titus* it is the sacrilegious assault on her beauty that evokes most precisely the situation of the old religion. When she is discovered by her uncle Marcus after the rape, there is no practical first aid of the sort that Gloucester receives in *King Lear* after losing his eyes. Instead, Marcus breaks into a long, lyrical lament—ludicrous in dramatic terms but strongly reminiscent of a lament in one of the Jesuit plays for the vandalism of a statue of the Madonna.[8] Indeed, Titus compares the bleeding but strangely unmoved Lavinia specifically to a picture, and later to the broken arches of a ruined church that once sheltered royal tombs.

> What stern ungentle hands
> Hath lopped and hewed and made thy body bare
> Of her two branches—those sweet ornaments
> Whose circling shadows kings have sought to sleep in . . .
> (*2.4.16–19*)

She is associated with common images of the takeover—Lucrece, Philomel, the plundered hives of the monasteries, 'pillage'. As with the church, the 'heavenly harmony' of her music has been silenced. Her spouts of blood twice evoke the word 'martyrdom'.

If Lavinia represents England's despoiled soul, the fate of the Andronicus family to which she belongs mirrors with Shakespeare's trademark chronological accuracy the fortunes of the old order during Elizabeth's reign, from the moment when it naively resigns power into the hands of an upstart faction—'strangers and more than so, / Captives . . . advanced to this height' (4.2.33–34), as Aaron proudly calls his own party—to the resolution so many longed for in 1594, the triumphant return of the exiled religion and a peaceful end to the schism.[9]

Titus himself, described as 'pious', mirrors the old, faulty but legitimate Catholic order.[10] He loses control of his inheritance through a series of blunders. Like the extremists under Mary, his religion demands the barbaric death of his enemy's son: Tamora's son must be 'lopped' and then burned, an echo of the martyrdoms of Protestants under Mary when some were burned, others hanged, drawn and quartered. By ignoring Tamora's pleas for mercy, Titus will incur her vengeance and, ultimately, his own destruction. The second blunder concerns the succession. When Titus unwisely declines the crown himself, he ignores the people's favourite, Bassianus, who is engaged to Lavinia and has inherited his family's ancestral ring: instead, blindly following precedent, he chooses the older brother. Here again, Shakespeare is dramatising a central argument from Persons's *Conference about the Next Succession*: the dangerously radical proposal that the legitimate heir to the throne was not necessarily the right choice.

No sooner has Titus given away power than he reaps the whirlwind. Saturninus's first act is to make a grab for the sacramental Lavinia. Here Titus makes his third misjudgement. As with the early conformist England under Elizabeth, loyalty to the crown overrides a deeper loyalty, and he angrily kills one of his own sons for the treasonable act of concealing the flight of the betrothed pair, Bassianus and Lavinia. His earlier piety forgotten, he even denies funeral rites to his son—another reference to an intense current debate, this time about rites of burial. His blinkered loyalty makes him a natural stool-pigeon for government plots, and he finds himself delivering a forged letter framing his own relative.[11]

The ugly bargaining that follows again mirrors the fortunes of Elizabethan Catholics. Naively, the Andronicus clan negotiates with the cynical Aaron to retrieve what has been unjustly taken from them—in the process, they lose more of their power and gain nothing except mockery.

This scene—where Titus loses his hand in exchange for two heads—reflects meek Catholic cooperation with the penal laws that banned priests and the Mass, laws that instead of leading to toleration were actually given new force by the 1591 'Proclamation against Recusants'. While presenting with physical accuracy Titus's reaction to losing a hand, Shakespeare makes the scene historically accurate as well. In his secondary role as old England, Titus falls, a 'feeble ruin' while holding 'one hand up to heaven' (3.1.207–208), recalling the broken arches of the ruined abbeys. Next, his sighs and Lavinia's dim the sky and blot out the sun, evoking smoke from great fires rather than sighs. There follows one of Shakespeare's most frequent images for the Reformation: Titus becomes a storm ('I am the sea') in which earth threatens heaven; and finally, retching was a metaphor used for the most awesome weather-event of Elizabeth's reign, the earthquake of 1580, seen as a momentous physical symptom of the country's spiritual upheavals. When Aaron returns the heads and the hand, adding insult to injury, Titus's response is that of many in England: 'When will this fearful slumber have an end?' (3.1.253).

On the allegorical level, the play has by now reached the point in the early 1580s when Catholicism licked its wounds after the persecution that followed Campion's death and began to consider how to resist.[12] Shakespeare continues to follow the sequence of events with absolute accuracy. Act 3 opens on a scene strongly suggestive of the claustrophobic world of Elizabethan catacomb Catholicism, the milieus, biographers now suggest, in which Shakespeare was brought up. Here it is presented as a world ridden with nostalgia, suppressed fanaticism, impractical and conflicting plans of action. Incongruously, the afflicted family are at a banquet, and Titus's commentary makes the banquet look very like a forlorn attempt to perpetuate the old forbidden Mass. 'Here is no drink', he observes; and advises his family to eat sparingly. Frequent communion, and above all, communion including wine, were both reforming innovations. Recalling the moment of sacrifice at the centre of the Mass, when the priest consecrates wine mixed with water that symbolises the water and blood that flowed from the side of Christ on the cross, Titus calls on Lavinia to pierce her own side so that the water of her tears can be mixed with blood; but of course without hands—on the allegorical level, without a priest—this is impossible. Titus breaks into a further lament, but he still treasures his daughter, however incapacitated, as a 'map' (3.2.12): just as, even though deprived of priests, spiritual England treasured the memory and the tradition of the Mass.[13] Here again, the allegory is extraordinarily detailed as Titus lovingly enumerates Lavinia's 'martyred signs' (3.2.36): closed eyes, bowed head, kneeling, gesturing. All these peripheral actions that accompanied the Mass, condemned by reformers as popish mummery, become doubly precious to Titus. Towards the end of his life Thomas More, though a reformer, adopted the same stance—once the essence of his religion was under threat, he began to defend even its accretions and ornaments.

The next development is again historically accurate, for while secretly struggling to practise their religion, Catholics in the 1580s were forced to supply the government with weapons against their co-religionists. In 1579, James Fitzgerald, backed by the Pope, landed an invading force in Ireland; the Privy Council's response was to finance the Queen's army by imposing a levy on English recusants. The money was rated carefully according to households, and was known as a levy for the Queen's Light Horse and Lances. By 1587, Catholics were offering further military support in the face of the Armada threat. At this point in the play, Titus inexplicably sends a gift of lances to the regime, to help resist his son's approaching army. Even more pointedly, Titus's present is accompanied by a letter attacking evil advisers, containing a coded reference to an ode by Horace that includes the line 'The pure and innocent man does not rely on the protection of the Moor' (4.2.20–21).

The account reaches 1589, the year when Southwell arrived in England. With great ingenuity Shakespeare dramatises Southwell's literary crusade, again at the correct historical point—immediately after the polemics and the military levies of the 1580s. Thus, Titus now urges his family to fire arrows wrapped with messages denouncing the regime into the Emperor's stronghold; but in order to reach the palace, he advises them to aim at the planets and stars in the sky above their heads, all named after classical figures—'Here boy, 'To Pallas'; here 'To Mercury'; 'To Saturn . . . not to Saturnine'. Instead of 'Well shot!', Titus implies the shot is a verbal one: 'O well *said*, Lucius!'. 'Good boy', he continues, 'in Virgo's lap!' (4.3.53-56). The volleys recall the literary attacks on Elizabeth's regime concealed within classical allegory.

The play now refers to the two occasions on which Catholics in England attempted to inform the Queen about the real state of the country. In 1585, Richard Shelley, a kinsman of Southwell's, was imprisoned for presenting a petition for toleration, dying later in jail without trial; and in 1592, Southwell wrote his doomed *Humble Supplication*. In an echo of these fruitless initiatives, the demented Titus accosts a simple countryman and asks him to deliver a letter that, like the first coded reference to Horace and the volley of allegorical flights, also contains a weapon, this time a knife—a hint at the barbed attacks contained in the appeals. The message is twice called a 'supplication'. For running this errand, the poor clown, who delivers the letter with a cheerful invocation to God and the martyr St Stephen, is hanged on the spot.

A central figure in this sequence of literary assaults on the regime is Titus's small grandson, the schoolboy Lucius. He makes a pathetic intervention during the family banquet, attempting to lighten the gloom by suggesting that they cheer Lavinia up with 'some pleasing tale' (3.2.47). This grandson is an intriguing figure—he represents the third generation of Catholics since Henry VIII's split with Rome, the first to grow up with no memory of Catholic England, and the generation to which Shakespeare and his contemporaries belonged. They remembered better times—just as Lucius, before the persecution, loved the aunt who was once his devoted teacher. Now, however, Lavinia terrifies him—he wants nothing to do with his dangerous and morbid inheritance. The stage direction at the beginning of Act 4 reads: 'Enter young Lucius and Lavinia running after him, and the boy flies from her with his books under his arm'. He seeks refuge with his great-uncle Marcus, who gently persuades him to face Lavinia and help her reveal the truth about her rape. Like Lucius, many of this third generation found their spiritual inheritance unbearably oppressive. The 1st Viscount Montague and the old Earl of Southampton had been intransigent men, not unlike Titus. John Donne remembers his own tutors as 'men of a suppressed and afflicted Religion, accustomed to the despite of death, and hungry of an imagined martyrdom'.[14] The year was 1592 in which Shakespeare's father, his fortunes in decline, became openly recusant. To this generation of English Catholics, dark prognostications like Titus's cheerless response to Lucius's proposal of a 'pleasing tale' must have been familiar: 'Peace, tender sapling; thou art made of tears, / And tears will quickly melt thy life away . . .' (3.2.50–51).

With a final glance at the role of government *agents provocateurs* in fomenting popish plots of revenge (Tamora's attempt to persuade Titus that she and her sons are the figures of Revenge, Rape and Murder, ready to perform his will), Shakespeare's account of the Catholic experience under Elizabeth has reached the early 1590s—the point at which the play was written. In Act 5, he moves on from exploring the history of suppressed English Catholicism to delivering a stark warning—on no account must they rebel; they must wait for rescue from abroad.

Like another celebrated figure of persecuted old England, Hieronymo, the hero of Kyd's *Spanish Tragedy*, Titus has gone through three stages—long-suffering loyalty, suppressed rage and madness. Now, quite deranged, he stages a second banquet. Here again, there are specific echoes of the Mass, but this time a black parody of the Mass. In a bid to shock Catholic extremists into recognising the evil of assassination, Shakespeare substitutes the divine sacrifice at the centre of the eucharistic ritual with a grisly sacrifice inspired by human vengeance. The horribly memorable spectacle could hardly be a more graphic illustration of the Catholic prohibition on murder: a sin that makes a mockery of everything the Mass celebrates.

The Mass text still refers to Old Testament precedents for Christ's sacrifice. In the murder of Tamora's two sons, Titus regresses to just such a primitive, pre-Christian ritual. The victims are bound and silenced like sacrificial lambs; Titus ceremonially cuts their throats while Lavinia, following the ancient Jewish custom, catches their blood in a basin. At the beginning of the banquet itself, Titus's clothes awake comment: 'Why art thou thus attired, Andronicus?' (5.3.30) asks the Emperor. Like Lavinia's veil, Titus's clothes in the original production may not have been the attire of a cook specified in the directions—but sacramental, priestly robes. For he is about to commit the final blasphemy, invoking 'A reason mighty, strong and effectual; A pattern, precedent and lively warrant, For me most wretched, to perform the like . . .' (5.3.43–45). This echoes not only the humble prayers by the celebrant in the earlier stages of the Mass but the rhythm and vocabulary of the words that immediately precede the consecration: '. . . benedictam, adscriptam, ratam, rationabilem, acceptabilemque facere digneris'.[15] The sacred words, the sacrificial victims, the unusual robes, the background of a meal all place the next horrific event in the context of what to Catholics represents the holiest moment of all—the consecration. For now Titus kills his own despoiled daughter—the symbol, as we have seen, for England's soul. He goes on to destroy the regime as well, but in the process destroys himself—the personification of the old Catholic order. Not for the last time, Shakespeare shows extraordinary prescience in his dramatisation of the disastrous effects of violent resistance on both the body and soul of English Catholicism. Years later, a leading Catholic, Francis Tresham, refused to take part in the Gunpowder Plot on the grounds, correct as it turned out, that such a course 'would not be the means to advance our religion but to overthrow it'.[16] Shakespeare's sensitive exploration of the fortunes of Catholicism in the earlier part of *Titus*, in particular the first, reverent re-enactment of a Mass without priests, would have made this horrific finale a doubly powerful disincentive to any sincere Catholic driven to considering a terrorist act.

The play ends with an assurance that rescue will come from abroad. The older Lucius's return at the head of an invading force is presented as the longed-for solution, which will rescue 'sad-faced men' from 'high tempestuous gusts' and 'knit again / This scattered corn into one mutual sheaf' (5.3.67–71). Lucius is 'Rome's young Captain' (5.3.94), proclaiming 'I am the turned forth, be it known to you, that have preserv'd her welfare in my blood . . .' (5.3.109–110). Soldier though he is, he stresses his own suffering, passive role, for he continues '. . . And from her bosom took the enemy's point, / Sheathing the steel in my adventurous body' (5.3.111–112). This healing restoration of native authority is presented in terms that pick up the central imagery of the play and align it with a description of the English situation in the 1593 '*Apology against the Defence of Schism*' by Henry Garnet, the gentle and scholarly head of the underground mission. 'If we cut ourselves off by heresy, by schism . . . we have no more the life, graces and fits of the Holy Ghost to merit life everlasting than hath the leg or arm cut off from the body'. In the play, Lucius's intention is to knit '[t]hese broken limbs again into one body' (5.3.72).[17]

So the play would have acted as a graphic warning to those English Catholics in the audience at the time who had followed the trail of allusions. In spite of the wickedness of the new regime, attempts at assassination would mean violating everything that was most precious and fundamental to Catholicism. But though it discourages rebellion, *Titus* encourages resistance—this was the line of leaders such as Campion, Persons and Allen. The propaganda campaign not only provides the Andronicus family with activity and something approaching entertainment while they wait for rescue—it effectively broadcasts the crimes of the regime, and unsettles Saturnine. The prospect of rescue itself did not look as impossible in the 1590s as it would with hindsight. France had just reverted to Catholicism; England's exiled Catholics had formed a regiment ready to spearhead the next invasion attempt by Spain; Persons was working on detailed contingency plans for Catholic rule should the invasion succeed. This hawkish policy depended on a sympathetic Catholic majority in England—but it was imperative, until the invasion or the coup occurred, that it should not be an actively rebellious majority.

A single hothead gave the government the excuse for widespread, crushing reprisals that risked breaking the Catholic spirit altogether. The message of the play can be summed up as: lie low, keep the faith, and wait for rescue.[18]

Was this all this seditious? Any advice, from any quarter, against active resistance would have been welcomed at this dangerous point by the Cecils; for whatever reason, Shakespeare's line at this point coincides with the aims of the regime.

There is no question, however, of any covert sympathy with the regime itself. Nowhere does he paint it in darker colours. He evokes the Tower of London, where Southwell was held, by repeatedly alluding to an evil 'pit' where innocent characters are trapped and killed.[19] The Pit was a dank well-shaft in the Tower, famous as the dungeon in which Campion, among others, was incarcerated. The pit in the play is mysteriously illuminated by Bassianus's ring in terms that echo the way the Mass was described as illuminating the experience of imprisonment for Catholics. Aaron is the most extreme of all Shakespeare's composite portraits of the dark forces that underpinned the government of Queen Elizabeth, his name an ironic reference to Moses' brother Aaron, an archetype for the priesthood according to church teaching. His comment 'My mistress is my mistress' (4.2.107) echoes Topcliffe's boast that he slept with the Queen, and his sadism, coarse jokes and Puritan cant are all in the style dubbed 'Topcliffian' by the Essex circle. In the manner of Puritan iconoclasts, of whom Topcliffe was one, Aaron despises his accomplices as 'white-limed walls' and 'ale-house painted signs'—common thrusts at moderate reformers who continued to use images, covering church decorations with a protective coat of whitewash instead of destroying them.

A related similarity between Tamora and Elizabeth is inescapable. This Elizabeth is not the familiar 'Gloriana' of the official version of Reformation history. She is the pragmatic queen, who, according to contemporaries, gave her favour to the man readiest to take the least popular measures; who was 'unwontedly merry' at the news of the capture of her distant kinsman, Southwell; and who complained when the numbers of Catholic executions fell. Tamora's key characteristics, like Elizabeth's, are intelligence and duplicity—she feigns a sympathy with her subjects for persecutions that she herself has instigated.

The painstaking detail of *Titus Andronicus* demonstrates Shakespeare's new resolve to record as fully as possible a saga that would never enter the history books. His later tragedies are much greater works of art than *Titus*—but the heartbreak of what was happening to England and frustration at the cover-up is nowhere better described, the simplicity of the language a long way from that of the court dramatist as he poses the unanswerable question: 'Or shall we bite our tongues, and in dumb shows / Pass the remainder of our hateful days? / What shall we do?' (3.1.131–132).

III

The Attempted Coup,

1595–1602

7

ADDRESSING THE QUEEN, 1595–1599

That Were Enough to Hang Us All

THE URGENCY OF the message behind *Titus Andronicus* implies
Shakespeare was by now addressing a dissident population close to
breaking-point. But by 1595, they had a focus for their hopes: the
Earl of Essex, though Protestant himself, promised to rid the Queen of her
unpopular advisers and establish religious toleration for Catholics as well
as Puritans. Malcontents from all sides gravitated eagerly to his cause.
Among them was Anthony Browne, the 2nd Viscount Montague, who had
just been released from a year's house arrest and was now working closely
with Essex and his chief supporter, the Earl of Southampton.

It was at this point that Shakespeare's plays evidently caught the attention of the Queen. Just as his patrons were moving towards a stance of
outright opposition, he himself was obliged by the knowledge that Elizabeth's eyes were on him to swallow the indignation and anger that inspired
Titus Andronicus and instead devise court plays that flattered the Queen
and actually paid tribute to the Cecils.

His unwelcome promotion followed Lord Strange's death, when the
regime was faced with the problem of what to do with his acting company.[1] The Privy Council had a choice—either to disperse the notoriously
seditious group or to keep them under close observation. They chose the
second. Shakespeare was one of the men selected to join a new company
under the patronage of Lord Hunsdon. Cousin and confidant of the
Queen, Hunsdon held the most senior office in the royal household, that
of Lord Chamberlain, organizer of court entertainment. From being on
the dissident fringe, the elite of Strange's old company suddenly found
themselves at the centre of life at court under the new title of the Lord

Chamberlain's Men. Shakespeare's next task would be the most difficult of his career: a celebration of the union between the Cecil family and the earldom of Derby, which had passed to William Stanley after the murder of his brother, Ferdinando, Lord Strange.

A ruthless contemporary comment survives on the role played by the Lord Treasurer, William Cecil, in Strange's death. 'It is no marvel', wrote Sir Richard Yorke in 1594 to Strange's exiled cousin, Sir William Stanley, 'when Machiavellian policies govern England. I durst pawn my life that the Lord Treasurer caused him to be poisoned that he being dead he might marry the young Lady Vere unto the brother of the said Earl of Derby'.[2] Yorke's suspicions were shared by many others. Among the benefits Strange's murder brought the Cecils was the chance to drive a wedge into a bastion of Northern English Catholicism by marrying into one of the wealthiest earldoms in the country. Elizabeth de Vere, the granddaughter of William Cecil, whom Southampton had paid so much not to marry, was known to be again on offer, and this time accepted by the new Earl. But there was a hitch. Ferdinando's widow vigorously contested the whole settlement, refusing to give up the earldom and claiming that she was pregnant with a Stanley heir. A ruinous lawsuit followed. In the end it became clear that the distraught dowager had simply made up the story of the pregnancy, and nine months later the path was cleared for the wedding to go ahead: it was celebrated at Greenwich Palace in the presence of the Queen on 26 January 1595. It appears that the Queen herself commissioned the evening's entertainment from the Lord Chamberlain's new company for her beloved 'spirit', the seventy-five-year-old William Cecil. Few tasks could have been less congenial to a writer who owed so much to the murdered Earl of Derby; few plays could have had a more intimidating first-night audience. Their reaction was critical to Shakespeare's future.

Foremost among the spectators would have been the Queen and the expectant William Cecil, not normally a great play-goer but eager to see his granddaughter's triumph fittingly celebrated: 'I am ready in mind to dance with my heart', he told the Queen when she teased him about dancing at the wedding, vowing that until the day "I will be a precise keeper of myself from all cold'. Then there were the Stanley relatives of the groom, on the alert to discover whether, now that Lord Strange's old protégé had changed masters, he had also changed his allegiance. There was a wide circle of clever, sophisticated courtiers, outwardly conformist, in fact connoisseurs of the artfully subversive drama in which Lord Strange's Men had specialised. Most daunting of all, there was Robert Cecil, aware of the company's seditious past and no doubt awaiting something that reflected more favourably on his family's rise to power than *Titus Andronicus* or *Richard III*.

Shakespeare's response to this test of loyalty and skill was one of his most brilliant achievements: *A Midsummer Night's Dream*. Acclaimed ever since as a great lyrical comedy, it is at the same time a dramatic conjuring trick that must have induced awe at the extent of Shakespeare's virtuosity and at his astonishing self-assurance. He presents the court with something completely new: a fairyland fantasy on the theme of English reunion, so rich in poetic language and imagery that the oblique asides would go unnoticed. The choice of the fairy world ostensibly pays homage to Elizabeth's chief advisers, both of whom she nicknamed 'Sir Spirit'.

The almost impudent daring with which Shakespeare opens the play heralds a period when his 'hologram' technique will be stretched to the very limit. 'O methinks, how slow / This old moon wanes!' laments the groom, 'She lingers my desires / Like to a stepdame or a dowager, / Long withering out a young man's revenue' (1.1.3–6). For the Cecil faction, the image would have raised a comical picture of the slow deflation of the story of the dowager's pregnancy and the simultaneous wastage of the Stanley fortunes; and of course the note of sensuous longing points forward to the couple's wedding night, so long delayed. But dissidents initiated into Shakespeare's writing would know that in his work the moon was always the Queen; they would recognise the familiar dissident profile of a barren old woman wearing out the patience of a virile younger generation as the exchequer was gradually drained by corruption at home and wars abroad. These carefully crafted lines announce the multiple strands that Shakespeare would develop in order to survive a testing period as dramatist in a court increasingly riven by the Essex-Cecil power struggle. Disarmingly, he shares his nerves with the audience. In a 'play within a play' that defers to his new patron's official role as organizer of court entertainment, a group of rustic actors fret about their performance: 'An you should do it too terribly you would fright the Duchess and the ladies . . . and that were enough to hang us all . . . That would hang us, every mother's son . . . I grant you friends . . . they would have no more discretion but to hang us' (1.2.66–71). Not so absurd, given the recent fate of men like Marlowe and Kyd.

Having drawn a laugh from both sides of the divide with his opening lines about the moon, Shakespeare goes on to initiate the theme of a marriage which would resolve old differences—'Hippolyta', says the groom, burying the hatchet between their two factions, 'I woo'd thee with my sword, / And won thy love doing thee injuries' (1.1.16–17). He next invites the audience to forget the sad event that lay behind the marriage, and instead enjoy the play: 'Turn melancholy forth to funerals' (1.1.14). The drama was developing exactly the way the Cecil faction might have hoped—and better was to come. Strange's old company had been infiltrated by such spies as the dramatist Anthony Munday, and it appears the authorities now knew a great deal about Shakespeare's dubious past, including his use of the code markers of high and low, dark and fair.³ Shakespeare accordingly makes a game of the whole business in this play, much of which takes the form of a light-hearted caricature of his own coded technique and his career with his previous acting company. At the same time he subtly re-aligns his customary treatment of England's dilemma so that it takes a form acceptable to the Cecils.

On comes the familiar quartet of two pairs of lovers, their tangled situation reminiscent of *The Two Gentlemen of Verona*.⁴ The Catholic Helena is in love with inconstant England, represented by the 'spotted' Demetrius; and the Protestant Hermia is pursued by the reformed Lysander. As the two women exchange insults, Shakespeare nonchalantly parades the code in terms so obvious they cannot be missed—the plaintive Helena is high, fair, 'dotes devoutly' and makes much of her martyrdom—Hermia calls her 'a tall personage', a 'painted maypole'. The 'heretic' Hermia is short and dark, 'a vixen', 'a tawny Tartar, 'an Ethiope', 'a bead, an acorn' (3.2.255ff). As usual, the rapid changes of loyalty reflect England's changes of religious allegiance—but the resolution diverges significantly from the resolution of the same quarrel in his earlier plays. Here the state, not the universal church, has ultimate authority over the quarrelling pair. Underlining the compatibility of the two faiths, Helena stresses their 'union in partition . . . due but to one and crowned with one crest . . . like coats in heraldry' (3.2.210–215). The meaning is cleverly ambiguous. The single crest could just refer to the country's 'ancient love'(3.2.215)—in other words, unified medieval Christendom—but the secular imagery strongly suggests the coat of arms now dominating parish churches, the heraldic device of the English Crown. Shakespeare plays on this ambiguity to the end. The quarrel is resolved, 'I wot not by what power— / But by some power it is . . .' (4.1.161–162).

The power in fact lies in the invisible fairy world that forms a shadowy background to the quarrel between the two pairs of lovers bewitched in a wood. Ornamental though it may seem at first, this other world is central to the play, for here a deeper quarrel is in progress that is the real cause of the dissonance in the mortal world experienced by the lovers—the quarrel between the fairy queen, Titania, and her dark husband, Oberon, an image of the deep forces dividing England.[5] When they first meet onstage, 'proud' Titania reminds Oberon of the catastrophic results of their quarrel—a dislocation of the natural world so severe that the sequence of the seasons is altered and 'the mazed world . . . now knows not which is which'; the 'nine men's morris is filled up with mud', 'no night is now with hymn or carol blest', 'the human mortals want their winter cheer' (2.1.98–117). These evoke the contentious results of the English Reformation: the dislocated calendar, the Puritan prohibitions on cheerful traditional customs such as Christmas festivities and morris dancing, even the storms and crop failures of the period that were seen by the superstitious as divine retribution on a godless country.[6] Their quarrel identifies dark Oberon and fair Titania as the factions that created the split in the psyche of England: they represent the power-mongering reformers and the aloof Catholic nobility, at odds over the country's religion. The cause of their quarrel is a tug of love over a mysterious changeling boy, on whom both Oberon and Titania have a claim. Just as in *Titus*, the dark-skinned child suggests England's new compromise religion. The plots of *Titus* and *A Midsummer Night's Dream* are both original: the idea of making a changeling child of mixed race the subject of intense disputes was Shakespeare's own.[7] When the pair at last agree (dark Oberon, like dark Aaron, gaining custody of the child), harmony is restored to the mortal lovers as well.

Unlike Oberon, Titania is accompanied by an elaborate entourage, reminiscent of the magnificent style of the Northern aristocracy, and there is a glimpse of the old religion when she is first announced: cowslips are her 'pensioners'—they wear her livery: 'In their gold coats spots you see; / Those be rubies, fairy favours, / In those freckles live their savours' (2.1.10–14). The five red spots in the centre of the cowslip recall the five wounds, once the object of intense devotion in England, and since the 1569 rebellion a banner of resistance to the imposition of the new order. Shakespeare uses the same allusion in *Cymbeline* in order to highlight the heroine's hidden identity. Slight though the reference is, it would have been enough to people who still remembered the 'superstitious' world of medieval plant symbolism, in which each aspect of the plant could be given a devotional meaning—in this context even the word 'savour' could have been heard as a pun on 'saver' or 'saviour'. The suggestion is that

Titania is on one allegorical level the Catholic tendency in England, doggedly retaining its claim on the spiritual half-caste.

Oberon's servant, Puck, is a comic portrait of Robert Cecil inspired by the Queen's nicknames for him: he was her 'Elf', her 'Pygmy', as well as her 'Spirit'. This portrait of 'Robin Goodfellow' was a brilliant stroke. The scheming aspect of the Queen's Secretary becomes benevolent rather than Machiavellian: his stratagems are all designed to solve the disputes of the squabbling lovers, and they cause harm only by accident. This was precisely the line put out by the Cecils—they were public servants working hard to create harmony and eradicate sectarian feuding: if their plans sometimes misfired it was not their fault. The action traces England's sectarian mix-up: at first both lovers pursue the Protestant Hermia; then, thanks to Puck's error, both fix on the Catholic Helena, worsening the web of misunderstandings. The imagery of oaths, perjury and double allegiance recalls the early comedies: 'One man holding troth, / A million fail, confounding oath on oath' (3.2.93). Finally, Puck gets it right: the pairs match up in Shakespeare's familiar, beguiling portrayal of the country's elusive goal: harmonious co-existence.

Towards the end, as he casts the magical spell over the audience, the figure of Puck, drawn from ancient folklore, comes to embody the numinous spirit of England; he is given the authoritative final speech. Robert Cecil would have been flattered. And so would his father. The immediate superior of the Queen's Secretary was the Lord Treasurer, William Cecil. Just so, Puck's master is Oberon, a charismatic prince of darkness pulling hidden strings, a characterisation to which the omniscient William Cecil would not have objected. But the Derby faction would have detected a sinister undertone to Puck's final speech. Spirits like him flee 'the presence of the sun' and 'follow darkness like a dream' (5.1.373–375) in the company of the creepy moon-goddess Hecate, patroness of ghosts, witches and the underworld, the object of fearful sacrifices at crossroads, the traditional site for executions.

The final settlement favours the 'dark' faction. Reconciled to Oberon, Titania gracefully relinquishes her claim on the half-caste child. Allegorically, the new ascendancy joins hands with the old order in the Stanley-Cecil marriage, and it is this new ascendancy, not a Catholic figure like Petruchio or the Abbess, that manages to resolve the sectarian quarrelling, re-establish national harmony and gain control over the spiritual direction of the country.

In the eyes of the authorities, this was the correct conclusion. Clearly,

Lord Hunsdon had his new company well in hand. Shakespeare stages him as Philostrate, 'Master of Revels to Theseus', amusingly doubtful about the quality of his foolish actors. Warily belittling his own pretensions, Shakespeare portrays himself and his company as the kind of rustic actors often encountered by the Queen on her progresses through the country: bumpkins clumsily attempting to perform before gentry. Here is Shakespeare humbly recommending himself and his fellows to the court in the style of contemporary literary dedications, apologising, as such dedications often did, for the quality of past work—seditious work in this case. The rustic's play, *Pyramus and Thisbe*, sends up the theme and many of the lines of Shakespeare's recent *Romeo and Juliet*—in reality a deeply serious work of art with undertones of martyrdom to which this parody makes distinct reference. There is a further parody of the intense effort that must have gone into the elaborate writing and staging of *A Midsummer Night's Dream* in an anxious rehearsal scene, in which the players' urgent call for an almanac and their arguments over how to dramatise the crucial image of the moon refer slyly to Shakespeare's problems of what to do with the political code.

The self-abasement went further still. Greene's famous dig at Shakespeare as 'an absolute Johannes factotum'—'in his own conceit the only Shake-scene in a country' had no doubt done the rounds and for many would have been all they knew of the company's writer. There may well have been truth in it—Shakespeare certainly ran rings around his theatre audiences, and what we know of his life indicates that the same was true of his dealings with bureaucracy. Shakespeare subjects this reputation to mercilessly comic treatment in the character of Bottom, leader of the troupe of rustic actors. Bottom embodies precisely Greene's caricature of Shakespeare, a bumpkin organising and outdoing 'in his own conceit' everyone in the company.[8] Oblivious that he is sporting an ass's head, Bottom complacently accepts Titania's brief infatuation, unaware of how foolish he and his country manners appear to her court. He recalls the event in the garbled language of St Paul's beatific vision. Those who had known Lord Strange would have seen this episode as the ultimate piece of self-mockery in which the Warwickshire actor-playwright relives the period when he was treated as an equal, perhaps a favourite, by the aristocratic Strange.[9] Bottom's muddled version of St Paul implies that Shakespeare's brief elevation to favour introduced him to doctrinal ideas that he was too unlearned to understand. By the end of the play, Shakespeare has disowned his company's past with its unreliable religious associations and well-worn coded themes; his association with Strange is derided for its pathetic delusions of grandeur. He has presented England in terms of a simple sectarian feud resolved, after a series of mishaps, by the Cecils. Only the most fleeting references, such as the hint that the play itself can be seen as a 'weak and idle theme / No more yielding than a dream' (5.1.416–417), suggest continuing disaffection.

It is probable that this brilliant play saved Shakespeare's professional life and that of his company. Both sides of the Cecil-Essex divide would have left the hall in Greenwich in the comfortable certainty that Shakespeare was speaking to them. The transition from seething dissident to equivocating courtier appeared to be effortless—and given the sparkling quality of *A Midsummer Night's Dream*, almost enjoyable. But it was not, according to his self-lacerating Sonnet 110, which refers to circumstances exactly like those of the mid-1590s:

> Alas, 'tis true, I have gone here and there
> And made myself a motley to the view,
> Gor'd mine own thoughts, sold cheap what was most dear
> Made old offences of acquaintance new . . .
> *(1–4)*

These lines apply accurately to this anguished moment—the attempt to please both sides at once; the strategic portrayal of himself as a foolish actor or 'motley'; the betrayal of his own convictions in his heartless skit of *Romeo and Juliet*.

Wake Diana with a Hymn

WHATEVER THE humiliations, Shakespeare's new position had the great advantage of bringing him close to the centre of power—of allowing him, now and then, direct access to the monarch. The nature of the role he was to take on, with one or two breaks, for the rest of his working life is suggested in a Latin play called *Captiva Religio* performed nearly twenty years later in Rome.[10] From the only surviving account, the drama was less than gripping: it opened on a scene of London dungeons filled with Catholics and took the form of a five-hour disquisition on the sorry state of the Catholic Church in England. But it contained an intriguing central role. The hero returns from

Rome to his native England to find Catholicism banned and its adherents persecuted. He becomes a jester in the Chancellor's household and uses his protected position to put their case. He prevents further persecution but fails to gain their freedom.

There was no official jester at the court of Elizabeth, but she allowed her court dramatists a degree of licence that horrified Puritans and surprised foreign visitors. Could the hero of *Captiva Religio* be based on entertainers like Shakespeare? The ridiculous Bottom is given a comic version of some serious resistance markers. On his entry he is associated with the 'shivering shocks' that 'break the locks of prison gates', echoing the rescue of St Peter, with the resistance hero Hercules (or 'Ercles'), with 'fair-coloured' beards, with the nightingale and the turtle dove, and boasts that he will go on roaring like a lion—but gently, so as not to incur hanging (1.2.25–74). It is at about this time that Shakespeare begins to introduce court fools into his plays—fools who mirror his own covert attempts to plead the Catholic cause. Though officially in the service of the Lord Chamberlain, Shakespeare studied how to turn the situation to advantage. And he came up with a bold strategy. The hidden level of Shakespeare's next play reveals him capitalising on the success of the obediently conformist *A Midsummer Night's Dream* in order to make a personal appeal to the Queen to show mercy to her desperate subjects—a rash entreaty, as it turned out.

His decision was prompted by an event that brought the steadily worsening Catholic situation to a head. *A Midsummer Night's Dream* was performed in January 1595; in February, Robert Southwell was finally released from the hands of Topcliffe to be hanged, drawn and quartered at Tyburn. Partly because of his wide circle of aristocratic connections, partly because of the exceptional savagery that accompanied his imprisonment and death, the result was a public outcry.

We assume that barbaric punishments inflicted in the name of religion were accepted in the sixteenth century in a way they would not be today. This was not the case. They clearly filled civilised onlookers at the time with the same revulsion felt by modern Muslims or Christians at the atrocities perpetrated by extremist co-religionists. Just as now, England thought of itself as essentially above such things. 'Our goalers are guilty of felony by an old law of the land if they torment any prisoner committed to their custody, for the revealing of his complices', wrote William Harrison in the 1587 edition of his *Description of England*.[11] It was not only humanist writers like Erasmus who protested; there is a vivid account of Walter

Raleigh's attempt to intervene at the foot of the scaffold to prevent the death of a priest, Father Oliver Plasden, at the hands of Topcliffe in December 1591. The heated debate conducted across the priest's hurdle almost ended in his release: 'Mr Sheriff', commanded Raleigh, having proved to the crowd Plasden's innocence of treachery, 'her Majesty desireth no more at these men's hands . . . I will presently go to the Court, let him be stayed'. But Topcliffe overruled him, applying the 'bloody question' of loyalty in its most literal terms; and the man was executed.[12]

The Merchant of Venice revolves round a law-court scene in which a reflective, innocent man is forced to bare his chest so that his enemy can slice off the pound of flesh nearest the heart. It is a play usually associated with an anti-Semitic mood following the Lopez affair, a shadowy intelligence operation that resulted in the execution of the Queen's Jewish physician, Roderigo Lopez, for an alleged attempt on her life. Shakespeare undoubtedly used the details of this plot in order to construct a play that would attract the interest of the Queen. But just as with his other two appeals to Elizabeth, *Love's Labour's Lost* and *Twelfth Night*, a cat's cradle of cryptic meanings and involved double identities lies beneath the great universal drama, their subtlety a reminder that the Queen took pride in deciphering codes and allegories that defeated her advisers.

Two modern scholars, Peter Milward and John Klause, have teased out a number of the play's hidden political threads, tracing the ways Shakespeare adapts the centuries-old religious division between New Testament Christian and Old Testament Jew to the sixteenth-century religious division between Catholics and scripture-conscious Puritans. With the privileged exception of such men as the Queen's doctor, Jews were officially banned from England, and most of Shylock's attributes would have reminded Shakespeare's contemporaries of a group closer to home— London's Puritan usurers, nicknamed 'Christian Jews'. They, too, kept themselves scrupulously apart from the idle and ungodly; they were 'precise' and legalistic; they, too, harboured vengeful hatred for the old order that had persecuted and burned them in Queen Mary's time and which now borrowed money from them while condemning the un-Christian practice of lending money at interest.[13] John Klause sharpens the contemporary application, identifying a rich seam of references that link the language of Shylock's opponents with the writings of Robert Southwell. There are further identifying touches. Shylock, like the Puritans, draws much of his language and imagery from the Old Testament. When the play's Christians respond, they play the favourite Catholic trick of quoting the Apocrypha, Old Testament books that Protestants excluded from the Bible, and which the Counter-Reformation defiantly promoted.[14] The love scene in the last act between the Christian Lorenzo and the Jewish Jessica is dense with liturgical reference from the Catholic Easter ritual, a ceremony that stresses the essential bond between Christian and Jew. The result is one of Shakespeare's idealized conclusions in which England's religious schism is resolved in the mutual embrace of a younger and more forgiving generation.

Just as in *Twelfth Night* and *Love's Labour's Lost*, Shakespeare is determined to persuade the Queen that she alone has the skill and the capacity to heal the country's divisions. In all three plays, the resolution of an apparently insoluble problem lies in the hands of a clever, witty, beautiful woman who runs a grand household and is besieged by unwelcome suitors. Cleverness is the particular quality stressed in *The Merchant of Venice*.

The first references to Portia chime with many other literary compliments to the Queen—she is a paragon courted by princes from the four quarters of the globe. The audience is told that they include 'many Jasons', who see her as their Golden Fleece (1.1.172). The Order of the Golden Fleece was an honour given to the highest ranks of the Catholic nobility and connected particularly with the Hapsburgs. And the Hapsburgs, led by Philip II, the Grand Master of the Order, had been among Elizabeth's most pressing suitors.

The Queen must have awaited with interest the actual appearance of Portia: and sure enough when she comes on, it is in a flurry of her own themes and catchphrases—she has a 'little body', 'weary of this world', she will die 'as chaste as Diana', she complains of the constraints of her office, her hosts of suitors are the subject of slightly heartless jokes with her lady-in-waiting. Her choice of spouse is 'curbed by the will of a dead father'— exactly Elizabeth's predicament, for Henry VIII's will stipulated that neither of his daughters should marry without the consent of a majority of the Privy Council. 'O me, the word choose! I may neither choose who I would nor refuse who I dislike!' (1.2.1–23).[15]

Portia's hand can be gained only by the suitor who correctly chooses one of three caskets, gold, silver and lead. Shakespeare adapts the old tale to Elizabeth's famous marital dilemma, enriching it with a wealth of contemporary reference, embodying in Portia's three suitors the three kinds of alliance contemplated by herself and her council. One of them is the 'Golden Fleece' Catholic Hapsburg suit that appears fittingly as the Prince of Aragon, the embodiment of Spanish pride. Next comes the Prince of

Morocco, whose darkness gives him a Protestant identity. Among the few foreign Protestants to seek Elizabeth's hand were Eric, Prince of Sweden, and his brother—their behaviour was so outlandish that Elizabeth ever afterwards referred to the hapless Eric as 'that barbarous King of Sweden'. An apparently extravagant flight of fancy connects the Moroccan prince to the Protestantism of Scandinavia, currently about to return to Catholicism: 'Make incision' beneath his dark skin, he says, and his blood will prove to be as 'red' as that of 'the fairest creature northward born, / Where Phoebus' fire scarce warms the icicles' (2.1.4–6).

Both these suitors, the Protestant and Catholic European powers, fail to win her hand. Who, then, is represented by Bassanio, the successful suitor? By 1596 it was clear that the aging Queen was unlikely ever to marry—indeed, in her own terms, she was married already. Nearly forty years earlier, when she had just ascended the throne and was under intense pressure from Parliament to choose a husband, Elizabeth is described giving her decision to the Commons in characteristically forthright terms:

> 'To conclude, I am already bound unto an husband, which is the kingdom of England, and that may suffice you. And this' quoth she 'makes me wonder that you forget, yourselves, the pledge of this alliance which I here made with my kingdom'. And therewithal, stretching out her hand, she showed them the ring with which she was given in marriage and inaugurated to her kingdom in express and solemn terms. '[A]nd so reproach me no more' quoth she.[16]

This early image, including the ring, was one she returned to repeatedly. To her many suitors, her marriage to her country appeared to be nothing more than a fanciful metaphor—but it was a marriage that was to last. 'Lady this long space / Have I loved thy grace', sings 'merry England' in a poem written by William Birch on her accession, and the Queen replies: 'Here is my hand, / My dear lover England, / I am thine both with mind and heart . . . until death us two depart'.[17]

'An husband which is the kingdom of England': this was how Elizabeth characterised the suitor who won her hand—and Shakespeare does the same. Bassanio represents exactly that loyal aspect of England that Elizabeth saw as her spouse. As in Birch's poem, the whole sequence of Bassanio's courtship in *The Merchant of Venice* mirrors Elizabeth's relations with her subjects. The flirtation is full of elaborate double meaning, designed to give the Queen pause for thought. Portia has been 'divided', she says, by Bassanio's 'eyes'. This is Elizabeth's experience, torn in two directions by England's reformist and Catholic extremes. In a sharper comment on the problems of loyalty she is Bassanio's 'torturer' but finds that even though he denies 'on the rack' that his love is mixed with treason, she is not satisfied for 'men enforced speak anything' (3.2.14–39). This was a shrewd touch, aimed at unsettling the Queen's faith in the current methods of her security service. Fresh in her mind was the admission of treason under torture by her trusted doctor, Lopez; in spite of assurances from her advisers, she refused to believe he was guilty. And on the eve of Southwell's execution, she had dispatched 'a nobleman of high rank' to his cell to discover whether he had indeed been intent on assassinating her. When Bassanio wins her at last, echoes of Elizabeth's Coronation Day fill the background, designed to recall the wave of popularity on which she came to the throne, when London did indeed greet her like a bride. The music that Portia summons to accompany Bassanio's study of the three caskets is 'Even as the flourish when true subjects bow / To a new-crowned queen'.[18] And having won her and listened to her acceptance, he feels as dazed with joy as her subjects did, 'a buzzing, pleased multitude', delighted 'after some oration fairly spoke / By a beloved prince . . .'.

While the tale of the wooing and winning of Portia unfolds slowly and enjoyably, bringing with it flattering echoes of Elizabeth's loving relationship with her country and in particular the honeymoon period surrounding her coronation, an altogether darker story fills the foreground.

The play has so far associated Bassanio with Elizabeth's loyal subjects. But she has other subjects, less loyal at the beginning of the play, though abjectly grateful by the end. Bassanio has a friend, Antonio, to whom he is bound by ties that rival those of marriage. Bassanio is only able to win Portia because of the self-sacrifice of Antonio, who, certain that his ships are returning laden with merchandise, mortgages himself to Shylock for a pound of flesh in order to furnish money for Bassanio's suit. The passionate relationship between the two friends suggests a homosexual subtext—but it represents with even more aptness the double character of England in which supporters of the old religion and the new were bound together by inextricable family and social ties.[19] Shakespeare artfully implies that Elizabethan England is under an obligation to the Catholics of Mary's reign. Like England, which gained its Protestant queen thanks to the early passivity of the old religion, Bassanio gains Portia thanks to the self-sacrifice of his friend. Just as English Catholics were exposed, on the accession of a Protestant Queen, to revenge from the Puritans they had persecuted, Antonio finds that as a consequence of his generosity to his friend he has been betrayed by the heedless Bassanio into the hands of his mortal enemy.

Shakespeare's treatment of Antonio's old-style Catholic identity follows familiar lines. At first Antonio suffers from some vague malaise; like the secular twin in *Comedy of Errors*, business worries in particular depress him. One friend remarks that his affairs must come between him and his prayers: the very stones of the church must remind him of the rocks that threaten his merchandise. This echoes the charge that pre-Elizabethan Catholicism had become worldly, and it points in particular to the reign of Queen Mary, when spirituality took second place to such political concerns as the re-structuring of the church's hierarchy and the restoration of monastic lands. Antonio also has a history of tormenting and abusing the usurer Shylock—an echo of the cruel treatment of Puritans under Mary. But like earlier Catholic characters, Antonio is reformed through hardship. As he gives his all for his friend, exchanging the melancholy of a rich man for the misery of a condemned one, he becomes a sympathetic character— though Shakespeare was careful, as Southwell was in his *Humble Supplication*, not to make the reactionary Catholic faction appear in any way a threat: Antonio is content to yield the limelight to Bassanio.

Against all expectation, Antonio's ships are lost, and he has to keep his side of the bargain with his creditor. The ghastly confrontation between Shylock and Antonio, with its suspended threat of legalised butchery, represents the kind of vengeful gallows scene that Raleigh had tried to prevent in his dispute with the Puritan Topcliffe. The situation is given contemporary application by the repeated insistence that the pound of flesh should be cut off 'nearest the merchant's heart'; the extraction of the still-beating heart was the last stage of the ordeal of 'merchants' like Southwell and Plasden. Here again, Shakespeare presents the solution in strictly secular terms. It is the Queen who must resolve the bitter conflict; a queen who on her accession had planted in her subjects' breasts 'a wonderful hope . . . touching her worthy government in the rest of her reign'.

Did Shakespeare need to be quite so secretive this time about the allegory behind the play? Partly, of course, its subtlety would have created a pleasing sense of complicity between the canny Queen and the calculating dramatist; partly, it would be convenient if the hidden meaning escaped the hard-line Puritans in the audience. But there was another reason. In Act 4, Portia triumphs, Shylock is confounded and Antonio freed, but that is not the end of the story. Shakespeare reserves his most daring variation on the role of Portia for the extraordinary Act 5, constructed on the fragile premise, cherished by many English Catholics, that the Queen secretly sympathised with their cause. It was an illusion assiduously fostered by the Queen herself: anecdotes of her resistance to hard-line churchmen and reassuring tales like that of her request that Magdalen Montague should pray for her must have spread quickly. Certainly the end of *The Merchant of Venice* adopts the assumption of appeals such as Southwell's *Humble Supplication* that it is only her advisers that prevent the Queen from reconciling the country with the universal church.

In Act 5, as Portia slowly makes her way home, Shakespeare deftly constructs around her allegorical shadow, Elizabeth, a suggestion of the Queen's true home—the sacramental religion in its most spiritual form. Even today, this part of the play reminds Catholics of the events of the Triduum—the Easter liturgy still clandestinely celebrated in the 1590s and familiar to the Queen's generation from their childhood. The symbolism of this ancient liturgy, its roots extending back to pagan times, was rejected as 'ornament' by the Protestant reformers, but for Catholics it continues to encapsulate the central truths of Christianity. On the night before Easter day, a fire is lit at the back of a darkened church and blessed along with baptismal water, the fire giving light to a single 'Paschal' candle borne in procession up the nave, lighting up individual candles as it passes through the congregation. The ceremony was designed to re-enact the entry of divinity into the world and to dramatise the Easter victory of light over darkness. The procession is followed by the 'Exultet', an early Christian hymn to the 'sacred night' of Easter preceded by a prayer from the cantor for the strength to perform it. Its celebration of divine rescue from death returns repeatedly in a single phrase, 'Haec nox est': 'This is the night Christ burst the bonds of death . . . this is the night of which scripture says And the night shall be bright as day and the night shall light up my joy . . . this is the night which at this hour throughout the world restores to grace those who believe in Christ . . . to ransom a slave, you gave up your Son'.

Act 5 opens by recalling this hymn. The famous moonlit exchange 'in such a night' between Lorenzo and Jessica, Christian and Jew, echoes the Exultet's themes of redeeming and rejected love, relating the Jewish Old Testament to the Christian Gospels. Next we are told of Portia journeying through the dark, periodically kneeling at 'holy crosses' to pray for 'happy wedlock hours' (5.1.30–32). The Good Friday tradition that preceded the vigil, 'Creeping to the cross', was one of the favourite targets of the reformers—kissing the feet of a crucifix summed up everything they meant by popish superstition. Next, Lorenzo and Jessica, like those at the Easter vigil, sit listening to music; the scene evokes the liturgical settings by Shakespeare's contemporaries, Byrd and Thomas Tallis, that are sung to this day at the Saturday vigil. They look up as they listen, and what they see—'the floor of heaven / Thick inlaid with patines of bright gold' (5.1.58–59)—is a description of the night sky in terms recalling the squares and bosses that chequer the wooden ceilings of medieval churches, once richly decorated with gold stars and angels to resemble the floor of Heaven. The passage ends with a veiled reference to the ban on the liturgy and its musical settings by black-robed reformers: 'whilst this muddy vesture of decay / Doth grossly close it in, we cannot hear it' (5.1.64–65).[20] Lorenzo's attack on those who are unmusical seems extreme: they are 'fit for treasons, stratagems and spoils' (5.1.85). But it makes more sense when applied to the vengeful Puritans, in particular the anti-musical Calvinists who ensured that the role of music was reduced to a minimum in the new Prayer Book. Shakespeare here exploits one of Elizabeth's chief quarrels with the reformers, for she loved and patronised church music.

When Portia finally arrives just before daybreak, she apprehends as if for the first time the quality of candlelight and music, their symbolic meaning enhanced by the darkness, and discovers a hitherto unnoticed beauty: 'How many things by season seasoned are / To their right praise and true perfection!' (5.1.105). The play on the words 'right' and 'season' point to the Easter 'rite'. Her famous line "How far that little candle throws his beams / Like a brave deed in a naughty world!" (5.1.90–91) recalls the most dramatic moment of the liturgy, when the Paschal candle, representing Christ's redemption, spreads its light to the watchers in the dark. 'Let me give light' she says a little later, 'but let me be not light' (5.1.129). Lorenzo has achieved his aim, to lead Portia home. It was at this annual vigil that converts were traditionally received into the Catholic Church. The same aim is true of the trance-like atmosphere of this final act—it is to lead the Queen back, by means of music and ceremony, to a recognition of the value of the older, endangered spirituality, 'seasoned' by persecution and now reaching 'true perfection'. 'Wake Diana with a hymn; / With sweetest touches pierce your mistress' ear / And draw her home with music' (5.1.66–68). As dawn breaks, the Catholic figures of Lorenzo and Antonio express their gratitude to the royal figure of Portia for the longed-for return of liberty and the Mass in two final references to the vigil readings: 'You have given me my life and living'; 'You drop manna in the way / Of starved people' (5.1.286–294).

The play began with an exploration of the corrupted spirituality of callous Catholics and vindictive Puritans; it paints an idealised picture of the merciful, clever Queen, utterly devoted to her adoring England, and the only hope of her divided subjects; but after her success in releasing Catholics from their Puritan tormentors, it sets her own position in an older, deeper spiritual context, into which the power of a monarch '[e]mpties itself, as doth an inland brook / Into the main of waters' (5.1.96–97). The judicious combination of flattery and daring advice was in the best tradition of Shakespeare's predecessor, the court dramatist John Lyly. In spite of the difficulties of working under the eyes of the Cecil faction, Shakespeare appeared to have found a new métier—that of highly placed apologist for the Catholic opposition.

By My Two Faiths

B
UT *The Merchant of Venice* went too far: someone must have objected. The elegantly encrypted appeals come to an abrupt halt. There is no doubt that Shakespeare was forced to concede defeat. *Henry IV* and *Henry V, Merry Wives of Windsor* and *Much Ado About Nothing* make no attempt to evoke the threatened Catholic spirituality conjured up in his recent plays; gone, too, is the heroic role of secret chronicler of the times. Instead they faithfully mirror the political concerns of Shakespeare's Protestant patrons, tempered wherever possible to avoid overt anti-Catholicism.

'Our bending author', Shakespeare calls himself in the epilogue to *Henry V,* writing with 'all-unable pen'. Did he give way under pressure, or did he genuinely convert to Protestantism? In the late 1590s, there was certainly a concerted effort by the government to cajole rather than coerce leading Catholics into adopting the new religion. Viscount Montague was a typical target. A manuscript book survives in his own handwriting, dated 1597, setting out all the arguments for Catholicism for his young daughter, warning her of the ploys of Protestant apologists.[21] It was a period when Shakespeare himself was unusually vulnerable. His company had lost the lease of the playhouse at Holywell, and a petition led by the Cecil faction successfully prevented them from using their new all-weather theatre at Blackfriars, a project on which they had spent an estimated £1,000. Shakespeare was therefore especially dependent on patronage. And at home, tragedy struck. In the summer of 1596 his only son, Hamnet, died at the age of eleven. Certain sonnets refer guardedly to this event,[22] and *Henry IV* and *Much Ado About Nothing* both include passages in which a heartbroken father rejects the efforts of well-meaning comforters on the death of his child.

He can have found little relief at court. 'It is a dangerous time here', wrote one courtier to an acquaintance abroad, 'for the heads of both factions being here a man cannot tell how to govern himself towards them. For here is such observation and prying into men's actions that I hold them happy and blessed that live away'.[23] For the next five years, Shakespeare was to be caught up in the bitter in-fighting between the two factions struggling for political supremacy, both of them led by Protestants: the aristocratic following of the popular Earl of Essex, already negotiating with Elizabeth's heir apparent, King James of Scotland, and the eerily omniscient Cecil faction, past masters at backstairs diplomacy and adept at manipulating both Essex and the Queen.

It is clear from his writings towards the end of Elizabeth's reign that Shakespeare took an active part in the struggle, promoting the cause of the opponents of the Cecil regime. Small pennants fluttering from the plays of the period announce that, like his patron, Lord Hunsdon, Shakespeare continued to support Southampton and Essex as they moved towards armed confrontation with Elizabeth's advisers. This required a continual balancing act: his work had to please Protestants without alienating Catholics. Rousing the country to the Essex banner remained the goal of many leading Catholics; but unlike Shakespeare's previous patrons, the bluff, soldierly Lord Hunsdon was a thoroughgoing Protestant and evidently had no time for papist nudges and winks about religious love and kneeling at crosses and suitors from Rheims. What he required from the Lord Chamberlain's Men was a bracing play about an English Protestant hero with chivalric features that would remind people of the Earl of Essex. It was equally important to remind the Queen of the key role played by himself and his son George in putting down the Rebellion of the Northern Earls back in 1570, the last stand of English Catholicism. Now that they were backing Essex against her favourite advisers, the Hunsdons needed to stress their unflinching loyalty to the Crown and their dislike of sedition. Also desirable would be a comedy that pilloried Spanish Catholicism and for once featured a dark, Puritan character as the persecuted heroine.

Just as with *Midsummer Night's Dream*, Shakespeare had to do more than conform in order to please his patron. Highlighting the military prowess of the Hunsdon family entailed celebrating their greatest triumph, the 1570 defeat of English Catholicism, whose forces had been led, among others, by the Percy family and by Magdalen Montague's brother, Leonard Dacre. Shakespeare was in a very difficult position: the commission would certainly not have endeared him to his Catholic protectors. The rebellion had been a serious threat, and his patron's decisive action had drawn an ecstatic letter of thanks from the relieved Queen: 'I doubt much, my Harry, whether that the victory were given me more joyed me, or that you were by God appointed the instrument of my glory . . .', she wrote. In *Henry IV, Part 1*, Shakespeare revives the Hunsdons' moment of glory in flattering terms, minutely linking their suppression of the 1569 rebellion with the royal suppression of a fifteenth-century rebellion led by the same Percy family. The play portrays many aspects of the Northern rebels in a negative light—like their sixteenth-century counterparts they are power hungry and divided, and the Catholic allegiance of the Welsh, who were the object of a determined government onslaught in the 1590s, is obliquely mocked in the superstitions of the boastful rebel Glendower. But Shakespeare also adroitly reminds the Hunsdons of the nobility of the rebels they defeated.

Henry and George Hunsdon found themselves campaigning against old friends when they took arms against the banner of the Five Wounds. Henry Hunsdon recorded his admiration for Leonard Dacre's cavalry charge at the Battle at Carlisle, and his courteous treatment of the imprisoned Thomas Percy led to suspicions of treasonable sympathies. The pair were disgusted by the nature and behaviour of their own allies. George Hunsdon wrote bitterly to London about the pathetic musters he had to lick into shape: 'Except it be a few protestants and some well affected to me, every man seeks to bring as small a force as he can of horsemen, and the footmen find fault with the weather and besides speak very broadly'.[24] They were appalled by the cruelty and greed of their reinforcements, a 'lusty southern army', as Henry Hunsdon sarcastically called them.[25] These men, arriving after the rebels had dispersed, looted and devastated the border country and took vicious reprisals on innocent towns and villages—there were 800 official executions, but many more were killed in the fields and forests. The cowardly knight Sir John Falstaff was Shakespeare's greatest comic creation; but his conscript 'scarecrows' and his cynical desecration of the body of Harry Hotspur, the courageous leader of the rebellion, would have reminded the Hunsdons of the tragic aspects of the campaign to put down English Catholicism.[26]

Similar contradictions mark Shakespeare's account of the great national hero Henry V. Essex's followers revelled in the character of Falstaff, a cheeky lampoon of the ancestry of one of Cecil's most hated supporters, Lord Cobham, and it was clearly for their benefit that Shakespeare linked Essex so explicitly with Henry V as he returns from the victory at Agincourt to a rapturous welcome in London. The Protestants behind Essex would have approved of Henry's 'reformed' identity, his story nicely linked with the favourite Protestant parable of the reformed Prodigal Son. But just as with the Northern Rebellion, Shakespeare refines the Protestant message. Critics note that Henry's glamour is accompanied by callousness and his brutality contrasts with the humanity of his tavern companions. He threatens the town of Harfleur with horrifying savagery; his rejection of his old drinking companion, Falstaff, is chillingly dramatised. The 'reformation' that Henry describes in *Henry IV, Part 1* as 'glittering o'er my fault' (1.3.206) makes him a great soldier, but an unlikable man. The careful avoidance of Protestant triumphalism would have pacified the many Catholics among Essex's supporters.

Much Ado About Nothing, written around 1598, continues to fulfill the tricky political brief. It gives a sympathetic portrayal of the unhappy cause of radical Protestants. By the mid-1590s, Archbishop John Whitgift had ruthlessly and at times bloodily suppressed the radical movement within the Protestant Church, dubbed 'Puritan' by some, but viewed by many others as the spiritual core of England's Reformation. Like Catholics, these fervent believers found themselves excluded by the rigid imposition of state conformity in religion. Shakespeare dramatises the predicament of England's persecuted radical Protestants in the sad fortunes of the 'dark' beauty, Hero, and demonises Essex's bugbear, Catholic Spain, in the stagily wicked Don John, a reminder of the famous contemporary hammer of Protestants, Don John of Austria. But he still has his Catholic audiences in mind. Hero and her lover, Claudio, are eclipsed by two of Shakespeare's most entertaining characters. The rapprochement between the quarrelsome lovers Beatrice and Benedick is not central to the plot, but it takes centre stage. And Shakespeare inserts a heavily coded passage into their courtship that would have signalled to Catholic spectators that his period of apostasy was coming to an end. Some time in the past, Benedick rejected Beatrice, a character with distinct Catholic markers— she is tall, sunburnt, fairer than her dark friend, Hero, and, like emblems of the phoenix, has a 'double heart', a symbol of rebirth. Moreover, in distinct contrast to Hero, she is 'merry'—the word is repeated a number of times. Benedick's friends tease him about his aversion to Beatrice. He is 'a heretic in despite of beauty'. In defence of his male chauvinism he will 'die at the stake'. If he ever does begin to 'fall from this faith', they speculate, he will 'look for an earthquake', he will 'temporize with the hours', he will lose his house, he will—and this last detail brings Benedick up short—sign a letter on 'the sixth of July'. 'Mock not, mock not' he reproves, 'ere you flout old ends any further, examine your consciences' (1.1.201–250).

On the meaning of all this, particularly the date and the 'old ends', the commentaries are silent. But the stream of banter has a topical undercurrent. It is a typical instance of Shakespeare's use of the extravagant language of arguments, fits of rage and flights of fancy as vehicles for inserting precise threads of coded reference into the dialogue. Initiated listeners would have understood that Shakespeare was associating the revival of Benedick's love for Beatrice with the experience of returning to Catholicism after a period of defection. Heretics who denounce beauty and die at the stake denote Protestantism—so Benedick's initial position is linked with the new religion. The earthquake associated with the 1580 mission, the Gregorian calendar, loss of property—all these, which he dismisses, denote Catholicism. But he checks when his friends throw in a date with a hidden significance—6 July. This was the date on which Sir Thomas More was executed. Its significance was deepened for Catholics when Edward VI also died on 6 July—clearly a judgement on his father, Henry VIII, for having condemned his saintly, 'merry' chancellor to death. For his friends to include this reference in their banter is going too far, Benedick decides. Mock not old *ends*, he says—More's death is not a laughing matter—and his parting shot, 'examine your consciences', is a reminder of the case of conscience that drove More to the scaffold.

The Montague household would certainly have picked up this allusion. One of their chaplains, Thomas More, was More's great-nephew, and they were closely connected with his recusant descendants, the Ropers. Other family friends—the Clitheroes—included an Elizabethan martyr. The Yorkshire housewife Margaret Clitheroe was pressed to death under heavy weights for refusing to plead when on trial for recusancy. Hers is another 'old end' 'flouted' by the unthinking Hero, who swears she will be 'pressed to death' with laughing. Her lover, Claudio, puns blithely on drawing and hanging apropos of a toothache. The play, in fact, is full of jokily secularised religious language, some of it about martyrdom but much of it

about the contemporary obsession with holding or changing faith—
'reforming', 'turning', 'reconciling'. 'By my two faiths and troths'
(1.1.195), swears Benedick, in two minds like so many of his onlookers.
Benedick does, of course, change faiths in the end when he and Beatrice
are tricked by their friends into revealing their love for each other. The
witty love-hate relationship between this pair is not only the essence of
romantic comedy—it evokes the complex emotions of many people in
England who over the years strategically abandoned their native religion,
while remaining secretly attracted to it.

This was the last play that Shakespeare wrote under duress. In 1599, his
company at last re-established their independence. One December night
in 1598, in a daringly resourceful move that was to prove the subject of
years of later litigation, the Lord Chamberlain's Men moved the timbers
of the redundant theatre from the disputed land in Holywell to a new site
across the river in Southwark, where it was triumphantly re-christened the
Globe.

This time, there was no mistake. The new theatre, though just across
the river from Westminster, was established outside the city limits in
Southwark, a stone's throw from two of the most notorious dissident centres in London—the Clink prison, and Montague Close. The period of
humiliating dependence on court figures and factions was over. Though
Lord Hunsdon remained the company's patron, they were no longer
working under the noses of the regime or dependent on the assistance of
other theatres: they had their own base again. Shakespeare was deeply
committed to the new enterprise: he rented new lodgings near the Globe,
in which he was one of the chief shareholders. The sense of a fresh start,
the impetus of convictions refined after years of questioning and debate,
are evident in his crystalline new play, *Julius Caesar*, which scholars believe
was written to inaugurate the Globe in 1599. But first he would have to re-
establish the credentials of his 'truant Muse'[27] with the supporters of the
cause he appeared to have betrayed.

The scars left by this period of defection clearly went deep. There had
been certain gains. Shakespeare acquired a first-hand understanding of
England's ideological deadlock, revealing his close acquaintance with the
mentality of reformers and reluctant collaborators in his next play. And he
was now clearly a trusted ally of the Essex party, whose cause he would
continue to support. But following on from the self-accusing Sonnet 110,
Sonnet 111 gives a further insight into what Shakespeare endured during
the late 1590s. Its highly specific allusions make sense only when it is read

as an appeal to one of his original protectors to forgive the 'harmful deeds' of his four-year apostasy, explaining that it was dictated by the demands of the 'public means' and 'public manners' on which his livelihood depends. The 'correction' he was forced to undergo was a penance to him, he claims, but he submits willingly to whatever penance is imposed on his return.

> O for my sake do you with fortune chide,
> The guilty goddess of my harmful deeds,
> That did not better for my life provide
> Than public means, which public manners breeds
> Thence comes it that my name receives a brand
> And almost thence my nature is subdued
> To what it works in, like the dyer's hand
> Pity me, then, and wish I were renewed
> Whilst like a willing patient I will drink
> Potions of eisell 'gainst my strong infection;
> No bitterness that I will bitter think,
> Nor double penance to correct correction.
> Pity me then, dear friend, and I assure ye,
> Even that your pity is enough to cure me . . . .[28]
> *(Source: Sonnet 111)*

The apologetic tone, the self-abasement, suggest that the rehabilitation would not be easy.

THE CATHOLIC RESISTANCE, 1599–1600

Friends, Romans, Countrymen

MOST BIOGRAPHIES of Shakespeare include maps showing the position of the original Globe Theatre on the south bank of the Thames. They give a clear picture of the route from the centre of London to Bankside: across London Bridge, then right past the church of St Mary Overies and Winchester Palace to the Globe, situated in a marshy district among a huddle of inns, brothels, smallholdings and gardens. But one significant landmark is often overlooked. Turning right after passing through the great archway that led off the bridge, the first building a sixteenth-century pedestrian would have encountered was Montague Close, a 'fine mansion' built for himself by Sir Anthony Browne, Master of the King's Horse, father of the 1st Viscount Montague.

Quick off the mark when it came to the division of monastic spoils, Sir Anthony had secured a prize site. The Augustinian Priory of St Mary Overies (St Mary 'over the water') was not only extensive, including church, hospital, refectory, dormitory, library and the outbuildings and gardens typical of ancient foundations dedicated to practical works of mercy, but it dominated the junction between London's single bridge and the main routes to the south of England, where his own lands lay. Sir Anthony's recusant descendants were to find the strategic position of Montague Close more useful still, for among its cluster of buildings, many of them sublet to relatives and retainers, were jetties and wharves that gave directly onto the river. For centuries these outlets to the Thames had been used for purposes other than the loading of spices, iron, fish and wool. St Mary's had been granted the right of sanctuary, which meant that its precincts traditionally provided a safe escape route for London's debtors. It was to became an invaluable resource for the Catholic underground.

Although aware that the sprawl of the old priory was now the headquarters of a nest of papists, the authorities found this part of Southwark impossible to police. Spies were stationed in the tower of the church in a vain attempt to keep a check on the comings and goings below. Identities were misleading. Montague's steward was a distinguished academic, Anthony Garnett, debarred by his Catholicism from his position as Master of Balliol College, Oxford. Among the servants who wore the Montague livery was a former pupil of Robert Persons at Balliol, the priest Simon Fennel. The library of Montague's chaplain, Alban Langdale, once arch-deacon of Chichester, was a rich theological resource seized on by Campion and Persons during their pamphlet war. Another 'popishly affected and suspect servant', Francis Gower, acted as an underground liaison officer, organising Masses and secret rendezvous all over Southwark. Francis Browne, the activist great-nephew of Lady Magdalen, set up a dissident printing press in the Close. It was here that the Jesuits held their 'synod of Southwark' in 1580, announcing a more assertive form of religious resistance, and here that Robert Southwell said his first Mass. Its proximity to the Clink prison provided the Close with yet another supply-line. Like London's other notorious prisons, the Fleet and Newgate, it was crammed with recusants, but in the Clink conditions were slack, the jailers no doubt under Montague influence. It rapidly became a 'Catholic think-tank', in which Mass was said openly and the policies and issues of the day hotly debated.[1] It was from the Clink that the Jesuit John Gerard organised his missionary network, establishing nation-wide links between Catholic recusant households and the Continent, and evading ubiquitous intelligence agents by setting up safe embarkation points on the beaches near Newcastle, along the Norfolk and Sussex coast, down the innumerable steps and passages that led from Catholic houses and 'liberties' to the Thames in London.[2]

The neighbourhood of the Globe Theatre is often described as London's red-light district, its brothels, leased out by the Bishop of Winchester, one of the scandalous legacies of the old church. But to the Privy Council and the city authorities, the real scandal of the south bank was the protection offered to dissidents by the Montagues. 'A forum for debate about the future of the Catholic community in England' is how one scholar describes their Southwark establishment.[3] This dissident powerhouse would have been an inestimable resource to the writers connected with the south bank theatres, keeping them in touch with the latest developments at court, in the south of England and abroad.[4] It was in this context that Shakespeare planned his first works for the Globe, plays that would form a decisive announcement of his return to the ranks of the literary resistance and which were ultimately aimed at persuading his native Catholic constituency to throw its weight behind the coming challenge to the Cecils by the Earl of Essex.

'Return, forgetful Muse', commands Sonnet 100, announcing a return to 'the ear that doth thy lays esteem', after wasting time on 'base subjects'. The tone catches the mood of Shakespeare's move across the river, and it evokes the quintessentially Catholic choice of subject for his first play. By 1599, the chief threat to Catholicism was the deceptive promise of a more tolerant form of Protestantism that would indeed become the defining characteristic of Anglicanism, but not for another twenty years. Shakespeare offers a forceful critique of the compromise by reminding Catholics of the bedrock issue that divided them from the sinuously attractive new Protestant image: the issue of papal authority. The narrative he adopts for his allegory is the story of Julius Caesar.[5]

It is thanks to the ferment of his own recent past that Shakespeare is able to create such powerful drama out of errors made by passionately idealistic men in *Julius Caesar*. The conspirators who assassinated Caesar believed their action would rescue the Roman republic from tyranny: in fact, it brought about civil war and the downfall of the Roman republic. The theme of error runs right through the play, recalling the great errors behind England's Reformation—the corruptions of the church and the crassness of church reformers. Everyone in *Julius Caesar* gets things wrong: Cassius's 'sight is thick'; Caesar is deaf in one ear; Brutus's eyesight is weak; both factions misread the portents. Even Cassius's suicide is a mistake. As the conspirators wash their hands in Caesar's blood, one of them foresees their moment of glory re-enacted down the centuries, unaware that it will be re-enacted as tragedy. Brutus's speech on seizing the moment—'There is a tide in the affairs of men' (4.3.216)—is fatally mis-timed: the tide in their case leads not to victory but to defeat.

Shakespeare gives an unmistakably Protestant profile to the Roman conspirators, drawing on his own recent experience of the reformers—intelligent, persuasive men who believed that in dismantling the edifice of the medieval English church they would bring about a new dawn. He does full justice to the strength of their opposition to blind obedience to authority and to their championship of the individual conscience. In the opening scene, they castigate 'servile fearfulness', unauthorised holidays and the worship of images—a classic anti-Catholic stance. They are lean, intellectual, independent-minded—Caesar complains that they think too much. Cassius in particular is too clever, 'looks quite through the deeds of men', dislikes music and 'loves no plays' (1.2.201–204). The combination of visionary drive and cold pragmatism that marks their discussions gives a vivid glimpse of the way the ideals of the new religion interacted with power politics in the Protestant circles Shakespeare had left behind at the court at Whitehall. Even Brutus, the noblest conspirator, carries a symbolically significant flaw: he is uncertain about times and dates. The calendar controversy was a doubly ingenious marker, for Julius Caesar, like the sixteenth-century pope Gregory XIII, also initiated a reform of the calendar, known as the 'Julian' calendar ever since. In a country that of necessity had constant recourse to the almanac, one of the best-selling books of the period, the confusion neatly linked the whole Brutus-Caesar opposition with that of England-Rome.

The great arguments of the age spring to life when the conspirators define themselves in relation to Shakespeare's favourite emblem of the Reformation, a storm, its duration and violence a demonstration perhaps of the special effects that were possible at the Globe. Just as the visionary Luther had described his moment of revelation that led him to defy the authority of Christendom as a literal thunderbolt, the chief conspirator, Cassius, dares heaven, baring his head and chest to the 'cross blue lightning' (1.3.50), deriding superstition and re-interpreting the signs and portents himself with an audacity that drives his colleague Casca to warn him, 'It is the part of men to fear and tremble' (1.3.54). Casca's own attitude is that of the unawakened pre-Reformation man, cowed by the 'tokens' and 'heralds' of the gods. As the huddled conspirators gather in Brutus's house, lit by the lightning, the intense intellectual debate on dismantling authority conjures up both the passion of the early reformers and their dangerous obsessiveness. The phrases Brutus uses in his attempts to moderate their proposals have a chilling association for late-sixteenth-century England: they must not 'dismember' Caesar, or 'hew him as a carcase fit for hounds' or 'cut the head off and then hack the limbs / Like wrath in death and envy afterwards' (2.1.163–174). After the murder, Mark Antony evokes the Queen's nickname for the Cecils—Sir Spirit—when he addresses the murderers as 'the choice and master spirits of the age' (3.1.164).

It is the conspirators who hold our attention and often our sympathy, their conflicting characters sharply individualised and affectingly human. Shakespeare underlines the dedication of the reformers and by contrast the weaknesses of the Catholic position, presumably those that he had found most difficult to defend against Protestant apologists over the previous few years. He alters Plutarch's complex, heroic Caesar until he resembles the monolithic late medieval Catholic Church—'ageing and somewhat ossified' is the way one editor sums up his character. Shakespeare subtly introduces the effect of institutional rigidity by making Caesar refer to himself repeatedly in the third person. He praises his own constancy and authority in objective terms. 'I am as constant as the Northern star . . .'. It is his complacency and pride—the 'smiling pomp' that Sonnet 124 attributes to the worldly church—that motivates the conspirators to decide on assassination. His claims to supremacy are undercut by such human weaknesses as deafness, epilepsy, timidity. While Plutarch stresses Caesar's toughness, Shakespeare surrounds him with 'men who are fat', a reminder of the venal princes of the unreformed Roman curia; his friend Antony is a reveller and a wastrel; Caesar has fallen away from what he was—a frequent Shakespearean marker for unreformed Catholicism: 'He is superstitious grown of late / Quite from the main opinion he held once / Of fantasy, of dreams, and ceremonies' (2.1.197).

The significance of Caesar's role, however, becomes apparent only with his destruction. Central authority, as it turns out, is indispensable—the empire falls apart without it, in the same way that the displacement of papal authority splintered Christendom into quarrelling sects. Moreover, as the faulty but divinely guided church, the figure of the Caesar in the play is seen, after his death, as the embodiment of the sacred. Here Shakespeare makes revealing changes to his sources. Plutarch specified twenty-three wounds in Caesar's body. Shakespeare alters this to thirty-three (5.1.53)—the sacred number of Christ's age at the time of his death.[6] The murder takes on a particular horror from its association with a theme that is to become increasingly powerful in Shakespeare's work: the murder of sanctity in England. By dwelling on the images of hanging, drawing and quartering, Brutus associates Caesar's death with the 'savage spectacles' at Tyburn, and this association deepens with Antony's prophecy of a time when mothers shall watch their 'infants quartered', when pity shall be 'choked with custom of fell deeds', a time of 'carrion men, groaning for burial' (3.1.255–276). The custom of pressing forward at such executions to dip handkerchiefs in the martyr's blood or to obtain 'tinctures, stains, relics and cognisance' (2.2.89) is connected several times with Caesar's death.

Both sides of England's religious divide are delineated in recognisably topical terms, resuming the consistent thrust of Shakespeare's hidden work, suspended in recent years. Bookishness, asceticism, a horror of image-worship, opposition to holidays, confusion over the time, distaste for music and plays, and above all, impassioned individualism coupled with contempt for unthinking submission—these markers accompany characters associated with the Protestant side of the great debate of the day, symbolised by a tempest. Balancing them are equally familiar Catholic markers applied to Caesar and his entourage: universal authority, but also pomp, superstition, degeneration, frivolity, vanity, deafness to appeals. However, the play is more than an even-handed examination of the Reformation debate. Shakespeare gives rein to a revived sense of vocation in lines so powerful that for many they are all they remember of his plays. When, after a bitter period of enforced conformity, Mark Antony resolves to set the record straight about his friend's assassination, he is also announcing the resistance manifesto of the leading dramatist of the new south bank theatre.

This is done without any sense of self-congratulation. As in *A Midsummer Night's Dream*, Shakespeare slips elements of an unflattering self-portrait into the character of Antony, using the role to explain his own apparent past defection. Unlike Brutus, Antony is not a straightforward man, but a clever dissimulator. Somehow he finesses his way out of the awkward spot in which he finds himself, that of a key supporter of Caesar after Caesar's assassination. Like so many in Shakespeare's position, he conforms publicly to save his skin. But, just as Shakespeare confided his self-disgust to his sonnets, Antony curses himself in private for shaking the bloody hands of the men who murdered his friend. He resolves to use his skills as an orator to broadcast the crime, reminding the audience of Shakespeare's promise in *Rape of Lucrece* to use the stage to convey the true version of a forbidden history. Only 'vassal actors', says Lucrece, can transmit the truth. Shakespeare will continue his mission of transposing their sly techniques of mime, grimace, emphasis and double-entendre into the more lasting medium of the printed text.[7]

Antony's histrionic soliloquy over the 'ruins' of Caesar's body uses significant terms to lament his murder. Caesar's mortal injuries are 'dumb mouths', he says, that 'beg the voice and utterance of my tongue' (3.1.255–262). His words announce Shakespeare's renewed decision to give voice to Elizabeth's silenced subjects and outlines the kind of drama audiences can expect in the 'confines' of the Globe: a repertoire of resistance plays, with their representations of nemesis and ghosts 'ranging for revenge' (3.1.271–273). Antony uses language that differs from the crisp diction of the rest of the cast—it is the emotive rhetoric of the manipulative dramatist, highlighted a little later when Brutus addresses the crowd in prose, but Antony in blank verse.

The famous piece of theatre beginning 'Friends, Romans, countrymen' (3.2.73–230) follows, a classic illustration of Shakespeare's cryptic dramatic method. An address to the crowd that appears to endorse the death of Caesar in fact does the opposite. Caesar's murderer, Brutus, having spared Antony's life, leaves him to address the mob unsupervised, merely asking him not to blame the conspirators, 'and say you do't by our permission' (3.1.248, 3.2.58). This may well have been the line taken by liberal patrons like Lord Hunsdon, who evidently turned a blind eye to what went on over the river so long as the company behaved properly at court. Antony keeps scrupulously to the letter of these conditions, but uses every trick in the actor-dramatist's book to undercut them, including abandoning the 'pulpit' to clear a space for street performance and setting up a complicit meaning for a single word: in this case 'honourable', which becomes, through crafty use of context, a savage indictment of the conspirators.

It is Antony and his allies who triumph at the end of the play. Divided, confused, haunted by the ghost of Caesar, the conspirators perish on the battlefield. But there is nothing triumphalist about the play. None of the victors can match Brutus in nobility and depth of character. He is torn between his condemnation of the old order and his distaste at the methods of its enemies. His complex, attractive personality, his dialogue with the ghost of Caesar, his intellectual soliloquies all look forward to Shakespeare's deeper exploration of the same anguished standpoint in *Hamlet*. Error and doubt mark Brutus's final decision to throw in his lot with the reformers. Already, Shakespeare is beginning to suggest that this hesitancy is the cause of a paralysis that would prove fatal to the country.

There is a new mastery and discrimination in the way that *Julius Caesar* presents the latest development of the Reformation debate. It inaugurates Shakespeare's decisive return to an intellectual position that he will retain—or, using the contemporary phrase, 'remain constant'—to the end.

The Good Man's Feast

RESTATING THE Catholic position in these clear, uncompromising terms was one means of convincing his co-religionists of Shakespeare's newly 'reconciled' position. But there was a more effective method of confirming that he had been welcomed back into the fold and was no longer working for both sides. This was to write a play demonstrating that he was fully informed on the latest developments in the political and literary Catholic underground. Most of the talk in houses like Montague Close would have revolved around a single topic—exile. Shakespeare's earlier work touched repeatedly on the pains of banishment: now he devotes an entire play to the subject, interspersing it with digressions exploring the latest developments in London's literary underground.[8] The play has remained ever since one of his most popular comedies: *As You Like It.*

By the turn of the century there can have been few English Catholics of any means who had not at some point considered the subject of exile; but leaving England in those days was a drastic step. William Cecil, writing to dissuade Sir Thomas Copley from leaving the country, spelt out the hazards:

> And now, Mr. Copley, wherein make you the difference so great in matters of religion . . . that you will for that lose the sweet benefit of your native soil, your friends, your kindred, yea, incur the infamy that wilful exile doth bring, to be accompted, if not a traitor, yet a companion of traitors and conspirators, and subject to the curses and imprecations of zealous good subjects, your native countrymen, yea, subject to lack of living by your own and thereby compelled to follow strangers for maintenance of livelihood and food? The cause must needs be of great force to induce you thereto.[9]

The exact number of those who left the country on religious grounds in Elizabeth's reign has never been determined, but it ran into tens of thousands. Because English Catholics were debarred from school and university education, many of them were students. At first, most families had found ways to circumvent the restrictions on education, but the rumour that William Cecil was considering the forcible removal of Catholic children from their parents in order to bring them up as Protestants prompted Robert Persons to found the first English Catholic school abroad in 1582 at Eu, in the Low Countries. By the turn of the century, the schools and seminaries had grown and multiplied in spite of stringent legislation forbidding education abroad, and the original trickle of boys, young men and young women who slipped quietly overseas had become a flood.[10]

The State Papers of the time reveal the contemporary alarm at this development: 'Here were lately 15 or 16 youths of good houses taken as they were going over to the seminaries', writes one observer in 1601.[11] In 1606, the *Journals of the House of Commons* note that 'over the past two years 2000 children under the age of 16 were gone beyond the seas', urging yet again that 'some course must be thought on for their returning home'.[12] Such students at least had somewhere to go. The educational foundations at Douai, Rheims, St Omer, Rome, Valladolid and elsewhere were all supported by funds from willing Catholics in England and abroad. But there was a second, less fortunate group—those who left their country simply in order to practice their religion unmolested. Unlike the industrious Huguenot artisans coming the other way to find refuge in England, many of these were members of the gentry who had no means of support or of earning a living—among them, Sir Francis Englefield, a Privy Councillor under Queen Mary, and Lady Dormer, both relatives of the Montagues. These distinguished figures provided a focus for the earliest group of exiles at Louvain. In the beginning, their high-level Spanish connections obtained pensions for English refugees, but such support dried up as time wore on and the numbers increased.

Anyone who had military training gravitated towards Sir William Stanley. Stanley was a brilliant soldier related to the earls of Derby, praised by the Earl of Leicester as being 'worth his weight in pearl' and knighted for his services in Ireland, where the loyal expertise of such a staunch Catholic supporter of the Crown was especially commended by William Cecil. But during the campaign in the Low Countries in 1586, he became the centre of one of the scandals of the decade when he defected to Spain with a number of his soldiers, handing over the city of Deventer in the process. 'Before I served the Devil, now I serve God', he said afterwards. Abroad, Cardinal Allen published a defence of his actions, but in England he became a byword for treachery. His 'Spanish regiment' was put at the service of Philip II of Spain, and he joined the group of high-ranking Englishmen attempting to persuade the Catholic powers to come to the aid of their stricken co-religionists in England.[13] Life for Stanley's followers was not easy as they impatiently awaited the invasion of England: they were never quite trusted by the Spanish, and their wages were fitfully paid.

Moreover, they were caught up in Philip II's often savage campaign to repress Protestantism and establish Spanish control in the Low Countries. Among their number was Charles Browne, one of the Montague family, struggling to maintain his seven children. Yet another Montague relative was Francis Dacre, who along with Thomas Fitzherbert and Englefield himself was petitioning foreign contacts for help in recovering his confiscated estates, his only hope of income. The families they had left behind in England were often reduced to dire financial straits, and a number of such exiles were reduced to beggary and died of disease or starvation. There were many poignant encounters between them and their more conformist countrymen. As far east as Prague and as far south as Sicily, English travellers came upon pockets of expatriates of all descriptions, from the aristocratic and scholarly to soldiers and sailors who had absconded. Their chief concentration was in the Ardennes area towns of Liège, Douai, Louvain and nearby Rheims. These were already on the English tourist route, for they were not far from Spa, a favourite health resort situated in the wooded Ardennes foothills. Here the exiles often found themselves in the awkward position of seeking hospitality from people with whom their country was officially at war; and here they witnessed at first hand some of the atrocities inflicted on Protestants by the Hapsburg Catholic powers.

For relatives unable to attach themselves to diplomatic or military missions, obtaining permission to travel abroad was often impossible, and the lack of news must have been agonising. Not surprisingly, then, when a book came out in 1595 by Sir Lewis Lewkenor entitled *The Estate of English Fugitives under the King of Spain and his Ministers*, it was snapped up at once, running into four editions over the next two years. Its picture of life among the exiles must have sent a chill down the spines of anyone with Catholic friends or family abroad. Published with the aim of discouraging the exodus, it was written with the authority of one who had returned to conform after himself living as an exile. He describes 'my unhappy countrymen (some of whom were gentlemen of good houses in England) wandering in poor habits and afflicted gestures heavily groaning under the burden of an extreme and calamitous necessity . . . daily overlooked by the proud eyes of disdainful Spaniards'. He highlights bickering among the factions, lack of leadership, the ubiquity of 'certain ambo-dexter fellows . . . feeding either side with news'. He reserves particular venom for Stanley's lieutenant, Jaques, a cosmopolitan soldier brought up in England who had fought in Ireland and was a popular figure in the Spanish regiment: 'As for Jaques . . . let him likewise attend that scourge and punishment which ever followeth such infidelitie'.

Anxious Catholic readers of Lewkenor's tales of misery and exile may well have turned back for reassurance to a more comforting book that painted a golden picture of life abroad. *Rosalynde*, a popular pastoral novel, was originally published back in 1590 by the Catholic playwright Thomas Lodge, by now an exile himself, studying medicine at Avignon. The embodiment of Catholic loyalty, he would later return to his native country to treat victims of the plague. Curiously, *Rosalynde* was written on a long and dangerous trip to the Indies of which Lodge was one of the few survivors. Apparently an escapist romance, it contains an allegory that examines the central concern of his own life: the dilemma of all those who believed that Truth had been driven from England by the Reformation and could see no other course but to follow her. A poem published when he was safely abroad, 'Truth's Complaint over England', sums up the situation in a nutshell: Truth, 'refused, disdained and set at naught' is forced 'to seek for rest in place unknown', leaving her supporters who try to restore the Mass to 'dance in shade', and announcing as she spreads her wings, 'You Islanders adieu, / You banished me before I fled from you'.[14]

Rosalynde is a difficult read these days. Even at the time, its deliberate artifice must have been off-putting. But this may not have been what drew people to the book. Buried amid ludicrously repetitive strings of conceits and sententious maxims there are familiar landmarks. Lodge, it emerges, was using the same code terms as Shakespeare. He plays on the same concept of the twinned Puritan and Catholic aspects of spiritual truth that Shakespeare developed in *The Comedy of Errors*: Lodge calls the linked, spiritual figures 'two bodies and one soul'. He employs the usual epithets for Catholicism—swan, goddess, phoenix and saint, but to her enemies 'a painted shrine full filled with rotten treasure'. There is the same artful use of tell-tale topical detail: an earthquake, a synod, a Knight of Malta; the fleeing hero escapes 'knowing full well the secret ways that led through the vineyards'—'vineyard' being a favourite Jesuit term for a missionary field.

Above all there is the name Rosalynde. It is no coincidence that variants of Rosalynde appear in the works of many of Shakespeare's contemporaries. Spenser, Daniel and Drayton all mourn a lost beauty named Rosalind or Rosamund. Characters in Kyd's and Shakespeare's plays sadly recall '[t]hat sweet lovely rose': 'Let her not wither, Lord, without increase', prays Robert Chester. It seems the red rose represented true holiness, the ideal of Catholics and radical Protestants alike.[15] The origin of the name may lie in the red rose of the House of Lancaster, effectively eradicated in the course of the Reformation by the white York rose represented by Henry VIII and his children. Its return, with the ascendancy of Lancaster descendants such as Lord Strange, was the cherished dream of many in England. Shakespeare has already given the name Rosaline to the unattainable 'dark' Genevan love of one of the students in *Love's Labour's Lost*; and another Rosaline has an off-stage role in *Romeo and Juliet*, where Romeo sentimentalises about her in terms very like Spenser's and Drayton's. Now Shakespeare gives humorous self-awareness to this hackneyed personification of exiled and threatened Truth. Rosalind, the heroine of *As You Like It*, laughs at her own allegorical significance while quietly highlighting it, Shakespeare's typically deft method of rejuvenating clichéd allegorical concepts: 'I was never so berhymed since Pythagoras' time that I was an Irish rat, which I can hardly remember' (3.2.163). Rosalind's light glance at Pythagoras's theory of reincarnation underlines her hidden identity as perennial spiritual truth.

Finally, there is the plot of Lodge's novel. Beneath the idyllic, jewelled pastoral is a story simply adapted to the situation of English dissidents. The persecuted figures of twinned holiness, Rosalind and Aliena flee their home, pursued by Rosalind's similarly persecuted lover. They undergo various trials in exile: the disguised Rosalind teases her lover in order to test him; he selflessly rescues his wicked brother from a lion; finally, all embrace in a harmonious happy ending. Shakespeare follows Lodge's plot so closely that in many ways *As You Like It* can be seen as a tribute to the exiled writer. But at every point, Shakespeare's wittily oblique system of reference contrasts strikingly with Lodge's traditional method of using elaborate and often empty verbiage to camouflage the simple messages within.

Shakespeare begins his tale on a sharply topical note. No less than seven times within the first few speeches, Orlando fumes that he has been deprived by his jealous older brother of education—the principal reason so many Catholics fled abroad. He escapes to follow the banished Rosalind in the company of a devoted family retainer, Adam, embodiment of the despised virtues of upright old England. The exiles find themselves in Arden, the name a thinly veiled reference to Ardennes, the region of northern France that was the centre for English exiles.[16] On the brink of starvation, Orlando and Adam are rescued by a banished duke and his outlawed followers; the suspicious exiles drop their guard after exchanging an identical greeting, suggestive of a password: 'If ever you have looked on better days, / If ever been where bells have knoll'd to church, / If ever sat at any good man's feast, / If ever from your eyelid wiped a tear . . .' (2.7.113–116).[17]

The anonymous duke's hidden identity is revealed in a tableau that sits awkwardly in the universal play, but its conspicuous oddity underlines its important purpose: to connect the duke with the figurehead for Catholic exiles, Sir William Stanley, and to defend Stanley's damaged reputation (4.2.1–18). A group of foresters cross the stage bearing the head of a stag for the duke to wear as a 'branch of victory'. They sing a song praising the stag's head: its antlers are not a shameful 'crest', they assert, not 'a thing to laugh to scorn'. 'Thy father wore it', they say mysteriously, 'And thy father's father wore it . . .'. They hail the duke as a 'Roman conquerer'. To those who knew William Stanley, the scene would have been poignant: his family crest was the head of a dead stag, 'its tongue hanging out', and his military prowess did indeed qualify this Catholic soldier as a 'Roman conquerer'.[18] The formal, emblematic moment of tribute confirms that the target audience for this play was the recusant elite. They would have picked up further Stanley references: Rowland Stanley was the name of Sir William's father, who was in his eighties when the play was first performed. Orlando's father, 'old Sir Rowland', is mentioned with deference no less than eight times, while the hero's own name, Orlando, is a derivation of Rowland.

Shakespeare applies delicate treatment to Sir William Stanley's political position. Regretting the necessity of killing deer to survive—a surprising scruple for the time—the duke calls his victims 'the native burghers of this desert city' (2.1.23). The reference is to Stanley's military dilemma: as an ally of Spain, he now had to fight against Protestants who were demanding the same religious freedom for their native cities as Catholics were in his own country. The tone of remorse is shared by the duke's followers. 'We are mere usurpers, tyrants, and what's worse, / To fright the animals, and to kill them up / In their assigned and native dwelling place' (2.1.60–63). Shakespeare develops the 'deer' parallel to cover the desperate case of many exiles in a passage sympathizing with a wounded stag, 'abandoned of his velvet friends', a 'poor and broken bankrupt', bitterly castigating his fellows, 'full of the pasture' who ignore him: 'Ay, sweep on, you fat and greasy citizens; 'tis just the fashion . . .' (2.1.45–60). Name-play identifies some of Stanley's companions in exile. Three characters are called after his controversial lieutenant, Jaques, while Orlando's father is given the surname de Boys ('of the wood')—the pseudonym of Stanley's most active colleague, Hugh Owen.[19]

The comedy begins when Rosalind, disguised as a boy, begins to tease her unwitting lover. Orlando unwisely allows her to stand in for the apparently absent Rosalind so that he can conduct an imaginary courtship; to test his love, Rosalind plays the part of a cruel lover. Allegorically, this is an attempt to make light of the most painful aspect of the English Catholic experience. In spite of thirty years of promises, the Catholic powers had so far failed to do anything for their English co-religionists. For both exiles and those in England, the uncertainty was agonizing. How long would they have to suffer poverty and banishment? What had happened to all those promises of diplomatic pressure, of Catholic marriage alliances, of invincible armadas? Writing eight years after Lodge, Shakespeare intensifies the concept of Truth tantalising her lover: for by this time, with the looming succession in doubt, the tension was becoming acute. By representing this long delay as part of a loving stratagem on the part of Truth to test the mettle of those who seek her, both Lodge and Shakespeare echo the explanations of missionary priests labouring to keep up the spirits of English Catholics—the years of uncertainty were sent by Providence to teach them the virtues of fortitude and perseverance.

Towards the end of the play, Orlando nobly rescues his cruel brother from a lioness, 'royal . . . with catlike watch . . . with udders all drawn dry' (4.2.113–114)—a daringly topical variation on Lodge's lion, relating the emblem of England to Elizabeth. And Shakespeare adds a further detail— the sleeping brother's neck is entwined by a snake that approaches his open mouth 'nimble in threats' (4.2.107), bearing the green and gilded Tudor colours; a reminder of the green and gilded snake that symbolized the security services in Elizabeth's Hatfield portrait. Orlando is wounded as he rescues his brother from the snake and the lioness, and Rosalind is smitten with remorse. Where Lodge labours to build up the image of exiled Truth agonizing over her martyred followers, who braved death to preserve their countrymen from the 'spiritual death' of heresy, Shakespeare uses a single stroke to gain the same effect: his Rosalind faints at the sight of a handkerchief soaked in Orlando's blood. In the England of the time, a blood-soaked handkerchief had only one connotation, already exploited in *Julius Caesar*—a relic obtained at the foot of the gallows.

Ever since its invention by the Greek poet Theocritus, the pastoral genre had been associated with the discussion of writers and literature under the guise of shepherds and their songs. The pastoral setting of *As*

You Like It gave Shakespeare the opening he needed to proclaim his close engagement with the latest developments in resistance writing in England. Marlowe's poem *Hero and Leander* had just been posthumously published, and it is quoted in the play. The context suggests that to Marlowe, brought up a Catholic, his first 'love' was in the end his most important allegiance. 'Dead shepherd, now I find thy saw of might: / "Whoever loved that loved not at first sight?"' (3.5.80–81) says Phoebe, quoting the poem as she falls for the charms of the figure of Catholic spirituality, Rosalind. And Marlowe's murder, recalled in *Romeo and Juliet*, resurfaces in a wry allusion to the fictitious argument over a tavern bill, or 'reckoning', said to be the cause of his death: 'The oath of a lover is no stronger than the word of a tapster; they are both the confirmer of false reckonings' (3.4.27–29).

But the play's most interesting literary character is a rising star on the Catholic side of the literary divide, a man who according to one account was Shakespeare's protégé. This was Ben Jonson. Eight years younger than Shakespeare, Jonson had just made his name with *Every Man in His Humour*, a brilliant and original comedy staged by Shakespeare's company, Shakespeare himself taking a leading role—very possibly Prospero, whose role in the play is that of a friend of a character not unlike Jonson himself, Lorenzo. These two figures amuse themselves by observing the follies of the rest of the cast in an influential form of English social satire popularised by Jonson based on the theory of 'humours'. His second attempt, *Every Man Out of His Humour*, was a failure like so many sequels, but it again features two characters who act as observers: 'Asper', one of Jonson's many portraits of himself as the fearless satirist, and the more experienced, restraining 'Cordatus', who again resembles Shakespeare, his brief comments full of cautious Catholic 'markers'. The friendship and rivalry between the two writers is the subject of many anecdotes. Though diametrically opposed in character, there were similarities in their background. After a grammar school education, Jonson fought in the Low Countries before coming home to work as a bricklayer. He moved on to become an actor, then a playwright, in and out of prison for various offences, including killing a fellow actor in a duel. During one of these spells in the Marshalsea—a prison close to the Clink in Southwark—he met an imprisoned priest who converted him to Catholicism; a year later he presented Shakespeare's company with the script for *Every Man in His Humour*. This vociferous Catholic, whose young followers, the 'Tribe of Ben', sat at his feet as he took on all comers in the Mermaid Tavern, was the subject of considerable pressure from the regime; in the end, in spite of his combative stance and two politically explosive plays (*Sejanus* and *Eastward Ho*), he proved no match for Robert Cecil. By 1606, he is to be found mysteriously under Cecil's wing; praises for the great statesman begin to flow from his pen; his plays become nonpolitical; in time he is persuaded to return to the Protestant religion. All this, however, lay in the future: in 1590, the fiery Jonson had only just erupted onto the London literary scene, a new Catholic literary champion. "A great lover and praiser of himself, a contemner and scorner of others, given rather to lose a friend than a jest, jealous of every word and action of those about him, especially after drink' is how he was described by one acquaintance[20]—yet Jonson clearly had magnetism, for he was friends with most of the literary figures of the day and found ready patrons throughout his long life, among them the Sidneys, the Earl of Pembroke and the Countess of Newcastle.

In the character of Jaques, Shakespeare sketched his own portrait of Jonson—largely overlooked, though the identity is unmistakable. Around 1599, a contemporary dramatist represents Shakespeare scoring a hit against Jonson—'Our fellow Shakespeare hath given him a purge that made him bewray his credit'.[21] 'Bewraying credit' was Elizabethan slang for overfilling the jakes, or chamber-pot—strongly suggesting a pun on 'Jaques'. As in Jonson's early plays, the sketch forms one half of a double portrait, for the inept courtier Touchstone—as scholars have noticed—is a typically self-deprecating caricature of Shakespeare himself. But if Arden is Ardennes, what is Jonson doing in the world of the exiles? He certainly knew it well because he fought with the English forces in the Low Countries and his first role in the play is to give an analysis of the condition of the exiles there. Tellingly, he is not onstage at this point—and is described as lying 'under an oak whose antique root peeps out / Upon the brook . . .'. In the simplified language of an emblematic woodcut, he is in England, symbolized by the oak, and is reluctant to join the 'disputable' exiled duke, whose stance, nonetheless, he later supports—it is Jaques who orchestrates the scene in which the foresters honour Stanley's crest.

Every detail of Jaques's manner and role is designed to recall Jonson. Jonson's prologues in particular are full of swaggering egoism as he tirelessly proclaims his own artistic manifesto: 'With an armed and resolved hand / I'll strip the ragged follies of the time / Naked as at their birth';[22] 'Let envious censors . . . look through and through me . . . I would give them pills to purge . . .'; 'I will scourge those apes / And to these courteous eyes oppose a mirror / As large as is the stage whereon we act / Where they shall see the time's deformity . . .'. Shakespeare catches this kind of thing perfectly as Jaques outlines a similar bombastic credo—'Give me leave / To speak my mind and I will through and through / Cleanse the foul body of the infected world' (2.7.58–60); 'I must have liberty withal, / As large a charter as the wind, / To blow on whom I please . . .' (2.7.47–48).

This being a pastoral, Jaques's satirical approach to drama sets off a literary debate that resurfaces periodically throughout the play. The jocular duke reminds Jaques that he is as guilty of vice as his victims. 'Thou thyself hast been a libertine . . .' (2.7.65). But Jaques ignores the barbs, sweeping on with his exposition of a satirical method that coincides exactly in its aims with Jonson's theory of the 'humours', based on deniable types rather than particular individuals. 'Why who cries out on pride / That can therein tax any private party? . . . / What woman in the city do I name / When that I say the city-woman bears / The cost of princes on unworthy shoulders? Who can come in and say that I mean her?' (2.7.70-86). Jaques shares Jonson's fascination with types: the Duke's remark about his fondness for lists of human failings, or 'headed evils' (2.7.67), pinpoints one of Jonson's favourite techniques. The famous speech 'All the world's a stage' (2.7.139-166) parodies the method. A similar Jonsonian list of types crops up further on when Jaques analyses the various species of melancholy. By making Jaques both describe and embody the humour of melancholy—'a melancholy of my own . . . a most humorous sadness' (4.1.10–18)—Shakespeare is recalling the originator of the fashion for 'humours' and lightly subjecting him to his own treatment. There are other entertaining personal markers. Jaques's sudden passion for motley—'Motley's the only wear . . . I am ambitious for a motley coat' (2.7.34–43)—highlights Jonson's pride in his acting ability, not great according to the seventeenth-century diarist John Aubrey, but written into the prologue to *Every Man Out of His Humour*, where Asper vanishes importantly to put on his costume. There is a hit at Jonson's still greater pride in his classical learning when Jaques uses a nonsensical 'Greek invocation to call fools into a circle' (2.5.55). Shakespeare even manages a discussion of metre. One of the innovations of *Every Man* was its avoidance of blank verse, based on the five 'feet' of iambic pentameter. The duke associates Jaques with 'the license of free foot' (2.7.68), and Jaques pointedly recoils from the threat of Orlando's love poetry: 'Nay then, God buy you [good-bye] an [if] you talk in blank verse . . .' (4.1.28).

The most intriguing literary figure is Touchstone, a 'motley-minded gentleman' interpreted by many as a typically modest self-portrait of a glib countryman who has left his rural self behind to become a courtier, 'very swift and sententious' (5.4.60), using his folly 'like a stalking-horse'(5.4.100), a self-appointed expert in the great contemporary game of quarrelling in print 'by the book' (5.4.85), which he describes with comic precision. 'O knowledge ill-inhabited' (3.3.7), groans Jaques. There is an autobiographical element in Touchstone's patronising dismissal of the inarticulate rustic, William, his rival for the affections of the ignorant 'country wench', Audrey. Touchstone's marriage to Audrey is ill-starred: Audrey is clearly better suited to William, a caricature of the simple countryman the sophisticated Shakespeare left behind. Audrey has no understanding of poetry—conversation with her on the subject is a fate Touchstone equates with the death of Marlowe: 'When a man's verses cannot be understood . . . it strikes a man more dead than a great reckoning in a little room'(3.3.9-11). Jaques, increasingly religious after his encounter with the love-struck Orlando, does his best to drag the pair off to 'a good priest that can tell you what marriage is' (3.3.72–73): but he foresees marital problems for the mismatched couple. These entertaining scenes may have been intended to make light of gossip about the state of Shakespeare's own marriage. For all his failings, Touchstone, like Mark Antony, has the one virtue that would recommend him to a Southwark audience: he is the close and valued companion of Rosalind and Celia, and his role is to amuse them as he shares their chequered fortunes.

These two plays publicise Shakespeare's own return to the company of Catholic resistance writers, but more important, they confirm the common identity of underground and exiled Catholicism, dramatising its essential doctrines and its trials with informed sympathy. Reinforcing the sense of communal solidarity was vital: Catholics, particularly those living in London, would shortly be called on to stand up for their beliefs. By 1601, a political crisis was imminent. The Earl of Essex had returned from Ireland in disgrace after a failed campaign and, seconded by the Earl of Southampton, had turned his house into a centre for dissidents of all persuasions. His mood was dangerous: 'The man's soul seemeth tossed to and fro, like waves of a troubled sea', wrote the witty courtier John Harington, a godson of the Queen.[23] If his initiative was to succeed, he would need the full support of both Catholic and radical Protestant. But how many dissidents were there? Essex had to be sure of his power-base before he moved against the Cecil faction. Everything depended on an unknown, much-debated factor: the true allegiance of middle England.

CHAPTER

9

APPEAL TO THE UNDECIDED, 1600

THERE BE MANY close Papists in England, that are content for a while to temporize, waiting for an houre, which I trust they shall never see' commented one observer at the turn of the century.[1] But exactly how many 'close Papists' were there? The precise number had become the subject of desperate calculation on all sides by the year 1600. Essex and Cecil were on a collision course; the aging Queen Elizabeth still refused to name a successor; Ireland was rebelling against Protestant English rule; and in Spain, Philip III, the son of Philip II, was preparing a third Armada to attack England. Yet the country's majority were silent. No one knew for certain whether dissent or loyalty to the Crown would prevail. Many Englishmen seemed caught in an agony of indecision; they were biding their time, or temporising.

The Jesuit Jasper Heywood, uncle of John Donne and a diehard idealist who abandoned a career at court to become a missionary in England in the early 1580s, had a go at this cautiously silent majority in his ironic poem 'The Lookers-on', which attacks those who criticised the more dynamic 'makers and doers' while keeping their own heads down in order to 'have the fruit, yet free from blame'.

If thou in surety safe wilt sit,
If thou delight at rest to dwell:
Spend no more words than shall seem fit,
Let tongue in silence talk expel.
In all things that thou seest men bent
See all, say naught, hold thee content.[2]

Shakespeare himself knew all too well what it was to temporise. The 'lookers-on' composed a group so wide and various that it could be said to have embraced most of his generation: even Campion and Persons went through periods of outward conformity and inner struggle before sacrificing their careers and leaving the country.[3] Did Shakespeare realise when he decided to appeal to those caught in this essentially English predicament by reworking an old drama known to scholars as the *Ur-Hamlet* that he would be producing not only his own finest play but one of the greatest works of literature ever written? For in cautiously universalising his analysis of the complex psyche of his country at the end of the sixteenth century he would find himself dramatising a timeless human dilemma—nothing less than the situation described by his contemporary, Fulke Greville, as the 'wearisome condition of Humanity! / Born under one law, to another bound: / Vainly begot, and yet forbidden vanity; / Created sick, commanded to be sound'.[4]

One reason for the unprecedented brilliance and subtlety of *Hamlet* lies in the character of its temporising hero. Shakespeare modelled him on a man who for many both at home and abroad epitomised the very best of Elizabethan England—and, in spite of the mystery surrounding his short life, one who continues to exert a spell to this day. In the words of a recent biographer, this contemporary of Shakespeare's was one of those rare figures who was 'fully human. His voice speaks for the best in us and the best in human society'. What makes him 'modern' is his 'concern with man as a rational being' and 'the fact that his writings remain profoundly secular despite his strongly religious nature'.[5] He was the poet, scholar and soldier Sir Philip Sidney, who had died fifteen years earlier but since his death had become a legend. Describing Sidney, many biographers cannot resist turning to Ophelia's description of Hamlet:

> The courtier's, soldier's, scholar's eye, tongue, sword
> Th'expectancy and rose of the fair state,
> The glass of fashion and the mould of form
> Th'observed of all observers . . .
> *(3.1.151–154)*

Though Shakespeare's literary debt to Sidney has often been acknowledged, scholars have stopped short of identifying Hamlet with Sidney's own life and character. The popular view of Sidney has always been that he was the very reverse of the disinherited and brooding Hamlet. Sidney is traditionally portrayed as the quintessential Protestant hero, the chief adornment of Elizabeth's court, a soldier and a gentleman who died fighting for the English Protestant cause and who was honoured with one of the most spectacular funerals of the period. But here again, history written by the winners of the struggle denies us the full context for men like Sidney and plays like *Hamlet*. Recent, more carefully researched biographies of Sidney suggest that his was a fitful form of Protestantism—one biographer suggests that he 'was a discreet Catholic fellow-traveller for a while' and that 'it may have been precisely to allay suspicions that he was in fact a crypto-Catholic that Sidney felt obliged to introduce hard-line Protestant remarks into those of his writings that were to be read at Court'.[6] His father, Sir Henry Sidney, on the surface a model of selfless loyalty, was marked down by Spain as a potential ally, 'held to be Catholic', said to be ready in the year 1574 to serve the Spanish King with 'six thousand chosen English soldiers'.[7] Philip was named after his godfather, King Philip of Spain, and for many years the boy's future looked brilliant. For most of his life he was heir to the childless Earl of Leicester, and the on-off relationship between Elizabeth and Leicester, which continued until the Earl's death, meant that Philip had the perceived status of England's crown prince. But as time went by and Protestantism took hold, Sir Henry adopted the new religion, though he was always suspected of 'favouring recusants', patronising Edmund Campion among others. An upright, able soldier and administrator, he spent much of his own money suppressing dissent in Wales and Ireland on behalf of the Crown. Like so many in his ambiguous position, young Philip was drawn into the Cecil web of influence, attending lessons in Cecil House and in his early teens entering into some kind of engagement to William Cecil's granddaughter Ann Cecil, who went on instead to make an unhappy match with the Earl of Oxford. At seventeen, just after the failure of the Northern Rebellion in 1572, Philip was dispatched on a three-year trip abroad, under the watchful eye of the Protestant scholar Hubert Languet. He made lasting friendships in courts and universities all over Europe, before returning to marry Frances, daughter of Sir Francis Walsingham.

But his position was a curious one. For some reason, he was not trusted, and it appears that Elizabeth actively disliked him. Much of his adult life was spent waiting fruitlessly for advancement. In spite of his erudition, charm and influence abroad, he was never given a proper position at court or in the government. He was also forbidden to leave the country unsupervised. The most accomplished of riders and swordsmen, he was the star performer at events like the Accession Day tilts; yet he was slighted by grander men and constantly in debt. He found himself humiliatingly restrained from joining Sir Francis Drake's expedition to Virginia and instead was sent to join Leicester on campaign in Flanders in 1586, where, in his early thirties, he died of a wound received in an indecisive action at Zutphen.

Kicking his heels for long months in the country, he turned to writing; and it is his writing that preserves for us the distinctive charm of his 'human' personality. His essay *A Defence of Poesie*, colloquial, graceful, at once casual and learnedly authoritative, is in the witty tradition of Erasmus and Montaigne; it is also a bastion of civilised common sense, written in reply to a crude attack on the theatre cheekily dedicated to him by the establishment hack, Edmund Gosson—an attack already countered, less ably, by Thomas Lodge. Though Sidney's early sympathies may have been Protestant, he is likely to have followed the enlightened humanist Protestantism of his tutor Languet, whose work included an indictment of tyrants who persecute their subjects on the grounds of religion. Sidney's writings, however, which are for the most part elaborately allegorical, suggest a gradual disillusion with English Protestantism, and a growing sympathy with the plight of Catholicism. It was an open secret that the 'amour lointaine' of his sonnet sequence *Astrophel and Stella* was his childhood friend Penelope Rich, Essex's intelligent and beautiful sister, and an active member of his dissident circle. She was married and had a lover, so Sidney's passion was famously unrequited—but like so many highly placed women with dissident backgrounds, she may well have been providing acceptable cover for poetry that was in fact political and religious.[8] The best evidence that Sidney may have been more in sympathy with the old religion than establishment Protestantism occurs in the course of his first diplomatic mission abroad in 1577. When he reached Prague, Sidney gave his minders the slip and had several meetings with Edmund Campion, then teaching at the university there and shortly to return to martyrdom in England. 'Their meeting . . . was difficult', wrote Robert Persons, 'for Sir Philip was afraid of so many spies set and sent about him by the English Council; but he managed to have divers large and secret conferences with his old Oxford friend. After much argument, he professed himself convinced, but said that it was necessary for him to hold on the course which he had hitherto followed; yet he promised never to hurt or injure any Catholic, which for the most part he performed'. Biographers believe that it was as a result of these meetings that the regime back in England lost confidence in Sidney: Campion's verdict bears out their suspicions: 'He had much conversation with me—I hope not in vain, for he was most eager . . . if any one of our labourers sent into the vineyard from the Douai seminary has an opportunity of watering this plant, he may watch the occasion for helping a poor wavering soul. If this young man, so wonderfully beloved and admired by his countrymen, chances to be converted, he will astonish his noble father, the Deputy of Ireland, his uncles the Dudleys, and all young courtiers, and Cecil him-self. Let it be kept secret'.[9]

Were these interviews the basis for Hamlet's dangerous exchanges alone with the ghost on the battlements? 'It waves you to a more removed ground But do not go with it' urge his companions. 'What if it tempt you toward the flood my lord, / Or to the dreadful summit of the cliff . . . and there assume some other horrible form / Which might deprive your sov-ereignty of reason / And draw you into madness' (1.5.61–74). But Hamlet shakes them off—'Hold off your hands . . . my fate cries out!'—only to shrink from the mission imposed by the ghost: 'O cursed spite, / That I was ever born to set it right' (1.5.189–190).

Was the 'wavering soul' of this remarkable and highly intelligent man a model for Hamlet? Shakespeare surely meant his audience to think so, and therefore to identify Hamlet with the man who more than any other embodied a covertly disaffected group of what we would now call Eng-land's intelligentsia. As Sidney had died when Shakespeare was only twenty-two, it is unlikely they met. However, Sidney's closest friend and biographer, Fulke Greville, was a writer and a Warwickshire man, one of a dissident circle centred on the Pembroke family that could well have sup-plied Shakespeare later on with the string of details linking Hamlet with Sidney. Most of these attributes, in any case, were well known. Early in the play, in a fanciful conceit of the ghost's, Hamlet's hair is compared to quills upon the fretful porcupine. This is one of Shakespeare's heraldic references. The porcupine was Sidney's family crest, well known to the public because it illustrated the frontispiece to the 1593 version of *Arcadia*, tethered beneath Leicester's rampant bear and the lion of England. Next, there is the vexed question of Hamlet's age.[10] He is a university student, treated by Gertrude and Claudius as an unstable adolescent; yet in two places it is made unnecessarily clear that he is thirty years old. Sidney, who had to work hard to overcome his boyish appearance, died at the age of thirty-two. At thirty, during a year when England was braced for a Spanish invasion, he was writing a new version of his *Arcadia*, one in which 'the problems and dilemmas faced by the characters are often insoluble; there is no 'right' course of action'.[11]

Sidney's most celebrated role as patron and practitioner of literature is recalled in the extended passages in the play concerning drama in which Hamlet reproves Polonius for failing to show due respect to actors. Ophelia twice uses the word 'rich' to describe Hamlet's letters to her, a reminder of the famous puns on the word in Sidney's love poems to Penelope Rich. The cult of Sidney was assiduously fostered for years after his death by Fulke Greville, who had been his close friend since their schooldays. Like Greville, the character of Horatio, Hamlet's 'fellow-student', is instructed by Hamlet on his death to 'absent thee from felicity awhile, / And in this harsh world draw thy breath in pain, / To tell my story' (5.2.339–341). This is just the elegiac tone in which Greville always spoke of Sidney. Early biographers note Sidney's habit of jotting down ideas on notepads in the oddest circumstances—'he was wont even while hunting . . . to take his Table book out of his pocket, and write down his notions as they came into his head'.[12] In the first act of the play, Hamlet's bizarre first instinct when the ghost leaves him is to take out his 'tablets' and note that 'one may smile and smile and be a villain' (1.5.108). The 'peculiar volatility' of Sidney's temperament coincides strikingly with Hamlet's—it was one in which 'periods of melancholy lethargy alternated with bursts of manic energy'.[13] He was also subject to sudden psychotic fits of rage: twice in the play, Hamlet also exhibits a manic loss of temper, requiring physical restraint. Hamlet's position as a slighted prince was Sidney's: he is without a role, he is a prisoner, he 'lacks advancement', he is 'promise-crammed'. In an extended interchange—one of the most amusing of the play—Hamlet mimics the affectations of the courtier Osric, who arrives to invite him to fight a duel with Laertes. This was the kind of man who maddened Sidney during his long periods of enforced idleness at court, and may have reminded onlookers of Sidney's famous enemy the Earl of Oxford, described by one contemporary as a 'ridiculously foppish Italianate courtier'.[14] (A quarrel with Oxford over precedence on the tennis court almost ended in a duel. Oxford swore instead to have him murdered.) Like Sidney, 'wonderfully beloved and admired by his countrymen',[15] Hamlet is loved of the distracted multitude' (4.3.4), so much so that Claudius is afraid to take him on openly. He is despatched abroad by a nervous regime, and returns a changed man. Like Sidney, he dies of an infected wound; and Hamlet, like Sidney, is accorded the honor of a soldier's funeral—a strangely incongruous honour, in Hamlet's case. His epitaph, 'The rest is silence' (5.2.349), is a reminder of the enigmatic motto that adorns the superb portrait of Sidney in the National Portrait Gallery—'Caetera fama'. (The rest is fame—or rumour).

But the most remarkable parallel between Hamlet and Sidney, the element that gives the play its unique depth, lies in their intellectual style and standpoint. If we want to hear the voice of Hamlet beyond the play, we have only to turn to Sidney's engaging *A Defence of Poesie*, a vindication of the power of literature, whose subtitle could have been Hamlet's admonition to Horatio: 'There are more things in heaven and earth . . . / Than are dreamed of in your Philosophy' (1.5.166–167). The manner of almost all Hamlet's digressions echo passages in this work, in particular Sidney's comments on drama, and throughout, the cast of mind is strikingly similar. Sidney's unexpected turns of wit, his combination of eager curiosity and serious speculation, his air of learning lightly worn, and the occasional flash of patrician authority are all Hamlet's, and the book ends on the same note that concludes Hamlet's advice to treat actors well, for 'better a bad epitaph than their ill report while you live' (2.2.520).

The character of Hamlet, then, might have been glamorised by its reminders of Sidney, but many of his generation could also have identified with his situation—those who had talent, intelligence and integrity, and found no place in Elizabeth's England. What, then, would the play have meant to them?

England — There All Men Are As Mad As He

THE SETTING WAS instantly familiar in 1600. The country is on military alert: shipwrights are working round the clock, there is the 'daily cast of brazen cannon' (1.1.73). The threat is from the warlike Fortinbras, taking up the cause of his father, also called Fortinbras— an echo of the imminent threat of Spanish invasion by the warlike Philip III, who has just succeeded his father, Philip II. In the foreground there is a sense of unease—'something is rotten'. There are spies everywhere: the monarch is an uneasy usurper, and relies on his aged Secretary of State for advice, a character commentators have periodically associated with William Cecil, whom he closely resembles. Hamlet and his companion Horatio have, like many of their audience, been raised in the reformed religion—they are students at Wittenberg, cradle of Lutheranism. But if they are Lutheran, they are lukewarm students, severed, like the English, from the original source of the Reformation. Hamlet is prevented from returning to university; Horatio, like Sidney in *A Defence of Poesie*, 'in part' believes the myths dismissed as superstition by reformers; he too fails to return to Wittenberg, has 'a truant disposition' (1.2.169), and is finally 'more an antique Roman than a Dane' (5.2.333). Hamlet's first appearance would have struck another chord, for the secret cause of his melancholy would have had a familiar allegorical ring: his uncle, whom he suspects of murdering his father, has usurped the throne and married his mother. His mother's easy capitulation so disgusts him that his life has lost its meaning. Here again, embodied in Gertrude, is fickle England, irresponsibly embracing the new order, forgetful of the virtues of the old. Sidney reproaches England in the *Defence* as the 'mother of Excellent minds' who has unaccountably proved a 'hard Stepmother', while polemicists often portrayed England's relationship with the church or the monarch as a marriage. The dark usurper, Claudius, is given the marks of the new Protestant regime. Hamlet contrasts him with his predecessor in familiar terminology—low, dark, bestial, he is a 'satyr' compared with the sun-god Hyperion: later he is a 'moor', with its connotations of a dark man and a flat landscape, compared with a 'fair mountain' (3.4.66).[16] High-low, fair-dark—the old markers established, the inner 'map' of the play begins to take shape, and the concealed rage and disgust of Hamlet's first soliloquy would have had powerful political resonance for those who blamed their country for what had happened since the Reformation. An aspect of Shakespeare's work that will become increasingly dominant from now on is indignation at the folly of England, expressed in Hamlet's utter incomprehension of his mother's motives—'Have you eyes? . . . What judgement / Would step from this to this? . . . / What devil was it / That thus hath cozened you at hood-man's blind?' (3.4.65–77).

When his father's ghost appears to him from Purgatory, the terrible region where, according to Catholicism, souls destined for Heaven expiated their sins through suffering, Hamlet instinctively replies in kind, calling on the angels, banned prayers for the dead, and St Patrick, the patron of souls in Purgatory. All this was out of bounds to a student from Wittenberg, for the doctrine of Purgatory was denied by reformers. Stern, chilling, majestic, his dead father calls for revenge. His ghastly account of his own death is a prime instance of the way Shakespeare repeatedly blends the imagery of the Reformation assault with a rape or a murder (1.5.60–73). Here the poison, equated with the spoken word, enters through the 'porches' of the king's ears and courses like quicksilver or curdled milk through 'gates' and 'alleys', covering the red-blooded body with a white 'crust'—a marvellous rhetorical feat, using the whitewashing of a church as an image for the suppression of the old religion, both contained within a medically accurate description of the effects of poisoning. Once he has vanished, he continues to call for revenge from various points under the stage. This curious device evokes the call from the active Catholic resistance, which at different points and from various underground cells continued to call on England to rise up in arms against tyranny. But it was a call to which England failed to respond: and the play's minute depiction of Hamlet's sequence of reactions to the ghost's command add up to a searching exploration of the reasons for this.[17]

His instant response is horror—both at the enormity of the crimes of his uncle and the suffering of the ghost—but horror, too, that he is being called to take action. In the same way, Sidney's generation recoiled both from the extremism of the Cecil regime and from the question of whether and how to unseat it. Another calendar 'marker' links their task with Hamlet's (setting the calendar 'right', of course, meant aligning England with Catholic Europe) when he says—'The time is out of joint, O cursed spite / That I was ever born to set it right' (1.5.190–191).

The prosaic character of many of the regime's 'new men' made them easy targets for sophisticated mind-games, evident in the writing and the coterie gossip of the time and dramatised in Hamlet's insolent displays of intellectual superiority over Polonius. His weapon against Claudius is a covertly topical play, *The Mousetrap*, which parallels reality so precisely that it provokes a tacit admission of guilt from Claudius. Everything about this vividly realised scene is a demonstration of the way Shakespeare and his contemporaries used theatre to perform a political function. Shakespeare takes particular pains to make the episode as contemporary as possible, alluding to rival theatre companies and to the techniques of imposing and avoiding censorship. Hamlet offers the same defence that Shakespeare had prepared for himself were he to be accused of sedition by the regime: any offensive material is the fault of the source.[18] In addressing his mother, like writers of the day reproaching England, Hamlet uses graphic illustrations and extreme language to wake her up to the reality of what she has done. But his hand is held back by the ghost: against his mother he must 'speak daggers but use none', just as Catholic dissidents could condemn the regime but not resort to assassination.

Under suspicion, Hamlet is 'confined' to the court of Claudius and forbidden to return to Wittenberg. This confinement of men of uncertain loyalty was a favourite technique—the heirs of great estates, particularly in the North, were advised to remain in their London houses; Catholics were confined to within five miles of their homes, difficult Catholic noblemen and women were confined in the houses of hapless relatives: without a government pass, it was impossible to leave the country. 'Denmark's a prison' (2.2.242), Hamlet comments, just as the priest John Pibush did: 'England is one vast prison for all who profess the faith'.[19]

By the time *Hamlet* was being written William Cecil was dead, which may explain why, in the characters of Polonius, Ophelia and Laertes, Shakespeare dared to include such a clear parallel to the Cecil family.[20] The position of Polonius as key adviser and policy-maker, his bonhomie, his fussy pedantic diction and his pragmatic amorality are a clear parody of William Cecil in his old age. Throughout the play Polonius, like Cecil, is ceaselessly occupied with spying, listening, plotting, watching. He sets up a spying operation, involving an *agent provocateur*, to keep watch on his own son, to whom he gives advice that in its limited outlook and sententious style caricatures William Cecil's own letter of advice to his oldest son, Thomas, who was in his younger days worryingly licentious. Laertes resembles Thomas, a man of action rather than thought, who, though never as brilliant as his younger brother Robert, eventually became a soldier and Member of Parliament. Laertes suggests the Protestantism of the new regime in a speech full of Lutheran overtones, its fatalistic belief in predestination a contrast with Hamlet's scruples about morality and the afterlife: 'Conscience and grace to the profoundest pit! / I dare damnation. To this point I stand . . . let come what comes . . . my will, not all the world's' (4.5.129–130). He usurps the authority of the church, using an age-old ecclesiastical image to describe himself: 'the life-rend'ring pelican' (4.5.143).[21] Ophelia herself plays an ambiguous role similar to Ann Cecil's in the life of the young Philip Sidney. But she also symbolises something deeper—the still-new establishment religion into whose embrace those in power were attempting to draw Sidney's generation, the policy caricatured by Donne in his *Third Satire* as an arranged marriage. For all her beauty and pathos, the passive Ophelia is a lifeless heroine. Her thoughts are often half-finished or uncertain; she follows her father's Machiavellian instructions without protest. She is associated not simply with chastity but with sterility and childlessness. She exemplifies a form of naïveté that in the old days would have found spiritual direction in the nunnery; in the world, she is a pawn in a power game,

paradoxically sanctioning and furthering corruption. By the end of the
sixteenth century, the English experiment of combining what Donne
defined as the 'honesty' of Geneva with the 'beauty' of Rome had still not
succeeded—'Your honesty should admit no discourse to your beauty',
Hamlet tells her bitterly; 'This was sometime a paradox, but now the
time gives it proof. I did love you once' (3.1.107–115).[22] All this, along
with her eventual derangement and death, symbolise the tragic loss of the
stillborn Reformation ideal, originally a thing of beauty, but rendered
gradually meaningless and empty once it had been taken over by the
state.[23] Ophelia's relationship with Hamlet, in which a subtle exploration
of the spiritual issues of the day is integrated with a failed love affair, typifies the delicacy with which Shakespeare blends the political and the universal throughout the play.

Meanwhile, the plot continues to trace the reactions of England's unde-
cided 'lookers on' to the call of the resistance. As Claudius and Polonius
urgently discuss ways of silencing Hamlet, he debates suicide in the play's
most famous speech—'To be or not to be' (3.1.54). This speech has
recently been re-examined as a debate about the morality of revolt—the
subject of intense debate among Essex's followers in 1600, aware that
Robert Cecil was plotting against them and corresponding secretly with
their own candidate for the throne, James VI of Scotland. The momentous decision is whether to risk damnation by taking life—a mortal sin in
the eyes of the church—and by taking life, to escape afflictions that apply
more to Elizabeth's oppressed subjects than the prince of Denmark:
'Th'oppressor's wrong, the proud man's contumely . . . / The insolence of
office, and the spurns / That patient merit of th'unworthy takes'
(3.1.71–75). Seen in this light, the speech addresses exactly the great unanswerable question of Shakespeare's time, never better expressed than in
this adroitly ambiguous speech. Was it immoral to rebel against a tyrant?
Was it a duty?

Was it wishful thinking on Shakespeare's part to portray Claudius as
actually smitten with remorse by Hamlet's play? Sidney's principal
defence of literature is that it persuades people to turn from vice to
virtue—showing Claudius absorbing the full horror of 'a brother's murder' after watching *The Mousetrap*, Shakespeare demonstrates the power of
drama to move a guilty man to tears—and, he may have hoped, to hold up
a mirror to the guilty men in England. Fawning courtiers have just advised
Claudius to banish Hamlet on the grounds that 'Holy and religious fear it
is / To keep those many many bodies safe / That live and feed upon your

majesty' (3.3.7–9). But secretly Claudius knows there is nothing sacred about his position, achieved by means of a criminal act. Yet he cannot repent. A genuine penitent would make restitution; but Claudius is 'still possessed / Of those effects for which I did the murder' (3.3.52–53). In the same way, Elizabeth's new regime owed its very existence to the wealth of the despoiled church, and legitimacy for the despoliation depended on the monarch's assertion of supremacy over the church. A change of religion was simply not possible without a change of regime. The similar difficulties of those Catholics who held monastic lands was being addressed at this point by Persons in his 'Memorial', a blueprint for the government of England in the event of a successful invasion, and they are mentioned again in one of Shakespeare's next plays, *Troilus and Cressida*. The viewpoint of those who had profited from the Reformation is put as graphically in Claudius's agonised speech (3.3.35–72) as the viewpoint of the resistance in Hamlet's.

Hamlet is despatched to England, a place where—a joke that hints at Hamlet's essentially English dilemma—'all men are as mad as he' (5.1.149). He returns from abroad a changed man. He has resolved his dilemma in the same way as thousands of those similar Englishmen who, following the advice of their spiritual leaders, committed their cause to providence and confronted the regime, not with an army but 'naked' and 'alone' (4.7.51–52). His spiritual serenity vanishes, however, when he comes on Laertes lamenting the dead Ophelia. He flies into a rage, claiming he loved her more. They come to blows over the body, the language—'Thou pray'st not well' (5.1.253)—recalling the sectarian squabbling as the vision of a new English spirituality died away. Paradoxically, the quarrel is followed by a rapprochement that echoes the way Puritans and Catholics came to sympathise with each other's predicament. 'By the image of my cause I see / The portraiture of his' (5.2.77–78), acknowledges Hamlet.

In the story of the *Ur-Hamlet*, the prince kills his uncle and takes his rightful place as king of Denmark. But in Shakespeare's play, all the protagonists die—and Fortinbras, the man of action whom the fatally inactive Hamlet names as his heir, arrives to make a new beginning. But though Claudius is a casualty of the final bloodbath, so is the truth. The dying Hamlet realises that only the friends he has sworn to silence know the truth about the murder of his father and his own struggle to avenge him. One of the most prophetic lines in Shakespeare's work is Hamlet's 'O God! Horatio, what a wounded name, / Things standing thus unknown shall live behind me!'(5.2.336–337)—the epitaph of resistance England, misrepresented ever since. He commissions Horatio to 'report my cause aright'. And Horatio vows to do so: his last speech talks of a 'bloody question', he promises to tell the 'yet unknowing world' of 'carnal bloody and unnatural acts', and 'deaths put on by cunning and forced cause' and 'purposes mistook fallen on th'inventors' heads' (5.2.372–377).[24] In real life, Fulke Greville did indeed tell the story of Sidney, but continually revised it as the new religion took hold; Greville became a successful establishment figure, concerned to give Sidney and himself impeccable Protestant roles.[25] The same fate met the deeper, allegorical story. Only now 400 years later do phrases like 'the Bloody Question' and 'unnatural Acts' and 'cunning and forced cause' begin to alert us to the 'alternative' history of the period and suggest that the playwright himself is acting as a Horatio, attempting to 'truly deliver' the story of a lost cause.

In performance, one of the most poignant moments of the play is the point at which Hamlet stands between his weeping mother, who implores him to come to his senses, and—invisible to her—his ghostly father, who urges revenge. Hamlet is here a living emblem of the torn loyalties that form the subject matter of so much of Shakespeare's work. This tableau, and the choice of Sidney as a model for Hamlet, suggest that Shakespeare himself was also at this point torn between loyalty to his country and his religion—an anguished 'looker-on'. But his treatment of the play's famous central theme—that of death and burial—makes it clear that this is a committed play with a Catholic Counter-Reformation message.

One of the aims of the Counter-Reformation was to rehabilitate the distinctive Catholic doctrine of Purgatory, stripped of the abuses that precipitated the original Reformation and presented instead as an essentially merciful concept that allowed souls to expiate sins committed on earth and to interact with the living, whose prayers could hasten them on the way to Heaven. The reformers denied the existence of Purgatory, asserting that souls were predestined either to Heaven or to Hell, and therefore had no need for chantries or prayers. But by the 1560s, there was a renewed proliferation across Europe of confraternities founded specifically to pray for the dead. The ghost of Hamlet's father brings the pains of Purgatory vividly to life, evoking from Hamlet traditional phrases from prayers for the dead.

One of these phrases—'hic et ubique' (1.5.156) (here and everywhere)—comes from a prayer in the Roman Missal for those buried in unconsecrated ground. In Shakespeare's England, burial in churchyards was permitted only for those who consented to a Protestant funeral rite—

impossible for Catholics. The stress on the 'maimed rites' of Ophelia's funeral, that of a suicide, artfully conveys the perceived inhumanity of the new curtailed funeral service, which lacked the singing of a requiem, charitable prayers, the strewing of earth—'Must there no more be done?' (5.1.213–228) asks her scandalised brother. All over England, many others felt the same. In the early days, aggressive groups of mourners defied the minister and conducted the burial in their own way 'compelling him to withdraw himself from the tumultuous assembly'.[26] But this was risky— parties of zealous Protestants could exhume the body in the night. Often, Catholics filled the official coffin with stones and secretly buried their dead elsewhere using the old rites, in fields or remote places, strewing earth from the churchyard 'for they say they are thus buried in consecrated earth'. Those who were able to even took the body abroad; it is possible that some were buried at sea, perhaps 'full fathom five'. As time went by, the ban on Catholic burial became less, not more bearable, and violent quarrels reminiscent of Hamlet and Laertes fighting in the grave frequently broke out in churches. The provocation could be extreme. Sir George Browne, one of Viscount Montague's uncles, was exhumed from his tomb in St Mary Overies on the orders of the Archbishop of Canterbury 'that the churchwardens might assure him that the body was there . . . not a log, and the body . . . carried beyond the sea'. The body was then commanded to be buried 'neither in church nor churchyard' but on the highway: 'so he lieth above ground where the sexton layeth the spades and shovels'.[27]

This is a play, then, that analyses in depth the course of the 'wavering soul' of England towards the end of the sixteenth century and sets it in the spiritual context of the writings of missionaries and exiles like Allen, Persons, Gregory Martin, Southwell. It contains Shakespeare's exploration of the reasons men like Sidney failed to take the lead and reclaim their inheritance from what they considered a usurping and tyrannical regime. Onlookers likely to connect Hamlet's incongruously military funeral in the play with Sidney's may also have remembered a small but significant fact. At his death, Sidney left his sword to the Earl of Essex; and in the year *Hamlet* was first staged, Essex was at last deciding, late in the day, to take up arms against the regime. The following year Essex requested a performance of *Richard II*, including its perilous deposition scene; already *Henry V* represented an Essex-like figure borne in triumph through the London streets. *Hamlet* is more radical. It was the first of Shakespeare's plays to suggest that passive resistance may not be enough. The original germ of *Hamlet* may well have been yet another request from Essex and Southampton: for a play that would demonstrate that civilised restraint was proving to be the death of spiritual England and that would prepare the minds of the most peace-loving spectators for the momentous approach of a justified military coup.

CHAPTER

IO

FAILURE, 1601–1602

B UT IN THE END, the long-awaited coup was foiled. To anyone in sympathy with the opposition cause, accounts of Essex's rebellion make painful reading; Shakespeare was shortly to dramatise the events leading up to the fiasco in his most disillusioned play. At every point, Essex's tactics were anticipated by Robert Cecil, who disposed of his rival with the finesse of a master duellist.

Early in 1601, Essex was still mustering support and negotiating for Scottish and Irish assistance when he found that his hand had been unexpectedly forced. He was secretly warned of an attempt on his life, and received a summons to appear before the Privy Council. A few weeks earlier his lieutenant, the Earl of Southampton, had been attacked by an armed gang in the Strand; only a brilliant feat of swordsmanship allowed him to escape. That night Essex summoned his chief followers to Essex House, his base on the north bank of the Thames near the centre of London, and the next morning, gambling on his popularity in the city and the court, he prepared to storm Whitehall Palace at the head of the municipal officials and crowds who normally attended the Sunday morning sermon in the nearby square outside St Paul's Cathedral. But the plan went wrong. As they hurriedly conferred at Essex House, a group of senior government ministers arrived to invite Essex to confer with the Queen, among them Egerton, the Lord Privy Seal; Lord Popham, the Chief Justice; and William Knollys, Comptroller of the Royal Household. Pushing through the growing crowds at the door, they demanded an interview. Essex was forced to imprison them in his house, a treasonable act. He now had almost 300 men behind him, but instead of riding immediately to Whitehall, which lay upriver, he walked straight into Cecil's trap. They made for the city centre, Essex crying, 'For the Queen, my mistress!'—but the streets were ominously empty, and when they reached St Paul's they found that the sermon had been cancelled, and every street and passageway barricaded.

Even so, such was the reputation of Essex inside and outside the palace that it was hours before the ministers plucked up courage to go out—only the Queen talked of going in search of the rebels, and 'not one of them would dare to meet a single glance of her eye; they would flee at the very notice of her approach'.[1] Essex returned home to find his men had released the hostages and that most of his support had prudently vanished. He and Southampton barricaded themselves in, but after a long parley from the rooftops, they and their remaining handful of followers were forced to yield. At the request of Robert Cecil, Southampton's sentence was commuted from death to imprisonment; but any hope of mercy from the Queen towards Essex died away when witnesses were found who gave evidence that Essex had called the Queen 'an old woman, as crooked in mind as she was in body'. After that, his declarations that his goal had been merely to rescue her from the parasites who surrounded her fell on deaf ears, and on 25 February 1601, he went to the block. There was an outcry at his execution. In the historian John Lingard's words, '[T]he popularity of the queen, which had long been on the wane, seemed to be buried in the same grave with her favourite. On her appearance in public, she was no longer greeted with the wonted acclamations; and her counsellors were received with loud expressions of insult and abhorrence'.

But Robert Cecil had never been concerned about popularity. The removal of Essex gave him control over the succession, and he was already preparing the Scottish King for the handover. The opposition, once potentially formidable, led by men of noble blood who had always despised him, had utterly collapsed. Those who escaped execution were dependent on him for survival. It was no doubt due to his personal insistence that from this point on Southampton's compliance on matters of religion was no longer in question; the assumption ever since has been that he had always been Protestant. Many other public figures were similarly bound to Cecil. Even his father had never enjoyed such complete political power. At the same time, Robert Cecil was beginning to gain the upper hand over his more shadowy enemy, the underground Catholic resistance. Here again, his technique was that of an expert swordsman, whose skill lies in exploiting his opponent's weakness—an easy task, in the case of English Catholics after Essex's death.

As with so many resistance movements, it was pressure from within just as much as enemy persecution that eventually proved fatal to the English Catholic community. A disagreement over strategy split the Catholics. Back in the 1580s and early 1590s there had been consensus: resistance to the regime, in some form or other, was the obvious course. But by now, things were less clear-cut. Towards the end of the 1590s, a group of 'secular' priests (regular clergy who did not belong to a religious order) had been led to believe that Elizabeth would follow the example of Henry IV of France and introduce a measure of religious toleration. The naive optimism of these priests added fuel to their long-standing feud with the Jesuit-educated missionaries, who irritated them with their born-again enthusiasm and dangerous thirst for martyrdom. The more old-fashioned Catholic clergy felt snubbed by these disciplined idealists.

The conformist priests had strong support from what Jasper Heywood called the 'lookers-on', the Catholic nobles and gentry who had gained from the spoils of the Reformation, who attended Protestant services in public and Mass in private, and who needed household chaplains who would give their blessing to their politic compromise with the regime. To this anxious group, 'Hotspur Jesuits and the Spanish' were to blame for everything that had gone wrong. The failure of Spanish support from abroad and the increasing oppression at home had weakened the resistance of those English Catholic sympathisers who stopped short of wanting to challenge the Queen's right to rule. When the Pope appointed George Blackwell as an 'Archpriest' to unify the English mission in 1598, the more conservative secular priests and their backers took angry offence —Blackwell, they believed, was a Jesuit sympathiser.

Robert Cecil, spotting the rift, skilfully exploited it. In 1598, a pair of secular priests found themselves hurried off to Rome to appeal to the Pope against the Archpriest's appointment. The Appellants, as the conservatives became known, after this 'appeal' were encouraged by the Queen to believe that the regime would ease the terms of the oath in return for their loyalty. They were offered the use of the official printing presses to give vent to their views on the Jesuits, and, led by Thomas Bluet and William Watson, they jumped at the chance. Between 1601 and 1603, eighteen Appellant publications, some of them vitriolically effective, others, in Robert Persons' phrase, 'little barking pamphlets', attacked the Jesuits, papal authority, the theory of resistance, above all Robert Persons himself, by now a valued adviser on English affairs in Rome and Madrid. The seminaries abroad rose to the challenge with a volley of counter-publications; the public row that resulted had Elizabeth's counsellors rubbing their hands as they watched their own propaganda work being done for them by experts. The Jesuit scepticism about the motives of the regime proved well founded. In 1603, having done everything in their power to prolong the expectations of the Appellants, the government finally rejected the idea of toleration on the grounds that 'the strain of two religions would be the end of peace'. At the beginning of the next reign, the two most obstinate Appellants were executed.

Shakespeare dramatized these two catastrophic blows to the resistance movement in England—the Appellant Controversy and the Essex Rebellion. He reserves the full heartbreak of the Essex rebellion for a dark play addressed to the survivors: *Troilus and Cressida* is a dejected analysis of the failure of allies at home and abroad to come to the aid of the Earl of Essex. But his characteristic reaction was more practical. The collapse of the opposition meant that the final two years of Elizabeth's reign saw a number of direct appeals to the Queen to intervene personally to allow religious toleration. *Twelfth Night* contains Shakespeare's contribution to this last-ditch plea to the aged Queen.

Of all Shakespeare's shadow plays, these are the most international in their outlook, embracing figures representing Rome, Ireland, the Pope, Philip II and Robert Persons. Shakespeare marginalises the Appellants, presenting them as puppets of the vested interests of old Catholicism, vindictive enemies of true spirituality. The missionaries from the seminaries abroad are, by contrast, the source of renewed truth and holiness. He goes out of his way to emphasise the spiritual unity of English Catholicism, attempting to downplay its many divisions. Where he touches on the Jesuit-Appellant rift, his intention coincides exactly with the title of one of Robert Persons's contemporary publications—to present the Appellant cause as *'A manifestation of the great folly and bad spirit of certain in England'*.

A Wise Man's Art

SHAKESPEARE APPEARS to have survived the Essex debacle unscathed. In *Twelfth Night*, he resumes his old role of court dramatist for the first time since 1599. His alter ego in the play, the court jester or 'clown', Feste, a melancholy 'corrupter of words' associated with 'old' ways, has just reappeared at court, risking disgrace: he refuses to tell the servants where he has been. There is an echo of the humble apologies of *A*

Midsummer Night's Dream: 'You will be hanged for being so long absent . . .' they tell him, 'Make your excuse wisely, you were best' (1.5.14–28). With difficulty, he reinstates himself with his mistress, the rich countess Olivia: '. . . I'll no more of you', she scolds, 'besides you grow dishonest' (1.5.37).

Olivia has a point. Shakespeare has returned to the business of slipping elegantly concealed Catholic petitions to the Queen, risking disgrace in the knowledge that she prided herself on her ability to discover hidden meanings that eluded her advisers, and that even in her old age she liked to be 'well advertised of everything that happened in the world'.[2] Shakespeare's final plea to Elizabeth for the repeal of the punitive anti-Catholic laws and the return of the Catholic exiles is rooted in a diplomatic occasion: the visit of the young Don Virginio Orsini, an Italian nobleman, to Elizabeth's court on 6 January 1601—a date known as Twelfth Night. A reference in the play makes it probable that it was performed not on that day, but later that year. Twelfth Night 1601 may have held poignant memories for the Queen, for Orsini's visit had occurred only a month before Essex's rebellion and was one of the last official occasions in which she was seen in public before she took to her room, fallen prey to depression and illness.

The play bears all the hallmarks of Shakespeare's previous 'pleas' to the Queen. The flattery is expert. Here again is a clever, charismatic woman courted by unworthy suitors. Against a background of music, comedy and complex allusion, she, like Portia, discovers true love and in the process brings about the visionary rebirth of true England. The portrait was well timed. In spite of her failing health and moods of depression and rage, the Queen's mental faculties remained undiminished. She still flirted with the younger courtiers and diplomats. 'I think not to die so soon and am not so old as they think', she would say, and continued to hunt and dance, banning Lord Hunsdon from her presence for two days when he had the temerity to suggest she cut down on her riding.[3] But after Essex's downfall, her vitality visibly flagged. She wore black and went out less often, remaining, according to John Harington, 'shut up in a chamber from her subjects and most of her servants and seldom seen but on holy days'. Her control over her court was less certain, and she became increasingly dependent on such men as the Puritan William Knollys, Comptroller of the Household, to keep the quarrelling factions in check.

The relationship between Olivia and Feste gives insight into the complicity that existed between the Queen and the great musicians and artists she patronised in defiance of pressure from hard-line supporters. 'Now you see sir how your fooling grows old', she warns Feste when her Puritan steward Malvolio is out of earshot, 'and people dislike it' (1.5.103–104). By picking out the concealed plot it is possible to follow and appreciate the way Shakespeare combines adroit flattery of this melancholic, reclusive and touchy old woman with an undiminished determination to plead the cause of Catholic England.

With an eye on the damage caused by the Appellant uproar, Shakespeare's first concern is to ridicule the mischief-making group of reactionary Catholic gentry whom he represents as a major cause of England's problems. It is they who persecuted the Puritans under Queen Mary, and they who now set the secular clergy against the Jesuits. True religion has nothing to do with them, the play implies. Instead, it is to be found in exile and underground in England—a new form of Catholicism, still loyal both to the crown and the papacy but refined through suffering. The Queen's own position is given sensitive treatment. She is in a quandary. She has had to adopt the religion formulated by her father and brother, her country is riven by sectarian bickering, the hard-line Protestants are gaining the upper hand and both Appellants and Puritans believe she is secretly in sympathy with their cause. On top of it all, she has to fend off ceaseless pressure from the Catholic powers abroad to return to the fold of the universal church. Surreptitiously, Shakespeare offers the solution: lift the penal laws, recall the exiles and all her problems would be at an end. This ideal picture had just been described by Robert Persons in 1599 in *A Temperate Ward-word:* if toleration were introduced, they would see '[a]ll sorts of people merry, contented, loving and confident within the realm; all to laugh and sing together; all to pray to God most heartily for Her Majesty's health, wealth, and prosperous long continuance'.[4] It was extremely unlikely that the Queen would ever have read anything by the hated Jesuit, least of all *A Temperate Ward-word*. But would the same argument carry any weight coming from one of England's leading dramatists?

Twelfth Night sets England in the wider context of Catholic Europe, represented by Duke Orsino's Illyria. England itself is depicted as one small area of Illyria, the estate of the Countess Olivia. Elizabeth is Olivia, obstinately refusing to have anything to do with the Duke. In deference to her depression in the wake of Essex's execution, she is portrayed as a mourning 'cloistress' (1.1.28) who has partially withdrawn from her increasingly unruly and divided household. Matching her mood, the comedy is permeated with a sense of sadness, the keynote struck by Feste's songs,

'Come away, death' and 'The rain it raineth every day'. The text is sprinkled with personal markers that would have pleased the Queen: a compliment on her famously exquisite Italic handwriting—'I think we do know the sweet Roman hand' (3.4.28), says Malvolio archly; a reference to the 'schedules' of her face, standardised portraits issued by the court to counter the unflattering likenesses that were in circulation (3.4.228–233); Feste's nickname for her, 'Madonna' recalling the semi-religious cult of the virgin queen. Elizabeth's looks and her authority—both, in reality, on the wane—receive particular attention; ''Tis beauty truly blent', marvels Viola when the veil is lifted, flattery all the more acceptable for her initial, cheeky, 'Excellently done, if God did all' (1.5.221–223). This was the kind of brinkmanship with which, as in *A Midsummer Night's Dream*, Shakespeare liked to tease a court saturated with the language of flattery. Like the impatient Elizabeth, Shakespeare's Olivia is quick to cut short 'poetical' compliment—'It is the more like to be feigned' (1.5.183), she snaps. In spite of the chaos that reigns in her house, one visitor notes Olivia's 'smooth, discreet and stable' (4.3.19) government. The most engaging aspect of the portrait is its acknowledgment of the debt owed to the Queen by Catholic entertainers—particularly musicians, actors and dramatists. Malvolio's remark to Olivia about Feste—'Unless you laugh and minister occasion to him he is gagged' (1.5.82–83)—has a more literal application if the word 'you' is stressed. For this was literally true—only the Queen's protection secured acting companies from the authorities' attempts to shut them down. Feste reminds Malvolio—and the Queen—of this point again at the close of the play.

Mixed in with judicious compliments are some more pointed references, the first to the sorry consequences of Elizabeth's failure to marry. 'I have read it—it is *heresy*', says Olivia of Orsino's marriage proposal (1.5.214). This odd use of the word is one of the details in the courtship scene that evoke the religious differences between England and Catholic Europe. It is also a reproachful reminder of Elizabeth's Accession Speech, in which she promised to accept a husband, denouncing rumours that she would never marry as 'heresy'.[5] Shakespeare's implied reproach for the broken promise continues with an oblique reference to the reason for the succession crisis: Elizabeth's refusal to provide the country with an heir. 'Lady, you are the cruellest she alive / If you will lead these graces to the grave / And leave the world no copy' (1.5.225–226). Shakespeare approaches these forbidden issues in the style Elizabeth used for her own speeches, described by one biographer as 'involved and tortuous . . . requiring detailed sifting before they yielded up their true meaning'.[6]

With similar cunning Shakespeare sets about aligning Olivia with Catholicism, implying, just as he did with Portia, that this is where Elizabeth's heart really is, if only she realised it. 'You do think you are not what you are' (3.1.135), Viola tells her. Wearing black is irrational, says Feste; and so, Shakespeare demonstrates, is her affection for her steward Malvolio, a caricature of a time-serving, hypocritical Puritan, whom Olivia mystifyingly values at more than half her dowry. The complex images imply that she is Protestant only in name, that seclusion, darkness, mourning, the rule of her steward are all part of a meaningless inheritance handed down by her father and brother. In this play Shakespeare cunningly suggests that Elizabeth is one of the victims, not a champion, of the Reformation. Her signet ring is a Lucrece, his classic statement of violated purity, and her forged letter also associates her with Lucrece.[7] This was the strategy of all dissidents who diplomatically represented the Queen as a kind of royal hostage, imprisoned by her Reformation inheritance and her influential advisers.[8] As she gradually falls in love with Viola-Sebastian, Shakespeare edges Olivia into the realm of Catholic imagery. She marries Sebastian in a chantry, and twice calls the priest 'father'.

The court would have recognised not only the portrait of the Queen, but that of her household and by extension her country. The identity of her reprobate uncle, Sir Toby Belch, is clearly that of the riotous old order, sworn enemy to the Puritans. His famous attack on Malvolio— 'Dost thou think because thou art virtuous there shall be no more cakes and ale?' (2.3.110)—is designed to awake memories of more than the good life banned by the reformers. The lost Catholic rituals are recalled as well—'cakes' was the popular term for communion bread, and 'ales' the parish fund-raising celebrations. One of Toby's songs, 'Constant Susanna', referring like *The Merchant of Venice* to the story of Susanna in the Apocrypha, sounds very like a Catholic rebel song (2.3.78–79). He is associated, like the great houses on the troublesome fringes of Elizabeth's kingdom, with 'fining' and 'confining' and is only fit for 'mountains and barbarous caves' (4.1.47)—the hideouts of unhappy recusants under threat of government raids. His feeble-minded protégé, Sir Andrew Aguecheek, whom he hopes will secure his future by marrying his niece Olivia, resembles the vacillating form of conformist Catholicism promoted by some of these households, happy to sacrifice spirituality for an easy life, but too hidebound to let go of the old traditions. The extreme folly of Sir Andrew, dealt the standard Catholic markers—he is tall, with flaxen hair, and, for good measure, wears flame-coloured stockings—represents Shakespeare's first satire on the Appellant clergy.

Just as in his previous play for the Queen, *The Merchant of Venice*, Shakespeare is careful to deplore the barbaric treatment of Protestants under Mary. Along with the maid, Maria, Sir Andrew and Sir Toby play a practical joke on Malvolio that ends with his imprisonment as a madman in a pitch-dark cell. A string of references connect this episode with the persecution of the previous reign and glance lightly at the equally brutal Protestant backlash: like many Catholic apologists, Shakespeare represents the Marian burnings as a cause of the revenge persecution of Catholics under Elizabeth. In this small cameo of the past, Maria is given the shadowy profile of Queen Mary, once a lowly member of her sister Elizabeth's household (according to rumour, Anne Boleyn made her a chambermaid).[9] Maria is the instigator of the whole plot, and curious descriptive details contrast oddly with her light-hearted role in the play. She dogs Malvolio 'like a murderer' (3.2.71), a jest ends by characterising her, like Mary, as 'barren' (1.3.75), and she is associated with monarchy— she is Queen of the Amazons, her prank is 'sport royal' (2.3.161). Malvolio's experiences in his cell also echo those of all Tudor prisoners of conscience. Only agreement to an absurd theological tenet will secure his release; meanwhile, Feste follows standard procedure by catechising him—first using Spanish Catholic terminology ('Bonos dies' [4.1.120]) then Puritan cant ('Cease thy vain bibble-babble' [4.1.93]). Ominously, the play leaves the tit-for-tat quarrel unresolved. Malvolio's similarity to Knollys, the Comptroller of the Household involved in the downfall of Essex, has often been noticed; it would have given a sharply topical edge to this miniature morality tale discouraging sectarian revenge.

While the Puritan Malvolio and the Appellant Catholic Andrew Aguecheek vie for their mistress's hand, Count Orsino pays court to her through an ambassador. At the end of the play, he at last exerts himself to appear in person. And here we come to the reason for the title and perhaps the inspiration of the play. In the sixteenth century, the name Orsini was synonymous with the papacy. Their pedigree extended back to Roman times and included an illustrious roll-call of prelates, bishops, cardinals and three popes. Virginio Orsino's Twelfth Night visit was therefore symbolic of the long and fruitless courtship of Elizabeth by the Catholic powers, petitioning her return to the universal church. Persons was only one of many Catholic writers who represent this projected union in terms of a marriage, the papacy representing England's father, the Queen her mother.[10] The Orsino of the play has unmistakably papal markers. His envoy has the title given to papal ambassadors—a 'nuncio' (1.4.28)—and recalls the papal motto 'servus servorum' in an graceful turn of phrase—'Your servant's servant is your servant, madam' (3.1.99).

In spite of his exalted status, however, Orsino is no more attractive as a suitor than Malvolio or Sir Andrew. He represents the wealth, decadence and complacency of one aspect of the Counter-Reformation. 'Give me excess of it', he says of the music, and retreats to a room 'canopied with bowers' (1.1.1–40). Worst of all, from the point of view of English Catholics, he is unreliable and fickle. Feste finds him a generous patron, but calls him a man of 'changeable taffeta', his mind an iridescent 'opal' (2.4.74). Allusions to Orsino's noble fleets sunk by boats of shallow draft recall the failure of the military arm of the papacy—Spain—to come to the aid of English Catholics. A strange digression at the end of the play glances at the infamous papal interdict of 1570 that encouraged Catholics to rise against an excommunicated Queen. To spite Olivia, the 'marble-breasted tyrant' (5.1.118), Orsino resolves to kill his adoring Viola, 'the lamb that I do love' (5.1.124).[11] This was how England saw the Pope's move—a pointless response to Elizabeth's stance that only brought hardship and death to English Catholics.

So far, the parallel between the play and England's position in 1601 is clear. The comic treatment of Elizabeth's predicament is uncontroversial and so entertaining that the quarrel between Toby Belch and Malvolio remains one of the most popular episodes of all Shakespeare's plays. Even at the time, the tale of Sebastian and Viola may have been seen by many as a series of romantic interludes between scenes of hilarious topical comedy. In fact, like the last act of *The Merchant of Venice*, it represents another complex, ornamented Chinese box for the Queen to unlock. The story of the separated twins conceals an intense appeal for the return of the beauty and revived holiness of England's lost religion.

The bond between Viola and Sebastian is closer than that between any of Shakespeare's other twinned couples. This is because their hidden symbolism is almost identical—they represent Catholic spirituality at home, and Catholic spirituality in exile—they are one and the same, parted only by the tempest of the Reformation. More than in any other play, their *identity* is stressed. The final scene dwells at length on the amazement of the cast at their similarity—they are compared to such optical illusions as Holbein's famous distorted skull in his painting 'The Ambassadors'—'a natural perspective, that is and is not' (5.1.209). Shakespeare has a strong political motive for stressing the loving unity of Viola and her more assertive brother, Sebastian, a pair as indistinguishable as 'an apple cleft in two' (5.1.215). His aim is to emphasise the common identity of English Catholics at home and their more militant exiled brothers—a body that in fact, after decades of separation, was riven with mutual suspicions and recriminations.[12]

Twelfth Night passes over the darker realities of the troubled relationship between domestic and exiled Catholics. Instead Shakespeare celebrates the ardent, revived spirit of the resistance movement, dramatising its two aspects in idealised form: one half, Viola, living in disguise in England and longing for the return of a faith that had vanished overseas; the other, Sebastian, stranded abroad, longing to be re-united with England and with co-religionists at home. The twins are associated with love, beauty, persecution, and the freshness of the Counter-Reformation—an image designed both to attract the Queen and to revive the battered religious allegiance of watching Catholics.

Shakespeare begins by separating the pair in yet another Reformation storm. Viola quickly finds service in Olivia's household, disguised as a man and choosing the 'Roman' name Cesario. She is associated with the heraldic sign of the Five Wounds—Olivia enumerates her 'five-fold blazon' (1.5.277). Her beauty and integrity intrigue Olivia, who turns from the tedious attentions of Malvolio, Sir Andrew and Orsino, awakening to the discovery of a new paragon in her own household. This is what she has been unconsciously looking for; this, suggests Shakespeare, is the attraction Elizabeth finds in the many overt and covert Catholics in her entourage and among her friends. But, like such Catholics, Viola resists her mistress's increasingly pressing invitation to submit to her.

Shakespeare adds a sophisticated twist. Privately Catholic friends and protégés were not merely wooed by the queen—their mission was to woo her. For the duration of Elizabeth's reign, playwrights, poets and musicians had tried pleading with her by means of allegory, code, laments and prayers; they were highly placed advocates for Rome, commissioned to put the case for toleration. This role is represented by Viola. She must somehow woo Olivia for Orsino, the symbol of the universal church, and the focus of her own intense loyalty—while resisting the pressure to conform to Olivia's will. Byrd, Jonson, Tallis and many others exemplify the difficulty for leading Catholics of combining constancy to their faith with loyalty to the Queen. The passion and ambivalence of their work is evoked in Viola's famous 'Make me a willow cabin at thy gate' (1.5.253), a lyrical address to Olivia into which she pours all her hidden love for Orsino.

Jealousy of the favour Viola finds with their mistress prompts Sir Toby to play a second practical joke—one that illustrates in revealing detail the birth of the Appellant Controversy. Toby mirrors the absurd quarrel when he decides to trick Andrew and Viola into fighting each other—even though both are dedicated pacifists. Shakespeare is careful to make their timidity specifically clerical—Viola, already linked with the virginal willow, 'would rather go with sir priest than sir knight' (3.4.258–259) and is described as 'a coward, a most devout coward, religious in it' (3.4.373). Like the Appellants Watson and Bluet, Sir Andrew has 'license' to write and is ferocious on paper, though he writes at Sir Toby's dictation—'Be curst . . . taunt him with the license of ink . . . if thou thou'st him some thrice, it shall not be amiss; and as many lies as will lie in thy sheet of paper . . .' (3.2.37–47). The implication here is that the Appellants were the tools of the conformist Catholic gentry. In a neat touch, the reason for the duel in the end boils down to an oath—exactly the point of difference between Appellants, who recommended acceptance of the revised oath and the Jesuits, who opposed it. 'There's no remedy sir', Toby warns Viola; 'he will fight with you for's oath sake . . . draw for the supportance of his vow' (3.4.281–284). The unexpected substitution of Sebastian for his timid sister, Viola, ends in serious injuries for Sir Toby, suggesting that the return of the exiles will spell the end of the mischievous aspects of old Catholicism.

Sebastian has attracted the friendship of Antonio, a sea captain who saves his life and uses a religious term to express his affection—'I adore you so' (2.1.42). Their relationship illustrates the pull the new missionary Catholicism had for ordinary Englishmen, particularly men like jailers, merchants and seamen who came into contact with the travelling priests and often risked their lives to assist them. The mission depended on their goodwill—once he is separated from Antonio, Sebastian describes himself as 'racked and tortured' (5.1.226). When he encounters Orsino's men, however, Antonio has problems, for he captained one of the 'baubling vessels' of 'shallow draft and bulk unprizable' (5.1.47–48) that routed Orsino's fleet—he clearly represents the loyal English enemies of the Catholic powers who fought against the Armada, admired, as this passage suggests, even by their enemies. What would happen to them if England became Catholic once more? Shakespeare dispels the fears of those attracted by revived Catholicism but apprehensive about the implications of a deal with Spain. Orsino compliments Antonio on his gallantry and dismisses the quarrel.

Sebastian's return ingeniously resolves all the problems in the play. The homesick exiles are reunited with the Crown; Elizabeth can freely acknowledge her sympathy with new reformed Catholicism; she is worshipped by the returned exiles; underground English Catholics can openly acknowledge their spiritual loyalty to the papacy; the papacy and the English monarchy are at last in the correct, harmonious relationship with each other, that of brother-in-law to sister-in-law.

The Heart of Loss

T welfth Night, one of Shakespeare's most beautiful plays, presents a determined, optimistic portrait of how England might be reconciled. It is idealistic, hopeful. The reality, too demoralising for public consumption, was dramatised in a far less polished play that the prologue states was originally addressed to a small, elite audience. This was the remorseless *Troilus and Cressida*, which tells the inside story in such searching detail that it reads like a damage report for the shattered and despairing opposition. The prologue announces that it is 'borne from that sea which brought forth Venus', suggesting that it was written for a literary connoisseur who would not set foot inside a playhouse for the next three years—the Earl of Southampton, in 1602 a prisoner in the Tower for his part in the Essex Conspiracy.[13]

Troilus and Cressida is one of the most rewarding subjects for 'coded' reading. As in *Titus Andronicus*, the universal layer is unsatisfactory only because of the passionate debates, dense with coded topical material, lying just below the surface. They throw up an astonishingly vivid snapshot of England's relationship with Europe at the end of the sixteenth century, the leading players portrayed with the casual accuracy of a brilliant caricaturist. Wholly overlooked today, the political context would have been unmistakable at the time.

Troy was a conventional literary alias for England, derived from the legend that one of the refugees from Troy—Brutus—came to England, his name allegedly the origin of the term 'British'. Shakespeare elaborates the parallel, using the familiar markers in order to turn an old tale into an analysis of the complex causes of the Essex catastrophe. Without an understanding of the coded message of the play, all that survives is a tale of sombre nihilism—the quality that saw its popular revival in Europe after the First World War. Even with some knowledge of the code, unravelling the complex allegory would have whiled away some of the long hours Southampton was spending in the Tower.

The preface mystifies modern editors by describing this dark play—a love story that is unromantic, set amid a war that is unheroic—as a highly amusing comedy. Almost undetectable now, the humour lies in a brilliant series of contemporary political cartoons that would have been a gift to actors at the time. They include the Greek leadership, composed of Agamemnon and his advisers, Nestor and Ulysses, who appear halfway through the first act. They are discussing a matter crucial to Elizabethan Catholics—their failure to storm Troy, and their conduct of a seemingly interminable siege. The ponderous, fatalistic Agamemnon has all the quirks of the imperturbable Philip II, who famously barely looked up from his desk at the news of the destruction of the mighty fleet. He brushes aside criticisms of his leadership—his setbacks are trials from God, he says, who uses tempests to test the virtuous. His manner is pedantic and laborious; his utterances have elaborate Latinate touches; oddities like 'protractive', 'persistive' and 'tortive' occur nowhere else in Shakespeare (1.3.9–21). Nestor is an equally recognisable portrait of an elderly pope, using the papal 'we', referring to himself in the third person and replying to the question 'Shall I call you father?' with the paternal 'Ay, my good son' (2.3.250–252).

Most intriguing of all is Ulysses, who bears all the signs of a rare portrait of Robert Persons in his role as lobbyist for the English Catholic cause, tirelessly urging action in the face of obstructive bureaucracy in Rome and Madrid. Ulysses is an ideas man; he is carefully deferential to the two elderly windbags, Nestor and Agamemnon, but his urbane manner conceals an eager, driving, impatient mind. His speaks in focussed and highly persuasive language, using balanced antitheses and vivid images to convey his clear grasp of political situations—a tribute to Persons's admirable prose style. Many at the time would have recognised the central image of his speech on fame and oblivion, 'Time hath my lord, a wallet on his back' (3.3.145–170). It comes from Persons's forgotten spiritual classic, his *Christian Directory*, enormously popular at the time.[14] Ulysses's equally famous speech on the importance of social order, or 'degree', is usually quoted as an instance of Shakespeare's support for the Elizabethan regime—a supreme irony, for its standpoint is in fact that of the arch-enemies of the Protestant state. Its terminology and gist would have been familiar to all those who had worked for the previous forty years on plans for the return of English Catholicism—plans formulated under Queen Mary in the days of Cardinal Pole, and now revised and spearheaded by the Jesuits. In characteristic Jesuit terms, it makes a passionate case for the importance of hierarchy and military obedience, evoking not only the Jesuit founder Ignatius's new order with its references to schools, communities, 'generals' and 'superiors', but also the new network of city confraternities that Pole hoped would revitalise English spirituality. To the orderly mind of Persons, author of the lucidly argued *Conference about the Next Succession*, disregard for hierarchy is not only to blame for the problems of the English Catholic clergy, but it lies at the heart of two other major issues of the day—the failure of the Spanish enterprise, with its chaotic chain of command, and the vexed questions that hung over the succession to the English throne. 'O, when degree is shaked, / Which is the ladder of all high designs, / The enterprise is sick! / How could communities, / Degrees in schools, and brotherhoods in cities, / Peaceful commerce from dividable shores, / The primogenity and due of birth, / Prerogative of age, crowns, sceptres, laurels, / But by degree, stand in authentic place?' The speech ends with a verdict on the malaise within the Catholic enterprise to regain England that exactly coincides with that of modern historical scholars: Protestant England 'in our weakness stands, not in her strength' (1.3.75–137).[15]

An admiring Nestor contrasts Ulysses's sense and eloquence with the 'matter needless, of importless burden' (1.3.71) put forward by his opposite number 'rank Thersites', hanger-on to the great Greek champion Achilles. Cynical and foul-mouthed, Thersites is often seen as the 'fool' of the play, angrily highlighting the futility behind the heroics. Like Andrew Aguecheek he is a coward with a hint of homosexuality, and his effect, like that of the more overtly homosexual Patroclus, is further to demoralise the whole Greek enterprise. Name-calling and 'railing' are his forte, recalling the scurrilous anti-Jesuit attacks of the Appellants. He compares the Greek enterprise to an attempt to release a fly from a web with 'massy irons'. This is precisely the pacifist Appellant attitude: invasion was a disproportionate response to the quibble over words in an oath. The whole profile, strongly suggestive of men like Bluet, who put the Appellant case to the Pope, is underlined by a pun. A 'blewitt' is a kind of mushroom, and in an exchange of insults, Ajax calls Thersites 'Toadstool' (2.1.20)—a usage unique in Shakespeare's work.

So much for the Greek leadership, along with their advisers and critics, unable by now to find anyone who can still be bothered to take to the field on their behalf. Their usual champion is Achilles. But this Achilles is not the heroic figure of the Iliad. He refuses to fight, and instead lounges in his tent, encouraging Thersites's attacks on the war effort and amusing himself with Patroclus's comical imitations of the leadership. Moreover, in a startling break with Homeric tradition, a shameful secret lies behind his deliberate inertia. He is secretly in league with the enemy. The omniscient Ulysses exposes his covert romance with a Trojan girl, daughter of King Priam. His insubordination is described in Catholic terms—he is no longer as biddable as in the days when 'they used to creep to holy altars' (3.3.74).

Achilles evidently stands for Shakespeare's chief whipping-boy at this period, the English Catholic nobility. It was on this increasingly reluctant group that the Spanish had for decades depended for support in the event of invasion. It was they who ignored the Pope's encouragement to rebel, while leading peers refused offers from abroad to take on the role of English Catholic figurehead. And it was they who were in fact secretly compromised by hidden links with the English regime. Persons, Allen and the Spanish ambassadors failed to take one vital factor into account when they led Spain to believe that England would rise in support of the Armada: the extent to which the resolve of many leading English Catholics had been eroded by the passage of time and the manipulating skill of William Cecil. The critical issue of the passivity of these grand 'lookers-on' is explored with extraordinary elegance in Ulysses's description of 'Time' as a forgetful, fickle host.[16] It is Ulysses who suggests Ajax as a replacement for Achilles. In another departure from Homer, Ajax is on his first appearance a muscle-bound, moronic figure, aggressive, stupid and, worst of all, 'languageless' (3.3.263). Thersites mocks him relentlessly for being inarticulate. But he undergoes a change after accepting Nestor's invitation to become the new Greek champion. Suddenly he is capable of fine feeling and courtly exchanges; he is on a par with the chivalrous Trojan champion Hector, who cuts short their duel in order to embrace him as a cousin. It then emerges, in another sharp break with the traditional story, that Ajax has dual nationality—he is 'a blended knight, half Troyan and half Greek' (4.5.86). This is clearly an important detail, especially to Hector, for he repeats it seven times.

Shakespeare has adapted Homer's noble Ajax to match the profile of one of England's most serious adversaries: Ireland. It was to Ireland that Spain and the Jesuits turned once they realised they could no longer depend on the compromised English Catholic leadership. The play's portrait of a hybrid Ajax mirrors the way the international image of the Irish altered towards the end of the sixteenth century. At first, 'languageless' is a particularly apt insult, recalling the 'seven-foot' Shane O'Neill's spectacular appearance to do homage at Queen Elizabeth's court in 1562, when the revelation that, like most of the other Irish lords, he needed an interpreter and could only speak 'howling' Gaelic created a sensation. But in 1577, a more cultivated Irish envoy, Fitzmaurice, was authorised by the Pope to lead a holy war against Elizabeth. And by the 1590s, Ireland had a leader who exactly fits Hector's oddly emphatic label for the new, courtly Ajax: 'half Troyan and half Greek'. This was Hugh O'Neill, Earl of Tyrone. In an enlightened move on the part of the English government, the young O'Neill had been brought up as a Protestant Englishman—in the Sidney household, according to one account. This explains the reference to the upbringing of Ajax in the play: 'famed be thy tutor . . .' and 'he that disciplined thine arms to fight' (2.3.236–238). At the age of nineteen, O'Neill returned to Ireland, where for many years he appeared to act in accordance with English interests, campaigning at one point alongside Essex. But he remained a hybrid, apparently English Protestant, at heart Irish Catholic. His years in England served him well. Not only did he learn to speak English, but he learned to think as an English politician. As overlord of Ulster in the late 1590s, he continued to feign friendship with the English regime while urgently signalling behind their backs for the long-promised Spanish aid. When it eventually arrived, he led a united country under the Catholic banner in the most serious of the many rebellions against English rule there.

Down to the smallest detail, then, the Greek camp mirrors the dealings at the end of the sixteenth century between Spain, the papacy, England and Ireland, with witty glances at the role of the Appellant priests.

The scene inside the Trojan camp, where the leaders are wearily going over old ground, mirrors the situation in Elizabeth's Privy Council with the same ingenuity. Here, too, morale is at a low. The most perceptive character is their champion, Hector, an intelligent, over-chivalrous soldier, the very image of the way his supporters viewed the Earl of Essex. He argues for a peace treaty. The Trojan position, he says, is untenable. By seizing Helen they have appropriated 'a thing not ours, nor worth to us' (2.2.22). That seizure is against '[t]he moral law of nature and of nations' (2.2.185), terminology often used to denounce Henry's seizure of the English church. Hector's advice is uncompromising—'Let Helen go'

(2.2.27). But his fellow Trojans object. It is too late to return her; she is damaged goods: 'We turn not back the silks upon the merchant / When we have soiled them' (2.2.68–69).

Men like Southampton would have heard Essex's voice in this inconsistent speech, which begins by deploring England's appropriation of a spiritual authority that rightly belongs to the universal church but finds no solution to the problem of the monastery lands and church assets. The silks have been soiled. Too many people in England had profited from Reformation gains; there was no going back for the new landowners, busily constructing new farms and manor houses out of the ruins of abbeys and monasteries.[17] Abandoning moral issues, Hector resorts to simple patriotism: to surrender would be dishonourable, and besides, he himself would have much to lose: ''tis a cause that has no mean dependence / Upon our joint and several dignities' (2.2.192–193). But in reality he is no fool—he sums up the motives for continuing the struggle as 'pleasure and revenge' (2.2.171), the revenge being that of the Protestants for the atrocities under Mary, the pleasure the worldly enjoyment of assets originally intended for spiritual use. The enjoyment is evoked in the decadent scene of Paris and his followers carousing with the yielding Helen. The scene is larded with the coded terms that mark the spoils of the old church—'fair', 'sweet', 'love', 'music'—here staled with exaggerated overuse, 'fair' recurring no less than eleven times within the first few lines (3.1.40–152).

Finally Hector clashes with the half-Trojan Ajax, but before the long-awaited struggle gets under way, the great champion claps Ajax on the shoulder, calls him 'cousin' and cancels the fight. The onlookers are bewildered: 'There is expectance here from both the sides / What further you will do'. 'We'll answer it', replies the expansive Hector, 'The issue is embracement' (4.5.146–148). Every detail of this ingenious scene, especially Hector's insistence that Ajax is an honorary Trojan, would have had a bitterly familiar ring to men like Southampton. In 1600, Essex had left England to suppress the rebellion of the 'half-English' Hugh O'Neill. Instead of returning, as Shakespeare had predicted in *Henry V*, with 'rebellion broached on his sword' (Prologue, 5), he made a notorious and, to the English, shameful truce with the rebel leader, once his comrade-in-arms. What the terms really were is still unknown. They were discussed out of earshot—Essex standing on the banks of the Brenny River, and Tyrone on horseback midstream. The assumption among many was that Essex was negotiating for O'Neill's support in his coming rebellion.

Shakespeare again departs from Homeric tradition in his depiction of

Hector's death. Hector, now compromised by his truce with Ajax, is basely stabbed in the back by Achilles while he is unarmed. The scene highlights his naive self-exposure, a critical factor in Essex's downfall. But it also points the finger at the group evidently regarded by the survivors of the debacle as the true villains—the Catholic nobility who abandoned him at the last minute. Among the twenty-five peers before whom Southampton and Essex were arraigned at their trial were a number of their supporters, including the Hunsdons and such leading Catholics as Lord Lumley and the earls of Worcester, Oxford, Derby and Northumberland. One reason for this quiet, deadly defection is suggested in *Troilus and Cressida*. For all his promises, Catholics never quite trusted Essex. Many believed he revealed his true colours years earlier during his celebrated sack of Cadiz. Accomplished with the minimum of bloodshed, the operation was a testimony to Essex's humanity and his powers of leadership—but under his direction, not a church was left standing. It was after this iconoclastic purge that the damaged statue, the 'Madonna Vulnerata', was taken to Valladolid. The Jesuit Henry Garnet's verdict on the rebellion is a cold one—Essex was punished for 'the outrages, plunder and sacrileges committed at Cadiz'.[18] *Troilus and Cressida* confirms his analysis. It is revenge that at last rouses Achilles to seek out and kill Hector—revenge for the injuries Hector has inflicted on his personal troops, the Myrmidons. Shakespeare describes these injuries in terms designed to recall the ravages of iconoclasts: the Myrmidons are 'noseless, handless, hacked and chipped' (5.5.34).

Much of the bitterness of this play derives from the disastrous revelation that key English Catholics were too suspicious of Essex to seize their one opportunity to topple the fragile circle of advisers surrounding the Queen.[19] But there is a further layer of disillusion. The play's love story contains a spiritual morality tale, one that draws on Shakespeare's own recent exploration of the Protestant position. It suggests that Southampton—who at about this time abandoned Catholicism—was in the process of considering the latest Protestant arguments, no doubt pressed on him during his time in the Tower. If so, the play ends with the advice Viscount Montague passed on to his daughter—it is all a sham.

Hamlet portrayed the attempt, fostered by the Cecils, to create a diplomatic synthesis of Calvinism and Catholicism, an Anglican 'broad church' ahead of its time.[20] Nowadays it is difficult to revive the horror with which convinced Catholics and Puritans viewed the proposition that they should subscribe outwardly to something that inwardly they did not believe. The nineteenth-century historian Lingard recaptures the sense of moral injury: the assumption was, he says, that all the Queen's subjects should 'submit to the superior judgement of their sovereign, and practise that religious worship which she practised. Every other form of service, whether it were that of Geneva in its evangelical purity or the Mass with its supposed idolatry was strictly forbidden . . . If any man refused, the fault was his own; he suffered, not for conscience' sake, but for his obstinacy and disobedience. That this miserable sophism should have satisfied the judgement of those who employed it can hardly be credited'.[21] Lingard's indignation reminds us just how much of an affront this appeal to expediency represented in an age of belief.

The central story of *Troilus and Cressida* reveals Shakespeare's own passionate disgust at the political compromise masquerading as the long-awaited emergence of England's own version of the reformed religion. Troilus is a sketch of the English spiritual idealist, his integrity an affecting contrast with the rest of the cast. He has clerical overtones, comparing himself to a merchant seeking a pearl, a priest offering his own heart on an altar. But he has turned away from the conventional worship of the degenerate Helen; he is now impatiently waiting for his union with a new love, Cressida, 'somewhat darker' than Helen, an embodiment of exactly the broad-church compromise proposed to men like Viscount Montague towards the end of the century. The likelihood that this intense, bitter episode draws on a personal spiritual crisis is deepened by the fact that there are distinct echoes of the language in a number of Shakespeare's sonnets.

The opening scene portrays Troilus pestering Pandarus for the long-promised opportunity to sleep with his niece, Cressida. A coarser version of Polonius, the doddering Pandarus recalls William Cecil: His kindred are 'burs', he quips, punning on Cecil's title, Lord Burghley; 'they'll live where they are thrown' (3.2.107–109). And there is a dig at Cecil's reputation as the assiduous Master of the Court of Wards: 'if my lord get a boy of you, you'll give him me'. Troilus has to endure tedious arguments with him about Cressida's precise degree of 'fairness' before enjoying her, though Pandarus ends by claiming to be indifferent as to whether Cressida is a 'blackamoor' so long as the pair get together—an allusion to the essential expediency of the theological arrangement

Cressida, as the state compromise, is Shakespeare's most vacuous character, sprightly but reactive and empty-headed, her conversation a series of meaningless questions and self-contradictions, her only concern to cover up her inconsistencies. Her thoughts have been purged, as Whitgift purged the state religion of its dangerously radical Protestant essence—

'In faith I lie', she declares, an ingenious pun. 'My thoughts were like un-bridled children, grown / Too headstrong for their mother' (3.2.118–120). Within minutes of their meeting, Troilus subconsciously realises that he has been conned, and in the first of a number of poignant speeches evokes the sense of loss experienced by all passionately spiritual people trapped in a secular tyranny. The puns continue through the love-making, reflecting the theological haggling that went on as the state angled for the religious allegiance of its subjects: 'O virtuous fight, when right [rite] with right wars who shall be most right!' (3.2.168–169). Such puns also pervade the anguished passage in which Troilus tries to come to terms with Cressida's betrayal in the Greek camp, where it quickly becomes obvious that she is all things to all men, abandoning the Reformed purity that hoodwinked Troilus in favour of happy promiscuity among the Catholic Greeks—the same grotesque 'sharing' that threatened Silvia in *The Two Gentlemen of Verona*.[22] Shakespeare loads the language of a lover's disillusion with doc-trinal double-meaning. The spiritual idealist realises he has bought into a fake.

The man who opens Troilus's eyes to the truth about Cressida is Ulysses, the parallel to Persons. Persons not only wrote vigorously against the compromise settlement but contributed to the basis of a new Anglican spirituality with his *Christian Directory*, which under the colour of Protes-tant authorship ran to twenty-two editions between 1586 and 1640. Shakespeare presents the English Jesuits not as the arch-enemy but as the country's one reliable guide to the truth. However, *Troilus and Cressida* holds out little hope for the spiritual future of the country. Pandarus has the last word, sounding a note of revulsion and world-weariness—the mood, no doubt, of Essex's followers, brooding on the fiasco, enlightened but probably not cheered by Shakespeare's most disillusioned play.

Truth and Beauty Buried Be

THE EXCITED PREFACE does all it can to signal the concealed mean-ing of *Troilus* and to invite the reader to enjoy the witty carica-tures hidden within. There is more to comedies than meets the eye, it urges, 'especially this author's comedies'. 'Were but the vain names of Comedies changed for the titles of Commodities, or of Plays for Pleas you should see all those grand censors that now style them such vanities flock to them'. But by now Shakespeare was plainly finding it difficult to find any comic capital in 'the matter of England'. In 1601, his poem *The Phoenix and the Turtle* appeared alongside contributions by Jonson and Marston in *Love's Martyr*, a daring volume of dissident poetry anticipating James's succession. Recent studies have revealed its hidden significance: an elegy for a pair who symbolised all that was best in the separated halves of the Catholic resistance, the married couple Anne and Roger Line, parted by the Reformation troubles. Anne had just been executed in England for assisting the Jesuit mission: Roger had already died in poverty in exile. The lament over their ashes is set within a meditation on a Palm Sunday Mass evoking the mystical union of the separated couple. They are given the badges of the persecuted church and its followers—the born-again phoenix and the constant turtle-dove.

The poem provides an unusual glimpse of Shakespeare's own profound spirituality. The dense thought is original, and the intense language recalls Southwell's translations of the hymns of Aquinas, in particular a setting by William Byrd sung by Father Mark Barkworth as he awaited execution on the scaffold alongside Anne Line.[23] The poem's haunting tone takes us beyond the death of two remarkable individuals. Shakespeare is here confronting for the first time the possibility that the spirit of the Catholic resistance would be extinguished in England. He calls his poem a 'tragic scene'; its conclusion is resigned: 'Beauty, truth, and rarity, / Grace in all simplicity, / Here enclosed in cinders lie . . . / Truth may seem, but cannot be; / Beauty brag, but tis not she: / Truth and beauty buried be'.

One opportunity remained for English Catholics. Essex's leading supporters were still behind bars in the early weeks of March 1603 when a fellow prisoner, Father William Weston, recorded a strange phenomenon. He knew nothing of the Queen's last illness—'so completely was I cut off from converse with men . . . But this I did witness. During those few days in which she lay dying beyond all hope of recovery, a strange silence descended on the whole city, as if it were under interdict and divine worship suspended. Not a bell rang out. Not a bugle sounded—though ordinarily they were often heard . . .'.[24] On the morning of 24 March, he looked out of his cell window to see members of the Council assembling below his cell to proclaim the new King, James of Scotland, 'crying out and publishing the proclamation with great pomp'. Elizabeth's long reign was over—and with it their own confinement. In spite of the flood of poetry lamenting the Queen's death, the prevailing mood was not one of mourning—it was one of cautious hope.

IV

The Plea to King James,

1603–1608

THE KING'S MAN, 1603–1604

The Lightning Flash

W HEN AT LAST in the early spring of 1603 the old Queen died, James VI of Scotland ascended the English throne with an ease no one had anticipated—except, perhaps, Robert Cecil, the mastermind behind the transition. After the long years of persecution, both James and Cecil knew that a peaceful accession was wholly dependent on the promise of religious toleration: a promise the Protestant James had repeatedly and cheerfully given to Catholic envoys. Though some were sceptical, James may genuinely have intended to grant toleration, secure in the belief, deliberately fostered by Robert Cecil, that the majority of the country were contentedly Protestant. If so, his eyes would have been opened as the royal procession, with the pardoned Earl of Southampton prudently positioned at its head, made its way slowly through the staunchly Catholic Northern counties towards London. The King showered the towns through which he passed with honours, pardons and concessions, and he arrived in London with his wife and three children on a wave of national acclaim. He was overwhelmed. Not only had he been accustomed since childhood to violent hostility and deprivation, but the long years of attempting to establish royal control over Scotland had tested his exceptional talent for statecraft to the limit. Now, in his own words, he was 'like a poor man wandering about forty years in a wilderness and barren soil and arrived at the land of promise'.

The ground had been skilfully prepared. Protestants welcomed him as one of their own, a theologian and scholar brought up in the reformed religion. Catholics were also eagerly expectant. James was the son of Elizabeth's Catholic rival, the executed Mary, Queen of Scots. They believed his assurances that he would grant toleration to English Catholics and welcomed his announcement that, though Protestant, he considered the Roman Church the 'Mother Church'. There were even hopes that he himself might follow the example of his wife, Anne of Denmark, who had converted to Catholicism a few years earlier. The court was suddenly full of Catholic nobility associated with the cause of Mary, Queen of Scots, foremost among them the Howard family. Perhaps the shrewdest public relations move was the advance publication in England of James's *Basilikon Doron*, a guide to the art of kingship that he dedicated to his son. The book ran into three editions in 1603 and in the words of Francis Bacon, 'filled the whole realm as with a good perfume'. Idealistic yet practical, the book is a scholarly exploration of the obligations of the monarch, written in a brisk style that was clearly James's own. In Rome, Robert Persons reported that 'such applause was here generated at this new King's entrance as if he had been the greatest Catholic in the world . . . These bountiful beginnings raise all men's spirits, and put them in great hopes, insomuch that not only Protestants, but Papists and Puritans, and the very Poets . . . promise themselves great part in his favour'.[1] On his accession, the new king's deeds matched his words; he offered pardons to recusants and remitted their fines. 'Great fears were', wrote Henry Garnet, the Jesuit Superior, 'but all are turned into greatest security: and a golden time we have of unexpected freedom abroad'.[2]

The events that followed led directly to the sensational Gunpowder Plot in 1605 and are of fundamental importance to the hidden level of the plays Shakespeare wrote for James over the next three years. The exhilarating, long-awaited honeymoon was over almost before it began. In spite of restraining advice from leaders abroad, people came in such numbers to Mass that the King was alarmed. He was also unpleasantly surprised at the loss of recusant fines to the Treasury: he had discovered on his arrival in London that the royal coffers were empty and the Crown in debt.[3] Exiles made matters worse by dedicating books to James that suggested that if he adopted his mother's religion, he would be on the side of the majority of his people.[4] The wording was unfortunate—James had been assured that the numbers of English Catholics were relatively small. At the same time the King was having to deal with an even more pressing problem: the unexpectedly vocal body of Puritans in Parliament, intent on curbing royal authority over expenditure and over the church.

To all these domestic difficulties the Privy Council, led by Robert Cecil, supplied a characteristic solution—to divert the Puritan onslaught and increase the royal income by once again declaring open sea-son on Catholics. The deal for the Puritans was, in Lingard's words, 'if they were not suffered to purge the church from the dregs of superstition, they might still advance the glory of God by hunting down the idolatrous papist'. It is difficult not to see what followed as the completion of Cecil's Machiavellian accession game-plan, accompanied as it was by the timely exposure of two trumped-up plots, known as the 'Bye' and the 'Main', which disposed of the last of Cecil's enemies while increasing the King's dependence on his omniscient aide. The penal laws were not only revived—they were extended, and this time, pursuivants and fanatics were encouraged to enforce them to the letter. On the pretext that Catholics had taken liberties with the concessions offered by the king, £20 a month was again exacted, backdated to include the year of suspension. The slightest default in payment incurred forfeiture of all goods and chattels and two-thirds of any property. Recusants who escaped prison found themselves having to buy back basic necessities through friends. Six months later, the confiscation process was repeated so that, as Garnet said, 'If these courses hold, every man must be fain to redeem once in six months the very bed that he lieth on', adding that the furniture in the house he was writing from had already been redeemed twice.[5] Most galling of all was the fact that much of the money raised went to supply the wants of the rapacious Scots who had accompanied James to England. Again, Lingard sums it up: 'the sufferers bitterly complained that they were reduced to beggary for the support of a crowd of foreign beggars . . . But they complained in vain. The exaction of the penalties was too profitable to James and his minions to admit of redress by the king, and among the magistrates in every locality were found persons eager to prove their orthodoxy by tormenting the idolatrous papist, or to benefit their dependents and officials by delivering him up to the tender mercies of men who were careful to charge the highest price for the most trifling indulgence'.[6] Penalties were increased on the families of all those who had fled abroad, on the masters of ships who had illegally transported them, and on unlicensed private tutors at home, while a proclamation banished all Jesuits and seminary priests. Father John Gerard, under cover at the time, gave expression to the terrible sense of disillusionment:

But now what shall we think to have been the state of all Catholic minds when all these hopes did vanish away; and as a flash of lightning, giving for a time a pale light unto those that sit in darkness, doth afterwards leave them in more desolation. What grief we may imagine they felt generally when not only no one of these hopes did bring forth the hoped fruit, nor any promise was performed, but when on the contrary side his Majesty did suffer himself to be guided and as it were governed by those that had so long time inured their hands and hardened their hearts with so violent a persecution; yea when he did not only confirm the former laws with which we were afflicted but permitted new and more grievous vexations to fall upon us . . . [7]

Responding to the protests of foreign ambassadors, James explained that 'since Protestants had generally received and proclaimed him king he had no need of papists'. His tone towards Catholics changed completely: he now 'hated' papists, would disinherit any heir who might tolerate them. His reported words to the Irish delegation that asked for a relaxation in the law still strike a chill: 'had he to wade in blood up to his knees, had he but ten followers, and were such conditions his sole means for recovering his kingdom, he would lose what was left to him and his life as well rather than accede to their request'.

Aghast at this volte-face, English Catholics looked once more for support from their allies abroad. But their last hope had gone. In spite of persistent pleas, by mid-1604 a war-weary Spain was concluding a peace deal with England that made no mention of toleration for Catholics; and once the peace was signed, James brushed aside further requests. To reminders from the Pope of his pre-accession promises to concede liberty of conscience and educate the prince as a Catholic, James 'could not concede . . . for fear of tumults'.[8] The peace with Spain represented a final body-blow to the divided and dispirited resistance. Ominously, the list of Englishmen sent home empty-handed from Madrid and Valladolid included three names that would before long be on everyone's lips—Thomas Winte, Kit Wright and Guy Fawkes.

Worst of all, James was out of reach of all appeals. Now that he had discovered the ideal deputy in his 'little beagle', Robert Cecil, he seemed to think his arduous years of government were over. The Venetian Secretary reported that the King had 'sunk into a lethargy of pleasures and will not take any heed of matters of state. He remits everything to the Council and spends his time in the house alone or in the country at chase', consorting with 'people of low degree'.[9] He was 'bewitched . . . lost in bliss . . . he leaves them with such absolute authority that beyond doubt they are far more powerful than ever they were before'. And yet these deputies, he says, are the very men 'stained with the blood of his Majesty's mother'.

The Advocate

KING JAMES's all-consuming pleasure was hunting. He would spend days in the saddle, conducting business by letter with Cecil in the odd spare moment. One desperate subject tried to gain his ear by attaching a note to the collar of one of his beagles: 'Then let him hear, good God, the sounds / And cries of men, as well as hounds'. Other royal amusements, drama in particular, lent themselves more readily to such pleas. James is usually portrayed as a philistine when it came to the stage, and accounts of snores and royal outbursts in the middle of plays suggest a short attention span—'What did they make me come here for?' 'I marvel what they think me to be!' 'Devil take you all, dance!'¹⁰ But he watched certain plays with attention—it seems he was a discriminating spectator who 'liked and disliked as he saw cause'. And he clearly recognised the quality of Shakespeare's company. Ten days into the new reign, letters of patent were drawn up promoting the troupe to the status of 'The King's Men' and giving them the freedom to perform unhindered anywhere in the kingdom. Their duties went beyond writing and acting plays. James liked to have his 'servants' on hand at court. They were given the new title of Grooms of the Chamber and were expected to take part in various court functions: there are records of the red cloth they were given to wear in the Coronation procession and of payment for the often surprising services expected of them: one recorded commission was to welcome the Spanish delegation at Dover in 1604 and escort them to London at the beginning of their three-week visit to sign the momentous peace agreement with England.

Of all the gaps in the documents that survive from the late Tudor and early Stuart times, one of the most frustrating is the lack of anything recording relations between Shakespeare and King James. James was no stickler when it came to rank and was always ready to abandon protocol in the interests of a good debate, whether with Jesuits, witches, Puritans, fellow writers or visiting ambassadors. In Scotland he had been at the centre of a distinguished literary and intellectual circle, and his writings reveal an intimate knowledge of contemporary English literature—one of his sonnets parodies English metre, another celebrates the poems of Sidney. The

early implementation and expansive wording of the charter he gave
Shakespeare's company suggests warm appreciation. Biographers usually
dismiss the idea that the King took any personal interest in Shakespeare;
yet it is scarcely credible that a man with the intellectual vanity of James,
who had as one of his attendants a best-selling poet and personable actor
widely acknowledged to be England's foremost dramatist, could have
resisted the temptation of sitting down with him to discuss, at the very
least, his own work.

The familiar disadvantages of the conspicuous position of court playwright, which certain sonnets explore in a Stuart context, must have been
greatly outweighed for Shakespeare by the unique opportunity it offered
of influencing the mind of the King.[11] For years, James's conscience had
been the object of continual assault by highly placed Catholics.[12] The
exiled English poet Henry Constable was one. He spent long months in
Edinburgh in 1599, obtaining occasional inconclusive interviews with
the King, but in the end returned to France with the dispiriting verdict
that James would never tolerate Catholicism, let alone convert. In 1605,
Constable had just arrived at Whitehall from Rome and was attempting
to capitalise on a last brief period of royal favour. But, firmly ensconced
near the centre of James's court, Shakespeare evidently hoped to do better. He was by now expert in writing universal plays of unparalleled brilliance designed at the same time to persuade his audience to consider his
cause. *Othello*, *King Lear* and *Macbeth* are among his greatest master-
pieces, dramas that soar above the events of the day; but they contain forgotten evidence of one motive behind their extraordinary writing, an
intense, single-minded determination to counter the corrupting influence of James's new advisers and to make him listen to the 'sounds and
cries' of his suffering subjects. As in the case of Queen Elizabeth and
Love's Labour's Lost, *The Merchant of Venice* and *Twelfth Night*, they reveal
that the playwright had made a profound study of the psychology of his
patron, and that he used it to challenge, flatter and arouse the monarch's
formidable intelligence to an awareness of the damage that was being
done in the royal name.

His tactics were varied, but the most pleasing must have been that of
approaching James primarily as a writer and political theorist rather than
as a monarch. One by one, Shakespeare's first four plays make courteous
reference to the four books James published in England in 1603. *Measure
for Measure* takes its starting point from *Basilikon Doron*; *Othello* from *Lepanto* and the King's love sonnets; *King Lear* from *The Trew Law of Free*

Monarchies; and *Macbeth* from *Demonologie.* Shakespeare was evidently certain of his standing with the King, for within this framework he gets away with biting commentaries on England's current position, repeatedly querying the dangerous Stuart assumption that a monarch's status was guaranteed by divine right, rather than his capacity for responsible and enlightened leadership. These plays also reveal Shakespeare's growing disillusion with his increasingly callous and irresponsible patron. The series is concluded with *Timon of Athens,* a play which despairs of ever influencing the King.

The Hideous Law

THE FIRST OF Shakespeare's plays written for James was *Measure for Measure.* Performed at court along with *Othello* during the Christmas season of 1604, it is yet another conspicuous example of the way the incomplete history of the English Reformation has for centuries handicapped our appreciation of some of his cleverest work. The plot is one of his most cerebral, reflecting early Catholic hopes that the King might be brought to see reason by means of the kind of intellectual debate he loved. It presents a startling, unexpected angle on the events of his first year on the throne, giving full credit to his shrewd Scots cunning but opening his eyes to the fatal impact of his domestic and foreign policy on his Catholic subjects.

In the play, a duke delegates his entire authority to an untried deputy. The deputy protests at being granted such sweeping powers, but the duke hurries away: 'Your scope is as mine own', he repeats, telling him they will communicate by letter, as James did with Cecil. Left alone, the deputy reveals his true colours. A fanatical, though hypocritical, moralist, he revives a 'hideous law' (1.4.63) against illicit love-making and implements draconian penalties that the tolerant duke neglected. The first casualty is Claudio, who faces execution for sleeping with his fiancée. Claudio's sister, Isabella, about to join the order of Poor Clare nuns, is induced to plead for him with the new deputy—but in doing so, she inadvertently arouses his lust. Isabella indignantly refuses to save her brother's life by sleeping with the deputy—and is horrified to find her condemned brother guiltily wishing she would.

The play has reached the kind of moral question James found irresistible: is it right to risk damnation in order to save a life? But along the way the King's astute mind would not have missed those uncomfortable references. He too had delegated his authority to unworthy deputies, led by Cecil; his deputies too had revived dormant laws and given them new teeth; they too refused to countenance high-level pleas for mercy. In the play, the duke intervenes after secretly observing the conduct of his deputy and restores justice all round. As it turns out, it has all been a ducal ploy to test the deputy's character. Shakespeare suggests that this might be the case with James—that he too is about to reclaim the reins of power and restore justice.

Measure for Measure flatters James with the suggestion that he is the omniscient ruler who steps out from the shadows to awe his subjects with Solomon-like powers of judgment. He had impressed the country with just such a *coup de théâtre* shortly after his accession, reprieving three of Cecil's old enemies after a dramatic period of suspense on the scaffold. Similar moments would recur throughout the reign. James himself took centre stage at the 1604 Hampton Court Conference, in which he outwitted the Puritans in debate 'Delight to haunt your session and spy carefully their proceedings', James advised his son, 'be a daily watchman over your servants that they obey your laws precisely'. The play's 'old fantastical duke of dark corners' (4.3.152–153) embodies James's concept of kingcraft as described in *Basilikon Doron* but also exhibits James's own quirks of character, among them his fear of crowds and his notorious paranoia. James would have been on tenterhooks throughout the play to discover the fate of the backbiting Lucio, who sneers at the duke's reputation as scholar and statesman, opining that though 'the greater file of the subject held the Duke to be wise', he was actually 'a very superficial, ignorant unweighing fellow' (3.2.127–130). Lucio is sentenced to be hanged in the last scene: 'slandering a prince deserves it'. There are further flattering allusions—among them to James's deadpan sense of humour, and his idiosyncratic, speculative cast of mind: the duke is 'one that, above all other strifes, contended especially to know himself' (3.2.218–219).

As the plot unfolds, deft strokes of colour highlight the topical parallels—perhaps aware of James's reputedly short attention span, Shakespeare repeats his key point several times. The story of Angelo, the deputy, emphasises the central error of James's domestic policy—his unquestioning reliance on the civil service he found waiting for him in Whitehall. To underline the abuse of royal authority by James's advisers in reintroducing the penal laws, Shakespeare gives heavy emphasis to the theme of *Basilikon Doron*. Even the play's title comes from a passage in the book that specifically warns against delegating power to deputies who have scores to settle: 'And above all, let the *measure* of your love to everyone be according to the *measure* of their virtue . . . letting your favour to be no longer tied to any than the continuance of his virtuous disposition shall deserve, nor admitting the excuse upon a *just revenge to procure oversight to an injury*'. Shakespeare drives home the point by creating in Angelo a memorable portrait of a hypocritical, worldly Puritan. Remember what you wrote about justice, pleads the play—deal with Catholics yourself, don't hand them over to their traditional enemies. He spells out the precise dates of Angelo's revived statutes, relating them closely to the anti-Catholic statutes revived by Parliament in 1604 and reinforced by the Privy Council in 1605. One is '19 zodiacs' old, like the 1585 'Act against Jesuits . . . and suchlike Disobedient Persons' that made sheltering a priest a capital offence; the other, fourteen years old, matches the 'Proclamation' of October 1591, which invited the whole nation to hunt down recusants.

Further precise touches relate the bargaining over the fate of poor Claudio to the repercussions for English Catholics of James's foreign policy coup—peace with Spain. The nun's name, Isabella, linked with a Poor Clare convent, would have brought to mind someone as closely identified with Spanish Catholicism as the name Orsini was with the Vatican. Isabella Clara Eugenia, Archduchess of Flanders, was the sister of Philip III of Spain. A popular figure in Flanders and in England, she was renowned for her beauty, piety and common sense. The Spanish royal family, and Isabella Clara in particular, had close links with the Poor Clare nuns; among many other good works in Flanders, Isabella founded a number of convents for the Poor Clares. In spite of her Catholicism, her claim to the English throne had been supported at various points by Cecil as well as Persons. Though she resisted their diplomatic overtures, she was among the first to congratulate James on his accession, assured that he would bring toleration to Catholics. Yet she did nothing to bring it about; her brother's anodyne peace treaty with England went ahead without protest.

The ineffectual Isabella in the play, who has to be prompted and nudged into pressing her brother's suit, would have reminded English Catholics of the inexplicably half-hearted support by Catholic leaders abroad like Isabella Clara. They could not have known that even before the peace treaty was discussed, Spain had washed its hands of their cause. The Spanish Ambassador had reported that James would never relent, and the Primate of Spain shrugged off the whole business, arguing that Spain had no moral obligation towards a group that was not, after all, composed of Spanish subjects.[13]

This issue would have been particularly close to Shakespeare's heart. One of the tasks of the King's Men as they accompanied the delegation from Dover to London was to arrange for interviews between Spanish delegates and imprisoned priests and recusants, ostensibly an information-gathering exercise into the true state of English Catholics. This experience may account for the spine-chilling dungeon scenes in the play, in which the visiting Isabella's piously resigned platitudes meet Claudio's anguished 'Ay, but to die and go we know not where, To lie in cold obstruction and to rot . . .' (3.1.119–120).[14]

Abandoned by Spain, desperate English Catholics proposed that Rome should purchase toleration for them by bribing James's counsellors. Publicly, the papacy reacted with the same horror the nun in the play exhibited. The suggestion was 'unworthy and scandalous'. But secretly, the Church acted on it. Before long every influential member of the English government, Cecil included, was receiving hefty retainers from Spain in return for promises to work for toleration. *Measure for Measure* dramatises the one-sided bargain. Like Spain getting into bed with James's corrupt advisers, the saintly Isabella at last agrees to pretend to trade her virtue for her brother's life. And exactly like the advisers who took the Spanish money and did nothing to stop the persecution, the cynical Angelo beds 'Isabella'—in fact, his disguised ex-mistress—and goes ahead with Claudio's execution regardless. So Shakespeare reminds James about—or perhaps alerts him to—the grubby role played by his Privy Council in facilitating the peace treaty.

The play's minor characters give a further taste of the style of the Jacobean court. The two-faced courtier Lucio is a new and depressing variation on Shakespeare's sequence of 'Luke' names. He is a portrait of the rising breed of unscrupulous Catholic who came to prominence under James, the result of Cecil's skillful pre-accession window-dressing. The most conspicuous examples were the Howard family, who seized the opportunities offered by Cecil and made a fortune over the next decade, their greed and immorality dragging into disrepute both the public face of Catholicism and the already dissolute image of James's court. Equally topical is the fate of Mariana, Angelo's mistress, ditched the moment she lost her dowry. She is yet another image of the original Puritan ideal, outlawed by the state religion, its aims betrayed by worldly Puritan zealots such as Edward Coke, the

Attorney-General, and the Chief Justice, John Popham—the men who implemented the persecution of Catholics under James.

At first sight a flattering 'patronage' play, *Measure for Measure* contains not only urgent pleas to James to listen to the 'cries of men' but grim premonitions of the future position of the monarchy. It is a minutely political drama—the unlikely ending in which Claudio lives and the duke weds Isabella is one of the many aspects that make sense only on the allegorical level, expressing the longed-for solution to the whole unhappy problem— the re-union of Stuart England with the universal Catholic Church.

True Hearts Cannot Bear It

B UT ALONGSIDE *Measure for Measure*, a drama dominated by politics, Shakespeare was engaged on a greater work. It is difficult now to think of *Othello* as being in any sense a topical play. But to an audience in 1604, the year when dawning toleration altered abruptly to a persecution 'by many degrees passing all former times', the poetic language and resonant imagery of this agonising universal drama would have had a contemporary application. Those accustomed to Shakespeare's code would have seen in the tragic triumph of 'dark' over 'fair' the latest chapter in the story of their own country—a story of valour and nobility deluded by evil into murdering its own soul.

Though the many court Catholics would have been the first to grasp the full meaning of the play, its theme suggests that they were not Shakespeare's primary target: again, it was James. The extraordinary boldness with which he addressed the King in *Othello* reveals his genius at full stretch, fusing layers of political insight, covert supplication and oblique flattery into a timeless drama. Scholars have played down the extent to which *Othello* was designed for James, and in particular James the author of *Lepanto*, a poem marked by passages of often ridiculous doggerel. But there is nothing sycophantic about the intimate relationship between *Othello* and James's poetry. It reveals instead how intently Shakespeare applied himself to the task of manipulating the complex character of the king in the early years of the reign. Long experience of adroitly confronting Elizabeth with uncomfortable issues enabled Shakespeare to burrow deeply— in places, mercilessly—into his patron's psyche, gambling on the probability that a man like James—unpompous, good-humoured, intellectually curious—would be a willing subject, a man who 'strove ever to know himself'. It would seem the gamble paid off. *Macbeth* and *King Lear* continue the same vein, suggesting that the King may have valued his dramatist as much as an analyst and commentator as a court entertainer.

James's youthful poem *Lepanto* takes the form of an enthusiastic celebration of a great Catholic victory. It begins and ends in Paradise, where God and his angels, led by St Michael, stir up Christendom against the pagan Turk, supported by an Iago-like Satan—'deceiver, liar, hating men'. The narrative describes the battle of 1571 in which Don John of Austria, supported by the League of Catholic Princes, defeated the Turks and drove them from the strategically vital Venetian colony of Cyprus. Lepanto revived the quintessentially Catholic devotion to Our Lady of the Rosary to whom Pius V attributed the victory. Its hero, Don John, was a particular hate-figure for Protestants, who also viewed the papal and Spanish forces as representatives of the Antichrist. James's cheerfully ecumenical poem was omitted from the 1616 publication of his *Collected Works*.

Its publication in England in 1603, although prefaced with assurances that it was a Protestant allegory that in no way praised a 'foreign Papist bastard', looks like yet another of the King's pre-accession gestures to hopeful English Catholics. Shakespeare seized on it, setting *Othello*'s opening scenes in a Venice similarly under threat from the Turkish fleet. Its action, too, is driven by angelic and demonic forces, a satanic Iago feuding with a man whose first name, Michael, is that of *Lepanto*'s archangel. *Othello* is a tribute to James's authorship, but also a reminder of the misleading promises of toleration that smoothed his way to the throne of England.

Shakespeare again puts not just James's work, but James himself at the centre of his drama. The concept of racial 'blackness' evidently had an appeal for the royal couple, who commissioned four Africans to dance in the snow at their wedding in Norway. James and Anne resumed the theme when they arrived in England. The first recorded performance of *Othello*, featuring a Moorish hero, was at court in November 1604; the following winter saw a sequel, the *Masque of Blacknesse*, devised by Ben Jonson and Inigo Jones, which featured Queen Anne and her ladies as Ethiopian women, complete with black make-up. Jonson distanced himself from the concept behind the masque—'it was her majesty's will to have them black-amoors'. For Shakespeare the royal predilection for dark skin was a gift: he was able to use it to portray James as the embodiment of Northern Protestantism.

The plot is Shakespeare's simplest and most concentrated. Othello is persuaded by his evil lieutenant, Iago, to murder his adored wife, Desdemona. Iago has convinced him that she is conducting an affair with their closest friend, Michael Cassio. When he discovers the truth, Othello kills himself. So deeply moving is this great tragedy that for most of us, the force of the universal drama overwhelms any topical meanings it may once have held. Yet for Shakespeare's clever, uncertain patron it would have had added impact; his own portrait, his own personal dilemma, lay at the centre of this masterpiece.

Like the duke in *Measure for Measure*, Othello has some of James's most recognisable characteristics. A champion of the institution of marriage, James was fond of depicting himself and the realm as a married couple, and his subjects as his children. He saw himself as 'Husband of the whole Isle'. The play's image of a bridegroom allegorically embracing spiritual England corresponded with much of his own political rhetoric. Shakespeare gives a personal edge to the identification by linking Othello's courtship of Desdemona with James's courtship of Anne, reminding him of their affectionate early relationship. James's sonnets to his wife go beyond mere convention and suggest that she kept his inner demons at bay: 'Your smiling is an antidote against / The melancholy that oppresseth me', he writes. Anne's love calms the 'raging wrath' that reigns within him. She is his 'sweet Doctor' who can cure his 'heavy heart', she is his 'only lamp of light'. The tales that won Desdemona echo the anecdotes James liked to tell about his past and suggest that their original romance sprang from Anne's sympathy with James's wretched childhood and endangered later life. As Othello says of Desdemona, 'She loved me for the dangers I had passed; / And I loved her that she did pity them'. James, like Othello, suffered 'most disastrous chances' from his 'boyish days'; his 'hairbreadth escapes' included being 'taken by the insolent foe' (1.3.128–170).[15] The 'deserts', or 'deserted places', of Othello's past resemble the dangerous wilds of sixteenth-century Scotland repeatedly traversed by the impoverished Scottish King—'rough quarries, rocks and hills whose heads touch heaven'. Even the tempest that separates the honeymoon pair in the play may have recalled the circumstances of their engagement, for when James chivalrously decided to travel out to Norway to meet his bride, storms at first kept the pair apart. Other markers link James and Othello: his favourite oath, 'Zounds', for instance, figures often in the play. By the end of the first act, the King would have found it difficult to avoid identifying with Othello, a noble foreigner whose wife falls in love not with his looks but with his mind and his 'pitiful' past.

At the same time, he could not have failed to notice that his own name had been given to the villain—a character who embodied his darker nature, the coarse, blasphemous, flippant, Machiavellian already being satirised by his disappointed English subjects. The name 'Iago' was universally familiar as Sant' Iago, or St James, of Compostella, the greatest centre of European pilgrimage. Commentators note the aptness, for Sant' Iago was known as Matamoro, the Moor-slayer: and Shakespeare's Iago destroys the Moor, Othello.[16] If James detected the elements of his own personality in both Othello and Iago, he would have realised that on one level this tremendous play was dramatising the scenario of his own potential self-destruction. Though he frequently exaggerated the courageous feats of his youth, James had demonstrated fortitude and good judgment as King of Scotland, and his early married life had been happy. But the comparative luxury of the English throne was proving fatal to him. Estranged from his wife, surrounded by favourites, James was now being manipulated by adroit government ministers intent on pursuing their own political agenda.

In order to develop a pointed personal morality tale, Shakespeare sets his play within the complex psyche of his patron, a dark landscape in which James's better nature battles with his demons. A format for what looks like a distinctly modern type of drama in fact derives from the medieval tradition of morality plays such as *Everyman* and *Mankind*, in which a good and an evil spirit compete for the possession of a man's soul—a format known as a *psychomachia*, which Shakespeare alludes to several times in his work.[17] Cassio and Iago have the attributes of good and evil spirits engaged in a struggle over Othello's soul; and his soul is personified in Desdemona, whose name suggests that, like all souls, she is desired by demons. In the style of morality plays, Othello's fall begins when his evil spirit deposes his good angel.

At the opening of the play, the recently Christianised Othello is closely linked to the cerebral, musical, light-hearted Michael Cassio, who helped him win Desdemona.[18] But the storm separates Cassio from Othello; he proves no match for Iago, who in true Satanic terms hates the 'daily beauty in his life / Which makes me ugly' (5.1.20). Drunkenness undoes Cassio's 'higher' faculties, allowing Iago to debase the weakened Othello until he is misled into killing Desdemona. James would have found himself watching a story in which he himself loses his own integrity as his darker side overwhelms his 'free and open nature' (1.3.393). Iago repeatedly identifies himself with Othello's inmost self: 'I am your own forever'

(3.3.483), an identity Othello acknowledges in the line 'I am bound to thee forever . . .' (3.3.218).

But this perceptive piece of psychoanalysis, an illustration of the damage James was doing to himself, was designed to awaken in James a deeper awareness of the damage he was doing to the country. In this tightly plotted play, James's spiritual self-betrayal is closely linked to his betrayal of England, the moment when he yielded to the persuasion of Cecil and the Privy Council to break what Catholics saw as his nuptial vow to the country. The whole metaphor of a honeymoon gone sour exactly expresses the relationship between English Catholicism and James. Iago, chosen by Othello as his soul-mate in preference to Cassio and Desdemona, bears the marks not simply of James's own dark side but of the unscrupulous men on the make who now thronged the court and packed the Privy Council, entirely concerned, as foreign observers noted, with jockeying for position and making money, as Iago does out of bogus promises of patronage. His loathing for Cassio and Desdemona mirrors the loathing of many of them for Catholicism—a motive for Iago's famously motiveless malignity.

Cassio has a corresponding series of Catholic attributes. Bianca, his mistress, shares her 'fair' name with the Catholic figure in *The Taming of the Shrew*. He makes an elaborately spiritual speech on Desdemona's arrival in Cyprus, welcoming her in terms that appear wildly exalted: 'Let her have your knees. / Hail to thee lady! and the grace of heaven, / Before, behind thee and on every hand / Enwheel thee round!' (2.1.67–87). In the context of Cyprus and the Turkish fleet, Cassio's address would have brought the concept of Our Lady of the Rosary strongly to mind—the invitation to kneel, the central prayer 'Hail Mary, full of grace', the protective 'enwheeling' effect of the rosary's circle of beads, an image that was the subject of a number of Catholic engravings at the time.[19] As so often in Shakespeare's work, the purpose of extravagant language is to introduce specific references. In the wake of Lepanto, the rosary was thought of by many hopeful Catholics as a powerful spiritual weapon. Henry Garnet, leader of the Jesuit mission, printed his book on the rosary on secret presses shortly after his arrival in England in the belief that the spread of the devotion would dispel heresy.

Cassio's rhapsodic greeting identifies Desdemona as the essence of the Catholic faith, miraculously emerging from the tempest in spite of treacherous shoals and rocks. In a highly condensed phrase, he links her with the central Catholic doctrine of the Eucharist, which used Aristotle's distinction between essence and existence to express the way God was present within consecrated bread. Desdemona, he says, is one who 'in th'essential vesture of creation / Does tire [attire] th'inginer [Creator]' (2.1.64)—in other words, like the Eucharist in the Catholic Mass, she is the aspect of creation that provides an earthly garment for the creator. Anti-papist rhetoric further identifies Desdemona with Catholicism. Othello lashes her with the apocalyptic language extremist Puritans reserved for Antichrist and the Whore of Babylon: 'a she-devil', who has 'the office opposite St. Peter' (4.2.92–93). Her death is surrounded by images of martyrdom in a scene that suggests that Catholic England, having survived so much, failed to survive the Protestant embrace of the new reign.

Part of the poignancy of Othello's murder of Desdemona arises from the inspired inclusion of an element ignored by many embittered Catholics. This was the genuine idealism of many of the most destructive reformers. Shakespeare does more than protest at the assault on Catholicism by crude opportunists like Iago, who took a sadistic pleasure in the process. He enters into the mind of the visionary men who were originally responsible: intellectuals capable of appreciating and regretting the wealth of spiritual and aesthetic beauty that had to be destroyed for the sake of true Reformation. They approached the removal of the old order in the spirit of Othello entering Desdemona's chamber: 'It is the cause, it is the cause, my soul' (5.2.1.); for them it was not vengeful destruction but a 'sacrifice' of something they treasured (5.2.68).[20] However alluring its centuries-old beauty, they argued, medieval spirituality had become inwardly corrupt, worldly and compromised: 'she must die, else she'll betray more men' (5.2.6). As Othello recoils from the murder, he describes the sleeping Desdemona from the point of view of such reformers, for whom the breathtaking artistry of England's churches and monastic libraries was all hopelessly contaminated by the corruptions of Rome, the 'Whore of Babylon'. Desdemona is seen as a precious book, a piece of 'monumental alabaster' (5.2.5). 'Was this fair paper, this most goodly book, made to write "whore" upon?' (4.2.72–73). Shakespeare had known such men and had witnessed the change of heart many experienced at the beginning of the century. Just at the point when the government was setting about the final stages of the extinction of English Catholicism, many woke up to the fact—too late—that along with the abolition of abuses they were losing something irrecoverable and essential to the life of the country. Their position was that of the remorseful Othello, 'One whose hand, / Like the base Indian, threw the pearl away / Richer than all his tribe' (5.2.350).

Having wrecked the place 'where I have garnered up my heart, / Where either I must live or bear no life . . .' (4.2.58–59), Othello dwells on the terrible permanence of the loss: 'Once put out thy light, / Thou cunning'st pattern of excelling nature, / I know not where is that Promethean heat / That can thy light relume' (5.2.12–13).

The unexpected mouthpiece for the furious indignation aroused by Desdemona's murder is Iago's wife, Emilia, until her mistress's death a pragmatic, worldly character who laughs at the idea of self-sacrifice. Her sudden transformation is one of the most vivid portraits of the sense of outrage that drove thousands of ordinary men and women in England to take a stand at this period—her use of 'whore' and 'true' touch on the theological debate, and Shakespeare generalises her reaction, as in so many emblematic moments like these. 'My lord has so bewhored her . . . that true hearts cannot bear it' (4.2.115).

The personal morality tale contained within *Othello* is designed to hold the attention of a man 'who strove especially to know himself'; but once he has James on the psychiatrist's couch, Shakespeare delivers political as well as therapeutic advice. Like *Measure for Measure*, the play contains an urgent message for the King that was to be reinforced next in *Macbeth* and *King Lear*—royal authority must not fall into the hands of base men like Angelo and Iago; it must be exercised responsibly. In spite of his own excellent books on the duties of a monarch, James increasingly inclined to the view that a monarch ruled by divine right, irrespective of his obligations to his subjects. Shakespeare's repeated warnings reveal that from the very beginning, he had identified the chronic Stuart weakness that within forty years would lead the country to civil war.

THE POWDER KEG, 1605–1606

Groans and Complaints and Tears of Blood

SOMETIME IN March 1605, an interview took place between the Venetian Ambassador, Nicolo Molin, and Robert Cecil. 'I asked him', said Molin, 'what was the cause of this extraordinary movement against the Catholics, for I could see no reason which justified the persecution'. Cecil's reply was lengthy and considered but in the end unyielding: 'My lord, it cannot be helped: there are laws that must be observed'. Under further pressure, Cecil defended his recent record— 'Whereas under the late Queen the sequestered property passed to strangers who, in order to wring as much out of it as possible, ruined the houses and lands of the recusant, now the sequestered property will be let to its owners at a very moderate price'; nonetheless, he ended, 'there is no doubt but that the object of these laws is to extinguish the Catholic religion in this country'. 'My Lord', pressed Molin, 'it is a great matter, that though the Catholic religion is prohibited in many countries in none is it persecuted as here'. What had happened, he asked, to James's assurance on his accession to the English throne that he 'did not desire either blood or property of any man for religion's sake?' 'As far as blood goes', answered Cecil, 'rest assured, provided the Catholics keep quiet; but as regards property'—and here one can almost see the apologetic smile, the delicate shrug—'the laws must be enforced'.

Molin evidently left the interview in an agitated state. His house was a resort for dissidents and he was well aware of the desperate mood of English Catholics, abandoned by their foreign allies and now a soft target for their enemies at home. On 30 March, he wrote, 'The persecution of Catholics is vigorously conducted, all suspicious houses are searched and if crosses or anything indicating the Catholic religion is found, the owner is imprisoned'. A few months later he was comparing Cecil's assurance that no blood was shed on religious grounds with the reality. Not only were Catholics still being executed—in one case, merely for writing a letter persuading a friend to convert—but for many, imprisonment amounted to a death sentence. In certain prisons 'they are so closely guarded and so badly treated that they die of want . . . in this way they claim that they do not proceed with the blood penalty, but execution takes place all the same, and perhaps with even greater cruelty'. As for property, 'goods have for some time past been seized quite as rapaciously as ever in the late Queen's time'.

Nowadays the assumption is that James was a more tolerant monarch than Elizabeth—but records of the raids, seizures and imprisonments of the time suggest the reverse. Molin ends with a vivid picture of the state of English Catholics in the early months of 1605. 'Those who are touched in their property and person, torn by cruel rage and wounded by the government, cry aloud to heaven that they are abandoned. And so all about us are groans, and complaints, and tears of blood. They live in a perpetual dread of losing their property today, their liberty tomorrow, their life the day after, as has happened to many'.[1]

Others had similar premonitions about the political powder keg on which the king and his government were by now quite literally sitting; like Molin, they did their best to make the strongest possible case for toleration towards the King. Among them was Shakespeare. *King Lear* is one of his least cautious plays, an unvarnished dramatisation of the state of James's England, a final attempt before the catastrophe of 5 November to awaken the King to the intolerable humiliations and sufferings of his Catholic subjects. Here he exchanges the ingeniously coded themes of *Othello* and *Measure for Measure* for more direct tactics, doubling up two well-known allegories of the state of England in order to drive home an unpalatable message: England had shamefully mistreated its most loyal subjects and had betrayed itself into the hands of a group of amoral opportunists.

All Dark and Comfortless

THE POLITICAL THEME may be unusually explicit, but Shakespeare continues to deploy devious subtlety in attracting and holding the attention of the King—for though there is a record of a performance of *Lear* by a recusant company at Gowthwayte Hall in Yorkshire before a Catholic audience likely to hang on every word, its primary target was clearly James, the man who could actually reverse the catastrophe. Nonetheless, it was a risky undertaking: witnessing the second half of the play would have been an uncomfortable experience for a monarch who could not avoid identifying himself with King Lear. Perhaps not surprisingly, there is only one record of a court performance.

At the outset, James would have been an attentive spectator. His playwright had taken yet another of his own books as the starting point for his play—in this case *The Trew Law of Free Monarchies*, which characterised the monarch as a fond father, his subjects as devoted children, willingly bound to him by an oath of unconditional loyalty. Moreover, Shakespeare appeared to be making exactly James's own point about the perils of a divided kingdom—a timely reminder to a government debating James's pet project, the proposed union between England and Scotland.

Most of the audience would have known the old story, set in pre-Christian Britain, in which the aging King Lear decides to share out his kingdom among his three daughters, requiring in return only an avowal of their undivided love for their father. The older two, Goneril and Regan, comply readily, but Cordelia, the youngest, objects, pointing out that a daughter must reserve some love for her husband. The enraged Lear banishes Cordelia, who leaves the country to marry the king of France. Before long, the two older sisters show their true colours, callously evicting Lear and quarrelling among themselves. Cordelia forgives her penitent father, and in all previous versions of the story, Lear regains his throne.

Many of Shakespeare's alterations to the story were designed to encourage James to identify with Lear; and the most obvious would have been the addition of Lear's fool, a caustic character childishly dependent on his master. James arrived in England accompanied by the young Archibald Armstrong, a jester to whom he was deeply attached, the first official court fool since the days of Henry VIII. The extent to which he was indulged and, worst of all, enriched, disgusted the English court elite, whom Armstrong was permitted to insult at will. His patronage was sought on all sides—he even received a pension from Spain. In spite of his many enemies, his influence with the king continued throughout the long reign, and he went on to serve Charles I, publishing books of jests at the end of his life that closely resemble the weaker jokes of Lear's fool. Shakespeare dramatises James's fondness for his fool as a neat method of attacking the dark side of the new regime in the 'all-licensed' manner of Armstrong.

Other artful details would have caught and held James's attention—the first line, for instance, suggests that Albany and Cornwall are Lear's two heirs and that Lear favoured one above the other. As Cornwall and Albany were titles that belonged to James's two sons, and James was beginning to have trouble with the elder, this would have drawn him into the political background of a play that swiftly develops all the characteristics of James's court life—a background of hunts and hunting dogs, of a transient, shambolic royal household, of government conducted by correspondence, of hidden loyalties and underhand plots.

Above all, Shakespeare plays on the royal sense of injury. Dimly, James was beginning to realise the extent to which he was being cheated by the men to whom he had handed over the government of England. Years later, the courtier Anthony Weldon looked back on these years and recalled the gossip of the time: how all business passed through the hands of the 'great managers of the State', in particular Cecil, now politically unassailable and amassing vast sums from his control over the Customs farm and the Court of Wards as well as numerous lesser scams; how the King, 'though he enriched the elite he did beggar himself and the nation in general . . . so was the poor King and State cheated on all hands'.[2] In addition, James had already discovered that Parliament was unaccountably intent on reducing, rather than endorsing, the authority of their divinely appointed monarch. Goneril and Regan's charges of riotousness, their querying of royal expenditure—'What need you five and twenty [followers], ten or five / To follow . . . What need one?' would have been a bitter reminder to James of recent unseemly haggling with Parliament over—as James saw it—matters of bare subsistence. Like James, the Lear of the first two acts is a vigorous man, unable to come to terms with the premature loss of authority he himself has sanctioned and which is instantly exploited by unscrupulous subjects.

But the most important parallel between the play and the King's concerns was that between Cordelia's refusal to make a public affirmation of unconditional love and the refusal of Catholic and radical Puritans to affirm their loyalty by taking the Oath of Supremacy. Shakespeare encourages James to make the connection by creating a certain sympathy with Lear's shocked reaction. He emphasises the unexpectedness of Cordelia's refusal, the element of unnecessary soul-searching over what to everyone else was merely formal procedure. Older stories include an explanation for Cordelia's refusal—but Shakespeare makes it come as a bolt from the blue. His Earl of Kent, too, is rude and confrontational in his defence of Cordelia. James could have safely identified with a king 'more sinned against than sinning' right through to the storm scene in Act 3, seeing in Cordelia's exile to France the exile of wilfully obstinate Puritan and Catholic dissenters. Continuing to appeal to the self-interest of his royal audience, Shakespeare goes on to paint an extended picture of the disintegration of a monarch and a country that deliberately alienates its most loyal subjects, forcing men like Kent and Edgar, Gloucester's son, to adopt disguise in order to serve their country and delivering supporters like the Earl of Gloucester into the hands of vengeful sadists. It was a line of approach designed to associate in James's mind the return of Catholicism with the return to full royal authority, free from the constraints imposed by an unfilial Parliament and offering deliverance from a clique of power-hungry counsellors. It is possible that pleas like Molin's and Shakespeare's had an effect, for at about this time James set about re-drafting the Oath of Supremacy as an Oath of Allegiance, allegedly to make it more acceptable to Catholics.

But though James was a key target, Shakespeare had a wider audience in mind. The Elizabethan dissidents who had been reinstated at court under James included many long-term aficionados of the hidden levels of such literature as Shakespeare's plays, a form of writing in which many of them were adept. These sophisticated spectators might at first have been surprised at Shakespeare's choice of subject. They had heard it all before. Only a year earlier an anonymous play had been published entitled *King Leir and his three daughters*. Versions of the old story were commonplace— but this one contained an even clearer allegorical treatment of the banishment of Catholicism than Shakespeare's. At first sight it appears that Shakespeare simply took over *King Leir*, complete with allegory, and developed it for court performance.

As so often, however, Shakespeare is not borrowing from his source but responding to it. The intellectual elite among his audience and his readers would have been alert to every nuance, more aware than we are of his position in the great debate that lay just below the surface of the literature of the time. And in his answer to the earlier *Leir* they would have read a harrowing expression of the despair felt by James's more humane subjects in the early years of his reign.

Though superficially similar, the allegories of the two plays in fact contradict each other. *Leir's* Cordelia is more explicitly Catholic than Shakespeare's. Surrounded by the vocabulary of recusant literature, she is banished partly because her sisters are jealous of her beauty and piety. Her behaviour, too, identifies her as exiled Catholicism, because, in disguise, she revives the exiled Leir with a meal symbolising the forbidden Mass— like the food of Elias or Aeson, it is 'blessed manna', which, Leir realises gratefully, 'hath recalled my spirits home again'. Then, in a scene that is ludicrous on the naturalistic level, *Leir* picks up the topical subject of the oath, emphasising Persons's and Allen's solution to the key question of Catholic allegiance by making father and daughter kneel continuously to each other, Leir acknowledging his daughter's spiritual ascendancy, Cordelia honouring her father's material support. Moreover, *Leir* ends happily. Cordelia and her husband, the French king, assemble a force to restore Leir to his throne—a force that includes resistance fighters under the banner of 'St Denis and St George' led by an English soldier, Lord Mumford, and containing a regiment of Gauls 'Sir-named Redshanks'.[3] 'Redshanks' is a crucial giveaway, as it was the nickname given to the bare-legged Catholic soldiers of the Scottish highlands who periodically joined forces with the Irish. The invasion is a walkover. Clownish watchmen abandon their Armada beacons and the play ends with the happy picture of the restoration of the old order. A benign Providence hovers over *Leir*, answering the prayers of the patient king and his virtuous daughter and justifying the doctrine of passive resistance, expressed in terms all too familiar to English Catholics: 'Let us submit us to the will of God, / Things past all sense let us not seek to know, / It is God's will, and there-fore must be so'.

One can only imagine the sense of hopelessness with which Catholic readers would have put down this outdated version of English political events, a reminder of everything they had lost. The truth was that the invasion never happened; there was no restoration; Providence had turned out to be deaf; the policy of submission had proved suicidal. It could well have been with something of the same anger that was by now driving plot-ters against the King that Shakespeare took a heavy pencil to the idyllic Elizabethan *King Leir*, scoring through the delusion and replacing it with the harsh Jacobean reality. To add force to his case he added a parallel alle-gory from Sidney's *Arcadia*, a tale of a mistreated father succoured by a misunderstood child. Shakespeare's final version of the story of Lear is densely peopled and uncharacteristically diffuse; it has had mixed reviews ever since. For once, Shakespeare's dramatic control falters. His correc-tions reveal that he was aware that the play was too long, that it lacked momentum, that parts of the scene on the heath were unactable. But as a piece of writing, the consensus is that it is his most moving piece of work—intolerably moving to readers like the great eighteenth-century critic Samuel Johnson, who 'could not endure to ever read again the last scenes of the play'.[4]

Shakespeare's *Lear* retains the central allegorical theme of *Leir:* the exile of spirituality through England's crass demand for unconditional allegiance. But though King Lear recognises his error, the invasion fails, its defeat announced by Cordelia in terms that would have gone straight to the heart of a Catholic onlooker: 'We are not the first / Who with best meaning have incurred the worst' (5.3.3–4). This time, the heavens are not obviously just. Far from assisting the oppressed, Providence in Shakespeare's play acts exactly as it appeared to do to England's Catholics—with almost perverse cruelty.

As in *Titus Andronicus*, Shakespeare compresses into the plot a coded history of England's Reformation experience—one reason behind the extended spectacle of Lear on the heath, his madness the vehicle for a wealth of topical reference. Early in the play, Lear's Stuart characteristics become subsumed into a grander figure, that of England. 'Come not between the dragon and his wrath', growls Lear as he banishes Cordelia, evoking England's old heraldic device—the dragon under which England fought such battles as Crécy and separated from the universal church under Henry VIII (1.1.121). Shakespeare's 'low'-voiced Cordelia has fewer Catholic markers than *Leir's*; she incorporates all whose conscience forbade them to take the oath, representing the concept of banished truth rather than simply banished Catholicism. And now Shakespeare embarks on one of his compressed, emblematic histories, designed for the attentive reader rather than the stage. Having uprooted the source of its spirituality, the country, personified by Lear, spirals downwards through all the stages of disintegration lamented by critics of the Reformation. Instead of escaping abroad, Shakespeare's Lear remains in England, his 'thin helm' (4.7.36) exposed to the full brunt of a Reformation tempest that eventually destroys him. Like the reformers in *Julius Caesar*, Lear at first urges on the storm—his rhetoric is that of the early Levellers, wildly invoking apocalyptic destruction of a corrupt social and religious order. Briefly, he experiences a genuine Reformation change of heart, sympathising with houseless wretches, attacking injustice, vowing to 'shake the superflux' (3.4.35) of society to the suffering poor. But before long, just as with England, narrow Calvinism takes hold as Lear recoils from women, devils and the flesh, setting up a commission to judge and 'anatomise' (3.6.75) his daughters. When Cordelia at last finds him, he is a broken victim of the tempest, crowned with 'idle weeds' (4.4.5) that entwine the corn, like the wicked biblical tares. He has reached the state of the country described by many at the end of the 1590s—psychologically adrift, with a self-seeking cabal at its head. Though Cordelia restores him to fragile health, the pair fail to unseat the new regime and are led off to prison. Lear fondly imagines the simple contentment they will find there in each other's company, sustained by the spirituality that did indeed light up prison life for English dissidents. But the gods destroy even this humble vision of the survival of old ways—'and so we'll live, / And pray, and sing and tell old tales' (5.3.11–12)—Cordelia is hanged, and Lear dies of a broken heart. On the allegorical level, the message is clear: the destructive force of the Reformation has extinguished integrity and truth in England.

However, one often unnoticed form of goodness triumphs at the end of the play. Edgar, the virtuous son of the Earl of Gloucester, defeats the regime's champion in single combat and inherits the kingdom. Critics have problems with this bizarre character. His actions much of the time are completely inexplicable. His nonsensical ravings prolong the scenes on the heath; his treatment of his blind father is grotesque; his grave soliloquies are at odds with his unpredictable actions. Yet he, too, represents a carefully worked parallel to a certain aspect of post-Reformation England—for on the covert level the story of Edgar mirrors in every detail the story of the Counter-Reformation Jesuit underground mission to England.

The record of the Jesuits in England was one of the chief talking points in the first years of James's reign: James himself was intrigued by their erudition and enjoyed testing them out in theological debates. One veteran just released from prison was Southampton's Jesuit cousin Thomas Pounde, a man who may well have been known among friends and family as 'poor Tom', for he had spent thirty years in no fewer than fifteen jails and now in his late sixties had been released, only to be tried by the Star Chamber and sentenced to lose his ears and stand in the pillory for protesting against the treatment of Catholics.[5] Robert Southwell was again in the news: his *Humble Supplication* had just been published, though it was rapidly suppressed. In 1603, Father William Weston, a long-term prisoner and Catholic figurehead, was mobbed by supporters as he left jail, a blind and broken man, to go into exile. His dynamic colleague, John Gerard, was still moving undetected among the governing elite, making conversions through effective use of St Ignatius's *Exercises*, a spiritual handbook that contained powerful meditational techniques verging on what we would now call self-hypnosis. In spite of long periods on the rack, Gerard managed a spectacular escape from the Tower and, like Weston, survived to write a vivid account of his years in prison and on the run.

There is an unmistakable link, noted by all the commentaries, between Edgar and these men. As 'poor Tom', he uses many of the phrases that Samuel Harsnett attributes to Weston, Campion and Persons in his attack on Jesuit exorcisms, *A Declaration of Egregious Popish Impostures*. The phrases would have set up in the minds of many in the audience an association—though a safely critical one—between the disguised Edgar and the underground priests, alerting them to the fact that Edgar's 'pilgrimage' (5.3.196) through the play mirrors in careful detail the biographies of such priests. The parallels begin with the breathless scene in which he escapes pursuit—a scene that mirrors accounts at the time of the hue and cry that followed the hunted priests, during which the ports were put on alert and proclamations and descriptions posted everywhere. The many narrow escapes in the autobiographies are echoed in the desperate Edgar's quick-thinking stratagem to disguise himself as a mad beggar to avoid capture. His decision to mortify the flesh with nails and pins and to embrace destitution specifically recalls the exacting rule of the Society of Jesus, described with feeling by Southwell in his *Humble Supplication*. Edgar later talks of 'My oath, and my profession' (5.3.130). Loss of estate, in particular the loss of name for missionary Jesuits, is a frequent attribute of such figures in Shakespeare's plays. "Edgar I nothing am' (2.3.21), he declares, and later, in more chivalric style: 'Know, my name is lost, / By treason's tooth bare-gnawn and canker-bit' (5.3.121–122), although—an important point for Southwell, indignant at William Cecil's characterisation of the priests as dissolute and baseborn—'Yet am I noble as the adversary / I come to cope' (5.3.123–124). Edgar's privations as a wandering beggar, subsisting on vermin and stagnant water, have been carefully selected to recall the experiences of imprisoned priests, tortured, starved and reduced, according to Southwell, to licking moisture from the walls. Edgar's allusion to the demon who inflicts the 'web and pin' (3.4.115)—the contemporary term for 'cataract'—was particularly apposite to Weston, blinded by cataract and haunted by devils. Edgar intersperses his ravings with the simple Christian precepts disseminated by the Jesuits in such books as Persons's *Christian Directory* and Southwell's *Rule of Good Life*, works designed to replace the loss of credible communal worship with guides to domestic piety. The identification of Edgar with the covert missionaries also explains the oddity of his self-appointed role as spiritual guide. To Lear, Edgar is a 'philosopher' (3.4.168), a 'discarded father'

(3.4.71) with whom he wants private conversation, but the character to whom he is a genuine spiritual guide is his own father, the Earl of Gloucester.

Gloucester's sufferings are those of indignant bystanders driven by common humanity to assist recusants. He is incredulous at the outrageous response: 'When I desired their leave that I might pity him, they took from me the use of mine own house, charg'd me, on pain of perpetual displeasure, neither to speak of him, entreat for him, or any way sustain him . . .' (3.3.2–6). Gloucester's words echo the wording of acts and proclamations of the time. Most interesting of all, a Jesuit identification for Edgar gives a new context for the strange episode in which he allows his father to attempt suicide over an imaginary cliff. The inspiration for Edgar's conduct of Gloucester through despair to blind trust, acceptance and wisdom can be found in the influential *Spiritual Exercises*. Ignatius's classic work uses exactly the kind of intense visualisation Edgar conjures up of Dover Cliff and, like Edgar, employs the image of the soul poised between a good and evil spirit. Its aim is to induce a sense of wonder and an awareness of 'the end for which we are created'—the 'ripeness' acknowledged by Gloucester, preceded by the discovery that 'thy life's a miracle' (4.6.65). Moreover, Edgar invokes the aura of chivalric romance with which schoolboys at Douai and Rheims were taught to associate the enterprise of winning back their country to the faith. 'Childe Rowland to the dark tower came' (3.4.178), he says on the heath, as he escapes the 'bloody proclamation' (5.3.183). And it is this embattled figure, the image of the Ignatian soldier-priest, that routs the new order in Britain in single combat with his corrupted illegitimate brother, Edmund.

Edgar is too late to save Lear or Cordelia: but the Duke of Albany, the disillusioned remnant of the unpopular regime, his conscript army dispersed, welcomes the victor with open arms. Albany is designed to appeal to the better nature of the new wave of Catholic nobility who now held high office under Robert Cecil. In a moment of sudden clarity towards the end of the play, the sickened duke sees his allies for what they are. Oswald, Goneril's steward, has already been attacked by the loyal Kent as a Reformation time-server: 'Such smiling rogues as these, / Like rats, oft bite the holy cords a-twain / Which are too intrinse to unloose' (2.2.68–70). Albany is more succinct, damning Oswald as a man 'turned inside out'. And it is Albany who echoes an extended passage in the earlier *King Leir* that describes the dehumanising effect on England of the loss of the sacramental Cordelia—its well-spring poisoned, dame Nature's 'sweet milk' soured, a lament sounded throughout Shakespeare's work. Goneril is a monster, Albany says, because she has cut herself off from humanity's essential sustenance: 'That nature which contemns its origin / Cannot be bordered certain in itself; / She that herself will sliver and disbranch / From her material sap perforce must wither / And come to deadly use' (4.2.32–36). This was such a familiar attack on the English Reformation breach that Goneril brushes it off as a 'text' (4.2.37).

The gloomy landscape of *King Lear* bears out Albany's insight—it represents Shakespeare's fullest dramatisation of the amoral wasteland outlined in his two narrative poems, a country from which enlightened, humanist Christianity has been banished. It has been replaced by a vague belief in supernatural forces—the gods, the stars, fate—beliefs lightly derided by both Kent and Edgar. In this nightmare vision, humanity is cut off from its life-giving source and preys on itself 'like monsters of the deep' (4.2.50). The tempest on the heath and the abortive landing at Dover portray in literal form the effects of the breach: the Reformation storm and the foreign landing at Dover, which in the event brought not rescue, but a shameful peace deal.

If *Lear* was intended as a warning, it came too late. Shakespeare may still have been putting the finishing touches to the play when the tension highlighted by the Venetian Ambassador finally snapped. In the resulting fallout, even the heroic mission embodied in the figure of Edgar, the last glimmer of optimism for English Catholics, was to be damaged almost beyond repair.

Dire Combustion and Confused Events

At first sight, *Macbeth* seems almost carelessly put together. The text features extreme language, abrupt syntax, severed lines, violent oppositions. At the centre of the drama, oddly out of place, is a long debate on the nature of kingship. It is the shortest of Shakespeare's plays, and scholars detect in it signs of considerable cutting and rewriting. And yet the effect is overwhelming—it has the impact of a waking nightmare. Even allowing for the superstitious reputation of the play, based on its hair-raising invocations of the forces of evil, it has a mysterious extra dimension: behind the text, noted the nineteenth-century critic Bernard Maeterlinck, there appear to be 'a great host of hidden powers'.

The argument of this book is that 'hidden powers' lie behind every play. But *Macbeth* is an extreme case. Destined to be performed at court along with *King Lear* in the winter season of 1605–1606, the horrors of its original script were overtaken by a Catholic conspiracy to blow up the House of Lords, discovered and prevented at the last minute on 5 November 1605. The first court performance of *Macbeth* is thought to have been during the summer of 1606, giving Shakespeare time to work a commentary on the near catastrophe into an already complex play. One reason for the ruthless disregard for dramatic decorum, the abruptness, the deliberate lack of polish of *Macbeth* could be its concern to encompass the pain, anger and despair of English Catholics in the wake of the events of 5 November, when overnight, according to Ben Jonson, their religion numbered 'five hundred gentlemen less'.[6]

The most effective method of isolating Macbeth's 'Gunpowder Plot' commentary is to reconstruct the way a pre-Gunpowder Plot *Macbeth* may have looked. The fourth in the quartet of 'Stuart' plays based on the King's own works, it includes a string of reminders of James's treatise on dark forces, a subject on which he was an expert. James's *Daemonologie* takes the form of an encyclopaedic question-and-answer session in which the obliging King identifies a wide range of supernatural phenomena with the confidence and precision of an ornithologist. "I think ye take me to be a Witch myself', he jokes as he responds to pressing requests to discourse still further on 'the four principall partes' of one particular branch of 'the Devil's School'. He works his way through diabolism, possession, witchcraft and necromancy, returning several times to a theme Shakespeare picks up in *Macbeth*—the ease with which evil spirits lure weak characters who 'find their practice to prove true in sundry things' to follow the 'slippery and uncertain scale of curiosity to satisfy their restless minds' and in the end to become 'bond-slaves of their mortal enemy'. Though parts of the book sound sensational and prurient, James had in fact acquired his expertise through first-hand experience. Since childhood, he had been the nervous target of spells cast by such enemy necromancers as the 'Wizard' Earl of Bothwell. In 1590, convinced that witches were behind the storms which kept him from sailing to Denmark to meet his bride, he himself interrogated suspects at their trial at Berwick, publishing his findings in another book on witchcraft, *News from Scotland.*

The semi-historical plot assembled from Holinshed's Scottish chronicles —themselves a grisly saga of regicide and supernatural omens—would have added further interest, for, on the surface, the story pays graceful homage to James's kingship. Encouraged by the prophecies of three 'weird sisters', the soldier Macbeth seizes the Scottish throne, having murdered not only the virtuous King Duncan but his own friend Banquo, who suspects Macbeth and whose descendants, according to the sisters, would inherit the throne. While Duncan's supporters re-group abroad, Macbeth embarks on a rule of terror in Scotland. But he and his wife are haunted by their crimes: unable to sleep, they relive the murders in horribly vivid form. Deluded to the end by diabolic prophecies, Macbeth is killed by his avenging enemies.

It is a plot that revolves round a powerful piece of Stuart propaganda. Banquo was James's remote ancestor, and in a visually striking scene the witches conjure up before the horrified Macbeth a vision of Banquo's Stuart progeny, an endless line of kings stretching out until 'the crack of doom' (4.1.117). This was a tribute to the stable succession promised by James's growing family. The circumstances of the play's regicide also link James with Duncan, for they resemble in many details the circumstances of one of the most famous events in King James's Scottish past, his narrow escape from death in the Gowrie Conspiracy, the assassination attempt in a remote castle in 1600 foiled only by the presence of mind of the king. Historians in fact question James's often-repeated account of his own role. The episode may well have been a trap set for, rather than by, the Gowrie clan, who were ruined as a result. Certainly a play staged by the King's Men in 1604 entitled *The Gowrie Conspiracy* had to be withdrawn after two performances, and the players were warned to avoid dramatising contemporary politics in future. Nonetheless, the 'unnatural and vile' conspiracy continued to be commemorated: once a year on 5 August the country gave public thanks for the deliverance of their King.

But as James would by now have realised, flattery from Shakespeare came at a price. Like *Othello* and *Lear*, the play features a trail of reminders of how very far James had strayed from his own image of the ideal king. One of Shakespeare's fortunate finds in the Scottish Chronicles was a passage on the qualities of a ruler, quoted at length in Act 4. Surreptitiously, he infiltrates an invented conclusion, attributing to Malcolm precisely those virtues of constancy and integrity that Catholics accused James of lacking: 'I . . . never was forsworn, / Scarcely have coveted what was mine own, / At no time broke my faith, would not betray / The devil to his fellow . . .' (4.3.126–129). The exiles in the play lament the condition of their country in just the terms the exiles under James lamented the state of England. Daringly, Shakespeare introduces insomnia, a condition from which James himself suffered, as a symptom of the Macbeths' guilt, and the cause of the couple's descent into hallucinations and despair. At the very least, this would draw from the king a reluctant empathy; at best, it might induce some personal soul-searching on the consciousness of crimes that 'murder sleep'. This, then, would have been the gist of the original *Macbeth*—compliment combined with strands of criticism. James could safely identify with Banquo and Donald, but he would have been aware that the portrait of a tyrannical reign would have struck a chord with many of his subjects, who served the regime not out of 'honour, love, obedience', but with 'Curses not loud but deep, mouth-honour, breath . . .' (5.3.25–27). Occupying the foreground were the horrors of *Daemonologie*, spiced with a new psychological depth and topicality, a suggestion that evil was not something that made an occasional and sensational appearance in the Scottish Chronicles but was an ever-present reality in the English court.

But this original version of the play has clearly been radically altered in the light of the Gunpowder Plot. However spine-chilling the content of the King's treatise on witchcraft, a line towards the end of the play contrasts it with the far more horrific impact of the events of the winter of 1605. 'The time has been . . . my fell of hair / Would at a dismal treatise rise and stir / As life were in't. I have supp'd full with horrors; / Direness . . . cannot once start me' (5.5.10–14). At this distance in time, the momentous impact of the Gunpowder Plot is difficult to recapture. The atrocity was, after all, averted, making it the last in a long line of assassination plots that historians can now demonstrate were deftly infiltrated, nurtured and exposed by the intelligence service.[7] But in spite of attempts at the time, and ever since, to blame the whole thing on Cecil, the evidence is inescapable: the plotters were utterly dedicated men; most of them died resolutely defending their actions. It was this group of desperate extremists, not the government, that brought about the downfall of English Catholicism in what James called their own 'direful Domesday'.

The most horrifying element of the plot was the number of innocent victims who would have been killed along with the King. Guy Fawkes was arrested in the act of detonating enough gunpowder to blow up the entire House of Lords, including not only the Privy Council, but the Queen, the eleven-year old Prince Henry and, among the Lords, many close friends of the plotters, including the Earls of Southampton and Worcester. Pressed at their trial on the subject of the massacre, and particularly the murder of children, the conspirators replied simply that desperate diseases required desperate remedies.

The second shocking aspect of the affair was the profile of the plotters themselves. They were not hardened soldiers of fortune but a cross-section of Catholic gentry from the Midlands, their respectability marred only by the presence of the shady Thomas Percy, the most likely to have fallen under government influence. Among the plotters was Sir Everard Digby, young, handsome, happily married to an enchanting wife, 'the goodliest man in the whole court'. All had suffered loss of estates or prospects for the sake of their religion. And most of them lived or had rented houses within thirty miles of Shakespeare's Stratford, a base from which they planned to kidnap James's daughter, the Princess Elizabeth, from nearby Coombe Abbey and rouse the country immediately after the explosion. From Shakespeare's own point of view, the shock must have been profound. Some, such as the scholarly John Grant of Norbrook and the Wintour brothers, were well-known local Stratford figures, and the Catesbys would be connected to Shakespeare's family through his daughter Judith's marriage. Also executed in the wake of the plot was the innocent Henry Garnet, known to many covert Catholics as the long-term head of the English Jesuit mission, who had done what he could to dissuade the conspirators. In London, the plotters used the Mermaid Tavern, frequented by Jonson and Shakespeare, as their meeting point. Shakespeare would have had to have been a very retiring man indeed not to have known at least some of them well.

It looks as if he moved quickly, retrieving the script of *Macbeth*, still unperformed at court, in order to proclaim his revulsion for the inhumanity of the plot and to distance himself from a terrorist group with whom his connections were uncomfortably close. Hence, he created one of the most famous allusions in the play. In a curiously comic scene immediately after Duncan's murder, often thought to be a later interpolation, the castle porter struggles to answer a knocking at the gate, parodying stock characters from the mystery plays, the minor devils who keep the gates of Hell. A famous sequence of references to the trial of Henry Garnet, including a play on his alias, 'Farmer', and on his defence of equivocation, make it clear that the porter expects Garnet to join him in Hell, at first glance a clear indication of whose side Shakespeare is on. Other allusions contribute to the same impression. 'Light thickens, and the crow / Makes wing to th'rooky wood' (3.2.50—51) introduces the murder of Banquo with a reference to Ambrose Rookwood, one of the conspirators. Macbeth is encouraged by his wife to 'look like th'innocent flower, / But be the serpent under't' (1.5.62)—a reminder of the medal struck in memory of the plot, a Catholic serpent hiding under a lily.

Images of dead children and murdered boys fill the play, echoing one of the chief talking points of the time, the callousness of including James's popular young heir, Prince Henry, among the victims. Lady Macbeth's mistaken reaction to a cry in the dark aligns her with the plotters— 'Th'attempt and not the deed / Confounds us' (2.2.10–11). There is a mention of 'dire combustion and confus'd events / New hatch'd to th' woeful time' (2.3.56–57). Then, as now, darkness and 'confusion' surrounded the whole affair. 'Confusion now hath made his masterpiece' (2.3.64) is the first reaction to Duncan's death, a reference to the assumption that Cecil had a hand in the affair. Bonfires were lit by royal command on the night of the discovery, inaugurating an anniversary recalled in a grim comment of Macbeth's when the witches disclose the indestructibility of the Stuart line: 'Let this pernicious hour / stand aye accursed in the calendar' (4.1.133–134)—as indeed, in England, it still does, 5 November annually connecting English Catholicism in the most graphic form with treachery.

Further shafts of imagery briefly illuminate the painful episodes that followed the discovery of the plot. The fleeing conspirators spread out their own supplies of rain-soaked gunpowder to dry in front of the hearth at Holbeach, near Stratford. A spark caught, the gunpowder exploded, and in a grotesque stroke of poetic justice, John Grant, the conspirator Shakespeare was most likely to have known, was blinded. Catesby and Percy were shot and killed by government troops in a last stand at Holbeach, but the blinded Grant stood trial and was hanged, drawn and quartered with the rest, an object of pity as well as horror. His fate haunts the play. 'Thy crown doth sear my eyeballs' (4.1.113), says Macbeth, whose bloody hands have earlier threatened to pluck out his own eyes.[8] In a dazzlingly intense and ambiguous speech that outlines not only the murder of Duncan but the failure of the Gunpowder Plot and the belated explosion, Macbeth imagines an 'even handed justice' (1.7.10) returning to plague the inventor and predicts that 'pity, like a naked new-born babe, / Striding the blast . . . / Shall blow the horrid deed in every eye, / That tears shall drown the wind' (1.7.21–25).[9] The speech ends with a dark pun on contemporary headlines about '[t]he Devil in the Vault' when Macbeth foresees the 'fall' of his own 'Vaulting ambition' (1.7.27).

The fleeting note of pathos in the images of blinding suggests a more complex reaction to the plot than the grave public condemnation by men like the great preacher Lancelot Andrewes ('In darkness they delighted, dark vaults, dark cellars and darkness fell upon them for it'). What did

Catholics among the audience make of a drama that is still seen as a glori-
fication of Stuart authorship and the Stuart line, punctuated by black jokes
at the expense of Catholic plotters who 'roast their goose' (2.3.17) in Hell?
To those familiar with the code, a grim line repeated throughout the play
in various forms said it all—'Fair is foul, and foul is fair' (1.1.10). The
basic component of the code had become inverted. The old religion,
thanks to men like John Grant and Everard Digby, who had once epitomised its image of grace under pressure, was now blackened beyond
repair. The first two acts of *Macbeth*, in which Shakespeare convincingly
reproduces the familiar sensations of sickening apprehension in the run-
up to a dreaded event, reveal the intensity with which he, like many others, dwelt on the subject and asked himself the question: how could
apparently normal people—people he probably knew—have contemplated such an atrocity?

On the surface, then, *Macbeth* has little to offer the shattered Catholic
community beyond sharing and dramatising their incomprehension and
despair. But the Catholic audience was accustomed by now to looking
below the surface, and there they would have found what they were
searching for. At the centre of *Macbeth* lies a deeper drama that uses the
discredited idiom and theology of the old religion to set the crimes of
tyrants and iconoclasts, as well as terrorists, against a backdrop of merciful
judgment. Apocalyptic language was of course the order of the day in
1606: but Shakespeare avoids the biblical imagery of Revelations and the
Protestant doctrine of predestination. Instead he revives an iconography
familiar to us through medieval and Renaissance art, and familiar to his
own generation not simply through the secret practice of Catholic devotions but also through memories of banned country rituals. *Othello*
revealed Shakespeare's renewed interest in the idiom of medieval drama:
in *Macbeth* he goes a great deal further. Exercising an elaborate ingenuity
that we usually associate with poets like Donne and George Herbert, he
interweaves the action of four of the final plays of the mystery cycles into
the existing plot of *Macbeth*. This is the source of both the disjointed text
and the sense of 'hidden powers' identified by Maeterlinck. The familiar
echoes would mean nothing to a Protestant audience, but they would do a
number of things for a Catholic one. They would have reminded the community of the banned expression of a core of belief that still held them
together, and the wit and control with which Shakespeare introduces
them, setting the catastrophe of the Gunpowder Plot in the light of eternity, would have given the kind of cathartic relief he described himself in

The Rape of Lucrece, a poem clearly at the forefront of his mind at this point, as he quotes it in both *Macbeth* and *Othello*.

The relevant mystery plays are the last ones in the mystery cycles, those that dramatise the doctrines of redemption, mercy and judgment: *The Death of Christ*, *The Harrowing of Hell*, *The Resurrection* and *The Last Judgement*. Shakespeare accompanies their theme with imagery of the end of the world, of time buckling and disintegrating until evil is overwhelmed and the 'pearl' of a new Paradise is established. Protestantism denounced as superstitious much of the material in these plays, drawn from sources like the apocryphal Gospel of Nicodemus. Startling and often primitive, these apocalyptic mystery plays give vivid expression to the Catholic doctrines of divine judgment and forgiveness. The inclusion of their strange, often dream-like images in *Macbeth* is inspired, for they are at once stark and profound, lending a primeval spiritual dimension to the themes of guilt and retribution. Christ is often portrayed as a soldier going to do battle on the cross; the cross itself is animate, capable of soliloquy or of playing tricks on the soldiers hammering in the nails. A blind centurion recovers his sight when he is made to pierce Christ's side. Christ's wounds are wells or fountains for sinners to bathe in. His death sets in motion the last battle between the forces of good and evil. While his body lies in the tomb, Christ leads the forces of light to Hell accompanied by trumpets, where after battering on the gates and parleying at length with obstreperous devils, he rescues sinners waiting for redemption. During this titanic battle, the climax of the mystery cycles, the earth awaits the resurrection in darkness and confusion. When the dead emerge to put on flesh, they find that the resurrected Christ has appeared in red robes drenched with 'wounds wet and all bloody', a terrifying judgment on those who caused his death.

As always in Shakespeare's plays, the opening scene flags up the hidden theme. 'What bloody man is that?' (1.2.1), it begins, a question asked before the Last Judgment in the great medieval poem *Piers Ploughman*. He turns out to be a man who 'like a good and hardy soldier fought / 'Gainst my captivity' (1.2.4–5). In a further reference to the redeeming death of Christ, Banquo and Macbeth intend to 'bathe in reeking wounds / Or memorize another Golgotha' (1.2.40–41). After this prelude, the theme goes underground until Duncan's death, when all the portents accompanying Christ's death in the mystery plays are unleashed: the sun, moon and stars vanish, the temple is damaged, the dead walk 'like sprites', the earth shakes, 'The wine of life is drawn' (2.3.93), 'The spring, the head, the fountain of your blood / Is stopp'd' (2.3.96–97).[10] The good characters put their trust in God: Macbeth utters the words of the wicked souls in the plays, who wish they had never been born: 'Had I but died an hour before this chance / I had liv'd a blessed time' (2.3.89–90). Shakespeare sticks faithfully to the medieval sequence by recalling the battle between Christ and the underworld in *The Harrowing of Hell* with the incongruous comedy of the porter and the otherwise puzzling stress on the knocking at the gates and the panic within the dark castle. The role of the devil-porters was to heighten the drama by failing to answer Christ's repeated knocking at the gates, a knocking that, like that of Lennox and Macduff, is intended to raise the dead. 'Wake Duncan with thy knocking! I would thou couldst!' (2.2.74), Macbeth comments. Lady Macbeth's description of the 'hideous trumpet' that 'calls to parley the sleepers of this house' echoes exactly the demons' reports to Satan of the trumpet blasts that accompany Christ's repeated assaults on Hell's gates in order to rescue, not the damned, but the 'sleepers' of limbo—Adam, Moses, John the Baptist. Seen in this context, the presence of Garnet takes on an entirely new meaning, comprehensible only to Catholics. To Protestants, the equivo-cating Jesuit is rightly consigned to Hell—but to Catholics, Shakespeare presents him as one of those awaiting the rescuing hand of Christ and the words 'Peace to thee, Adam, my darling, / And eke to all thine offspring / . . . To bliss now I will you bring'.[11] One reason for introducing the mystery play theme was that in this scene, it enabled Shakespeare to convey covert assurance of Garnet's innocence to English Catholics, many of whom knew him well during his long underground ministry in England.

The battle of the forces of light and dark come to a head in *The Harrow-ing of Hell* when the gates of Hell burst open and light floods in, a moment reproduced when the porter opens the gates to Lennox and Macduff and allows the light of dawn into a castle that so far has been seen only in dark-ness. *The Resurrection* comes next in the cycle, the medieval Christ return-ing as a triumphant wounded warrior, a 'bloody man', bearing the marks of the passion. Eerily linked to this majestic image, the avenging ghost of Banquo appears at Macbeth's feast with 'gory locks' (3.4.51) that 'might appal the devil' (3.4.59). Here the bloody man coming in judgment is a figure of terror, seen through the fearful eyes of the damned. Shakespeare carefully infiltrates phrases from the resurrection accounts into Macbeth's hysterical reaction. Once, he babbles, 'the man would die / And there an end; but now they rise again . . .' (3.4.78–80) 'our graves must send / Those that we bury back . . .' (3.4.70–71). Macbeth echoes the medieval image of the speaking cross or 'tree' and the narrative of the stone moved from Christ's tomb at the resurrection: 'Stones have been known to move, and trees to speak' (3.4.123). The empty tomb was discovered at sunrise, the point at which this scene ends: 'What is the night? . . . Almost at odds with morning, which is which' (3.4.126–127).

The increasingly polarised forces of good and evil battle it out for the rest of the play, drawing on the imagery of the final mystery play, *The Last Judgement*, in which the damned lament: 'sore may we wring our hands and weep . . . Now mun never soul ne body die'. Macbeth, envying the sleep of the just, endures 'the torture' of a mind 'full of scorpions' and suffers 'restless ecstasy' shaken by 'terrible dreams' (3.2.18–36), while Lady Macbeth rubs imaginary blood from her hands at night. Images of doomsday multiply as the play moves towards 'the last syllable of recorded time' (5.5.21). Part of the horror of the play arises from the skill with which Shakespeare links conditions of insomnia and depression familiar to most of his audience—and particularly to James—with the graphic mystery play accounts of the terrors of damned souls.

Audience reaction at the time would have been complicated further by his daring use of the hologram technique at the moment of Duncan's murder. Shakespeare ensures that at the very moment we witness the atrocity planned by the plotters, the angle shifts to remind spectators of the greater atrocity that drove them to such extremes. The murder of Duncan, like that of Richard II, has overtones of the destruction of the old religion, in particular the removal of the Real Presence from the centre of English spiritual life: 'Most sacrilegious murder hath broke ope / The Lord's anointed temple, and stole thence / The life o' th' building' (2.3.65–67). This line highlights the brutal aspect of the persecuting regime. Twice Macbeth is associated with the hanging, drawing and quartering reserved for Catholic traitors—his 'hangman's hands' (2.2.27) are bloody; in battle he 'unseam'd' his victim from the 'nave to th' chops' (1.2.22) before sticking his head on the battlements. Both the government and the extremists are invited to witness their own crimes and their nemesis in the rise and fall of the Macbeths.

The underlying mystery play sequence would have carried an element of consolation for Catholic onlookers. Not only is Garnet numbered among the just, but the terrible story of the Plot is lifted beyond the painful context of the times into the familiar imagery of a transcendent dimension, reminding them at the same time of the idiom of the old religion, still intact in spite of the cataclysm of 1605. Nonetheless, the cataclysm has taken a heavy toll. In the past, whenever Shakespeare has approached the possibility of the total loss of the old religion, he calls up the image of permanent darkness. Tarquin, whose 'ravishing strides' (2.1.55) are quoted in Macbeth, 'sets his foot upon the light'; Othello blows out the light before he murders Desdemona; the light in the cave in *Titus* is extinguished before the murders; light vanishes on Adonis's death. The moral darkness that follows sacrilege is described at length in *Lucrece* and at the end of *Venus and Adonis*. In *Macbeth*, written at a moment when the worst fears of the Catholic community had become reality, literal and metaphorical darkness envelops the entire play. The worst aspect of all was that when the catastrophe finally happened, it was self-inflicted. It would be years before Shakespeare could bring himself again to associate any aspect of Catholicism with unequivocal purity and innocence.

THE POST-MORTEM, 1606–1608

Nothing Left Remarkable

IN THE YEARS that followed the Gunpowder Plot, a change comes over Shakespeare's writing, a change so marked that some critics have detected a different hand in his later plays. He starts to break rules. In the first place the blank verse, already fragmented in *Macbeth*, becomes increasingly fluid. Overruns from one line to the next increase; so do lines with weak endings; compound words multiply; to the despair of literature students, the thought is occasionally so compressed that it defeats the syntax. In places, commentators have to take on the role of translators. A similarly casual attitude towards rules characterises the plots and the stagecraft. Shakespeare never bothered much about dramatic decorum, but from this point on he appears to go out of his way to incorporate all the faults Sidney condemned in early Elizabethan drama. 'The miserable beholders', complained Sidney, were subjected to 'grosse absurdities' of time, action and place in plays 'where you shall have Asia of the one side, and Affricke of the other, and so many other under kingdomes, that the player when he comes in must ever begin with telling where he is or else the tale will not be conceived'. This passage from his *Defence of Poesie* reads like a blueprint for Shakespeare's later plays. There are other changes. His main characters become opaque, even sketchy. One critic remarks that Cleopatra is the last of Shakespeare's fully naturalistic characters. 'Cleopatra, an astonishing act of human invention, was Shakespeare's farewell to his richest gift, and I wish we could surmise why this was, or perhaps had to be'.[1]

In their search for evidence of some parallel trauma in his personal life, biographers have scoured the complex images and savage language of the plays and poems written in the early years of James's reign. Theories include venereal disease, alcoholism, incipient blindness, family bereavement, exhaustion. At the top of the list is an unhappy love affair, strongly suggested by a literal reading of certain sonnets, which taken together appear to tell a story.[2] The poet, who describes himself as 'old', introduces a 'fair' young man whom he adores to a 'dark' mistress to whom he is reluctantly tied. The mistress seduces the friend, leaving the older man heartbroken. Certain sonnets clearly are biographical; but those who have followed the code through the plays will recognise in this particular story a trauma that goes beyond the private life of the author: it points to the downfall of the 'fair' English Catholic revival at the hands of a 'darkened' England, the mistress to whom 'old' Catholics owed unhappy allegiance. The despair suggested by these sonnets, published in 1609, was a despair shared by many men and women in England after the events of 1605.[3] The consensus of most readers and critics is that the daringly mannered development of Shakespeare's later work is marked not by loss of grip but by increased mastery. What has altered is not his artistic capacity, but his target audience. He is no longer writing for the King, but for his fellow Catholics. For his approach to these demoralised spectators, he chooses a mercurial, supple, exploratory style—an ideal medium for issues that for many of them would have been almost unbearably painful.

Since the death of Queen Mary in 1558, Catholicism in England had remained loyal to a vision of its religion as the vessel of sacramental reality. But on a political level, the Catholic Church had repeatedly misled its English adherents, its professions of encouragement and solidarity sickeningly at variance with its actions. In the end it appeared to have abandoned them, risking the extinction of English Catholicism for the sake of peace with the new regime and precipitating the terrorist outrage of 5 November. Political pragmatism obscured a vision of truth and beauty that for many had been the reason for their existence. How could such a fickle, fallible church be the one, true, apostolic foundation of Christ? Perhaps there was truth in the increasingly influential atheistic argument—perhaps faith itself was an illusion. A measure of the extent to which English Catholicism had been shaken by recent events is the fact that Shakespeare's next play queries the very foundations of religious belief.

Our Faith Mere Folly

Antony and Cleopatra is more loosely worked than the densely layered *Othello* or *King Lear*; perhaps because it was written rapidly: long passages of the love affair are purely naturalistic; the narrative remains close to Plutarch, who is occasionally quoted verbatim; the style is light, humorous and fluent. The theme, however is profound. It is a story of two aging lovers who deliberately close their eyes to their mutual betrayals and instead create a vision of each other as grandly romantic figures whose passion transcends the banality of real life. The question asked by the play is whether the vision is an illusory fantasy or whether it is a glimpse of a deeper truth. Cleopatra asks whether the superhuman Antony she loved ever really existed:

> His legs bestrid the ocean; his rear'd arm
> Crested the world. His voice was propertied
> As all the tuned spheres . . . For his bounty,
> There was no winter in't; an autumn 'twas
> That grew the more by reaping . . . realms and islands were
> As plates dropp'd from his pocket.
> *(5.2.82–92)*

No, comes the prosaic answer—there never was such a man. Cleopatra responds furiously: 'You lie, up to the hearing of the gods' (5.2.94). She defends her dream by giving emotional expression to the standpoint that has so far underpinned Shakespeare's entire work. A visionary ideal that eclipses the natural world and that outsoars the human imagination implies a transcendent reality, a substance beyond the shadows. It must be true.

> But if there be nor ever were one such
> It's past the size of dreaming. Nature wants stuff
> To vie strange forms with fancy; yet t'imagine
> An Antony were nature's piece 'gainst fancy,
> Condemning shadows quite.
> *(5.2.95–99)*

A similar point is made by Hippolyta at the end of *A Midsummer Night's Dream*.[4] But there is a difference between Cleopatra's lonely vision and the visions of Bottom and the lovers in the wood. In *A Midsummer Night's Dream* the vision is a communal one. Having witnessed the supernatural events earlier in the play, the audience knows that the lovers have not been dreaming—what the bemused quartet dimly remember as they wake up has been real to the play's onlookers. Moreover, Hippolyta observes that their stories all agree—therefore, however unlikely, they must be true. Up until now, whenever he brings up the theme of shadow and substance, this has been Shakespeare's consistent position: that of a Catholic humanist who believes that the collective vision handed down by the church's evangelists, saints and teachers bears convincing witness to spiritual reality. As Hippolyta puts it: 'All their minds transfigur'd so together, / More witnesseth than fancy's images, / And grows to something of great constancy' (5.1.24–26). In *Antony and Cleopatra*, however, the dream is uncertain and defiant. No one else shares it. The audience knows that the lovers' romantic views of each other are no more than 'fancy's images'; and they know that, underneath all the rhetoric, the lovers realise it, too. Love—on the hidden level, faith—is no longer a ladder to the divine; it is a brave illusion.

But *Antony and Cleopatra* maintains that constancy to a vision of goodness and beauty, however illusory, is the only noble response in a world emptied of meaning. Without it, 'there is nothing left remarkable' (4.15.67). Antony's joke that a crocodile 'is as broad as it hath breadth . . . and the tears of it are wet' (2.7.41–48) underlines the relativism of the play, with its dizzying sequence of contrasting backgrounds and conflicting points of view. Things are only what they are. Antony's pragmatic follower Enobarbus derides the irrational idea of embracing a lost cause or a meaningless belief in a line that would have had a painful resonance for English Catholics suffering for their religious allegiance: 'The loyalty well held to fools does make / Our faith mere folly' (3.13.42–43). But then he changes his mind: 'Yet he that can endure / To follow with allegiance a fall'n lord / Does conquer him that did his master conquer / And earns a place i'th'story' (3.13.42–46). Typically for this disillusioned play, however, Enobarbus does in the end abandon Antony.

The examination of loyalty to a lost, possibly pointless cause in *Antony and Cleopatra* dramatises the crisis of faith and allegiance that was being discussed after 1605 in great households like that of the Montagues. The tale of Antony and Cleopatra had long been an accepted vehicle for covert comment on the condition of England. Fulke Greville, concerned as ever to leave what he called 'fair weather' behind him, destroyed his own play on the subject in case it was misconstrued as an allegory on Elizabeth and

Essex and the 'vices in the present governors and government'.[5] In 1590, Mary Herbert, Philip Sidney's sister, had adapted a French play on the subject, *The Tragedie of Antonie*, which illustrates exactly the kind of dangerous allusiveness Fulke Greville refers to. The lofty, sententious speeches periodically touch on contemporary English politics. There are points where Octavius Caesar becomes a cold representation of the new order; Cleopatra's laments become the cries of helpless England, in the person of Queen Elizabeth, held hostage by ambitious counsellors. Cleopatra's children will have to endure capture, shame and the 'caitiff knife' under the new tyranny: 'This realm have I to strangers subject made / And robbed my children of their heritage', she mourns. Antony becomes the old aristocratic order displaced by the Cecils, unmanned by the blandishments of a vacillating Queen. Samuel Daniel, a member of the same circle, continued the theme in his 1594 poem, *Cleopatra*, following Mary Herbert's advice 'to sing of State and tragicke notes to frame . . . to chase away this tyrant of the North, gross Barbarism'.

As well as exploring the whole question of religious faith, Shakespeare follows these writers in depicting the political circumstances of the downfall of the old order, using two of Mary Herbert's identities— Antony as the old order, Caesar as the new. The play opens with the deepening opposition between the aging Mark Antony, a celebrated and much-loved soldier, and the young, humourless Octavius Caesar—briskly efficient where Antony is raffish and glamorous. Their attempt at power-sharing fails. Antony is hopelessly distracted from affairs of state by his dalliance with the Queen of Egypt. In spite of Antony's attempt to reconcile with Octavius by an expedient marriage with his sister, Octavia, Caesar turns on his rival and defeats him in a sea battle in which the besotted Antony relies on Cleopatra's support: her navy disperses at the height of the action. While lamenting her lover's defeat in extravagant terms, Cleopatra quietly makes a pact with Caesar. Shakespeare's tale is that of the prolonged and tragic downfall of a once great man, tied to a woman's apron-strings.

Antony has been called 'a magnificent ruin . . . a man on whom the sun is going down',[6] common images used by historians to describe the state of English Catholicism after 1605. Others use the theme of contraction— late Elizabethan Catholicism is 'like a great lake subject to a newly hostile climate', beginning to shrink.[7] The same idea of melting, dissolving, 'discandying', runs through the play. Antony 'cannot hold his visible shape' (4.14.14), comparing his decline to a cloud that takes on one shape after

another: the first is the 'dragonish' emblem of old England, the last a vanishing horse, the symbol of lost political power. Mary Herbert's Antony
anticipated his fate in terms of Tyburn and the rack: 'limb after limb will
be rent'. Shakespeare's Antony repeats this echo of the fate of dissenting
England in a brilliant two-word pun: 'That which is now a horse, even
with a thought / The *rack dislimns*, and makes it indistinct . . .' (4.14.9–10).
His gradual decline and slow death, the 'miserable change' at his end, such
lines as 'O, my fortunes / Have corrupted honest men!' (4.5.16–17) would
have had a personal application for many, who, like Enobarbus, were
reluctantly abandoning their old convictions at this point. Shakespeare
sharpens the application when Antony makes his political marriage of
convenience with Caesar's sister, who is linked, like Ophelia, with the
compromise religion: she is torn between the two extremes 'praying for
both parts', discovering that there is 'no mid-way / 'Twixt these extremes
at all' (3.4.14–19).

But Cleopatra is given a new and unexpected identity. Well aware of the
dangerous path he was treading with his Catholic audience, Shakespeare
sticks close to his source in his portrayal of her, in places merely versifying
Plutarch's original text. She is clearly not the helpless Elizabeth-as-England
of Daniel and Mary Herbert. Courtesan, gypsy, empress, seductress, her
vibrant entourage is contrasted with the stern repressiveness of Caesar's
Rome, a contrast deliberately intensified by constant intercutting between
the two. Not until the third act does Shakespeare signal her allegorical
identity to those familiar with his code. In a long deviation from Plutarch,
Cleopatra interrogates a messenger about Octavia's appearance, and in the
process reveals her own. The markers make their appearance. Octavia is
not as tall as Cleopatra—'dwarfish', Cleopatra concludes; her brow is low;
and her hair, Cleopatra is delighted to learn, is brown, the implication
being that Cleopatra's is fair—she was, indeed, traditionally represented as
blonde, being descended from the Greek line of the Ptolemys. The darkness of Cleopatra's skin aligns her with other sunburnt Shakespearean
heroines—Beatrice, Julia and Rosalind. This battery of Catholic markers
gives a new significance to earlier attributes. Cleopatra made her entry in
the second act with a languid line that is a direct reminder of Orsino's
opening speech in *Twelfth Night*—in sybaritic mood, both characters call
music the food of love. Orsino represented Counter-Reformation
Europe; Cleopatra does the same. The repeated epithet 'gypsy' defines
her still further: another ingenious pun, it derives from the word 'Egyptian', but it also has Spanish connotations. Expelled from most sixteenth-

century European countries, gypsies settled in Spain, bringing flamenco music and dance to the native culture. Thus, Shakespeare once again sets English politics in an international perspective. The richness of Cleopatra's court—the elaborate barge, the fortune-tellers, music, dances, eunuchs, the atmosphere of extravagance, beauty, wealth and wit all evoke imperial Egypt—but they can apply with equal aptness to imperial Spain.

Not all the English of Shakespeare's day viewed Spain as the Great Satan. A number had spent long periods as envoys and ambassadors there. Until the Reformation, Spain had been England's traditional ally, and even now, diplomatic, social and mercantile connections were still close. In areas such as painting, architecture, theatre, fashion and literature, Spain and Italy were the acknowledged arbiters of European taste. The play's emphatic contrast between the two settings—technicolour Egypt and black-and-white Rome—applies equally well to the contrast between the exuberance and dangerous allure of Counter-Reformation Spain and the restraint of Protestant England.

The more one looks at the play in the light of relations between Spain and the old order in England, the more ingenious the parallel becomes, a perfectly judged offering to a sophisticated audience made up of survivors of the resistance, elegantly shadowing the sequence of accidents, misjudgments and betrayals that punctuated the two countries' long and ultimately tragic alliance. The love affair between Antony and Cleopatra sheds further light on the extraordinarily skilful technique that earned Shakespeare the repeated epithet 'witty'—meaning not humorous, but intellectually ingenious—from his fellow writers. The gist of this hidden narrative is that Catholic England met its downfall by depending on Spanish support instead of its own resources. Shakespeare announces the doomed relationship in the opening scenes, which recall the 'dotage' of England's close links with Spain under Philip and Mary, during whose reign the weakened country lost Calais, its last military foothold in France. Cleopatra tells Antony that they must 'find out new heaven, new earth' (1.1.17)—a magnificent line, setting in motion the lovers' theme of transcendence. But it is also an echo of one of the most famous emblems of the day—Philip II's 'Non sufficit orbis', meaning 'The world is not enough'. Antony's next step, a marriage of convenience to Caesar's passive, hesitant sister, echoes Catholic England's initial acceptance of the compromise religion on Elizabeth's accession. Like Philip II, who instantly set about wooing the country back to Catholicism, Cleopatra determines to win back her lover. Antony's gradual submission to his mistress, and his accompanying loss of judgment and authority, mirrors the increasing dependence of dissident England on Spanish support up to the point when English exiles prepared to return to their country at the head of Spanish forces. The fortunes of the Armada are precisely recalled as the couple prepare to take on Caesar's regime. In the manner of propaganda accounts of England's victory, Caesar scornfully enumerates the vast levy of Egyptian forces against him, observing that Antony 'gives his potent regiment to a trull' (3.6.95); these terms recall the ignominious fate of the regiment of English exiles headed by Sir William Stanley, their lives and reputations ruined under indecisive Spanish command. Wind scatters Cleopatra's navy; like the Spanish fleet compared with the English, her ships are heavy and manned by conscripts; Caesar's are swifter and have experienced crews. After this, Cleopatra's political flirtation with the young Caesar's regime and her ultimate betrayal of Antony follows the twists and turns of Spain's dealings with Cecil leading up to the Peace of 1604.

The elegiac grandeur of Antony's passing, with its repeated lament—'I am dying, Egypt, dying' (4.15.18, 4.15.42)—evokes the improbable and awesome spectacle of the old order foundering, and with it the traditions and heritage, now dispersed and shattered, of the medieval English Church. In the scene in which Antony's god leaves him, Shakespeare replaces the Mars mentioned by Plutarch with Hercules, symbol of religious resistance to the 'hydra' of heresy,[8] vanishing underground like the ghost in *Hamlet*. Rage, folly and ineptitude characterise Antony's suicide, and though he calls on Hercules, 'all labour / Mars what it does' (4.15.47–48). And there is a suggestion in one of the last lines of the play that on a certain level, Cleopatra, like slippery Catholic Spain, lives on unscathed—in death 'she looks like sleep / As she would catch another Antony / In her strong toil of grace' (5.2.344–346).

It is not difficult to imagine the passionate arguments raging at this point behind closed doors all over the country. How much was the downfall of English Catholicism self-inflicted? How much was Spain to blame? Was there any point in enduring further hardship for the sake of a cause that was now clearly lost? And in any case, did it mean anything anymore? Shakespeare's own standpoint is revealed only in the resonant language of Cleopatra and Antony, persuading audiences that however deluded the two lovers may be, it is a finer thing to side with them than with the pragmatic victors. Blind faith may be, in Enobarbus's words, 'mere folly' (3.13.43), but to abandon it is to 'joy no more' (4.6.19).

Preparing Fire

C oriolanus dramatises the final phase of the tragedy of Catholic England, the events leading up to the Gunpowder Plot. This play, written sometime after 1605, represents Shakespeare's considered analysis of the plot's political causes. Looked at as a universal drama, it is an unsatisfactory play. Coriolanus himself is a puzzling hero, at once noble and repellent; the characters are schematic and appear to stand for various ideological positions; much of the language is that of closely reasoned political argument. But seen as a topical play, these elements all make sense—and the title's topical significance would have been recognised at once. Just as with *King Lear* and *Antony and Cleopatra*, it is taken directly from the political debate of the day, in this case a classical story closely associated at the time with the Gunpowder Plot.

The tale of Coriolanus is set in a Rome in which the old patrician order is under threat from the new republican movement. The young nobleman, Coriolanus, embodies the old order. An accomplished soldier, he scorns the ignorant plebeians and the upstart tribunes who represent them. So long as Rome is at war, Coriolanus is valued for his military skills; but when peace comes, public resentment at his arrogance forces him into exile. He defects to Rome's enemies and returns at their head, bent on razing the city to the ground. In the end he yields to pleas from his family and spares the city, dying at the hands of his frustrated allies.

At the time of the Armada, the tale of Coriolanus was used by Protestants to highlight the danger to their own country of exiled Catholic soldiers such as Sir William Stanley.[9] By 1604, thanks to the strenuous diplomatic efforts of King James, the country was at peace abroad; but this merely exacerbated the more immediate threat of Catholic aggression at home. Strict enforcement of the penal laws meant that by the end of the sixteenth century, soldiering was almost the only profession left to young Catholic gentry. Orlando in *As You Like It*, kept unschooled 'like a peasant' at home, has only one means of earning a living abroad—by the 'base and boisterous sword' (2.3.32). The leading gunpowder plotters were outstanding swordsmen and had fought either for Essex or in the Low Countries. Two of them, Guy Fawkes and Thomas Wintour, had switched sides to fight alongside Sir William Stanley, Fawkes by all accounts a man of 'exemplary life' and 'extraordinary fortitude', whose prowess had earned him 'considerable fame' among soldiers. As early as 1604, two writers with

Catholic connections, Thomas and Dudley Digges, had been using the Coriolanus theme in their *Four Paradoxes* to highlight the problem of disaffected subjects deprived of the safety valve of military action, arguing that war was healthier for society than peace and that the country should 'mother-like respect those sons that are her champions'.

But as an analogy for the simmering violence of the Gunpowder Plot, anti-Catholics used a different analogy—a classic tale defending centralised authority. In this story, the more active parts of the body rebel against the apparently idle, greedy stomach and starve it of food, only to realise that without it the whole system fails. In 1606, Edward Forset's *True Form of Commonwealth* uses the tale of the belly to denounce Catholic opposition to state authority in England, presenting the problem in terms of a cancer, threatening the body of the country.

Shakespeare opens *Coriolanus* with an unmistakable signal that the play is to be another contribution to this topical debate: he retells the story of the belly, putting it into the mouth of an elderly Roman patrician, Menenius, who is attempting to quell an imminent revolt against old-style Roman authority by a restless plebeian mob, their heads filled with new republican ideas. Shakespeare uses the scene to turn Forset's parable on its head. To polemicists like Forset, the authority of the new Protestant English state was under threat from reactionary Catholics. Shakespeare instead uses the old story to remind us of its wider application: the threat to the traditional authority of Christendom by rebel Protestant states.[10] He does this by using markers to link the plebeian mob in *Coriolanus* with the popular movements that brought reform to Protestant states in Europe. In a passage hinting at self-parody, not one has 'fair' hair: some are 'brown, some black, some abram [auburn], some bald' (2.3.17–18). He portrays the mutinous crowd happily admitting that the wits within their heads are just as 'diversely coloured'; their idea of consensus is to be simultaneously at 'all points of the compass' (2.3.19–23). Their leaders are keen on grafting old crab-trees with new relish, the women are veiled against the sun. To Rome's patricians, these tradesmen 'reek of fens' and are redolent of 'the dead carcasses of unburied men' (3.3.123-124)—suggestive of two attributes popularly applied to reformers, that they flourished in the fens of East Anglia and the Low Countries, and that they disapproved of burial rites. Their leaders are a pair of crafty, power-hungry tribunes, linked by the epithet 'Foxship' with the old 'Fox', William Cecil (4.2.18).

Turning to the patricians, Shakespeare develops the context of the Reformation split with a delicately shaded picture of the position of English

Catholicism at the beginning of James's reign. Menenius, the elderly, humorous senator, has features of the more acceptable older patriarchs of English Catholicism, men like the genial and eccentric Sir Thomas Tresham, father to one of the plotters, Francis Tresham. Menenius praises Coriolanus in terms that bring to mind two plotters in particular, the society darlings Everard Digby and Robert Catesby, the latter a young nobleman seen by many as the future hope of Catholicism: 'The only sun that must ripen our harvest'.[11] Through Menenius's fond eyes we see the best of Coriolanus. But his attempts to restrain the uncompromising younger man fail. Reluctantly, he agrees to his exile and shares Rome's relief at Coriolanus's departure, though his feelings are mixed: 'All's well, and might have been much better if / He could have temporiz'd' (4.6.17). The mannerisms of Menenius are so distinctive that he was evidently meant to bring a particular figure to mind: 'You have made good work' is repeated six times and sounds like a well-known catchphrase.

Historically, the complex relationship between Menenius and Coriolanus is one of the most interesting in the play. Even more illuminating is the role of Coriolanus's mother, Volumnia, whose vivid character is Shakespeare's own invention. Like earlier resistance heroines, she is connected with Hecuba. For decades, women like Magdalen Montague had formed the backbone of the Catholic resistance, holding together the impoverished households of their imprisoned or banished husbands, sending their children on dangerous journeys to be educated abroad, tirelessly pursuing loopholes in the penal laws and pleading the family cause with men of influence, protecting priests at great personal risk and doggedly perpetuating the banned practice of their religion. Not all of them can have been easy characters; over the years, as the situation steadily worsened, their endurance may well have hardened into intolerant rigour. The families of the plotters feature a number of such women—heroic in many ways, but quite possibly as off-putting in the flesh as Volumnia. One was Ursula Wright, mother of Kit and Jack Wright and mother-in-law of Thomas Percy. Her granddaughter describes her as a 'great prayer' who spent whole nights on her knees and did what she could to relieve Catholic prisoners in the notorious blockhouses in nearby Kingston-on-Hull. There, behind walls fifteen feet thick, deprived of light or ventilation and subjected to flooding in spring, many either suffocated from the stench or starved to death—intolerable conditions that could well have induced angry extremism in those who witnessed them. Other pillars of Catholic recusancy were Catesby's mother, the widowed

Anne Throckmorton, and Jane Ingleby, member of a large Yorkshire recusant clan and mother of the two Wintour brothers. Thus, five of the leading plotters had mothers who were defiantly recusant, an element in the background of the younger generation of Catholics that may have inspired Shakespeare's distinctive portrayal of Coriolanus as a man who owed his militant character to the formative influence of his mother.

The nature of this influence on the surface seems purely class-conscious —Coriolanus inherits Volumnia's scorn for 'woollen vassals'. But Volumnia's snobbery is as much sectarian as social. She sniffs that the mob 'buy and sell with groats', they yawn and look around ignorantly 'in congregations' (3.2.7–11). In other words, they are an unthinking flock who know about trade, but not about how to behave in church—another typical Catholic jibe at commercially minded, upwardly mobile Protestants. Reminiscent of the style of recusant matriarchs, an incongruously grandmotherly manner accompanies her most bloodthirsty speeches—she clucks fondly over a tale of her promising grandson tearing apart butterflies with his teeth. This portrait of uncompromising feminine recusancy is tempered by the accompanying sketch of Virgilia, Coriolanus's passive, nervous wife. 'O Jupiter! No blood!' (1.3.38) is her response to her bullying mother-in-law. She says little, bowed over her needlework as she awaits her husband's return. She seems literally unable to leave the house, refusing to go out in spite of being told, 'You confine yourself most unreasonably' (1.3.76). The pair are described as 'manifest housekeepers' (1.3.51)—along with the word 'confine', the allusion points to recusants forbidden by law to move beyond their home.[12] The robust Volumnia pays no attention, but Virgilia obeys: 'Indeed I must not'.

Shakespeare accentuates the features Coriolanus shares with the leading plotters: youth; rashness; noble birth; a powerful physical presence; a reputation for fine soldiership; a profound sense of injury and wounded pride; obsessiveness. He too has been fitfully educated: 'He has been bred i'th'wars / Since 'a could draw a sword, and is ill school'd / In bolted language' (3.1.320–323). While giving full play to his phenomenal military ability and powers of leadership, Shakespeare makes it clear that there is something inhuman about Coriolanus: he returns from one engagement head to foot 'a thing of blood' (2.3.106).[13] His opposition to mob rule, a line Shakespeare elsewhere endorses, is narrow-minded and excessive: arrogance characterises his every action. The characteristics that Shakespeare adds to his source point directly to men like Catesby. The terrifying imperviousness of Coriolanus as he approaches Rome, that of a man on a suicide mission, ties in with what we know about the plotters, bound by sacred oaths, their swords engraved with scenes from the passion of Christ. Coriolanus becomes 'a kind of nothing, titleless, / Till he had forged himself a name i' the fire / Of burning Rome' (5.1.13–15). A messenger describes his strange behaviour: 'I kneel'd before him; / 'Twas very faintly he said "Rise"; dismissed me / Thus with his speechless hand' (5.1.65–67). Shakespeare's most striking addition to his source is the theme of destruction by fire—fire is mentioned fourteen times towards the end of the play, and the overtones are of the deliberation of a plotter rather than the blind rage of an indiscriminate destroyer. 'My son!' says the weeping Menenius, 'Thou art *preparing fire* for us' (5.2.68–69). The apocalyptic rhetoric that drove the plotters pervades the language of the avenging Coriolanus, while the indifference with which he dismisses the deaths of friends and family would have aroused memories of the callousness of the plan to destroy the entire House of Lords—'he could not stay to pick them in a pile / Of noisome musty chaff' (5.1.25–26).

However, Menenius's reaction to news of the 'intended fire' is revealing. He describes it as an appropriate punishment for the cowardice of nobility like himself. "If he could burn us all into one coal, / We have deserved it (4.6.138–139); 'If he were putting to my house the brand / That should consume it I have not the face / To say "Beseech you cease"' (4.6.116–118). Menenius's elated image of the avenging Coriolanus as the resistance hero Hercules shaking down 'mellow fruit' (4.6.100) suggests that after half a century of indecision, even moderate Catholics felt a guilty surge of exhilaration at the rumour that violent action of some kind was on the way. An unjust country, along with its inert nobility, was about to get what it deserved: 'The gods be good unto us', prays the tribune, Sicinius, and gets the flat answer from Menenius: 'No, in such a case the gods will not be good unto us. When we banish'd him [Coriolanus] we respected not them; and, he returning to break our necks, they respect not us' (5.4.31–33). In the end, his mother dissuades Coriolanus from destroying Rome, using arguments that would have been deployed by fellow Catholics who, like Garnet, tried desperately to dissuade the Plotters. The fire would destroy women, children, his own family, she urges, and his 'noble name' will be 'abhorred' forever. One passage in particular conjures up the idealistic style of men who attended Mass and adopted biblical terminology while planning the explosion: 'Thou has affected the fine strains of honour / To imitate the graces of the gods / To tear with thunder the wide cheeks o'th'air / And yet to charge thy sulphur with a bolt . . .'

(5.3.149–152). One theory about the disclosure of the plot is that pleas such as Volumnia's persuaded at least one of the plotters to give the game away. If so, as with Coriolanus, his decision proved suicidal.

Coriolanus is a chilling protagonist. No one following the hidden narrative could accuse Shakespeare of outright sympathy with plotters like him. But in his sensitive treatment of the elements that lay behind the plot—the political context, the indoctrination and the character of the plotters, the subtlety of their opponents, the obduracy and subjection of female recusants, the conflicting motivations of the ineffectual Catholic nobility—he reveals himself as a man with an insider's knowledge of the background to a watershed event in English history, one that remains to this day the subject of intense controversy.

The Second Hope

NO ONE KNOWS when the incomplete *Timon of Athens* was drafted, but it was very possibly in the wake of the plot that Shakespeare added some of his darkest material to a piece of work that scholars believe he started earlier and then abandoned. The text of the play was included in the First Folio only as an afterthought. It sketches out two themes, the fall of a great man, undone by his naive open-handedness, and the revenge of a banished soldier, both of which Shakespeare developed more fully in two separate works, *King Lear* and *Coriolanus*. The first theme was clearly aimed at King James, whose reckless generosity was legendary; it is an attempt to awaken him to the true state of his fiscal affairs and to encourage him to identify with his dispossessed subjects.[14] The second dramatises another famous instance of a noble exile who turns on his country—Alcibiades, a man Plutarch couples with Coriolanus.

Having abandoned the project, Shakespeare continued to tinker with the draft in a way that suggests that, for once, he was not writing with a particular audience in mind but was giving vent to the same emotion that took over towards the end of the *Rape of Lucrece*, and on the same subject: the nightmare of a country that has lost all concept of spirituality. Timon's diatribes recall other satires of the time that portrayed commerce as the new religion. But Shakespeare's attack goes deeper. The ancient Christian concept of a physical universe held together by love is replaced with a vision of a predatory world built on avarice and lust. Timon's hatred of life, underscored by the misanthropy of the philosopher Apemantus, spills beyond the confines of the play as he becomes a vehicle for passage after passage of utter disillusion. Taken with recent work in which Shakespeare repeatedly extinguishes the embodiment of holiness, it is difficult not to feel that this writing represents the depression and anger of someone who had lost all hope for England's spiritual recovery.

The mood behind *Timon of Athens* appears to have been widespread. The angry frustration of Shakespeare's ignored Alcibiades finds echoes in the writings of many humane men of influence in the first decade of the seventeenth century as persecution of Catholics continued unchecked in spite of all pleas. Yet another stringent act against recusants was passed in 1606, and the activities of pursuivants, sanctioned by the wave of revulsion at the Gunpowder Plot, became more brazen than ever. Confirmation that this was the end of the road as far as appeals to James were concerned came with his revised version of the Oath of Supremacy: the Oath of Allegiance, imposed in 1606. It made the promised distinction between spiritual and temporal allegiance, but Catholics were now asked to reject traditional papal claims as 'heretical', 'damnable', and 'impious'. Pius V responded immediately, forbidding Catholics to take it. Hopes that James was not personally responsible for the drafting were dashed when his book *An Apology for the Oath of Allegiance* was published the following year, hotly defending the terms of the oath and denying any challenge to papal authority.

James's book stirred up an international hornet's nest. Responding to his *Apology*, intellectuals all over Europe joined battle yet again across the familiar Reformation fault-lines. The leading Catholic apologist, the Italian Cardinal Bellarmine, spearheaded the opposition, arguing that the Pope had the right to depose a monarch who broke his coronation oath and persecuted his subjects; Persons followed up by recapitulating the entire Catholic case against Protestantism and denouncing in graphic terms 'the persistent plague of Calvinian seducement'.[15] Persons argued that where Protestant and Catholic were so interconnected, the persecution of one would inevitably hurt the other. 'Who knoweth not, but that the bowels of England are so combined and linked together at this day in this point as hardly can the sword pass the one but it must also wound the other'.[16] John Donne, eager for promotion, wrote his *Pseudo-Martyr* defending James's stance, though his poetry, published much later, revealed that he was privately agonising over whether or not to conform.

As James emerged from the fray as champion of international Protestantism, calling for an ecumenical council to unite Christendom, the

effect at home was to increase the intellectual and moral pressure on
leading recusants; many of them would have agreed wholeheartedly with
Persons that '[n]o violence is like to that which is laid upon men's consciences'. Among those caught in the tightening net were a number of
recusants closely linked to Shakespeare. His daughter Susannah was cited
in 1606 as a 'person Popishly affected'; so were the godparents of his
twins, Hamnet and Judith Sadler. Ben Jonson was another casualty. After
his years of regular debates with a group of divines who included the
Dean of St Paul's, Jonson finally gave way in 1609 and abandoned
Catholicism. Another victim of the times was George Blackwell, the
imprisoned leader of English Catholics, who was coerced in 1606 into
accepting the Oath of Allegiance. A fresh generation of churchmen was
brushing up the intellectual appeal of the new religion—but the depressing reality was that a brutally intolerant form of Calvinism still held sway.
It would be the bigoted George Abbot, not Lancelot Andrewes, who
became Archbishop of Canterbury in 1612.

   In desperation, leading Catholics turned their attention to a potential
new champion: James's son and heir, Prince Henry, already courted by the
group of dissidents who had gathered round Essex. Among them was a
man whose political and religious outlook closely resembles Shakespeare's.
The writer and courtier Sir John Harington is best known as the inventor
of the water-closet, which he described in a risqué book on the subject
published in 1596, *The Metamorphosis of Ajax* (a pun on 'jakes', or chamber-pot). He was briefly banished from court on its appearance—it is
always assumed because of its bawdiness. In fact, as recent scholars have
pointed out, it is a thinly disguised satire on the use of libel and torture as
tools of terror under Elizabeth's reign.[17] His handwritten marginal notes
indicate that his opinions were shared by an influential circle of men with
Catholic sympathies who met to discuss them, including Southampton,
Montague, the Arundel family, Sir John Petre, Sir John Spencer, Lord
Lumley and the earls of Northampton and Worcester.

   In his 1602 *Tract on the Succession*, confident of the sympathy of the
future King James, Harington puts a passionate case for toleration: 'I have
said it and therefore I may well write it, that these rigorous laws, these odi-
ous terms of traitors used to Papists by those that have been Papists and
served Papists themselves, hath both increased their number and their
malice'. He highlights, just as Shakespeare does, the dangers of enforcing
cruel laws on so many subjects and laments the ruinous costs of the
Protestant campaigns in the Low Countries and Ireland that forced the

Queen to extort money from her poor subjects by means of 'base shifts . . . that perhaps she knows not of . . . while the pulpit sounds nothing but faith, and peace, and plenty in her ears'. He clearly fumed throughout the obligatory sermons and instead praises Campion's eloquence and singles out Persons as the best writer of English of the age. He followed this book with a series of equally passionate verses presented to James on his accession, denouncing the old reign and full of hope for the new. They depict England as a corrupt land full of 'base spies' and 'forged wrongs' where 'law with lust and rule with rape is yoked', a land 'abounding with abomination'.

But after the renewal of persecution of 1604, Harington, like so many others, gave up on the King. He rededicated the book to Prince Henry, aged eleven at the time. The handwritten dedication copy still exists in the Folger Library. A picture of the rosary introduces the volume, which includes poems recalling the old religion with nostalgia. He appeals to the boy prince to rescue the country from the regime to which his father had just given new powers.

There are critics, led by Samuel Johnson, who puzzle over the startling contrast between Shakespeare's next three plays and the sombre, increasingly intellectualised work of the previous seven years. Shakespeare begins to produce fairy-tales. The first of them, *Pericles*, is almost childishly naive in its presentation and narrative form—so much so that it is widely accepted that the first part of the play is the work of another author. But once detected, the course of Shakespeare's long career as Catholic apologist provides a motive for this abrupt transition. Shakespeare, along with a large number of other highly intelligent contemporaries like Harington, was about to devote all his powers of persuasion to restating his case in terms designed to appeal to a fourteen-year-old boy.

V

THE LOSS OF PRINCE HENRY,
1608–1616

14

THE SECOND HOPE, 1608–1610

Prince Henry

JAMES I, whose appearance and temperament resembled those of an eccentric academic rather than a monarch, had fathered a captivating heir. 'Will he bury me alive?' he groaned, when after a day's hunting with his son, most of the party disappeared yet again to the Prince's own establishment at St James's Palace. Portraits of Henry bear out contemporary reports of his athletic figure, his physical grace and poise, his olive skin and grave, angular features, strongly reminiscent of his mother's family. He was in every way the antithesis of James. Where James was gauche, Henry was an outstanding athlete and dancer; where James was scholarly, Henry had a practical, scientific turn of mind; where James was peace-loving, Henry revelled in arms, chivalry and the art of war. Unlike his father, Henry combined an enquiring mind with considerable organising ability, ordering his household and keeping meticulous accounts from an early age. Perhaps in reaction to the sleaze of James's court, he himself was a model of moral rectitude, even installing a 'swear box' in St James's Palace, where those caught using foul language were expected to deposit a voluntary fine.

Not only did he resemble his mother physically, he shared her aesthetic tastes and, it was noted, treated her with the deepest respect, though James had done his best to keep the pair apart, removing the baby Henry from her Catholic influence at an early age and placing him in the austere Calvinist household of the Earl and Countess of Mar. The policy appeared to work. Henry grew up surrounded by Protestant divines and showed no sign of favouring his mother's religion. Nonetheless, he remained throughout his life an enigmatic character. A common observation was that he combined a deliberate, formidable manner with 'a close disposition, not easy to be known or pried into'.[1] Francis Bacon wrote, 'There were indeed in the Prince some things obscure and not to be discovered by the sagacity of any person, but by time only, which was denied him'.[2]

The period of unique Stuart promise proved tragically brief. At the age of eighteen, Henry caught typhoid fever after swimming in the Thames and after a long struggle died on 6 November 1612. There was a national outpouring of grief. To those accustomed to the corruption of James's court, this upright, reserved, determined young man had come to embody all the half-forgotten virtues of the ideal monarch. A Protestant hagiography sprang up around him immediately after his death. It was said that he refused to have papists in his court; that he would never allow 'two religions in one bed' by marrying a Catholic; that he had planned a Protestant crusade against the Hapsburgs. 'A chosen instrument . . . to work the Restoration of his Church and the Destruction of the *Romish* Idolatry' is the climax of a typical paean of praise.

The legend has survived to this day, the portrait of the militant, puritanical prince forming yet another jigsaw piece in the official version of the history of Shakespeare's times. But a recent biography reveals a more complex character.[3] Though Henry did indeed hope to re-establish England as a political force in Europe, spearheading a Protestant alliance against the Hapsburg ascendancy, aesthetically his home was the Counter-Reformation South. His interest in soldiering had an anachronistic, chivalrous streak. He consciously modelled himself on Sidney and Essex, and his head was filled with the kind of romance literature deplored by the strict Puritan churchmen who were his chaplains. Stories of Bevis of Hampton, Guy of Warwick and King Arthur were deeply suspect to such men: 'spiritual enchantments' written by 'idle Monkes or wanton Canons'.[4] Henry was a reluctant scholar, but he loved romances and did his best to bring them to life. He and his mother patronised a new form of court masque—elaborately staged performances that employed allegorical poetry, music and special effects to celebrate the royal family but also to advocate a revival of old ways and a rediscovery of vanished beauty and virtue. He himself starred as Meliadus, a lost prince who returns to reclaim his own, or as Philisides—Philip Sidney's poetic alter ego. A number of Henry's masques and tournaments take up the central theme of *Arcadia*: a mysterious prophesy that promised the recovery of something stolen but not lost. Shields at the tournaments set the tone with mottoes such as 'I revive the ancient glory'.

Such events appeared purely decorative at first sight. But Henry's Protestant tutors were right to be wary. Elizabethan romances were rarely escapist. Sidney's *Arcadia*, however decorative, was not what he called a 'trifle, triflingly handled'. It was a coded vehicle for his reflections on the matter of England that he refused to publish because, he warned, its chief safety 'shall be the not walking abroad'. There were a number of survivors of the Essex and Sidney circles at Henry's household, which was beginning to be a magnet for cultivated nobility and artists of all shades of opinion who found there a civilised refuge from the dissolute, Howard-dominated court at Whitehall. These were just the people to initiate Henry into the meaning of the elaborate Elizabethan idiom he adopted. The writer Matthew Gwynne was one, a close friend of Sidney's who back in 1590 had been one of *Arcadia*'s original editors.

Henry's strong aesthetic side led him into even more suspect territory. As his boyhood friends grew up and travelled, he pored over their long letters describing—with careful disclaimers—the glories of the Counter-Reformation courts of France and Italy, the splendour of their spectacles, their theatres, their gardens, architecture, paintings, sculptures. Detained in England by strict guardians, he imported Renaissance sculptors, artists, architects and inventors from abroad. Not only was his court alive with Italian artists and designers, but in spite of later denials, many of his courtiers were Catholic. Among them was the elderly Lord Lumley, a scholar and aesthete who had travelled widely in Italy after being imprisoned during Elizabeth's reign for his alleged part in the Ridolfi Plot against the Queen's life. He was now one of the Prince's tutors and spent his time collecting paintings, studying history and medicine, and developing the first Italianate garden in England at Nonsuch Palace.⁵ The prince's admiration for him amounted to discipleship; one scholar has said Henry was Lumley's 'ideological heir'. Lumley left Henry his collection of priceless books, which was to become the foundation of the modern British Library. Other Catholic associates included Ben Jonson and Inigo Jones, the brilliant team behind the development of court masques. Jonson's lyrics intrigued Henry, who in 1609 requested an annotated transcript of his *Masque of Queens*. The Queen's protégé, Samuel Daniel, master of elegantly concealed Catholic subtexts, also worked closely with Henry. The prince was evidently not put off when the first work Daniel dedicated to him, *Philotas*, almost landed the author in prison on a charge of subversion. He commissioned another subversive, John Hayward, to write a true history of medieval and Tudor England, the subject that had earned Hay-

ward several years in the Tower during the previous reign.[6] Other Elizabethan dissidents who gravitated towards the Prince included John Harington, Thomas Arundel and the Earl of Southampton.

To men like these, Henry offered genuine hope. Here at last was a
future ruler who avoided favouritism and opposed corruption. In 1606,
the French ambassador reported that 'he is already feared by those who
have the management of affairs, and especially the Earl of Salisbury
[Robert Cecil]', noting that he 'shows little esteem for his lordship':
indeed, he boldly tackled Cecil over his profiteering from Crown preroga-
tives. His great hero was Henry IV of France, a liberal-minded Catholic
whom he looked on as his 'second father'.[7] Like Henry IV, and in spite of
years of sectarian indoctrination, Prince Henry's attitude to religion was
pragmatic. Ignoring the protests of churchmen, he accepted his father's
decision that he should marry a Catholic: arrangements for his marriage
with Maria of Savoy were settled just before his final illness.

The First Approach

I T WAS WHEN Henry was approaching his fifteenth year in 1608 and
was beginning to attract dedications from all sides that Shakespeare's
work altered from dark, complex drama to consciously naive
romance. The change is not usually associated with the character of the
prince as presented by Protestant historians. But it was perfectly tailored
to the fuller portrait uncovered by recent research. Designed to play on
Henry's interest in mythic romance, authentic history and noble feats of
arms, the freshness and energy of these late plays mirror the great hope
that the Prince might come to the aid of a cause that seemed otherwise all
but dead. The code reveals a pressing hidden agenda: to set before Henry
the suppressed version of the story of England from the dawn of the
Reformation until the day when the young Prince, as England's champion, would step out from the shadows and come to the country's rescue.

Critics often note that the late romances revisit earlier plays and repeat
old motifs leading to the suggestion that Shakespeare has 'run out of
ideas'. In fact, the impression of a new beginning is deliberate: the first of
these plays even uses the same source material as his earliest work, *The
Comedy of Errors*. For years he had been addressing audiences of initiated
Catholics or erudite spectators like Elizabeth and James, able to detect his
hidden meaning from the slightest reference. But by 1608, Shakespeare

faced a new audience: a boy with no pretensions to scholarship. Accordingly, the next four plays reduce the whole convoluted history to its barest essentials, Shakespeare doing his utmost at every point to restate its complexities in terms likely to appeal to Henry. The result is timeless. Shakespeare takes the story of England's break with Rome and the period in the wilderness and universalises it into the saga of fall, suffering, rescue and homecoming that underlies all great myths. Yet the story of the age is clearly sign-posted in each of the plays, the subtext growing in sophistication as the Prince matures.

All four stories—*Pericles, Cymbeline, The Winter's Tale* and *The Tempest*—begin with horrors that soon become a thing of the past, proceed through a stormy period of suffering and remorse, and finish in the sunlight of a prolonged happy ending. The original crime is deliberately nebulous, its cause obscure; it is the unfinished, messy business of an older generation. Nonetheless, its effects poison the lives of the aging protagonists—a phase that evokes the waning spiritual life of the country under Elizabeth. Without knowing it, the children who grow up under the shadow of these dark events are cut off from their natural roots. But a youthful Counter-Reformation dynamism breaks the curse. Virtuous and constant, the children overcome evil, find their way back to their true home and in the process heal the wounds of the chastened older generation. The transcendent final acts of these great universal plays would have been more moving still to audiences that recognised the story of their own times—worldly, often disillusioned spectators who saw in the golden boy in their midst the chance of just such an ending.

Pericles is additionally an ideal entertainment for a boy with a passion for antiquity, adventure, tournaments, the sea, and no time for the depth of analysis that characterises Shakespeare's earlier plays. The play was mocked by Shakespeare's jealous rivals because like many works written primarily for the young, it became a byword for popular success, shown 'divers and sundry times' at court and at the Globe. It was also acted by recusant players and by English schoolboys in Catholic colleges abroad, which included *Pericles* on their syllabus—a tribute not simply to the pace of the narrative but to the clarity and occasional depth with which it recapitulated the stormy fortunes of recusant England. Tempests, abused love, earthquakes, a spiritual daughter who kneels to her earthly father—all these familiar code themes were now adapted to appeal to the young Henry, Shakespeare displaying again the extraordinary sensitivity to the character of his target audience evident in plays written for Elizabeth and James.

Vivid accounts survive of the energetic fourteen-year-old in 1608, itching to leave the confines of the schoolroom. 'I know what becomes a Prince', he bursts out after being scolded for neglecting his studies, 'It is not necessary for me to be a professor, but a soldier and a man of the world!' His passion was ships and the sea; his ambition was to renovate England's navy, and he was already expert in the details of boat-building. On his tenth birthday he had been given a miniature ship, the *Disdain*, which he sailed proudly along the Thames at London. Shakespeare accordingly bases his play on an eventful sea saga from a fourteenth-century poem by John Gower. Throughout, he adds small schoolboy touches. The sports-mad prince would have appreciated the inelegant description of Pericles as a ball tossed around the world's 'vast tennis court'; a pun on a 'vile' viol refers to the instrument Henry was learning at the time. But there are also emblematic episodes with deeper meanings for Henry to explore—among them a tournament and the discovery of a suit of armour retrieved from the sea.

Perhaps aware of a natural resistance on the part of the Prince and his tutors to a work by a writer known to plead the Catholic cause, Shakespeare barely reveals his hand in the first two acts of *Pericles*, which retell Gower's old story in such archaic terms that, even allowing for Shakespeare's skill at pastiche, many scholars believe Shakespeare did not write them at all. But in spite of the simple diction, Shakespeare's control is evident from the first moment. The character of Gower himself introduces each act with clarity and charm, the actors illustrating difficult bits of his brief narratives with mime. The 'restorative' freshness of his first speech sets the tone for all three romances—all the more stimulating set beside the highly involved despondency of Shakespeare's most recent works.

The play opens arrestingly on a dark stage bristling with heads on stakes. The royal children would have been gripped. The heads are of the victims of a tyrant who executes suitors for his daughter's hand who fail to answer a riddle. Pericles, a young 'Hercules', quickly discovers that those who succeed also die, for the answer contains a horrible secret. The king and his daughter are incestuous lovers—hence the 'curious pleasures' (1.1.16) Pericles reads in her face. Wisely, he bolts—but only just in time. The effects of the discovery are to haunt him until the final act. Only initiates would have recognised fleeting references to Henry VIII's original crime in this familiar instance of abused love, and a hint at the persecuted resistance in the young 'Hercules'.

Pericles becomes an exile. Pursued by the tyrant, he leaves his kingdom and flees overseas. The first of the play's storms, full of Reformation resonance, tosses him on the shore of Pentapolis. Shakespeare here arrests the action in order to dwell on a scene that does not appear in Gower. It is often quoted as evidence of alternative authorship; in fact, it is intended to give a hidden Catholic slant to Henry's favourite theme of ancient chivalry resurrected. The jocular fishermen who rescue Pericles retrieve his rusty armour from the sea. They announce the discovery with a cryptic phrase: 'Here's a fish hangs in the net like a poor man's right in the law' (2.1.115–116). Pericles tries to reclaim it. The armour was his birthright, he protests, given to him by his dying father, who told him it would always protect him from death. 'It kept where I kept, I so dearly lov'd it' (2.1.128). But the fishermen object. Their labour in retrieving it means that it is theirs as well. In another riddling image, they compare it to clothes that they have remade with the 'seams' of the sea: 'Ay, but hark you, my friend; 'twas we that made up this garment through the rough seams of the waters' (2.1.146–147).

In the Prince's court at St James's there would have been many ready to explain the riddle. The fish was the oldest image for Christianity, and fishermen for apostolic Christians. Earthy and good-humoured, the fishermen retrieve the rusty armour entangled in nets—the ancient Christian 'fish', caught in the mesh of English anti-Catholic legislation. This bare, rusted 'rite' is the Mass, stripped of ornament by the storm of persecution. The exiled nobleman recognises his once-rich inheritance and reclaims it. But he is not allowed to forget the new Counter-Reformation emphasis on poverty. The point of the scene is that it was ordinary people who painfully preserved and renewed the 'poor man's rite' in the course of the Reformation tempest. The incongruous debate was intended to prompt questions from Henry, obsessively expert when it came to armour.

His armour and his faith restored, the chastened Pericles becomes a guest at the court of the just Simonides, ruler of Pentapolis, and takes part in a tournament: another densely worked allegorical set-piece, evoking one of the first havens for English exiles, the English College at Rome, run by the Jesuits, known as the 'soldiers of Christ'. Shakespeare substitutes knights for Gower's naked gymnasts; and he adds the idea of a birthday celebration. When Elizabeth I's birthday replaced that of the Virgin in the calendar, English colleges abroad countered by celebrating the birthday of the Virgin with redoubled pomp, designed to rival the Queen's tournaments with more erudite, literary tournaments of their own, featuring a spiritual version of the same processional emblems.[8] The deeds of the play's 'right courteous Knights' (2.3.27) are described with reference to artists, volumes, title-pages, 'laboured scholars'. The glittering company casts Pericles into gloom, as he contrasts it with his own country. It all reminds him of the days of his dead father: 'in that glory once he was' (2.3.38). He himself, he realises sadly, is 'like a glow worm in the night, / The which hath fire in darkness, none in light' (2.3.43–44). His experience is that of impoverished Catholic exiles blinking at the splendours of Counter-Reformation Rome, suddenly aware of the extent of the revival that had passed England by. The conversation turns to the subject of treachery, the first talking point for English Catholics abroad.

Pericles leaves for home with the princess Thaisa as his wife—the embodiment of the revived faith he discovered at Pentapolis. But a second storm strikes, again from the 'grizzled north' (3, prologue, 47–48). Thaisa dies giving birth at sea, and her body is cast adrift while Pericles is left with a 'piece' of the dead queen, a 'fresh-new seafarer' (3.1.17–41)—their daughter, Marina. On land at Ephesus, men wonder at the force of the storm, and its accompanying earthquake. Like Juliet's, Marina's birth evokes the earthquake of 1580, the year of Campion's and Persons's seminal English mission.[9]

In a scene full of sacramental Catholic markers, the physician Cerimon finds and opens Thaisa's coffin and revives her. Unknown to Pericles, she retires to a convent—a common refuge for women exiled from England.[10] Meanwhile, Pericles leaves their baby in the safekeeping of the king of Tarsus and his wife, Dionyza, as he journeys sadly onwards. He is now in the position of returned exiles who lose their faith in a new storm of persecution and who despair of its revival.

But Marina, 'all that is left living' (3.1.20) of Thaisa, grows and flourishes. Gower appears in order to waft us forward to the moment when she is about to be killed on the instructions of the cruel Dionyza, a 'harpy' with 'an angel's face'—a punning allusion to the English coin, which had an angel on one side and Elizabeth's face on the reverse (3.3.47–48). Marina has been reared with Dionyza's own daughter but is like a dove beside a crow, eclipsing the other's 'graceful marks' (4, prologue, 36).[11] Marina's life is that of Catholics born in the 1580s, who, like Shakespeare's recusant daughter Susannah, had known only persecution—'born in a tempest . . . / This world to me is like a lasting storm' (4.1.19–20). She pleads with the murderer, but he is 'sworn' and 'will despatch'—only a timely kidnapping by pirates saves her. She exemplifies the heroic virtue of many underground Catholics around the early 1600s, for in spite of the persecution the number of missionaries grew steadily. It was during these years that Mary Ward, relative of the Gunpowder Plotters, founded her group of 'English Ladies'. She faced strong opposition from the church. Nuns were traditionally enclosed, but Mary Ward's order lived and worked exposed to the temptations of the world. Patronised by English nobles and gentry, they educated Catholic girls abroad along the same lines as boys in Jesuit schools. The controversy surrounding these new initiatives is recalled in the comic sequence that follows. Marina is sold to a brothel, where she converts all her clients, including the governor, and before long has set up a school, teaching divinity, music, sewing and other virtues: 'deep clerks she dumbs' and 'pupils lacks she none of noble race / Who pour their bounty on her' (5, prologue, 1–10).

In the moving final scene, Pericles's ship returns. Believing both daughter and wife are dead, he has fallen into a trance of grief. The governor proposes Marina try to rouse him—as she sings, Pericles gradually recognises her. On the hidden level, he represents those Catholics who despaired after the Gunpowder Plot but now encountered a vigorous influx from abroad of the next generation—a miraculous revival among their children of the faith they believed had foundered in spite of all their efforts. That Marina stands for this second and more spiritual generation of missionaries is made clear in the lyrical lines with which Pericles embraces her: "O, come hither, / Thou that beget'st him that did thee beget; / Thou that wast born at sea, buried at Tharsus, / And found at sea again' (5.1.193–196). The pair go to Ephesus to sacrifice to Diana, and they fall into the arms of the 'nun', Thaisa, who has been living in the temple there. Here again, as in *The Winter's Tale*, Shakespeare lays stress on the fact that the active, missionary Marina and the contemplative, mystical Thaisa are one and the same. 'Flesh of thy flesh, Thaisa', says Pericles, like Marina: 'My heart / Leaps to be gone into my mother's bosom' (5.3.45–48).

The lengthy last acts of these plays, which celebrate the 'great miracle' of reunion, give the impression of a writer who cannot bring himself to sign off.[12] Just as a personal despair overflowed and distorted works like *Timon of Athens* and *The Rape of Lucrece*, here a lingering, restorative delight, a rebirth of hope, overflows the bounds of the fifth act: 'New joy wait on you', Gower says to the audience as he departs.

England's Champion

A MOULDY TALE', Jonson called *Pericles:* and many later scholars, baffled by the point of the play, have taken their cue from his patronising tone. Criticism for Shakespeare's next play, however, has been much more forthright. Its moments of sacramental beauty apart, *Cymbeline* on the whole gets even lower marks than *Titus Andronicus*. Dr. Johnson explains why: 'To remark the folly of the fiction, the absurdity of the conduct, the confusion of the names, and manners of different times, and the impossibility of the events in any system of life, were to waste criticism upon unresisting imbecility, upon faults too evident for detection, and too gross for aggravation'.[13] Others can defend it only on the grounds of self-parody. More than any other play, *Cymbeline* is cited as evidence that Shakespeare retired early from the stage because his powers were exhausted.

Yet the hidden level reveals that the opposite was the case. Seen as the second stage of an intensive campaign to influence the outlook of the Prince, it becomes clear that the reason for its shortcomings is not that Shakespeare's grip has weakened: it is, as so often, that he is trying to do too much. It seems he had had an encouraging response to *Pericles*. The young Prince was trained to look for the deeper meanings behind fables and histories, and he plainly enjoyed it: there are accounts of Henry and his young nobles telling 'every one an History by turne, all of them delivering some observation upon the History told'.[14] Shakespeare's intention now was to provide the Prince with a much fuller version of his country's recent past, and to 'theme' it on the first great official occasion for the heir to the British throne, Henry's coming investiture as Prince of Wales in 1610, when he would be sixteen.

He chooses the setting of ancient Britain under assault from Rome: in this case, it is the Britain of the mythical first-century king, Cymbeline, a man dominated by his wicked queen. The Romano-British period was a well-worn staple of polemical debate. Ever since the first edition of *The Mirror for Magistrates* back in the days of Edward VI, it had been a stalking-horse for discussions of England's relations with Catholicism. Protestant writers identified the imperial Roman attempts to invade Britain with the ambitions of papal Rome and associated Britain's refusal to pay tribute to Caesar with contemporary England's defiance of the Pope. *Cymbeline* contains an entertaining parody of the style of this 'Roman Britain' debate.

Henry would certainly have been familiar with the crude Armada rhetoric that opens Act 3, when England's wicked queen and her simple-minded son insult a courteous Roman envoy, withholding tribute in terms that lampoon the more jingoistic anti-Roman poems in *The Mirror for Magistrates*. Even today most scholars take these speeches at face value, forgetting that they are put into the mouths of contemptible characters. Instead, the speeches of the villainous pair are said to express 'the same simple pride that all men of the age took in their country's history and good fortune'.[15] This was far from accurate.

One of the central messages of *Cymbeline* is that there was nothing simple about being a patriotic Englishman in the early years of the seventeenth century. Confirmation that this painstaking exploration of England's situation is intended to counter crude Protestant propaganda comes at the end of the play, which proposes what many saw as the ideal answer to the vexed problem of Britain's relations with Catholic Europe. In battle, the newly united country trounces Rome, but at the same time acknowledges a deeper allegiance. On equal terms after its dramatic victory, Britain volunteers to pay its 'wonted' tribute to the Roman overlords, 'from the which / We were dissuaded by our wicked queen' (5.5.460–461). This was an emphatically pro-Catholic gesture. The payment or withholding of tribute from Rome was the decisive factor in the 'Roman Britain' debate, determining the author's allegiance. It is a solution that would have satisfied Henry, longing to take to the field against the Hapsburg powers in Europe, yet not averse to marriage with a Catholic.

For connoisseurs of the coded technique, *Cymbeline* is a delight, its broad overview a comprehensive update on the way Shakespeare now looked back on the past two decades. In order to engage the attention of the royal family in this reassessment of the country's problems, he gives distinct Stuart traits to certain key roles, capitalising on the family fondness for acting out their own finer qualities in court masques.

The first strand of the plot restates Shakespeare's consistent theme, his 'noted weed [familiar clothes]', as he calls it ruefully in Sonnet 76, a subject so obsessive it 'almost tells my name'. This is the persecution and banishment of England's native religion, including the latest, most dangerous development: the mistrust that was poisoning relations between domestic and exiled Catholics. Addressed to the royal children, the tale takes adventurous form in *Cymbeline*, following the turbulent fortunes of two lovers: the high-spirited princess Imogen and Posthumus Leonatus, whose name suggests the rebirth of leonine English valour. Separated by the wicked queen, the parting of the secretly married couple, full of references to ancient liturgical prayers, sets up their Catholic identity. Posthumus falls prey to backbiting in an international college abroad, where an urbane slanderer persuades him that Imogen is unfaithful to him. The naive Posthumus instantly sees 'a million turns' in Imogen's alleged betrayal, just as the English exiles were led to believe that millions in Elizabeth's England wholeheartedly adopted the new religion.[16] Meanwhile, pursued by the queen and her son, stricken by her lover's lack of trust, Imogen embarks on a dangerous, disguised underworld existence. The couple's complex story and the bitterness of their rift emphasises the seriousness with which Shakespeare viewed the rifts between English Catholics. He reserves one of his finest lines of poetry for their reunion on an immovable 'rock'—'Hang there, like fruit, my soul, till the tree die' (5.5.264–265).

The second strand, directed particularly at the two Stuart princes, concerns the true heirs to Britain, menaced by the upstart order promoted under Elizabeth. Cymbeline's two noble sons have been spirited away by the resentful, dispossessed courtier Belarius, to be brought up in the wilds of Wales. Here Shakespeare inserts an in-joke for aficionados of the code, calling Cymbeline's seizure of his subject's lands 'a storm, or robbery, call it what you will' (3.3.62).[17] Cymbeline's second wife is an evil and nameless sorceress who intends to marry her gross son Cloten to Imogen. She maintains her power through schemes, potions and herbs; in an image of Elizabeth's paralysing hold on the country, her ultimate plan is to bring about Cymbeline's slow death through poison. Years after Elizabeth's death, Shakespeare has no qualms about sketching this venomous portrait of her. She is the image of duplicity: 'Dissembling courtesy. How fine this tyrant / Can tickle where she wounds!' (1.1.84–85), exclaims Imogen. It is she who alienates the country from Rome. Equally vicious is the play's portrayal of Elizabeth's legacy. Tactfully silent on the role of King James, who appears later on as Jove, Shakespeare portrays her son Cloten as the coarse new order now threatening England. Intended to remind the fastidious Henry of everything that repelled him in his father's court, Cloten particularly objects to being criticised for swearing, an allusion to Henry's expletive-free household that must have caused family amusement: "A whoreson jackanapes must take me up for swearing . . . when a gentleman is disposed to swear, it is not for any standers-by to curtail his oaths' (2.1.3–11).

Entertainingly repulsive though he is, Cloten has a strangely contradictory nature. He woos Imogen with a lyrical song about 'Mary buds' and 'chaliced flowers': surprisingly Catholic terminology. He pursues her to Wales dressed in Posthumus's clothes, about which he has developed an absurd fixation. His impersonation of Posthumus is one of the most subtle aspects of Cloten's identity as the upstart order. Shakespeare's last plays continue to address the growing threat to Catholicism from what was seen as a crafty, facsimile religion—the Protestant 'middle way', which adopted the appearance, vestments and ritual of the old religion while rejecting papal authority and the Mass. This is the reason behind Cloten's obsession with imitating Posthumus. His disguise eventually deceives Imogen when she finds his headless body and believes Posthumus is dead—a brilliantly condensed coded image typical of the play. The loss of Cloten's head, highlighted several times in Imogen's hysterical reaction to the discovery, would have reminded those with a knowledge of the theological disputes of the time that a body without a head symbolised a church without central authority.[18]

The country's true heirs are, of course, Cymbeline's two sons, the two princes, who are given the characteristics of Henry and his younger brother, Charles, destined to become King Charles I. The cameo of their isolated life in a cave near Milford Haven in Wales pays tribute to the future Prince of Wales, descendant of Henry VII, who landed his invading troops at Milford Haven, a reference used by other writers celebrating the investiture.[19] Isolated victims of a sententious old tutor, impatient to see the world, the princes' upbringing would have echoed with Henry. 'We have seen nothing', they complain (3.3.39). Belarius is a caricature of the royal tutors, with whom Henry had a playful love-hate relationship. The old man moralises ceaselessly, and his curriculum features Henry's pet subjects—the art of perspective, tales 'of courts, of princes, of the tricks in war' (3.3.10–15). In contrast to the verbose Belarius, the diction of the older prince, Guiderius, is direct and to the point—again, a characteristic of Henry, who made up for a slight speech defect with a gift for succinct witticism. He effortlessly kills Cloten for insulting his honour: 'I have spoke it and I did it', he says calmly to a later, horrified audience (5.5.290).

Another gesture to Henry lies behind the unusually distinctive character of the princes' sister, the disguised Imogen. Her playfully extravagant, exclamatory manner distinguishes her from Shakespeare's other youthful heroines and recalls contemporary accounts of the person who meant most to Henry—his sister Elizabeth, later the 'Winter Queen' of Bohemia. One acquaintance reported that she was 'like a schoolboy'—a good description of Imogen. The introduction of her buoyant character and distinctive mannerisms into the main theme of *Cymbeline* would have been a shrewd method of retaining the Prince's attention throughout the complexities of the plot.

As in previous plays intended for the eyes of the court, Shakespeare diplomatically places the solution to the country's problems in the hands of the monarch—and, in this case, of his children. Posthumus's hopelessly tangled situation—by the end of the play, that of an anguished triple defector—is resolved by a James-like Jupiter, who descends from Heaven in a vision to save him. The princes also have their moment of glory. Supported only by Posthumus and the elderly Belarius, they defeat the Roman army and save the country single-handed.

Cymbeline is a play the bickering Stuart family would have loved. With the exception of the Queen, each of them has a role in the establishment of a peaceful future for England. In many places the coded scenarios appear almost too compressed, but Shakespeare knew his audience, and no doubt Henry, the 'ideological heir' to the sophisticated Renaissance scholar Lord Lumley, would have enjoyed working out their hidden meaning. He would have known that Milford Haven, towards which deluded Imogen toils to meet her lover, was an invasion target, not just for his ancestor but for Spain; and he would therefore have appreciated the fact that, like the resistance deluded by Spanish promises, Imogen is unwittingly travelling to her death. And he would have known enough about the iconoclasm under Edward and Elizabeth to appreciate the significance of the scene in which the slanderer Iachimo prowls wickedly around the ornamented bedroom of the sleeping Imogen—a scene full of historical clues. Imogen, whose 'eyes are weak' (2.2.3), has turned down her book of Ovid at the rape of Philomel, the page to which the raped Lavinia pointed in *Titus Andronicus*. *The Rape of Lucrece* is recalled: 'Our Tarquin thus', gloats Iachimo, 'did softly press the rushes' (2.2.12–13). Like Desdemona, the vulnerable Imogen is compared to a monument in a chapel. Iachimo notes her church-like surroundings and attributes—the incensed breath, the candle, the 'canopied eyes', their lids like 'windows white and azure, laced / With blue of heaven's own tinct' (2.2.21–23), above all her mole evoking the Five Wounds: 'cinque-spotted, like the crimson drops / I' th'bottom of a cowslip' (2.2.38–39). Shakespeare briefly gives Iachimo the character of one of Elizabeth's ecclesiastical commissioners, writing 'all down' in 'mine inventory' and referring officiously to 'above ten thousand meaner movables' (2.2.23–30). The whole scene is designed to appeal to Henry's love of objets d'art, and to remind him of the destruction and greed that lay behind England's Protestant Reformation.

The elaborate denouement of *Cymbeline* would have left Henry in no doubt about the network of divisions within the country he would one day inherit. But at the same time it set before him an appealing goal: a glorious victory over everything that threatened England, and a reunion with its native faith.

It Is Required You Do Awake Your Faith

S HAKESPEARE'S GREATEST story of crime, exile and revival, written around 1610, is *The Winter's Tale*. The transcendent ending of this play, in which lost mother and exiled daughter embrace, has already been examined in relation to Magdalen Montague, who had recently died. It contains a second vindication of the essential continuity of Catholicism. In a charming pastoral debate at the centre of the play, the chaste heroine Perdita pointedly prefers the pure stock of country flowers to the 'grafted' varieties proposed by her more sophisticated visitors. The language of the debate comes straight from the theological argument of the day, in which the 'grafted', 'hybrid', 'spotted' state religion was denounced by both Catholics and Puritans.

The Winter's Tale presents the suppressed history of Reformation England in romantic and aesthetic terms that reveal, on the hidden level, that Shakespeare was not simply addressing the recusant community, though there was much in it for them—he still had the rapidly maturing Henry firmly in his sights. By 1610, the question of the Prince's marriage was uppermost in everyone's minds. For years James had been intent on fulfilling his dream of a grand dynastic double wedding for his two elder children, one to a Protestant, the other to a Catholic. His project sent waves of horror through anti-papist churchmen and administrators. It was rumoured that the Queen had secretly assured the Pope that her son would convert if he married a Catholic. There were continuous diplomatic comings and goings between Whitehall and the Spanish and Italian courts, inspiring a spate of anti-Medici plays from the many who opposed the project. Meanwhile, there were rumours that the Prince, until now a byword for chastity, had been seduced by one of the more promiscuous women at court, Frances Howard.

The chaste love story at the centre of *The Winter's Tale* coincides with this new phase in the life of the Prince. It is sufficiently idealised to suit either his own or his sister's wedding, featuring some of Shakespeare's finest love poetry and his most evocative English setting. In the end it was performed for the Princess Elizabeth's marriage to the Protestant Elector Palatine in 1613. Typical of Shakespeare's method of highlighting significant points for his target audience, the play's most profound moment includes a specific appeal to Henry's interest in Italian Renaissance art. The scene in which the statue comes to life is the only point in his work where Shakespeare mentions an artist by name:—the 'rare Italian master, Julio Romano'. Henry was particularly interested at this point in perspective and trompe l'oeil, fields in which the sixteenth-century artist and engineer Julio Romano was the acknowledged master. Henry was also devoting huge sums to a garden modelled on those of the Medici palaces, which featured special allegorical effects in the form of moving statues and automata. In choosing to dramatise an animated statue with a symbolic meaning and to attribute the finishing touches to Julio Romano, Shakespeare could not have made a more direct appeal to the Prince's tastes. In contrast to the dark contemporary dramas of Cyril Tourneur and Webster, the play reinforces everything Henry admired about the Medicis. Though directed now at a sophisticated young man, the scene has the same purpose as the rescue of armour from the sea in the boy's play, *Pericles*, and the killing of Cloten in *Cymbeline*, the play for the young Prince of Wales: it was to alert the future ruler of England to the role he could play in reversing the threatened extinction of the country's spirituality— still, for Shakespeare and his patrons, the one paramount issue.

Whatever Henry's reaction to this prolonged assault, it was clearly not discouraging. In planning the next play, *The Tempest*, Shakespeare kept up the pressure, continuing the theme of chaste courtship and marriage and taking as its subject the Prince's new obsession: he was fitting out a ship to travel to the New World. As an entertaining, romantic court play, it was a great success. *The Tempest* was played at court at the Princess Elizabeth's betrothal and her marriage. But Prince Henry, who threw himself into the preparations for the great event, did not live to see it. By the beginning of November 1612, he was in the final throes of typhoid fever. Elizabeth's wedding was deferred until some months after his death. When the muted celebrations took place, the change in the ideological climate was already evident: the masques Henry had planned with such care to celebrate his sister's marriage were replaced by performances that were more nationalistic and sectarian than anything that had taken place under his humane patronage. The French Ambassador was in no doubt as to their author-ship: they were the work, he reported, of 'les ministres protestants'. The last hope of a harmonious future for the country had vanished. For dissi-dents of all persuasions, a new dark age had begun.

CHAPTER

15

SILENCED, 1610–1611

Victory Against Dissidents

IN EARLY 1610, Shakespeare, only forty-five years old, was at the height of his powers. One of his greatest plays, *The Tempest*, lay ahead of him. He was the court's favourite playwright; in the popular theatre, his dramas were to remain for many years the mainstay of the King's Men, a byword for box-office success. Where Jonson's 'tedious' and 'irksome' plays 'scarce defrayed the Seacoal fire', wrote one admirer, 'Let but Beatrice And Benedick be seen, / Loe in a trice The cockpit, galleries, boxes, all are full . . . you scarce shall have a room / All is so pestered'. Not only was Shakespeare's work high on the reading list of the literati of the day, but judging by the slavish adulation of the would-be poet in *The Return from Parnassus*, he was already in a league of his own. Ben Jonson has to distinguish his own discriminating appreciation of Shakespeare from the uncritical acclaim of such admirers: he 'loved the man', he said, 'this side idolatry'. Yet all the evidence suggests that in the year 1610, Shakespeare wrapped up his affairs, left London and went back to Stratford. The remaining plays, *Two Noble Kinsmen* and *Henry VIII*, were completed by an inferior dramatist, John Fletcher.

A host of theories surrounds his sudden departure. Recent interest in Shakespeare's shrewd business dealings has led many to see it as the logical move for a man now rich enough to retire. They link it with another apparent indication that Shakespeare was more interested in social status than the fate of his plays—the fact that it was not until 1623, seven years after his death, that his fellow actors published the first collected edition of his work, the First Folio; in other words, it is only thanks to the posthumous efforts of friends that many of his plays survive at all.

One aspect of his retirement is rarely noted in the many accounts of his life. With one conspicuous exception, the same biographical pattern applies to almost all the leading dramatists of Shakespeare's day. From 1610 onwards, the subtle, obstreperous voices begin to fade out—Chapman, Marston, Daniel, Thomas Dekker, Tourneur, Middleton, Drayton, Webster, John Ford. They crop up occasionally over the next ten years, writing the odd court masque or meekly collaborating in politically correct plays with John Fletcher; but it is not until 1622 that they return, industriously publishing a backlog of poems and plays and writing new ones, some of them, such as George Chapman, producing serious work well into the 1630s. The year of the First Folio—1623—saw the long-delayed publication of Webster's savage *The Duchess of Malfi* and Daniel's quietly subversive poetry; in 1622, Dekker and Philip Massinger brought out a startlingly explicit play about persecution of Catholics, *The Virgin Martyr*. Had Shakespeare and Daniel lived, they too might have returned to work like the rest in the 1620s. There was only one major writer who kept going throughout the dark second decade of the seventeenth century: Shakespeare's most famous contemporary, Ben Jonson.

Jonson plainly struck gold after publicly renouncing his Catholicism in 1610. The enfant terrible now became a high-profile, token dissident, enjoying a degree of licence in return for toeing the party line. A trip to France, during which he took on a French Cardinal in debate while supposedly minding Sir Walter Raleigh's young son, was followed by two major plays, an Oxford MA, a London lectureship, and the post of England's first Poet Laureate, which brought with it a pension for life. In 1616, he became the first English author to publish his collected works. But he was clearly an unhappy man, recording the fact that, though 'reconciled' he is 'suspected still', and though financially secure, he has 'lost all his friends'.[1] His poems, prologues and recorded conversations are peppered with sour references to the new literary climate. He fulminated against his invidious position in a wonderfully eloquent outburst, 'To my Muse'. And for a few years after 1616, he too falls silent. In his 1623 tribute to Shakespeare, he laments 'the drooping Stage / Which, since thy flight from hence, hath mourned like night, / And despairs day, but for thy volumes light'.[2]

The cause of the despairing night was not a dearth of talent. It was a sudden change in the political climate. In 1610, Europe was convulsed by a shocking event: the assassination of Henry IV of France, the monarch whose combination of military boldness and diplomatic finesse made him a hero to young Henry Stuart and to everyone in England who advocated religious toleration. The murderer was a deranged friar, confirming King James's worst fears about the Catholic threat. It was a disaster that put an end to all hopes of freedom of conscience in England. James lost no time in cracking down hard on Catholics in his own country, and he began with a still wider and more stringent enforcement of the oath, this time including peers of the realm.[3] Many Catholic noblemen submitted; but Viscount Montague refused. He was sent to the Fleet prison and fined £6,000, a huge sum that entailed the lease and eventual loss of Montague House and its estate. His refusal, followed in 1612 by that of another leading London Catholic, Lord Vaux, made them heroes to the resistance and to Catholics abroad; but it spelt disaster for the many who had depended on them for protection. Among them may well have been Shakespeare.

Ever since Robert Greene's publisher had apologised back in 1593 for the dramatist's jibes about the newcomer from Stratford, Shakespeare had been protected from public attack. But after the death of Magdalen Montague in 1609, the great patronage network of the Montague family had been slowly disintegrating. The King had expressed irritation with the publication of the funeral eulogy of Lady Magdalen by her chaplain, Richard Smith, and even more annoyance at the number of priests sheltered in the Montague houses. The death in the same year of the Montagues' supporter on the Privy Council, Lord Buckhurst, left the family even more exposed. By the winter of 1609, their London houses were subject to repeated raids by enforcers and pursuivants; a series of arrests followed. 'No man can peep out of doors but he is caught' reported one of Lord Montague's servants. Before long the authorities had obtained valuable inside knowledge of the community from various disaffected priests. Houses of members of the entourage were ransacked; manuscripts and books, among them the work of suspect poets and dramatists, became more vulnerable than ever to seizure.[4]

The loss of such sanctuaries could not have come at a worse time. In the wake of the French assassination, executions resumed and the harassment and imprisonment of Catholics became continual. In 1611, James passed over the expected choice for the post of Archbishop of Canterbury, the moderate Lancelot Andrewes, and chose instead a well-known scourge of papistry, the Calvinist zealot George Abbot.

It was the ascendancy under Archbishop Abbott of the establishment hard-liners, old enemies of liberalism and Catholicism, that brought about the despairing literary 'night' referred to by Ben Jonson. Their methods of coercion remain unrecorded, but their impact on Shakespeare's fellow dramatists suggests a thoroughness that puts Elizabethan censorship in the shade. The renewal of dramatic activity eleven years later in 1622 coincided exactly with Abbott's fall from favour. By then, memories of the assassination had receded and James again began to consider a Spanish match for his heir, even contemplating religious toleration as one of the conditions. For a brief period in the early 1620s, Catholicism became almost acceptable, while Abbott's Calvinism began to give way to Archbishop Laud's much milder 'Anglican' form of Protestantism.

Like many others, then, Shakespeare withdrew from public life at the beginning of a highly restrictive decade; and the authorised publication of his work occurred, like theirs, the moment the hard line softened. The momentous implication, passed over by Protestant historians for whom such widespread dissidence and repression has always been unthinkable, is that Shakespeare did not retire—he was silenced.

Later comments imply that Shakespeare did not go quietly, but that to the end he refused to compromise, that force was used to get him either to conform or to leave. The first surviving indication that he had lost his protection comes in 1611 with John Speed's association of Shakespeare with extreme Catholicism. Raking up his identification of Robert Cecil's supporter, Lord Cobham, with the comic character of Falstaff, he accuses Shakespeare of being hand in glove with Robert Persons. He attacks 'this papist and his poet, of like conscience for lies, the one ever feigning and the other ever falsifying the truth'. Another suggestion that Shakespeare had become dangerously exposed occurs in 1614, in Jonson's prologue to his last great play, *Bartholomew Fair*. After a bruising introduction designed to flush out the spies and 'state decypherers' skulking among the spectators, Ben Jonson slips through to the Globe audience information many of them would have been waiting for about the disappearance of his famous rival. They can feel quite safe attending *this* play, he reassures them; there is nothing subversive here. The characters they are about to watch have no hidden identities. He is not as rash as some dramatists—those who write about tempests, tales and servant monsters—ridiculous subjects, of course, but also dangerous. The crowd need not wonder what 'great lady' is meant by the pig-woman, or 'what concealed statesman by the seller of mousetraps'. Some in the audience would not need reminding that *The Mousetrap* was the name of Hamlet's coded play exposing the usurper Claudius. No, Jonson goes on, reaching his angrily ironic climax, he is more prudent than such playwrights—unlike them, he is not about to risk 'mixing his head with other men's heels'. As he says elsewhere, a play-wright is one who 'takes private beatings and begins again'.[5] In other words, a dramatist who wrote the way Shakespeare did was likely to get beaten up.

Street violence was something Jonson knew all about, and in his later comments on Shakespeare, there is a recurrent note of irritation at his failure to use restraint and prudence, as Jonson did, once under pressure from the regime. He would not keep quiet, Jonson implies, and the result was that he ran into trouble. To the popular assertion that Shakespeare never crossed out a line, Jonson famously answered, 'Would he had blot-ted a thousand. Which they thought a malevolent speech.' In fact, the comment had nothing to do with professional jealousy, for he went on: 'He flowed with that facility, that sometimes it was necessary he should be stopped. *Sufflaminandus erat*, as Augustus said of Haterius. His wit was in his own power, would the rule of it had been so too'.[6] The reference to Augustus, the emperor who exiled Ovid, reinforces the suggestion that Jonson is talking about political indiscretion rather than artistic licence. There is an element of 'I told you so' here. As Shakespeare noted in *As You Like It*, Jonson liked to boast of the clever deniability of his own technique of satirising generalised 'humours' rather than coded characters and events, though as time went by a note of bitterness crept into Jonson's pride in his own canny professional survival.

Jonson's 1614 prologue also touches on the question of Shakespeare's allegiance to the old religion. Those who retain the standpoint of such resistance plays as *The Spanish Tragedy* or *Titus Andronicus*, it proclaims, reveal the 'virtuous and staid' ignorance of 'a man whose judgement shows it is constant, and hath stood still these five and twenty or thirty years'. This is clearly a particular man, with whom—if any in the audience are interested—Jonson is still in touch, for 'such a one the author knows where to find him'. He later accuses his rival of the same pig-headed con-stancy in his comment on Shakespeare's habitual line of debate that 'Cae-sar did never wrong but with just cause'.[7] Jonson's apparent air of superiority conceals genuine respect. For all the cautious disclaimers, such a stand, however self-defeating, actually embodied the unwavering virtues Jonson most admired. As he worked on altering *Every Man in His Humour* in order to include it in his own collected works, erasing both the Italian setting and the Catholic references, it is difficult to believe 'honest' Ben Jonson felt quite as pleased with himself as he liked to make out.

Shakespeare's Last Play

E very Man in His Humour, Jonson's first success, was also in Shake-speare's mind in the turbulent months of 1610 as the Montague households began to disperse, as Catholics everywhere took cover and as he prepared to re-draft what would be his last play. This time the hidden level is untidy and impressionistic; the magical universal play and the inner message do not always fit, and sometimes clash. But the outlines of the coded story are clear.

Just as in *Every Man in His Humour*, *The Tempest's* central character is called Prospero, and to reinforce the link, one of its fools is called after Jonson's foolish Stephano. The reason behind this was not simply a reminder of happier days. The cast list for Jonson's play suggests that Shakespeare acted the original Prospero: the re-use of the name is one of the many indications that *The Tempest's* Prospero was meant to be the author himself.[8] It was essential that the main character should be a recognisable self-portrait, for Shakespeare intended *The Tempest* to be his most autobiographical play. So far he had confined himself to a few self-deprecating bit parts: the deluded Stratford tinker, Christopher Sly; the bumptious director, Bottom; the rustic courtier, Touchstone, and William, the simple boor; the rejected entertainer, Feste; Mark Antony, the slippery master of double-speak. Now, in his farewell to his follow-ing, he adopts a major role in order to give a comprehensive coded apolo-gia for his life's work. It was considered so important that *The Tempest* was given the position of author's prologue to the rest of the plays in the First Folio.

In order to dramatise his own inner landscape, Shakespeare returned to the format known as the *psychomachia*, in which good and evil spirits strug-gled for possession over the soul. Shakespeare last used it in *Othello* to present James with a portrait of his imperilled self. Just as in *Othello*, Shakespeare goes one step further than other practitioners of this form of literary psychoanalysis, giving it several dimensions: personal, political and spiritual. Alongside James's disintegration, *Othello* dramatised the far more serious consequence—the disintegration of England. The intellec-tual Cassio was James's finer self, but also the spiritual side of England; the earthy Iago stood for the baser James, but also for the corrupt element that was destroying the country. Shakespeare uses the same technique in *The Tempest*. His own career as a professional dramatist is interlinked with something he considered far more important: the fortunes of the dissident English theatre.

In *The Tempest*, Shakespeare refines the *psychomachia*, retaining the 'angel-like' soul but representing it as suspended, not between two opposing spirits but between two opposing pairs of elements—the higher, intellectual faculties, and the lower, physical ones. John Donne describes himself as 'a little world made cunningly / Of elements and an angel-like sprite'. Prince Henry used the same motif: his proposal for a giant garden statue contained various rooms, with an airy dovecote for a head and damp, earthy caves at its base. The construction was another illustration of man as a microcosm of the universe, also composed of the four elements. Both Shakespeare and Drayton used the image in their sonnets, portraying their higher nature as fire and air drawn upwards by the angelic beloved, and their lower nature—earth and water—dragging them down.[9] This way of analysing identity is essential to Shakespeare's plan for *The Tempest*, which revolves around the higher faculties of air, fire and intellect, counterpoised by the lower elements of earth, water and the flesh, the lower elements forever threatening to despoil the 'fifth element'—the innocent and beautiful soul.

Shakespeare's tale begins with an island inhabited by Ariel, a spirit composed of air and fire, and Caliban, a monster associated with earth and water—Shakespeare's most extreme refinement of the principles of 'dark' and 'fair'. Two exiles land there, Prospero, the usurped Duke of Milan, and with him his daughter, Miranda, embodiment of beauty and innocence. The duke's learning and magical skill give him power over the island, and he becomes its king. As the action unfolds, seventeenth-century spectators would quickly recognise that the group represented the ingredients of a single personality. Prospero is Shakespeare's commanding self. Ariel represents both his intellectual, creative faculties and his command of the English stage at the turn of the seventeenth century. Caliban stands for his lower, physical side and for his own habitual characterisation of the dark side of the regime. The innocent Miranda is at once his soul and his concept of the spiritual essence of England. By means of this double allegory, Shakespeare's work is presented as integral to his nature.

Just as Shakespeare repeatedly conjured up the image of the Reformation in the shape of a tempest, Prospero raises a storm with the help of Ariel and summons to the island a shipload of characters from his own past, a company that echo Shakespeare's past plays at every turn. There is Prospero's wicked brother, Antonio, along with his equally wicked friend

Sebastian; the honest old courtier Gonzago, who saved Prospero's life; his political enemy Alphonso, Duke of Naples, and his son, Ferdinand; a fool and a drunkard, Trinculo and Stephano; finally, the boat's crew and boatswain, berated and obstructed by the passengers but still manfully trying to keep the ship afloat. Prospero's goal is the marriage of his daughter, Miranda, with his enemy's son, Ferdinand. He brings them together, tests their love and gives the union his blessing. Meanwhile, Ariel prevents the evil pair, Antonio and Sebastian, from murdering the duke of Naples; and only just in time, prevents the fool, the drunk and Caliban from murdering Prospero himself. In the end, Prospero reveals himself and is warmly reconciled with his old enemy Alphonso, a reconciliation confirmed by the marriage of their children. He retrieves his dukedom from his sullen brother; all of them prepare to leave the island.

From beginning to end, running jokes and puns remind the audience of yet another coded identity. The island has all the features of the stage, full of sounds that 'give delight and hurt not' (3.2.131), the magic at every point mimicking the illusions of the theatre. It features such props as musical instruments, a wardrobe of glittering costumes, a cell containing the dramatist's standby, his books. When Prospero's terrific tempest fails to wet the clothes of the shipwrecked men, Gonzalo notes that they are new-dyed like players' costumes. There is even a reference to the 'great globe itself' (4.1.153), threatened with dissolution. In the first act, two castaways criticise their island surroundings in the manner of seventeenth-century critics of the theatre (2.1.1–60). It lacks 'means to live', it stinks 'as if it had lungs, and rotten ones', the ground, like the pit of the open-air theatre, is 'tawny' with 'an eye of green in it'. *The Tempest* is a play about play-making.

The island's only native inhabitant—on the symbolic level, the only true native of the stage—is Ariel. Long before Prospero's arrival, Ariel served another visitor—'the foul witch Sycorax' (1.2.259), who arrived years earlier with her 'freckled whelp'. Ariel proved 'too delicate' to 'act her earthy and abhorr'd commands' and was imprisoned by her 'more potent ministers' (1.2.268–284). So effective was the imprisonment that Sycorax was unable to release him. 'With age and envy . . . / Grown into a hoop', Sycorax is connected with the moon, with wicked charms and with Algiers, a country just as notorious as sixteenth-century England for piracy. She and her son, Caliban, are extreme versions of the wicked queen in *Cymbeline* and her debased, idiot offspring—in other words, another angry caricature of Elizabeth and the blight she inflicted on England. The hidden reference therefore behind Ariel's imprisonment is to the attempts under Elizabeth to use the stage for Reformation propaganda, and when that failed, to stifle the country's dramatic creativity by banning all unlicensed drama and censoring whatever survived. Prospero's great achievement is to use his art to release Ariel when even Sycorax could not, an image of the way Shakespeare used his art to release the spirit of unfettered creativity that animated the lost world of popular drama. That he himself pioneered the consistent, covert allegorical technique is not only clear from the effect of his work on other writers, but he modestly alludes to it in Sonnets 78 and 79. So Ariel, the imprisoned spirit of the island, released and employed by Prospero, is also the silenced voice of the stage, released and employed by Shakespeare.

Ariel becomes a fascinating portrait of the way Shakespeare regarded his own creativity. 'I conceive', he says as he realises Prospero's plans with the speed of thought, originating and elaborating the action, requesting constant assessment and approval, his relationship with Prospero an accurate depiction of the interaction between the dramatist's will and his imagination. Prospero's attitude to his 'delicate Ariel'—by turns attentive, commanding, impatient and critically appreciative—is that of an artist exploiting his gifts to the full.[10]

By contrast, Caliban, constantly plotting to overthrow Prospero and regain the island for himself, represents Shakespeare's consistent leitmotif, the dark side of post-Reformation England, barbaric and politicised, intent on removing dissident drama from the stage. He is a 'moon-calf', a term used by Thomas More to describe Luther, and he is associated with the fens, homeland of the reformers (3.2.21). Like the early Levellers and the German peasants who rebelled in the 1520s inspired by Luther's doctrines, Caliban is a visionary who hates his enslavement and joins the rabble to overthrow his cruel master. He rejects manual labour, chanting 'No more dams I'll make for fish; / Nor fetch in firing / At requiring / Nor scrape trenchering, nor wash dish' (2.2.169–172). This is the very moment that the princely Ferdinand rolls up his sleeves to carry logs for Miranda's sake and reminds us that 'some kinds of baseness / Are nobly undergone' (3.1.2–3)—a deliberate contrast between the spiritual and political effects of the Reformation. From Aaron the Moor to Cloten, this increasingly brutal characterisation of England's intractable, destructive element is a motif of Shakespeare's work that he recognises in The Tempest as peculiarly his own. He lets Ariel go, but not his dark obsession, Caliban: 'this thing of darkness I acknowledge mine' (5.1.275).

At the same time, his 'servant-monster' embodies the earthy elements essential to Prospero, who cannot do without him: 'he does make our fire, / Fetch in our wood, and serves in offices / That profit us' (1.2.312). Moreover, Caliban's speech is full of a rich natural poetry, the complement to the ethereal songs of Ariel. But he also embodies everything associated with man's lower nature: sloth, lust, resentment, envy, drunkenness. These debasing tendencies are kept in check by the will: Prospero's rough enslavement of Caliban would therefore have been seen as entirely correct, an echo of St Paul's line, 'I buffet my body, and make it my slave'. There is something ominous, however, in Prospero's explicit appropriation of these lower elements at a moment of imminent 'despair' (epilogue, 15) when he has lost not only the intellectual, creative Ariel but the books without which, as Caliban knows, 'he's but a sot, as I am' (3.1.88–89).

Caliban attempts to rape Miranda. The hidden plot of *Othello* portrayed the soul overwhelmed by man's lower nature; and the same imagery is at work here. The attempted rape is not—as some scholars have suggested—Shakespeare's guilty admission of incestuous feelings for his daughter. Following the contemporary allegory of the elements as the play invites us to do, it becomes an image of his uncontrolled baser nature threatening to overwhelm his 'angel-like sprite'—his soul. Politically, however, the episode is designed to recall that characteristic Shakespearean theme: the campaign by the regime to take over and control the country's spirituality, in particular its representation on the stage. Finally, Caliban belongs to the great contemporary debate about the moral nature of savages, of deep interest to those like Prince Henry and the Earl of Southampton who were investing in voyages to the new world. As so often in Shakespeare's plays, the diverse dimensions combine to produce an extraordinarily resonant character.

Miranda herself is not only the embodiment of what Prospero loves most, his 'dear heart', his 'wench', his 'wonder'; she is also the last of Shakespeare's many incarnations of what England ought most to value—the vital force that he often portrays as the country's soul. A single humorous phrase—'the fringed curtains of thine eye advance'—lightly recalls the world of hyperbole he and many others used to evoke this spiritual figure (1.2.408). Along with her attempted extinction, he touches on a second motif—the dream of her eventual re-union with the country, reflected in Miranda's marriage to Ferdinand. As the virtuous son of Prospero's old enemy, Ferdinand represents the vision of a new national tolerance, his 'sweet beloved name' homage perhaps to the politique patron of

Shakespeare's early plays and one of the lost hopes of English Catholicism, Ferdinando, Lord Strange. In a stroke of brilliant literary shorthand, Shakespeare ends *The Tempest* with an emblem that resolves once and for all his fundamental theme, the problem of the irreconcilable differences between the 'dark' reformed religion and the 'fair' old faith (5.1.172–178). He represents it as a game of chess between lovers—the ultimate refinement of war between black and white, of conflict within harmony. The scrap of dialogue over the chessboard in which Miranda laughingly accuses a protesting Ferdinand of cheating has profound significance. Though Ferdinand may wrangle for 'a score of kingdoms', when it comes to 'the world' the pair are at peace: a brief vision of the perfect balance achieved at the end of *Cymbeline*, in which political power-games have no impact on matters of the soul. Black and white, instead of being forced to merge, here preserve their distinct identity within a context of mutual respect. This is another consistent position, unchanged since the days of *The Two Gentlemen of Verona* and *Love's Labour's Lost*, plays that allow equal dignity to the finest elements in both Lutheranism and the old faith, while deploring England's callous policy of repressing its native religion and abusing and enforcing the new.

The other elements of the plot recall further distinctive aspects of Shakespeare's hidden work, all of them orchestrated by Prospero himself, who from start to finish is actor, director and playwright, in complete command of the stage, working urgently and often irritably within the confines of the dramatic unities, particularly the unity of time, balancing the subplots and almost losing track of one of them, allowing Ariel free rein in certain areas, repressing him in others. His age as well as his name connects him with Shakespeare: Prospero is forty-five, as was Shakespeare in early 1610.

The whole business of Caliban's attempt to rob, murder and replace the island's master precipitates Prospero's abandonment of magic—a strong suggestion of actual pressure on the real-life dramatist. It is the recollection of Caliban's brutish attempt on his life that prompts the first of the three speeches in which Prospero resigns his power—speeches that refer unmistakably to the end of Shakespeare's own professional career. The first set-piece, 'Our revels now are ended' abruptly cuts short the play that has been enthralling Ferdinand, scattering the actors along with an unusually impressionistic stage direction: 'a strange hollow and confused noise' (4.1.138–163). The speech evokes the end, not simply of the play—'a vanity of my art'—but, in an anticipation of the coming suppression of all dissident drama, the end of the Globe Theatre and all it stood for. 'Like the baseless fabric of this vision . . . the great globe itself, Yea, all which it inherit, shall dissolve'. The lines are spoken in a fury, Prospero attempting and failing to regain his composure as he walks off 'to still my beating mind', summoning Ariel with impatient urgency: 'Come with a thought. I thank thee, Ariel; Come'. Though Caliban's plot has been foiled, Prospero rages on: 'A devil, a born devil . . . on whom my pains / Humanely taken—all, all lost, quite lost!' (5.1.188). Earlier in the play both Prospero and Miranda recall their attempts to educate Caliban, echoing Shakespeare's own attempts through his work to enlighten, cajole and humanise the brutal element in England that destroyed so much of the country after the Reformation. But—a characteristically precise pun—Caliban will not take 'any print of goodness' (1.2.352). The result creates an articulate opposition: 'You taught me language, and my profit on't / Is, I know how to curse' (1.2.364–365). Prospero's obsession with his failure to educate Caliban reflects Shakespeare's own sense of failure, for in 1610 it was clear that coarse extremism was by now more embedded than ever in the new order: 'As with age his body uglier grows, so his mind cankers' (4.1.191–192). And now there was a personal animus, evident in the hints from Speed of character assassination, from Jonson of assaults and threats, from *The Tempest* of an attempt to silence him. It seems there was a genuine threat of physical violence, and if the regime's intention was to cut short his career, it succeeded.

The second stage of the farewell is the speech at the beginning of the last act in which Prospero announces that he will bury his staff, drown his book and renounce his magic powers. It is preceded by a conference between Prospero and Ariel over how to resolve the drama, all the threads of which Ariel obediently holds in suspended animation. As he fumes over Caliban, Prospero has been planning revenge; but to his surprise, Ariel advises forgiveness. In a momentous revision of the plot, evidently involving a powerful effort of will, Prospero follows the advice of the servant who embodies his higher faculties: 'Though with their high wrongs I am struck to th'quick, / Yet with my nobler reason 'gainst my fury / Do I take part. The rarer action is / In virtue than in vengeance' (5.1.27–28).

The same effort of will is evident in the magnanimity and lack of recrimination that give such grandeur to this second speech of resignation (5.1.34–57). Its opening, 'Ye elves of hills, brooks, standing lakes and groves' would have alerted anyone with a grammar-school education to its original, Medea's famous speech from Ovid's *Metamorphoses*, foremost among the source-books Prospero, and Shakespeare, are about to renounce. Shakespeare uses the passage to review his own achievement in a catalogue that builds up to an electrifying crescendo with the evocation of the great image that gives the play its title, opens the First Folio and informs his work: 'I have . . . called forth the mutinous winds, / And 'twixt the green sea and the azured vault / Set roaring war. To the dread-rattling thunder / Have I given fire and rifted Jove's stout oak / With his own bolt . . .' (5.1.41–45). Like earlier references to midnight magic, none of this appears in Ovid but is added to remind the audience of particular works. The use of Jove's fire against his oak, for instance, recalls all the points in his plays, particularly *Titus Andronicus*, *King Lear*, *Timon of Athens* and *Coriolanus*, in which the English nation—the 'oak'—is bitterly attacked by its afflicted countrymen.[11] Ovid's Medea summons the spirit world in order to enact further magic: Prospero summons it only—in a tremendous and unexpected volte-face—to renounce it forever.

One of the features of *The Tempest* is its intimate relationship with the audience; not only is it first-class entertainment, fast-paced, funny, lyrical, tense, enriched with music and masque: it is a drama that abounds in soliloquies, knowing asides, comic by-play. More than any of his other works, this play about the theatre draws the audience into the action. And the relationship culminates with the final stage of Shakespeare's farewell, the epilogue, delivered sotto voce to the one audience he never lost sight of, even in the most elaborate of his court dramas—those standing in the pit of the theatre: not merely, as we now know, a place for groundlings but one of the best positions from which to enjoy the plays.

The short, simple speech begins with an invitation unique in his work: 'Please you, draw near'. His final words are the clearest indication that Shakespeare was not leaving voluntarily but had been given a choice: either to stay and confine himself to harmless subjects or to leave. He begins by confirming the rumour: 'Now tis true / I must be here confined by you / Or sent to Naples'. Unlike the Prospero in the play who leaves voluntarily for Naples, this one is 'sent'; he goes in order 'to please', though he does not say whom. Many must have pressed him to stay: he asks them not to 'confine him' on 'this bare island'—the imperilled English stage. Following theatrical convention, he requests the hands and voices of his audience, but instead of applause he unexpectedly asks for prayers in order to release him from a state of 'despair'. And not just any prayers: by using the inflammatory word 'indulgence' and asking for the kind of prayer that will release him from his purgatory in return for pardon for their own sins, Shakespeare concludes his work with a series of defiantly Catholic terms, invoking precisely the doctrines of Purgatory and the prayers for the dead known as 'indulgences' that triggered Luther's Reformation.

Given the intense personal emotion that underlies *The Tempest*, one has to admire the way Shakespeare's professionalism continued unaltered to the end. For his momentous withdrawal from public life forms merely one aspect of the drama, taking the place of the political commentary that usually lay below the surface of the plot. In every other way, the play represented a rich parting gift for the King's Men: entertaining on all levels and, like the other romances, crafted with court performance in mind.[12]

If, as he packed his bags for Stratford, Shakespeare took comfort from the fact that the worst was now behind him, he was wrong. For too long he had been a uniquely privileged thorn in the flesh of the country's new religious and political order. The same forces who were behind the changes to Princess Elizabeth's wedding masques were about to exact a perfectly calculated revenge on the writer who for twenty years had been their most subtle and formidable opponent.

CHAPTER
16

'THE LOST MAN', 1611 AND AFTER

The Forgeries of John Fletcher

ONE OF THE CRUELLEST fates for an artist who has managed, against all the odds, to preserve his integrity under a repressive regime is to be misrepresented as a collaborator. This was what awaited Shakespeare. Everything indicates that the authorities realised that their actions in silencing the country's foremost dramatist would make bad publicity. Better to let it appear that, like Ben Jonson, he had seen sense and decided to conform: better—and more satisfying. The instrument of their revenge was the versatile pen of John Fletcher.

Fifteen years Shakespeare's junior, he was the son of Richard Fletcher, the kind of worldly churchman who was the despair of genuinely spiritual Protestants. A corrupt and sycophantic Calvinist, Richard Fletcher exhibited what the *Dictionary of National Biography* calls 'the insolence of unfeeling bigotry', pestering Mary Queen of Scots with his 'unwelcome ministrations' at her execution. He beggared his diocese, spending most of his time and money at court, where according to John Harington, he 'knew what would please the Queen and would venture on that though that offended others'. But after a second marriage to a woman of 'low reputation', he was banished from the Queen's presence and never regained favour, in spite of 'illiterate, fawning' letters to William Cecil. He died in 1596 owing large sums of money both to the Crown and to other creditors, and he left behind him eight children, among them the seventeen-year-old John.

John Fletcher's inexplicably rapid rise in the world of the theatre suggests that the son repaid his father's debts in terms of services far more valuable than money. None of the plays he wrote unaided was successful, and he owed his reputation to the skills of his many collaborators, chiefly the more able Francis Beaumont. He was not above copying the manner of different writers and would occasionally publish his own work under their names: his *Cupid's Revenge*, for instance, is mostly by Beaumont. A clue as to why more talented men agreed to this parasitic partnership lies in the distinctive nature of Fletcher's contributions. His treatment of familiar controversial material is bland and sentimentalised, drained of the passion that often made political mine-fields of innocuous settings like Roman Britain or Arcadia. He specialises in marginal digs at the Catholic line on such subjects, revealing a well-informed mastery of the idiom of dissident writers. Typical hits include Boadicea's sneer, 'Your great saint Lucrece died not for love' and the advice to England's enemies to 'place in your Roman flesh a Briton soul'. Shakespeare was one of his early targets. The 1610 preface to his *Faithful Shepherdess* attacks plays that celebrate lost Catholic rituals under guise of a pastoral setting—exactly the technique of *The Winter's Tale*. His 1611 *The Tamer Tamed* reverses the subtext of Shakespeare's *The Taming of the Shrew*, featuring a Petruchio cowed by his second wife, the even more shrewish Maria, an accomplice of Bianca's who is given papistical Jesuit markers. It seems that after years of ineffective censorship, the regime had hit on the technique used later in Soviet Russia—that of infiltrating government men into the literary community and promoting their work at the expense of those who failed to conform. Fletcher, in other words, was the dramatists' 'minder', and collaboration with him was the way to survive in the later years of James's reign. Fletcher shared the credits with almost every leading dramatist of the day: Jonson, one of his reluctant partners, eloquently attacks his magpie technique in his poem 'Poet-Ape',[1] deriding his pretensions 'to be thought our chief'. Yet he succeeded. When Shakespeare left, it was Fletcher who became the leading dramatist of the King's Men.

He was the ideal instrument for delivering the coup de grace to his predecessor. Somehow, perhaps through the agents who were currently raiding great Catholic houses like Montague Close, Fletcher obtained drafts of Shakespeare's unfinished plays—what Jonson called 'shreds from the whole piece'—and somehow, between his many collaborations, found time to saturate himself in Shakespeare's previous work, achieving a remarkable mastery of his manner. One result was *The Two Noble Kinsmen*, published under the names of Fletcher and Shakespeare, but excluded from the First Folio. Most scholars agree that it is largely by Fletcher; some of it—the mad scenes and the pastoral—'undisguised, but mostly fatuous and provoking, imitations of Shakespeare',² some of it extremely skilful. The opening scene contains many familiar Shakespearean motifs: laments for the unburied dead, references connecting the mourners with ravaged beauty, with Hercules, with a courtly dispute over kneeling. But it is a superficial resemblance. Though Fletcher captures the rhythms and the density of Shakespeare's style, the images are two-dimensional and lead nowhere. Many critics, including William Hazlitt, have agreed with the poet Shelley's brisk dismissal: 'I do not believe Shakespeare wrote a word of it'.³ Perhaps aware of his shortcomings, Fletcher resorted to a low trick to establish the play's Shakespearean credentials. In a flowery, super-fluous passage, a character reflects on the death of her beloved twin sister 'when our count / Was each eleven'. Though Shakespeare never explicitly mentions it, acquaintances would have known of the death of his only son, Judith's twin, Hamnet, at the age of eleven, and would have seen this as a mark of his authorship.

The Two Noble Kinsmen may have been Fletcher's practice run. His tour de force was *Henry VIII*, destined to become the nation's flagship play. Yet he took no credit for his achievement. From the beginning, it was pre-sented as the work of William Shakespeare, and as such it was included in the First Folio at the end of the Histories. Fletcher's own hand in the play was not detected for centuries, during which, thanks to its effectiveness as stage spectacle, it continued to be a popular part of the Shakespearean canon. Only gradually did scholarly opinion begin to detect a number of passages in Fletcher's idiosyncratic style; it is now clear that much of the play is by Fletcher, while even the sections attributed to Shakespeare appear, on close examination, to be Fletcher at his most chameleon-like.

Why was Fletcher so uncharacteristically retiring when it came to tak-ing credit for what was possibly his most crowd-pulling play? Its 1613 per-formance at the Globe was an unusually grand occasion: someone put up a great deal of money for the lavish staging, which included real cannon and costumes that could well have survived from the court of King Henry VIII himself. The way was mysteriously cleared for its openly topical content, while the pre-publicity would have suggested that Shakespeare had at last returned from retirement with another play for the Globe. Sir Henry Wotton, who attended the performance, emphasised its almost unseemly extravagance: the impersonations of historical characters were so literal as to be 'ridiculous'.

In passing off such a vital work as Shakespeare's own, Fletcher may have been fulfilling his commitments to his real paymasters—not the playhouses, but the propagandists of the new regime so ringingly endorsed in *Henry VIII*. For the purpose of such a high-profile staging of a brilliant imitation of Shakespeare's work was nothing less than to proclaim to the world that the national poet was, after all, overtly Protestant. In the words of the critic Northrop Frye, the play is designed to reveal a 'providence who is ready to tear the whole social and religious structure of England to pieces in order to get Queen Elizabeth born'.[4] Given its unusually clear polemical nature, it is strange that for so long there were no doubts over its authorship, though there are deliberate echoes of Shakespeare's most conformist play, *Henry V*. The crass subtitle, *All Is True*, is diametrically opposed to Shakespeare's characteristic obliqueness, and the superior tone of the prologue again is the inverse of Shakespeare's. 'I come no more to make you laugh', it begins repressively, implying that the author of *The Tempest* has seen the error of his ways.[5] Ridiculing fights and comic fooling, it proclaims a loftier goal: that 'such as give / Their money out of hope they may believe / May here find truth too'. The word 'believe' sets in motion the sectarian rhetoric, and already the word 'truth' recurs with a confidence and regularity foreign to Shakespeare. By the time the play has reached its climax with Cranmer's patriotic hymn to Elizabeth and her successor at the end of Act 5, the author is well into his stride. Shakespeare, who had been publicly reproached for his pointed refusal to join the conventional outpouring of grief at Elizabeth's death now had to accept as his own a ludicrously extravagant panegyric of every aspect of her reign—exactly the kind of pulpit sycophancy that had so disgusted John Harington.

The crafting of the play shows considerable subtlety. The first scene, critical in establishing Shakespearean credentials, is a masterly pastiche; the pace of the dialogue and the condensed imagery is exactly in Shakespeare's style. Even here, however, Fletcher repeatedly verges on the ridiculous; and crucially, the complex diction is mannered and misses Shakespeare's concise intensity. Finally, certain 'code' ideas, treated with sophistication by Shakespeare, are unwittingly trampled on by Fletcher. The idea of exposure to the sun was one of these areas, the concept of closeness to the sun carefully reserved to mean closeness to God; Fletcher is ignorant of its significance, casually associating it with the venal Wolsey (1.1.55).

The play's most plausibly Shakespearean characteristic is its even-handedness: Wolsey, Norfolk and Buckingham are all given noble farewell speeches, though at the expense of convincing characterisation; and

Catherine of Aragon is a wholly sympathetic figure, the great speech at her trial taken almost word for word from contemporary accounts. But there is sleight of hand beneath the apparent impartiality. Archbishop Cranmer, architect of England's Reformation, is the play's hero, while the dazzling pageantry of Anne Boleyn's coronation represents the play's major set-piece, in which the presence of leading Catholic peers like Norfolk are repeatedly stressed. The last act contains references to a source unusual for Shakespeare, the Protestant propaganda classic, *Foxe's Book of Martyrs*; and though Catherine in fact died three years after Henry's marriage to Anne Boleyn, the play makes it appear that she dies at the same time, allowing greater legitimacy to Elizabeth's parentage. There is no mention of Elizabeth's older sister, Mary. As propaganda, the play is a masterpiece; it is, at the same time, an expert forgery. It makes brazen use of the name and style of a leading dissident author in order to give legitimacy to England's Protestant regime. Shakespeare's followers must have experienced shock and disillusion—the effect would have been that of a new novel by Boris Pasternak that glowingly endorsed the Communist regime and contained a sympathetic portrait of Lenin.

If this is the case, how did *Henry VIII* end up in the First Folio, edited by Shakespeare's old friends, the actors Henry Condell and John Heminge? The reason must be that it was too late to disown it. By 1623, the play had been acted many times under Shakespeare's name and was a major money-spinner for the King's Men. Even in more tolerant times, the censor could have read treacherous implications into the deliberate omission of *Henry VIII*. Its inclusion must have been a condition of publication. However, one cannot imagine Shakespeare ever authorising a volume of his works containing the play.

Ben Jonson's Pastoral Tribute

I F THESE WERE the circumstances of Shakespeare's retirement, his last five years must have been bitter indeed. When the sparks from a cannon fired during the 1614 performance of *Henry VIII* set light to the Globe Theatre and burned it to the ground, one is tempted to imagine a grim smile from the so-called author at the poetic justice of the accident. But there is no real evidence of how he felt. The notion of an alienated and disillusioned retirement is as much a guess as that of the shrewd and contented Stratford man of business. There are no known accounts of

Shakespeare in retirement, and he himself wrote nothing more. There is the odd anecdote—Aubrey's, for instance, that he died after a drinking bout with Jonson and Drayton. He was clearly not incapacitated, for surviving accounts and legal documents reveal that between 1610 and 1616 he was active at Stratford and continued to visit London. But in spite of all the attempts to read deeper meanings into his will and the epitaph on his tomb, his state of mind at the end of his life remains a mystery. Nonetheless, it may well be that we have always had in our possession an intimate portrait of Shakespeare in retirement, overlooked by scholars because it depicts, not the popular conception of the respectable, well-to-do retired dramatist, but the unfamiliar dissident Shakespeare of the hidden plays.

Ben Jonson's *Sad Shepherd* is a literary curio. Published posthumously, it breaks off abruptly in the third act with the characteristic words 'go hang thyself'. It is his only pastoral: and it takes the form of a vigorous counter-blast to Fletcher's *The Faithful Shepherdess*, replacing Fletcher's Arcadian daintiness with the robust, bawdy world of Robin Hood and his outlaws and celebrating everything Fletcher deplored in his prim preface— unfettered emotions, the language and customs of English country life, an explicit longing for the return of better times. In his own hard-hitting preface, Jonson implies that his play was originally written around 1612, not long after Fletcher's: 'Here's an heresy *of late* let fall, / That mirth by no means fits a pastoral, / Such say so, who can make none, he presumes . . .'.[6]

The heart-warming boldness, however, is deceptive, for Jonson's play remained unpublished, and there are no records of a public performance. This is Jonson as he longed to be, writing 'things manly and not smelling parasite'.[7] But its polish does suggest a private audience. The play is not merely a vindication of earthy English pastoral; it is a belated answer to Shakespeare's portrayal of Jonson in the pastoral play *As You Like It*. Jonson's central figure is Robin Hood, the outlaw to whom Shakespeare compared his exiled Duke; he too includes a lover who carves names on trees, and he makes elaborate play with Jaques' theme of deer and venison. The sad shepherd of the title is Aeglamour, 'who best could tread / Our country dances and our games did lead' but who has withdrawn into solitary depression. His departure strikes 'horror' into his friends; without him, 'the mirth is troubled much'. He believes that his beloved Earine has drowned and that life holds no more meaning. Although he is deceived (in an echo of *The Tempest*, Earine has been imprisoned in an oak tree by a witch who wants her own son to marry her), the play is cut short before

Aeglamour discovers the truth. His companions try to lift his depression but they fail; instead, he verges on madness.

There is a single literary precedent for the name Aeglamour.[8] He is one of Shakespeare's few entirely virtuous male characters: the generous, open-minded lover who courts Julia yet also assists the afflicted Silvia in *The Two Gentlemen of Verona*. And Shakespeare was the only writer Jonson acknowledged as pre-eminent—like Aeglamour, he 'our games did lead'. Critics have pointed out another link. Aeglamour's language is distinctly Shakespearean. Not only is it unusually lyrical for Jonson, but it is full of echoes from such plays as *A Midsummer Night's Dream*, *The Merchant of Venice*, *As You Like It*, and *Love's Labour's Lost*.

Unlike Fletcher, Jonson catches the true ring of Shakespeare's language in his portrayal of the melancholy Aeglamour. This is no mere imitation of his tricks of speech, but rather Shakespeare reproduced from the inside by someone who understood the way his mind worked.[9] Aeglamour's images may be bizarre, but they develop with Shakespeare's fluency and inner logic. And when it comes to code markers, Jonson brings them in with a knowing nudge, from the small signposts—'It will be rare, rare, rare!' 'In faith, in faith'—to the familiar penumbra of spiritual markers surrounding Earine. He gives us a portrayal of Shakespeare actually discussing his hidden methods, in particular such allegories of Henry VIII's takeover as those concealed within *The Rape of Lucrece*, *The Winter's Tale* and *Pericles*. Brooding on how to avenge his loss, Aeglamour returns obsessively to the idea of secret, deniable ways of communicating—'You know my meaning', he hisses in dark asides; 'No words!', as he hints at lust on holy ground and in king's palaces. Harking back to the heyday of resistance theatre on the south bank of the Thames, the half-mad Aeglamour devises a scheme to spell out his enemy's crimes in stones by the river bank 'till all the country read how she was drown'd!' There are other details that suggest not only the writer, but the man Jonson knew. One is Aeglamour's capacity for intense concentration, his desire to be left alone, noted by John Aubrey: 'I pray you give me leave, for I will study, / Though all the bells, pipes, tabors, timburines ring, / That you can plant about me; I will study'.[10] Another is the magnanimity, the 'free and open nature', to which Jonson allegedly owed his first break. Though in the depths of depression, Aeglamour gives the young shepherd Karolin a critical assessment of his naive poetry and tries to open his eyes to what love really means. But for Aeglamour, true love, in the shape of Earine, is dead; he has lost 'the treasure I had in her: now I am poor as you'. Earine's fate—apparently drowned, in fact penned into an oak tree—recalls the fortunes of Prospero's work: the drowning of his books and the threatened imprisonment of Ariel in an oak tree. By referring so precisely to Ariel's threatened fate, Jonson implies that the threat was actually carried out: far from roaming free after his release, Ariel/Earine, true spirit of the English stage, was successfully gagged. The witch who imprisons her is given some of Jonson's finest descriptive passages, full of Shakespeare's markers for the dark side of the regime—ruined abbeys, changelings, bogs and fens. In the machinations of her children, Jonson portrays the schemes of usurping playwrights: her daughter attempts to impersonate Earine by stealing her clothes; her son tries to make her his mistress.

All this fits in both with Shakespeare's work and with evidence of his character. But Jonson adds to the portrait an analysis of a state of extreme depression. He sets out to portray '[i]n one man / As much of sadness shown as passion can'. 'Alack', laments one shepherd, 'that ever such a generous spirit as Aeglamour's should sink by such a loss'. There is an indication that the loss is a recent event: 'His phantasie is hurt, let us now leave him; / The wound is yet too fresh to admit searching'. Aeglamour's desperation as he dreams up hopeless ways to avenge Earine's death suggests that the cause of his depression is as much frustrated creativity as passion: 'phantasie stopped will soon take fire, and burn / Into an anger, or to a frenzy turn'. His melancholy is well observed: he 'will scarce admit / The physic of our presence to his fit'; 'Sometimes he sits, and thinks all day, then walks, / Then thinks again, and sighs, weeps, laughs and talks'. Jonson opens the play with an introduction to the sad shepherd '[l]ike his woes figure, dark and discontent'. A stage direction follows: '*The Sad Shepherd passeth silently over the stage*'. Taken with the references to his mourning garb and wreath of cypress, this allusion to Aeglamour's 'woe's figure' sounds very like Shakespeare's Hamlet, his famous attitude of melancholy graphically conjured up in this brief preview.

'The lost man' is the way his fellow shepherds describe the distracted Aeglamour, doubting whether he will ever recover—they will never see him 'himself again'. Jonson's play reads partly as a bracing stimulus to his old sparring partner, an attempt to laugh him out of a state of depression; and partly as a more informal, private version of Spenser's *Astrophel and Stella*, the classic pastoral lament for Philip Sidney. It fits with the prospect of 'despair' Prospero foresaw at the end of *The Tempest*; and the heartbreak it describes, underlined by the absence of an ending, suggests that disillusion at the new wave of 'gross barbarism' that finished his career could well have been a factor in Shakespeare's early death. The final line 'Go hang yourself' is addressed to the witch's Cloten-like son.

The Rest Is Silence

BY THE TIME *The Sad Shepherd* was published in 1640, the hidden language had had its day. Gradually, a more humane form of Anglican Protestantism took hold and flourished, exploring an intimate relationship with God in the openly spiritual language of bolder Elizabethan writers such as Constable, Southwell and Persons. For such poets as George Herbert writing in the 1630s, there was no further need for the elaborate hidden symbolism of covert Catholicism. 'Must purling streams refresh a lover's loves? / Must all be veil'd, while he that reads, divines, / Catching the sense at two removes? / . . . Is there in truth no beauty?' Writing in 1631, the Protestant Thomas Carew congratulates Donne for turning his back on 'the subtle cheat / Of sly exchanges, and the juggling feat / Of two-edged words', associating the technique with the 'superstitious fools' of the old religion.[11] Catholic toleration had returned and along with the 'new apostasy', Carew deplores the return of Shakespeare's staple source of imagery—'the silenced tales of the *Metamorphoses*'. Fifty-six years on, when Dryden published his great poem defending Catholicism, *The Hind and the Panther*, he gave no indication that much of its idiom had once been part of a hidden coded language.

As the myth of a golden Elizabethan age became the foundation stone of Protestant historiography, memories began to fade of a time when such a hidden language could ever have been needed. After all, hadn't Shakespeare himself described his age in *Henry VIII* as a time when God was 'truly known', when 'each man sang the merry songs of peace to all his neighbours'?[12] Soon, what was seen as Shakespeare's gentlemanly silence on matters of religion and politics became the model for patriotic Englishmen who had no idea that in his day, discussion of such matters was forbidden to dramatists. His explicit support for authority was taken to mean support for the new Tudor state against the forces of insurrection: it was forgotten that the great debate of his time concerned the rival claims of papal authority and the individual conscience. By the nineteenth century, the Shakespeare industry was well under way, much of it based on fabrication. Reputed scholars such as John Collier and James Halliwell-Philips, who dedicated their lives to consolidating the legend of the English Bard, are known to have stolen, forged and destroyed numerous documents as they worked their way unsupervised through various libraries and private collections. The losses may have contributed to the spread of the strangely sanitised area around Shakespeare's life and personality, preserving the impression of neutrality that he himself so prudently cultivated. Only now is attention turning to scraps of evidence neglected over the centuries: to subversive texts and glosses that circulated in manuscript, the pervasiveness of double and triple meanings within printed texts, the impact on sixteenth- and early seventeenth-century literature of the wholesale repression unearthed by recent historians and biographers.

There is an argument that to resurrect the hidden language is to diminish Shakespeare's universality. Not to resurrect it, however, is to do him a deep disservice. Time and again Jonson and others draw attention to the importance and danger of concealed meanings in the works of their contemporaries. Discovering and following the concealed thread does more than open out a new dimension to Shakespeare's genius. It provides the key to the two elements missing from his work: the history of his own deepest convictions and the history of his own times. The hidden level makes it clear that for all his surface neutrality, the driving force behind Shakespeare's work was profound commitment to the traditional, sacramental life of the country, threatened in his day with extinction. Ironically, it was censorship by the regime he detested that drove him to transpose the narrative of its precarious survival into deniable, universal themes—into the myth of something incomparably beautiful and life-giving, of its irretrievable loss, of the improbable miracle of its return. Clearly he hoped that the brilliance of this universal level would induce readers to pursue and discover something hidden: a plea, and at the same time an elegy for the soul of his country. Historically, this hidden level still holds a vital significance for England, providing a first-hand, authoritative counterbalance to the 'Great Myth' created and perpetuated by Protestant historians. Above all, it throws light on the genesis of some of the greatest plays ever written. It reveals that it took not only intellectual brilliance but exceptional courage and constancy to produce them.

Appendix: Sonnet 152

A CLOSE LOOK at a single sonnet, hearing 'with eyes' and applying 'love's fine wit' as Sonnet 23 suggests, illustrates the often dangerous meanings that lie behind these highly wrought poems. Sonnet 152, which supplies subtitles for the first chapter of this book, yields up its secret because of the obvious political parallel: the national concern with the subject of reciprocal oaths at the beginning of the seventeenth century. The Crown was insisting ever more urgently on an oath of obedience; dissidents struck back by accusing the Crown of betraying its coronation oath to govern in the best interests of his subjects. Robert Persons argued that both Henry VIII and Elizabeth had broken their contract with their people by persecuting those who maintained England's traditional faith. This charge that sovereign had broken faith with subjects far more radically than subjects with sovereign came to a head in 1606 when James, who had promised toleration, extended the scope of the Oath of Supremacy in the form of a new oath—the even more stringent Oath of Allegiance.

Ostensibly, Sonnet 152 is a highly involved and condensed poem about double adultery. The hints that it was about something more would have been picked up at once by readers accustomed to code. A key indicator is the awkward and redundant phrase 'in act', which alongside the political echoes awakened by the association with a 'broken bed-vow' and 'new faith' in the same line, prompt the reading 'in Act'. 'An English Catholic Reproaches his Country' might have been this poem's manuscript title.

In loving thee thou knowst I am forsworn;
But thou art twice forsworn to me love swearing,
In act thy bed-vow broke and new faith torn,
In vowing new hate after new love bearing.
But why of two oaths' breach do I accuse thee
When I break twenty? I am perjured most,
For all my vows are oaths but to misuse thee,
And all my honest faith in thee is lost:

For I have sworn deep oaths of thy deep kindness,
Oaths of thy love, thy faith, thy constancy,
And to enlighten thee gave eyes to blindness,
Or made them swear against the thing they see:
For I have sworn thee fair: more perjured eye
To swear against the truth so foul a lie.

(Sonnet 152)

On a personal level, this is a strange poem. But read alongside the complex political situation in 1609, its unforced accuracy is striking.

Line 1: You know I am perjured when I swear the Oath of Allegiance;

Line 2: But in swearing love and allegiance to your subjects you are perjured twice over;

Line 3: First, in Henry's Act of Supremacy (the bed-vow broke) and then in Elizabeth's Act of Uniformity ('new faith' under Mary 'torn' on Elizabeth's accession);

Line 4: That is, in swearing to persecute subjects to whom you had just been reconciled (in Mary's reign).

In the second part of the sonnet, the speaker moves on from the worldly, legal oaths of the first part to the deeper oath involved in giving a personal word of honour.

Lines 5 and 6: But of the two of us, I am more perjured;

Line 7: For by swearing oaths of loyalty I have (disloyally) injured you.

Line 8: And, in the course of your downfall I have lost everything I sincerely believed in—my faith in you, and the Faith.

Lines 9 and 10: For privately—on the deepest level—I have sworn that in the end you would remain constant to the old religion and true to your own;

Line 11 and 12: By presenting you in this light I blinded others to the truth, and even made them deny the evidence of their own eyes;

Line 13 and 14: For I have sworn that you were just and at heart faithful to the 'fair' religion, Catholicism—nothing could be further from the truth.

This was exactly the situation of those who found in the end that they had actually worsened England's situation by persuading others to see the country's actions in the best light, by advising them to wait. For years they had counselled patience, persuading initially sceptical fellow Catholics that one day things would improve; that underneath all the changes, England would remain true. The sense of utter betrayal can be found time and again in the writings and in the catastrophic actions of Catholics from 1604 onwards, when James's brief honeymoon period was followed by even harsher penal laws.

The 'alternative' political reading of the sonnet gives in passing a fascinating autobiographical insight. Not only had he been a dupe, Shakespeare implies; he had been duped into duping others. The sincerity and authority of his 'deep oaths' had carried all too much weight; his artistic skill in 'enlightening' England was such that it had blinded others to reality. Unwittingly, he had contributed to the destruction of what he cared most about.

GLOSSARY:
A SELECTION OF CODED TERMS

THE LIST THAT follows merely hints at the complex hidden level that exists in the literature of Shakespeare and his contemporaries: it can be compared to a phrase-book designed to give an entry point to a long forgotten, almost foreign language, which survives today only in the arcane world of cryptic crosswords. But readers of this kind of literature need not despair—they have available to them the added assistance of context, often the chief ingredient in conveying secret meanings. The word 'pit', for instance, is innocuous in itself; but a pit that is described as the mouth to one of Hell's rivers, the scene of imprisonment, blood and death, would certainly have turned the minds of sixteenth-century Londoners to the notorious dungeon in the Tower known as the 'Pit', a disused well-shaft where Catholic prisoners were incarcerated.

Many more coded terms remain undiscovered, awaiting the kind of attentive, initiated readers to whom Samuel Daniel addressed his cryptic work: 'If only one allow / The care my labouring spirits take in this, / He is to me a Theater large ynow, / And his applause only sufficient is: / All my respect is bent but to his brow, / That is my all and all I am is his.'[1]

Body, parts of   An allegorical body had allegorical parts. If a woman represented England, then her hands could be her supporters, her eyes her intellectual leaders, her strands of hair her subjects. The frantic woman at the beginning of the poem that follows the Sonnets, *A Lover's Complaint*, is a typical example. The figure of Catholicism is given further ingenious attributes, some of them tasteless to modern readers. Robert Chester and Henry Constable eulogise her in language taken from the biblical Song of Solomon: her round, white breasts, for instance, are images of the host— 'crystal orbs from whence life's comfort springs', 'love lying in a bed of ivory', the resort of 'pilgrims'. Lips and kissing figure the act of taking holy communion, an image Rosalind plays on in *As You Like It* (3.4.15). See also **Eyes**.

Burial   The loss of traditional ceremonies and the ban on Catholic burial in churchyards was a major sectarian flashpoint, explored in *Hamlet* and *Cymbeline*. Webster's *White Devil* evokes the dilemma of 'the friendless bodies of unburied men' covered with leaves by 'robin redbreasts' only to be dug up by wolves. Like *Cymbeline*, Kyd's *The Spanish Tragedy* highlights the omission of a sung dirge (2.119); instead it is spoken, in forbidden Latin.

Caesar   Centralised Catholic authority (see also **Rome**). Marlowe's wicked Catholic Guise dies with the words: 'Vive la messe! Perish Huguenots! / Thus Caesar did go forth, and thus he died'.[2] The tales in *The Mirror for Magistrates* repeatedly give a Caesar the profile of a hostile Catholic power. He 'would bring in bondage valiant, worthy men'; he is a bloody, remorseless conquerer, proclaiming 'I set myself aloft the world to guide' . . .'My whole pretence was glory vain'.[3] After Shakespeare's death, Jonson reminisced about Shakespeare's 'ridiculous' defence of Julius Caesar. He recalled him taking Caesar's side in argument. 'As when he said in the person of Caesar, one speaking to him; Caesar, thou doest me wrong. He replied Caesar did never wrong, but with just cause and such like: which were ridiculous. But he redeemed his vices with his virtues'. Jonson is using the common code for papal authority, and, himself a reluctant Protestant conformist, is mocking Shakespeare's defence of the Catholic doctrine of papal authority in studied, extreme terms: such a stance, he says, 'could not scape laughter'.[4]

Calendar   One very conspicuous difference between England and Europe at this point was the discrepancy between their calendars, an inconvenience that meant that almanacs were among the best-selling books of the day. In 1582, Pope Gregory XIII announced the solution to inaccuracies in the calendar that had exercised mathematicians for centuries. In order to correct the gradually worsening chronological imbalance, it was declared that on 4 October 1582, the calendar would jump ten days to October 14. But the anti-papal regime in England refused to conform. As a result, for the next 150 years the country was sometimes as much as five weeks out of step with the rest of Europe. A country where characters are muddled about times and dates is always, in Shakespearean terms, Protestant. A typical Shakespearean joke about the calendar division occurs in *Love's Labour's Lost*, in which a character compares his dark love to an inaccurate German clock (3.1.192). Peace comes in *The Taming of the Shrew* only when Kate, the dark, quarrelsome shrew, gives in to her husband and calls the moon the sun. Hamlet is born into a time and country where 'the time is out of joint'. There are points when Shakespeare jokes about this favourite marker: an anachronistic clock repeatedly strikes in the calendar-conscious play, *Julius Caesar*, while *Cymbeline* parodies his coded technique in the melodramatic bedroom scene in which the villainous Iachimo disappears with the cry, 'Time, time!' The Reformation scholar Diarmaid MacCulloch takes the same line as Shakespeare: 'There could hardly be a better symbol of the way in which the Reformation tore apart the fabric of European society than this disagreement about dating'.[5]

Dark The 'dark' new religion, associated with black print and sober dress.

Dragon The ancient heraldic device of the dragon, supposedly that of the last native ruler of Britain, Cadwalader, was removed from the royal coat of arms by James I and replaced by the Scottish unicorn. Shakespeare compares the doomed heroes Antony, Coriolanus and Lear to dragons.

Earthquake Marks the year 1580, when Campion and Persons arrived in England. (See pp 315–316) *Venus and Adonis* accompanies the death of Adonis with an earthquake; it is used as a marker in *Romeo and Juliet* and *Pericles*.

Eyes Shakespeare and his contemporaries found these aspects of the allegorical 'body' particularly useful. The means by which the body is illuminated and guided, eyes could on one level mean leading intellectuals, thinkers or spiritual guides. Southwell appeals to 'the eyes of all antiquity' for evidence of England's 'blindness'.[6] Shakespeare frequently refers to the threat of blinding—an allegory of the loss and persecution of the country's most enlightened guides. *A Lover's Complaint* gives the image extensive treatment in Verse 4, where England's religious leaders are portrayed in a state of comic confusion. *Venus and Adonis* goes into similar detail: cowardly eyes hide in 'deep-dark caverns' to avoid seeing the 'bloody view' of a mangled body.

'Eyes' had a second, geographical, meaning. Capital cities were known as the 'eyes' of the country. London was the 'lightsome eye' of England, according to one of Shakespeare's contemporaries; a little later it was the 'eye and theatre of the world'.[7] In his cryptic autobiographical Sonnet 153, he decides that the 'bath' for 'my help' lies 'in my mistress's eye'—a place that is the source of 'new fire'. The lines are usually read as a series of bawdy puns. But they also suggest his decision to work as a dramatist at the theatre at Holywell, London, the heartland of the new religion.

Faded Beauty   An attribute of characters representing the despoiled, 'old' English church: examples are Julia, Hermione and Alice Montague in *Edward III*.

Fair   Coded attribute of Catholicism, taken from the stress placed by Catholics on outward beauty, parodied by Protestants as the 'Scarlet Woman'.

Fens   Associated with Protestant reform, which originally spread from the Low Countries along the east coast of England. Dryden calls it 'slimy-born'; Jonson's witch in the *Sad Shepherd* comes from 'fens and bogs', 'the drowned lands of Lincolnshire'.

Five   Devotion to the Five Wounds of Christ was widespread in England on the eve of the Reformation and was pictured on the banner of uprisings against the new regime. The patterned number—in a flower, birthmark or heraldic 'blazon'—is one of Shakespeare's Catholic markers.

Friars   Shakespeare barely mentions monks in his work, but friars appear often, particularly Franciscans, and are always positive characters. Here he follows the Counter-Reformation line, which promoted the newly reformed 'Christ-like' religious orders that took the vow of poverty.[8]

Gazers   A nickname for superstitious Catholics who 'gazed' on the host, the term occurs a number of times in contemporary polemical writing as well as in poetry and drama. The Parnassus Plays link Drayton with the phrase 'rash gazers'; the same term is later used by George Herbert, in a poem that suggests a rejection of the Catholic resistance stance: 'Sweet rose whose hue, angry and brave / Bids the rash gazer wipe his eye / Thy root is ever in thy grave / And thou must die.' Shakespeare's sacramental figure in *Edward III* 'doth dazzle gazers like the sun'.

Grafting   A metaphor for the way the new religion was seen by Catholics as a hostile parasite, altering the nature of the old: 'a bastard slip proceeding of another stock', wrote the Catholic exile Thomas Stapleton in 1594.

Shakespeare uses grafting in this same negative sense: the most famous example is the extended debate that forms the centerpiece of *The Winter's Tale*, in which the artless Perdita refuses to be persuaded of the virtues of grafting, in spite of pressure from her social and intellectual superiors.

Hallowmass   All Saints' Day on 1 November ('All Hallows'), and its vigil on 31 October ('All Hallows' Eve', or 'Halloween') were known collectively as 'Hallowmass', the feast when the Catholic Church remembered and prayed for the dead. But from the 1530s, 31 October became 'Reformation Day' to Protestants, as it was the anniversary of the day on which Luther nailed his ninety-five theses onto the church door at Wittenberg. The date symbolised the Reformation rift, when Luther defied church authority and denounced the custom of praying for the dead.

Hecuba   Like many figures from the tale of the Fall of Troy, this mourning widow had a contemporary significance: she symbolized widowed England, mourning the lost old order in the bloody deaths of her spouse and children. This gives a hidden resonance to Hamlet's question about an actor's tearful rendition of a speech by Hecuba: 'What's Hecuba to him, or he to Hecuba?'[9]

Hercules   The classical hero who fought the many-headed hydra, Hercules was a favourite Counter-Reformation image of resistance to the many heads of heresy. Shakespeare's Hercules, often a humiliated figure, is associated with various aspects of resistance to the Reformation in England.

'Here I Stand, I can no other'   The words with which Luther allegedly confronted the authority of the church at Worms in 1521. Shakespeare adapts the phrase, along with Luther's equally famous summary of his revolutionary doctrine—**Faith Alone**, and **Scripture Alone**—using them to highlight the Lutheran aspect of such characters as the shrew, Joan of Arc, Valentine and Laertes.

High   Catholic, or ceremonial, religion, still associated with the term 'High Church'. Shakespeare is always aware of this secondary meaning.

Holofernes   The story of Judith and Holofernes, taken from the biblical Apocrypha, was a resistance image used by Protestants abroad and Catholics in England. By cutting off the head of the tyrant Holofernes, who tried to force

her to eat forbidden food, Judith became the archetypal champion of freedom of conscience. Shakespeare named his daughter Judith, after her
Catholic godmother, and features a comic Holofernes in *Love's Labour's Lost*, a
foolish Protestant pedant who indoctrinates the young.

Interdict   The excommunicated state of England under Elizabeth I,
inviting parallels with the interdict imposed on King John. Kyd's *The
Spanish Tragedy* refers to a benighted country where 'the soul that should
be shrined in heaven / Solely delights in interdicted things'.

Love   Opposing fickle lust, the inconstant **Moon** and 'shifting' **Time,**
Shakespeare used what he called 'the ever-fixed mark' of true love as an
analogy for courageous allegiance to spiritual truth. Many other writers did
the same, but contemporaries characterise Shakespeare as a writer obsessed
with the subject of love. The censor in *The Return from Parnassus* shakes his
head over Shakespeare's writing—he might do better, he says, 'Could but a
graver subject him content, / Without love's foolish lazy languishment'.

Low   The new 'Low Church' religion, in which a simple communion
table replaced elevated altars.

Luke   St Luke's feast day had a personal significance for Robert Southwell. It was the day on which he joined the Jesuit order, a feast day shared
by St Faith, whose priory his unscrupulous grandfather had robbed to
build the family home. He and Garnet adopted Luke as the patron of their
dangerous enterprise; the pair attributed one of their narrowest escapes to
his protection. It is clear that Shakespeare knew of the dedication to St
Luke. He regularly attaches variations of the name to Catholic places and
characters—in his early work, twice within a single play *(The Comedy of
Errors, Titus Andronicus, The Taming of the Shrew)*.

Mass   Evoked through a sacred meal, manna, altars, the liturgy, the real
presence of the godhead. Ben Jonson's *Sejanus* daringly stages the ceremony in a chapel (5.4.) including the actual words of the Mass—'Accept
our offering'; 'Be present and propitious'. Here, as in *The Winter's Tale*, an
image comes to life. The tyrant, Sejanus, overturns the altar with its 'juggling mystery' 'superstitious lights' and 'cozening ceremonies', sneering
'Thou shalt stand to all posterity / The eternal game and laughter'. Shakespeare is equally explicit in *Titus Andronicus;* there is another suggestive

banquet in *The Tempest*, associated with the phoenix and the unicorn, both emblems of Christ.

Merchants   In coded Jesuit newsletters, souls were 'merchandise', priests 'merchants', pursuivants 'creditors'; Jesuits were 'journeymen', prison a 'credit house', the sacraments 'gems', the gallows at Tyburn in London 'a place of much trading'.

Miracles   Another doctrinal debating point. Protestants held that 'the age of miracles is dead', a question periodically raised in Shakespeare's work.[10] Though he dismisses fake miracles, his late romances emphatically vindicate the miraculous.

Moon   To represent Elizabeth, Shakespeare used the classic image of inconstancy, the moon. The beauty of this marker was that it had been sanctioned by the Queen herself, who was associated with Diana, the moon goddess, more often than with any other classical figure. Officially, the moon represented her virginal purity. But there were other aspects, developed by more critical writers. The moon ruled over darkness; it was barren; it was eclipsed by heaven's true light, the sun. Dryden, referring to the introduction of the new religion to England, later stresses that it shines with 'borrowed light'.[11] It was its inconstancy that Shakespeare stressed. In *Edward III*, a poet is forbidden to use the image in connection with true love: 'Out with the moon line, I will have none of it'. Juliet does the same: 'Swear not by the moon, th'inconstant moon'. Moonlight is cleverly ambiguous in plays clearly written for the Queen, such as *A Midsummer Night's Dream* and *The Merry Wives of Windsor*. Elsewhere, Shakespeare's moon is so negative that it forms part of the parody of his work in *The Return from Parnassus*, where a Shakespearean devotee, addressing his beloved, calls 'the moon in comparison of thy bright hue a mere slut'. After Elizabeth's death ('The immortal moon hath her eclipse endured' was his only epitaph), his references become darker still.

New Fire   Revived, post-Reformation spirituality, both Protestant and Catholic. Shakespeare keeps it Protestant. Edward Dyer and Sidney imply something more dangerous in two sonnets about a satyr who seizes new fire from heaven. Dyer's burns himself; Sidney's, in his 'Reply to a Sonnet by Sir Edward Dyer', has a 'coward mind' and 'for fear of maybe, leave[s] the sweet pursuit', 'thinking not why, but how himself to save'.

Nightingale   The story of Philomel, who was turned into a nightingale and sang plaintive songs in the night after being raped, was used as an image of the desecrated church and its covert protests.

North   Regularly associated with the 'Northern' Reformation in Shakespeare's plays, frequently linked with the **Tempest** in the form of the 'North wind'.

Oath   A consistent theme in the literature of the time, the word invariably conjured up the dilemma of divided loyalty involved in taking the Oath of Supremacy (later the Oath of Allegiance).

Old   Of the old religion. A Victorian critic notes that Samuel Daniel, Shakespeare's contemporary, is said to 'smack of the old cask'. Where Shakespeare pointedly couples 'old' with 'new' or 'young', he highlights the division in England. He repeatedly describes himself as old in his sonnets.

Ours   Jesuit code for their own priests.

Pelican   Emblem of self-sacrifice, applied both to Christ and the church: the mythical pelican fed her children with her own blood.

Phoenix   Image of purity and rebirth; a Christian symbol of resurrection adopted by the 'virginal' Elizabeth but reclaimed by Catholics as an emblem for the revival of the persecuted church. Shakespeare's poem 'The Phoenix and the Turtle' is a tribute to the two aspects of the resistance: the faithful turtle dove, exiled abroad, and the phoenix at home, which dies to be reborn. The same images run through *Love's Martyr*, the volume in which that poem was published.

Precise   Puritan.

Rare   Associated with Catholic poems, figures and situations. There may be a Latin derivation, linked with forbidden prayers for the dead. Jonson's famous epitaph, 'O rare Ben Jonson', can be read as 'orare (pray for) Ben Jonson'. Shakespeare includes the line 'O rare for Antony!' in *Antony and Cleopatra*.

Red and White   One of Shakespeare's most distinctive epithets, parodied in *The Return from Parnassus*. It had two applications that he orchestrated with witty precision, particularly in his poetry. The first was the vision of a united England: the red rose of Lancaster and the white rose of York had been briefly reconciled under Henry VII to form the red and white Tudor rose. By Shakespeare's day, the white rose was in the ascendant, and, trimmed with green, formed the livery of Elizabeth I. The second application was to the Catholic Church. In 1574, the Catholic writer Richard Bristow recalled the words of St Cyprian, who had said that the church lacked neither lilies nor roses, having the white of good works and the purple of martyrdom.[12]

Redbreast   Like other compounds of 'red' (redshanks, red lips, rosy cheeks), this had overtones of the old religion, with its red vestments and red-lettered prayer books. Shakespeare's contemporary, Robert Tofte, is referred to as a sorrowing redbreast in the preface to his 'Alba', a poem full of Catholic allusion.

Red Rose   An all-purpose image, but used specifically by Catholics for the old, 'beautiful' religion.

Revenge   An apparently motiveless or disproportionate desire for revenge in Shakespeare's plays refers to the revenge of Puritans for the persecutions under Mary—the shrew, Shylock, Malvolio, Aaron. The question of whether or not to take revenge explores the response to the more recent persecution of Catholics under Elizabeth—Hieronymo in Kyd's *The Spanish Tragedy*, Titus and Hamlet in Shakespeare's plays.

Right, Rite   A common contemporary pun, referring to the forbidden rite of the Mass.

Rome   Classical Rome was the simplest cover for discussion of the Church of Rome, Caesar representing the papacy. In the late 1560s, when he was considering exile, Edmund Campion dedicated a long manuscript poem to the 1st Viscount Montague, contrasting the ruins of imperial Rome with the survival of the Roman church, anchored in eternity; it was widely circulated among the aristocratic community, including Philip Sidney, the 3rd Earl of Southampton and Lord Lumley.[13] Spenser published 'The Ruines of Rome', a poem that boldly takes up Campion's theme by including in his lament for the ruined city a subtle, fleeting reference to the spiritual Rome that survives: the shepherds that once grazed the seven hills foreshadow Peter's successors, whose 'shepherdlike' role shows that 'all things turn to their first being'. Rome is cast as the villain in many of the Protestant poems in *The Mirror for Magistrates*, the imperial attempts to invade England closely paralleled with the Armada. Shakespeare's Roman plays exploit these political overtones; all of them are directed primarily at the 'Roman' Catholic community. See also **Caesar**.

Rosalind, Rosamund, and so on   Based perhaps on the lost red rose of Lancaster, these names are given by Shakespeare and his contemporaries to figures representing the country's spirituality, lost in the Reformation. She is the first love of Spenser's shepherd, Colin Clout; for the poet Daniel, she is shadowed under the figure of Rosamund the Fair, Henry II's mistress, whose love nest, suitably for Truth, was at the centre of a labyrinth, and who returns in his poem 'Rosamund' (1592) to lament the destruction of her tomb at Godstow, near Oxford, by the reformers. Drayton, too, takes Fair Rosamund as a paragon in his *Heroical Epistles* (1597), hymning the magical powers of 'that sweet name' in a litany that Shakespeare appears to parody in *As You Like It*. In *Rosaline's Complaint*,[14] a long poem that is a virtual compendium of Catholic imagery, Robert Chester prays for the survival of his imperilled 'phoenix' Rosalyne—'Let her not wither, Lord, without increase'. Shakespeare has no time for the nostalgia surrounding the name: Romeo sentimentalises it in a parody of the convention; Rosalind jokes about it, and in exile changes her name to Ganymede.

Shadow and Substance   Terms which evoke one of the key differences between Catholic and Protestant interpretations of the Eucharist. Catholics (and Lutherans) maintained that the substance of bread and wine changed at the act of consecration; Calvinists held that the change was purely symbolic—a 'shadow' of the original last supper. Shakespeare repeatedly uses the opposition in his plays and sonnets.

Sinon   The treacherous Trojan who persuaded his countrymen to allow the wooden horse, containing Greek soldiers, through the gates of Troy. He was compared by John Leslie, a resistance writer, to William Cecil.[15] Shakespeare also gives him Cecil features in *The Rape of Lucrece*.

Sunburn   The sun represented the divinity; like Cupid's blindness, sunburn suggested closeness to God. There was a scholastic precedent. In the

Bible's Song of Solomon, the beautiful Bride, classic image of Christ's Church, had become tanned through working in the vineyards, to which she had been banished by jealous brothers. 'Working in the vineyard' was a common Jesuit description of the English mission. Sunburnt characters contrast with those who adopt the 'new' fashion of masks or broad-brimmed hats to protect their faces from the sun. Beatrice, Rosalind, Cleopatra and Julia are all sunburnt. Shakespeare described himself as 'tanned' in Sonnet 62.

Sweet, Sugared   'Sweet' meant refined, or reduced to its essence. Often used by Shakespeare's contemporaries to describe literary works, the word appears to have similar overtones to 'distilled'. Shakespeare's sonnets differentiate between 'self' and 'sweet self'—the second being the inner, refined, spiritual self. The same applies to literature: 'sweet' writing has a spiritual core.

Tempest   The tempest was a widespread image for the Reformation upheaval in England, and it remains a central metaphor in the works of modern Reformation historians. It was often associated at the time with a tempest-tossed ship, image of the church. Petrarch uses a ship in the tempest as an image of the threatened church; Spenser takes up the theme; Protestant propagandists used a ship as an image of the Catholic 'bark of Peter'. Chronologically, *The Tempest* was Shakespeare's last work: its place at the beginning of the First Folio provides a subtitle to the book as politically loaded as *'The Blitz'* or *'The Troubles'* might be to a modern reader. His distinctive use of the term is explored at the end of Chapter 2.

Thirty-Three   The age of Christ at the time of his death. Southwell referred to it at his trial, associating it with his own age. Shakespeare alters his sources to include the number in *The Comedy of Errors*, where the abbess claims she has waited thirty-three years to be reunited with her family; in *Julius Caesar*, he gives Caesar thirty-three wounds. Sonnet 33 can be read as an expression of grief for the death of his son, which occurred in Shakespeare's thirty-third year—like Southwell, he linked the number with Christ's passion, a concealed theme in the sonnet.

Time   Shakespeare's sonnets dwell on a classic image of transience—that of *tempus edax*, or devouring time, an unusual theme for love sonnets. Here and in the plays, time is repeatedly given the characteristics of the new order, which, like time, defaces tombs and monuments, gouges lines on faces, alters royal decrees and historical records, 'diverts strong minds to the course of altering things'. Very often they are Cecil characteristics. Time is lame and has a 'wallet' on his back like the splay-footed, hunchbacked Robert Cecil, he is misshapen, slow-footed, never-resting, he has a deformed hand. William Cecil was an avid collector of clocks and incorporated them into spectacular new buildings like Burghley House—another element behind Shakespeare's figure of 'Old Time, the clock-setter'.

Troy   England was often poetically dubbed 'a second Troy', and London as 'Troynovant', for legend had it that it was founded by Brute, one of the descendants of Aeneas. The myth was given official backing after 1534, when Henry VIII declared that England was an empire; the pedigree legitimized his imperial ambitions. The anonymous play *True Trojans* is a typical version of militant Tudor nationalism, while *Troilus and Cressida* takes the propaganda myth of the English Troy as its starting point. Characters from the Fall of Troy were given contemporary identities. See **Sinon**.

Turtle Dove   A traditional image for the apostles, denoting loving fidelity; applied to those who remained faithful to their beliefs in spite of persecution.

Well-Dealing, Well-Wishing   Compounds of 'well' frequently occur in odd contexts in the works of suspect writers and have overtones of the holy wells that were centres of Catholic recusancy—chief among them Holywell in Wales.[16]

White and Green   The Tudor livery, used by Shakespeare in *Romeo and Juliet* and *The Merry Wives of Windsor.*

Winter   Catholic laments used winter as the obvious image of the sudden onslaught of the Reformation, when elaborate vestments and decoration were stripped from churches and replaced with whitewash. The murder in *The Spanish Tragedy* is followed by a speech about 'blustring winds' that have 'moved the leafless trees' and 'disrobed the meadows of their flowred green'. Shakespeare's Sonnets 5 and 12 lament 'sable curls all silvered o'er with white'; 'sap checked with frost'; 'beauty o'ersnowed' and 'bareness everywhere'.

Wrack, Rack   A common pun.

REFERENCE LIST

Airs, Malcolm. *The Tudor and Jacobean Country House*. Stroud, 1998.

Akrigg, G.P.V. *Shakespeare and the Earl of Southampton*. Boston, 1968.

An Anthology of Catholic Poetry. Edited by Shane Leslie. London, 1952.

Antony and Cleopatra. Edited by M. R. Ridley. London, 1965 (Arden Shakespeare).

Asquith, Clare. 'Oxford University and *Love's Labour's Lost*'. In *Shakespeare and the Culture of Christianity in Early Modern England*, edited by Dennis Taylor and David Beauregard. New York, 2003.

Aubrey, John. *Aubrey's Brief Lives*. Edited by Oliver Lawson Dick. London, 1987.

Averell, William. *A Marvellous Combat of Contrarieties*. London, 1588.

Black, J. B. *The Reign of Elizabeth*. Oxford, 1951.

Bloom, Harold. *Shakespeare: The Invention of the Human*. London, 1999.

Bossy, John. *The English Catholic Community, 1570–1650*. Oxford, 1975.

Breight, Curtis. *Surveillance, Militarism and Drama in the Elizabethan Era*. New York, 1996.

Browne, Anthony, 2nd Viscount Montague. *Instruction to my Daughter*. 1598. Holograph manuscript, Downside Abbey Library, Somerset, DAL 28000.

Calendar of State Papers Venetian. Vol. 10, 1603–1607. Edited by Horatio Brown. London, 1900. Public Record Office, London.

Camden, William. *Remaines of a greater worke concerning Britaine*. London, 1605.

Caraman, Philip. *Henry Garnet, 1555–1606, and the Gunpowder Plot*. London, 1964.

———. *John Gerard, The Autobiography of an Elizabethan*. London, 1951.

———. *The Other Face: Catholic Life Under Elizabeth I*. London, 1960.

———. *The Years of Seige: Catholic Life from James I to Cromwell*. London, 1966.

Carey, John. *John Donne: Life, Mind and Art*. London, 1981.

Cawley, A. C., ed. *Everyman and Medieval Miracle Plays*. London, 1956.

Cecil, David. *The Cecils of Hatfield House*. London, 1973.

Chambers, E. K. *William Shakespeare: A Study of Facts and Problems*. Oxford, 1930.

Chester, Robert. *Love's Martyr*. N.p., 1601.

Cole, Susan. *So Sweet a Star as Harry: A Consideration of Henry Frederick, Prince of Wales 1594–1612*. Royal Stuart Papers 39, 1992.

Collinson, Patrick. *The Birthpangs of Protestant England*. London, 1988.

Daniel, Samuel. *Poems and a Defence of Ryme*. Edited by Arthur Colby Sprague. Chicago and London, 1965.

De Chambrun, Clara Longworth. *Shakespeare: A Portrait Restored*. London, 1957.

Devlin, Christopher. *The Life of Robert Southwell*. London, 1956.

Donne, John. *John Donne, Complete Poetry and Prose*. Edited by John Hayward. London, 1967.

Dryden, John. *The Poems and Fables of John Dryden*. Edited by James Kinsley. Oxford, 1970.

Duffy, Eamon. *The Stripping of the Altars: Traditional Religion in England, 1400–1580.* New Haven and London, 1992.

Duncan, David Ewing. *The Calendar.* London, 1999.

Duncan-Jones, Katherine. *Sir Philip Sidney, Courtier Poet.* London, 1991.

———. *Ungentle Shakespeare.* London, 2001.

———, ed. *Shakespeare's Sonnets*, Arden Shakespeare. London, 1997.

Edwards, Thomas. *Cephalus and Procris.* 1595. London.

Elizabeth I. *Collected Works.* Edited by Leah S. Marcus, Janel Mueller and Mary Beth Rose. Chicago and London, 2000.

Erickson, Carolly. *The First Elizabeth.* London, 1983.

Febvre, Lucien. *Problem of Unbelief in the Sixteenth Century.* Translated by Beatrice Gottlieb. Cambridge, Mass., 1942.

Fraser, Antonia. *The Gunpowder Plot: Terror and Faith in 1605.* London, 1996.

———. *The Six Wives of Henry VIII.* London, 1993.

Gerard, John. *The Autobiography of an Elizabethan.* Translated and edited by Philip Caraman. London, 1951.

Graves, Michael A.R. *Burghley: William Cecil, Lord Burghley.* London, 1998.

Greenblatt, Stephen. *Will in the World.* New York and London, 2004.

Grigson, Geoffrey. *The Englishman's Flora.* London, 1987.

Haigh, Christopher. *English Reformations.* Oxford, 1993.

Hamilton, A. C. *Sir Philip Sidney: A Study of His Life and Works.* Cambridge, 1977.

Hamilton, Gary D. 'Mocking Oldcastle'. In *Shakespeare and the Culture of Christianity in Early Modern England*, edited by Dennis Taylor and David Beauregard. New York, 2003.

Haynes, Alan. *The Gunpowder Plot.* Stroud, 1994.

Herford, C. H., ed. *The Two Noble Kinsmen.* Temple edition. London, 1897.

Hibbert, Christopher. *The Virgin Queen: Elizabeth I, Genius of the Golden Age.* London, 1991.

Holden, Anthony. *William Shakespeare: His Life and Work.* New York, 1999.

Holmes, Peter. *Resistance and Compromise: The Political Thought of Elizabethan Catholics.* Cambridge, 1982.

Honan, Park. *Shakespeare: A Life.* Oxford, 1998.

Honigmann, E.A.J. *Shakespeare: The 'Lost Years'.* Manchester, 1998.

———. *Shakespeare's Impact on His Contemporaries.* London, 1982.

Hopkins, Lisa. *John Ford's Political Theatre.* Manchester, 1994.

Hutton, Ronald. *The Rise and Fall of Merry England.* Oxford, 1994.

Isham, Gyles. *Rushton Triangular Lodge.* English Heritage, London, 1986.

Janelle, Pierre. *The Catholic Reformation.* London, 1971.

Johnson, Poetry and Prose. Edited by Mona Wilson. London, 1970.

Johnson, Samuel. *General Observations on the Plays of Shakespeare.* London, 1756.

Jones, Edwin. *The English Nation: The Great Myth.* London, 1998.

Jonson, Ben. *Ben Jonson's Works.* Edited by William Gifford. London, 1816.

———. *Poems of Ben Jonson.* Edited by George Burke Johnston. London, 1954.

Kerman, Joseph. 'Music and Politics: The Case of William Byrd (1540–1623)'. *Proceedings of the American Philosophical Society* (September 2000).

Kernan, Alvin. *Shakespeare, the King's Playwright: Theater in the Stuart Court, 1603–1613.* New Haven, 1995.

Kilroy, Gerard. *Edmund Campion: Memory and Transcription.* Burlington, Vt., and Aldershot, 2005.

Knowles, David. *Bare Ruined Choirs.* Cambridge, 1959.

Kyd, Thomas. *The Spanish Tragedie.* Edited by Emma Smith. London and New York, 1998.

Lingard, John. *The History of England.* London, 1849.

Littlehales, Margaret Mary. *Mary Ward, Pilgrim and Mystic.* London, 1998.

Lyly, John. *Selected Prose and Dramatic Work.* Edited by Leah Scragg. London, 1997.

MacCulloch, Diarmaid. *Reformation: Europe's House Divided, 1490–1700.* London, 2003.

Manley, Lawrence, ed. *London in the Age of Shakespeare.* London, 1986.

Marlowe, Christopher. *The Plays of Christopher Marlowe.* London, 1939.

Martin, Patrick H., and John Finnis. 'Thomas Thorpe, "WS", and the Catholic Intelligencers'. *English Literary Renaissance,* vol. 33, no. 1 (2003).

Martz, Louis. *The Meditative Poem.* New York, 1963.

Massinger, Philip. *Plays.* Edited by John Monck Mason. London, 1759.

McCabe, William H. *An Introduction to Jesuit Theatre.* St. Louis, 1983.

Merriam, Thomas. 'The Misunderstanding of Munday as Author of *Sir Thomas More'.* *Review of English Studies,* New Series, vol. 51, no. 204 (2000).

Milward, Peter. *The Catholicism of Shakespeare's Plays.* Southampton, 1997.

Montague, 2nd Viscount. *Instruction to my Daughter.* Manuscript in his own hand.

Nashe, Thomas. *The Unfortunate Traveller and Other Works.* Edited by J. B. Steane. London, 1972.

Nelson, Alan. *Monstrous Adversary: The Life of Edward de Vere, 17th Earl of Oxford.* Liverpool, 2003.

Nicholl, Charles. *The Reckoning.* London, 1992.

O'Donoghue, Bernard. *The Courtly Love Tradition.* Manchester, 1982.

Palliser, D. M. 'Popular Reactions to the Reformation'. In *The English Reformation Revised,* edited by Christopher Haigh. Cambridge, 1987.

Penguin Book of Renaissance Verse. Edited by Henry R. Woudhuysen. London and New York, 1993.

Persons, Robert. *The Jesuits' Memorial for the intended Reformation of England under their first Popish Prince, presented to the late James II.* Edited by Edward Gee. London, 1690.

———. *Judgement of a Catholic Englishman.* 1608. Downside Abbey Library, Somerset, DAL 47519.

———. *A Memorial of the Reformation of England.* Unpublished ms., 1596. Downside Abbey Library, Somerset, DAL 26603.

———. *A Temperate Ward-word.* 1599. Downside Abbey Library, Somerset, DAL 47451.

———. *A Treatise tending to Mitigation.* 1607. Edited by D. M. Rogers. London, 1977.

Persons, Robert, under the name Doleman. *A Conference about the Next Succession to the Crown of England.* N.p., 1595.

Pilarz, Scott R. *Robert Southwell and the Mission of Literature, 1561–1595: Writing Reconciliation.* Burlington, Vt., and Aldershot, 2004.

Questier, Michael. *An English Catholic Community? Confessional Politics and the Aristocratic Entourage c. 1558–1640.* Forthcoming publication.

Rahner, Karl. *Greek Myths and Christian Mystery.* New York, 1971.

Read, Conyers. *Lord Burghley and Queen Elizabeth.* London, 1960.

Richmond, Velma Bourgeois. *Shakespeare, Catholicism and Romance.* New York, 2000.

Rowse, A. L. *The England of Elizabeth.* London, 1950.

———. 'Queen Elizabeth and the Historians' (1953). In *Past Masters, the Best of History Today.* Edited by Daniel Snowman. Stroud, 2001.

Sams, Eric. *The Real Shakespeare: Retrieving the Early Years, 1564–1594.* New Haven and London, 1995.

Scarisbrick, J. J. *The Reformation and the English People.* Oxford, 1984.

Shakespeare, William. *Complete Works.* Edited by Peter Alexander. London, 1958.

———. *Edward III.* Edited by Eric Sams. New Haven, 1996.

Shell, Alison. *Catholicism, Controversy and the English Literary Imagination, 1558–1660.* Cambridge, 1999.

Sidney, Philip. *Defence of Poesie.* 1595. Edited by Richard Bear. Available: http://darkwing.uoregon.edu/%7Erbear/arcadia1.html, 1992.

———. *The Old Arcadia.* 1580. Edited by Katharine Duncan-Jones. Oxford, 1994.

Sohmer, Steve. *Shakespeare's Mystery Play: The Opening of the Globe Theatre, 1599.* Manchester and New York, 1999.

Somerset, Anne. *Elizabeth I.* London, 1991.

Southern, A. C., ed. *The Elizabethan Recusant House, comprising The Life of the Lady Magdalen Viscountess Montague (1538–1608).* London, 1954.

Southwell, Robert. *An Humble Supplication to Her Majesty.* 1595. Edited by R. C. Bald. Cambridge, 1953.

Spenser, Edmund. *Poetical Works.* Edited by E. De Selincourt. London, 1912.

Stribrny, Zdeneck. *Shakespeare and Eastern Europe.* Oxford and New York, 2000.

Strong, Roy. *Henry, Prince of Wales and England's Lost Renaissance.* London, 2000.

Taylor, Dennis. *Shakespeare and Religion in Reformation and Post-Reformation England: A Chronology with Special Emphasis on Shakespeare's Catholic and Protestant Contexts.* Available: http://www2.bc.edu/-taylor/shakes.html.

The New Oxford Book of English Verse, 1250–1590. Edited by Helen Gardner. Oxford, 1972.

The Norton Shakespeare. Based on the Oxford Edition. Edited by Stephen Greenblatt et al. New York and London, 1997.

Vickers, Mark. 'Saint Polydore Plasden'. In *The Forty-Four.* Farnborough, 2000.

Waugh, Evelyn. *Edmund Campion.* London, 1935.

Weldon, Anthony. *The Court of King James.* London, 1650.

Wilson, Ian. *Shakespeare: The Evidence: Unlocking the Mysteries of the Man and His Work.* London, 1993.

Wilson, Richard. *Secret Shakespeare.* Manchester, 2004.

Wood, Michael. *In Search of Shakespeare.* London, 2003.

Wooding, Lucy E.C. *Rethinking Catholicism in Reformation England.* Oxford, 2000.

NOTES

Introduction

1. Curtis Breight, *Surveillance, Militarism and Drama in the Elizabethan Era* (New York, 1996).

Chapter 1: The Silence of John Nobody

1. For the headings in this Chapter, see Appendix: A Note on the Sonnets and *A Lover's Complaint*.
2. David Knowles, *Bare Ruined Choirs* (Cambridge, 1959), p. 265.
3. Edwin Jones, *The English Nation: The Great Myth* (London, 1998), p. 16.
4. Ibid., p. 17.
5. Christopher Haigh, *English Reformations* (Oxford, 1993), p. 173.
6. Elizabeth's Secretary of State, William Cecil, did not mince his words. His 1584 'Memorial' to the Queen states: 'Your strong, factious subjects be the Papists: strong I account them, because both in number they are (at the least) able to make a great army, and by their mutual confidence and intelligence may soon bring to pass a uniting; factious I call them, because they are discontented'. He considers, and rejects, the final solution—a massacre. Given their numbers, this would be 'as hard and difficult as impious and ungodly'. Instead he discusses removing their children, confiscating their armour and weapons, dividing their loyalty by means of the Oath of Supremacy (Petyt ms., quoted in Christopher Devlin, *The Life of Robert Southwell* [London, 1956], pp. 330–332). The Catholic threat remained William Cecil's major concern throughout his political life.
7. See the writings published abroad by exiles such as Robert Persons, Gregory Martin, John Leslie, Thomas Hide, William Allen, and covertly in England by such missionaries as Robert Southwell and Henry Garnet. Allen describes the 'extreme misery' in which 'the greatest part of the country should be Catholics in their hearts, and in their mouths and actions, Protestants' (see the year 1581 in Dennis Taylor, *Shakespeare and Religion in Reformation and Post-Reformation England: A Chronology with special emphasis on Shakespeare's Catholic and Protestant contexts*, available: www2.bc.edu/-taylor/shakes.html). In England, Viscount Montague spoke openly in Parliament about the pernicious effect of the oath. Philip Sidney described Catholics as men 'whose spirits are full of anguish . . . being forced to oaths they account damnable' (see the year 1579 in Taylor, *Shakespeare and Religion*). Robert Persons portrays them as being 'in continual torment of mind' (see 1580 in Taylor, *Shakespeare and Religion*). William Allen (*A True, Sincere and Modest Defence*, 1584) and Robert Southwell (*An Humble Supplication*, 1591) both highlight the way the Oath of Supremacy divided the Elizabethan English from 'the

ancient Catholic Faith in which their forefathers lived and died these 1400 years' (see 1591 in Taylor, *Shakespeare and Religion*).

8. Diarmaid MacCulloch, *Reformation: Europe's House Divided, 1490–1700* (London, 2003), p. 24.

9. Lucien Febvre, *Problem of Unbelief in the Sixteenth Century*, trans. Beatrice Gottlieb (Cambridge, Mass., 1942), p. 8.

10. Haigh, *English Reformations*, pp. 152–154. In 1538, the Six Articles enshrined Catholic theology in statute, including transubstantiation, clerical celibacy, masses for the dead and communion under one kind. Denial of transubstantiation was punishable by burning; denial of any of the other articles incurred hanging or life imprisonment. In 1540, Henry demonstrated his royal 'middle way' by executing three Lutheran reformers alongside three papalist Catholics.

11. MacCulloch, *Reformation*, p. 127.

12. An estimated 207 Catholics were executed during the following reign under Elizabeth, though many more died in prison and in exile. Her chief minister was well aware of the propaganda value of martyrdom, warning the Queen that persecution was considered one of the 'badges' of the true church. See 'Memorial', in Devlin, *Life of Southwell*, pp. 330–332.

13. Scripts were not preserved, which is why their influence has been forgotten.

14. Haigh, *English Reformations*, p. 223.

15. The best account of the political chicanery that secured the vote is given by John Lingard, *The History of England* (London, 1849), vol. 6, pp. 2–19. Also see Haigh, *English Reformations*, pp. 238–241.

16. T. J. McCann, 'The Parliamentary Speech of Viscount Montague against the Act of Supremacy, 1559', *Sussex Archaeological Collections*, p. 108, quoted with further Montague speeches by Michael Questier, *An English Catholic Community? Confessional Politics and the Aristocratic Entourage c. 1558–1640* (forthcoming), chap. 4, pp. 12ff.

17. These lines are from a coded attack by Edmund Spenser, which resulted in his exile to Ireland ('Mother Hubberd's Tale', 1591, lines 1197–1200, in *Poetical Works*).

18. These included the 1559 Act of Supremacy, 1559 Act of Uniformity, 1563 Act for the better assurance of Royal Power, 1566 Ordinance for reform of disorders in printing. The Catholic threat was Cecil's abiding concern. In 1575, he reckoned the majority in the country would rally to a foreign invasion (Conyers Read, *Lord Burghley and Queen Elizabeth* [London, 1960], p. 235). By 1580, he had ensured that all the Privy Council members except one were more anti-Catholic than the Queen (ibid., p. 236).

19. Philip Caraman, *The Other Face: Catholic Life Under Elizabeth I* (London, 1960), p. 141.

20. Robert Chester's 1601 collection of poetry, *Love's Martyr*, plays on the image throughout and gives it a clear recusant subtext.

21. These tensions are explored in a classic account of English Catholicism, John Bossy's *The English Catholic Community, 1570-1650* (Oxford, 1975).

22. The quotation, from his famous 'Brag', or challenge to the government, ends on the gracefully magnanimous note that the Jesuit order consciously strove for, but which seemed to come naturally to Campion: '. . . If these my offers be refused, and my endeavours can take no place, and I, having run thousands of miles to do

you good, shall be rewarded with rigour, I have no more to say but to recommend your case and mine to Almighty God, the Searcher of Hearts, who send us His grace, and set us at accord before the day of payment, to the end we may at last be friends in heaven, when all injuries shall be forgotten' (Evelyn Waugh, *Edmund Campion* [London, 1935], p. 222).

23. See Philip Caraman, *Henry Garnet, 1555–1606, and the Gunpowder Plot* (London, 1964).

24. This is the number given by Clara Longworth de Chambrun, *Shakespeare: A Portrait Restored* (London, 1957), p. 7. There are of course no precise records of deaths in prison or in exile; but the consensus among recusant scholars is that tens of thousands died in this way under Elizabeth. Recent interest in local and family histories is beginning to build up a picture of the full extent of a persecution that touched all the Catholic families mentioned in this book; the death of John Donne's brother in prison is one instance; Mary Ward's grandmother, who spent fourteen years in prison, is another; recent biographies highlight the number of Shakespeare's friends and relatives who died or were imprisoned as a result of their religion. Among the many new and improvised prisons and prison camps all over the country, those at Wisbech and outside York are well known; but there were thousands of unrecorded deaths in lesser-known prisons such as the block-houses at Kingston-upon-Hull (Margaret Mary Littlehales, *Mary Ward, Pilgrim and Mystic* [London, 1998], pp. 18–19). The collection of recusant fines was often farmed out to private enforcers, so that the true picture of displacement and destitution went unrecorded.

25. In 1584, William Allen addressed William Cecil on the subject in his *True, Sincere and Modest defence of English Catholics*. He wishes fellow Catholics abroad could see with their own eyes what was happening in England: they might have more sympathy, he says, 'if they might see all the prisons, dungeons, fetters, stocks, racks, that are through the realm occupied and filled with Catholics; if they might behold the manner of their arraignment . . . how many have been by famine, ordure and pestiferous airs pined away; . . . how many gentlemen and other persons of wealth are wholly undone . . . how many of the most substantial, profitablest and persons of greatest hospitality in divers provinces are chased out of their own houses by spials, promoters, and catchpoles; how many wander in places where they are not known, driven into woods, yea, surely, into waters, to save themselves . . . how many godly and honest married couples most dear to one another, by the imprisonment, banishment, flight, of either party are pitifully sundered; how many families thereby dissolved; into what poverty, misery and mishap their children are driven; what number thereby run over sea into most desperate wars and fortunes . . .' (see the year 1584 in Taylor, *Shakespeare and Religion*).

26. Southwell, *Humble Supplication*, pp. 43–44.

Chapter 2: Secret Voices

1. Malcolm Airs, *The Tudor and Jacobean Country House* (Stroud, 1998), p. 6.
2. See Glossary, "Merchants," for the full Jesuit code.
3. Sidney, Philip, *Defence of Poesie*, 1595, ed. Richard Bear (available: http://dark-

wing.uoregon.edu/-rbear/defence.html, 1992), p. 24. Sidney goes on, 'There are many mysteries contained in Poetry, which of purpose were written darkly, lest by profane wits it should be abused', p. 31. He attacks the 'over faint quietness' of English writers, afraid of their 'hard welcome' in an England that 'now can scarce endure the pain of a pen', pp. 26–27.

4. 'Humanism' in Shakespeare's day meant a Christianity deepened by the exploration of Greek and Roman philosophy and literature (known as the humanities).

5. Shakespeare's own genius is partly to blame for this. His greatness and enduring popularity has eclipsed the work of his contemporaries and has partially erased his historical context.

6. See the Blackfriars epilogue to John Lyly's play *Campaspe*, 1583, in Lyly, *Selected Prose and Dramatic Work*, ed. Leah Scragg (London, 1997), p. 128.

7. Chester's terms feature throughout the Glossary and include 'Rosaline,' 'phoenix,' 'rare,' 'high hills,' 'breasts,' 'the fall of Troy,' 'Caesar,' 'the rape of Lucrece'.

8. Edmund Spenser, 'Mother Hubberd's Tale', 1591, *Poetical Works*, ed. E. De Selincourt (London, 1912), lines 1197–1200.

9. The earliest version, known as *The Old Arcadia*, contains a number of intriguing passages. The most striking is an allegory of Sidney's central dilemma. Faced with the choice between Catholicism (Venus) and Protestantism (Diana), his alter ego, Philisides, opts for a third figure, Mira, despised handmaid of Diana, who combines the beauty of the one and the chastity of the other. She vanishes, like the ideals of the English Reformation, and throughout his early life he pursues her in vain (pp. 290–296). On pp. 121–123, the shepherd Dicus offers advice to his friend Dorus, who laments the suppression of his 'due faith'. Dicus advises him to stand up for himself and not to fear 'a woman's moody eye': 'Silence doth seem the mask of base oppression'. Dorus hymns his love's 'rare gifts' in terms that evoke the works of recusant poets (p. 122). Among *Arcadia*'s many debates and songs on the subject, the antiphonal song of Strephon and Klaius is the most affecting, as the two benighted, storm-tossed shepherds lament the lost Urania— the name given to the 'tenth muse', the embodiment of theological truth who 'Christianised' the other nine (pp. 285–290). Sidney and Spenser portray her as the banished essence of both high and low religious tendencies. Chester describes her 'making their nine a perfect ten'. For the origin of the concept of Urania, see Alison Shell, *Catholicism, Controversy and the English Literary Imagination, 1558–1660* (Cambridge, 1999), pp. 65–67.

10. Recent research into the coteries of individual writers in the late sixteenth century now reveal the extent of closet Catholicism at the time. Lisa Hopkins (*John Ford's Political Theatre* [Manchester, 1994]) has investigated the 'tightly bonded homogenous group' of Catholic sympathisers behind John Ford, including the Pembroke circle; Michael Questier (*An English Catholic Community? Confessional Politics and the Aristocratic Entourage c. 1558–1640*, unpublished thesis) has demonstrated the extensive influence of the Montagues' patronage; Gerard Kilroy (*Edmund Campion: Memory and Transcription* [Burlington, Vt., and Aldershot, 2005]) reveals John Harington's influential Catholic network.

11. On 'Play-wright', see Epigrammes LXVIII, in *Poems of Ben Jonson*, ed. George Burke Johnston (London, 1954), p. 33.

12. Thomas Kyd, *The Spanish Tragedie*, ed. Emma Smith (London and New York,

1998), pp. 28–32, 60–64. Kyd uses the code to blame the Queen and her courtiers for failing to intervene: '. . . Yonder pale faced Hee-cat there, the Moone, / Doth give consent to that is done in darknesse, / And all those Starres that gaze upon her face, / are aggots [agates] on her sleeve, pins on her train, / And those that should be powerfull and divine, / Do sleepe in darkenes when they most should shine . . .' (p. 61).

13. Aubrey, John. *Aubrey's Brief Lives*, ed. Oliver Lawson Dick (London, 1987), p. 334.

14. For discussion of the 'Lancashire Shakespeare' hypothesis, see E.A.J. Honigmann, *Shakespeare: The 'Lost Years'* (Manchester, 1998), pp. 1–39 and passim; Park Honan, *Shakespeare: A Life* (Oxford, 1998), pp. 64–70; Michael Wood, *In Search of Shakespeare* (London, 2003), pp. 74–80; and Stephen Greenblatt, *Will in the World* (New York and London, 2004), pp. 93–117.

15. Among them were: Robert Debdale, a Stratford contemporary from nearby Shottery, later executed as a missionary priest; Simon Hunt, a schoolmaster who may have taught the young Shakespeare, and who left Stratford to study for the priesthood in Douai and Rome with Southwell; Thomas Cottam, brother of another Stratford schoolmaster, a missionary who was arrested on his return to Shottery and executed at Tyburn in 1582.

16. For Shakespeare's inside knowledge of Oxford University in the 1570s and 1580s, see Clare Asquith, 'Oxford University and *Love's Labour's Lost*', in *Shakespeare and the Culture of Christianity in Early Modern England*, ed. Dennis Taylor and David Beauregard (New York, 2003), pp. 80–102.

17. Honan, *Shakespeare*, p. 159.

18. This secondary reading of Sonnet 23 has been lost for centuries, as successive editors, convinced that Shakespeare's sonnets should only be read as love poems, have altered the keyword 'books' to the more romantic 'looks'.

19. Katharine Duncan-Jones in particular emphasises the canniness of Shakespeare's business dealings: see her *Ungentle Shakespeare* (London, 2001).

20. From *Greene's Groats-worth of Wit*, quoted in *The Norton Shakespeare*, based on the Oxford edition, ed. Stephen Greenblatt et al. (New York and London, 1997), pp. 3320–3321.

21. 'Satire III', *John Donne, Complete Poetry and Prose*, ed. John Hayward (London, 1967), pp. 128–129.

22. Allegorical figures specifically representing England's political and religious predicament occur in explicit form in Jesuit plays written in Latin by English exiles. One of the few to survive is *Psyche and her Children*, which gives a glimpse of the way recusants staged their own country's dilemma. England takes the form of Psyche, a sleeping soul. In her sleep she begs her three children to find the lost 'rose, the flower of the ancestral faith', source of faith and wisdom. These are the roses of Paestum, which bloom twice—an image of the Counter-Reformation revival of Catholic spirituality, which it was hoped would spread to England. But her children fall out—on their quest Heresy (Musus) sets traps for English Catholicism (Eros) and the Catholic exiles (Elpis). In the end, Philosophus comes to the rescue. The play is undated but was probably performed in Valladolid in 1615. These shadowy figures and concepts recur throughout Shakespeare's hidden work. Other Jesuit plays use the iconoclasts of Byzantium as an allegory for contemporary English iconoclasts and feature extended laments over mutilated statues of the virgin that closely parallel the laments for

the similarly mutilated Lavinia in *Titus Andronicus*. See Shell, *Catholicism, Controversy, Imagination*, pp. 187–193, a passage that illustrates the way exiled Catholics used allegory.

23. Jesuit drama provides the closest analogy to what Shakespeare was about to attempt (see Note 22, above). The genre began as a teaching tool in Jesuit colleges but rapidly spread to courts, universities and cities all over Europe, its playwrights patronised by Protestants as well as Catholics as their plays 'drew on a vast treasury of profane subjects rich in lessons of natural virtue' and were careful to involve 'nothing vile or unbecoming'. Scholarly attention is only now beginning to wake up to the significance of these plays and their relationship to dramatists working in England at the time. See William H. McCabe, *An Introduction to Jesuit Theatre* (St. Louis, 1983), pp. 23–24 and passim.

24. George Gascoigne (1534–1577), *Penguin Book of Renaissance Verse*, ed. Henry Woudhuysen (London, 1993), p. 61.

25. See Glossary, 'Sunburn'.

26. *The Duke of Milan*, written by the Catholic playwright Philip Massinger and published in 1623, pays homage to Shakespeare's use of code. It includes an argument between a tall fair woman and a short dark one—a pastiche of the quarrel in *A Midsummer Night's Dream*. The authoritarian Marcelina is a 'pinetree . . . a monster 3 feet too high for women', while the shrewish, contentious Mariana is a 'dwarf', a 'puppet', who imposes 'black livery'. Massinger was able to publish this, and other explicitly Catholic plays such as *The Virgin Martyr*, only because restrictions on Catholic publications were briefly lifted in 1623, the year Shakespeare's works were first published. The title of the play evokes Shakespeare's own Duke of Milan—Prospero, in *The Tempest*.

Chapter 3: The Protectors

1. Michael Questier's forthcoming publication (*An English Catholic Community?*) provides a rich fund of information about the Montague family network and their extensive contacts throughout the country.

2. The following descriptions of Magdalen Montague, as well as all related quotations in this chapter, come from a memoir by her chaplain, Richard Smith, written in 1609. See A. C. Southern, ed., *The Elizabethan Recusant House, comprising The Life of the Lady Magdalen Viscountess Montague (1538–1608)* (London, 1954), pp. 6ff.

3. Greene's plot contains a topical allegory. The trial of an innocent wife, accused of adultery by an irrational king, the dramatic appeal to an oracle, the oracle's vindication of the queen, the king's blasphemous rejection of the judgement and the consequent loss of a male heir—all this was the story, thinly allegorised, of England's break with Rome. Though not a Catholic, Greene, like many disillusioned Protestants, including Nashe, was critical of the effects of the Reformation on England.

4. *Edward III*, ed. Eric Sams (New Haven, 1996).

5. The dialogue anticipates the extended theological debate of *The Rape of Lucrece*.

6. Warwick's debate with his daughter throws a new light on Shakespeare's sonnets. Evoking the revulsion many felt for the iconoclasm initiated by the adultery of

Henry VIII, the pair use phrases that recur in the sonnets: 'That sin doth ten times aggravate itself / That is committed in a holy place / An evil deed done by authority/ Is sin and subornation . . . / Lilies that fester smell far worse than weeds.' (2.1.798–808). The debate ends with a final, unmistakable hit at the new 'dark' faction, which gained power as a result of Henry's break with Rome: Warwick says his blessing on his daughter will 'convert to a most heavy curse / When thou convertest from honour's golden name / To the black faction of bed-blotting shame.' (2.1.813–814).

7. Thomas Nashe, 'Pierce Penniless', in *The Unfortunate Traveller and Other Works*, ed. J. B. Steane (London, 1972), p. 113.
8. See E.A.J. Honigmann, *Shakespeare's Impact on his Contemporaries* (London, 1982), pp. 1–6.
9. See Thomas Edwards, *Cephalus and Procris*, 1595 (London).

Chapter 4: Reconciliation, 1588–1592

1. Anthony Browne, 2nd Viscount Montague, *Instruction to my Daughter*, 1598 holograph manuscript, Downside Abbey Library, Somerset, DAL 28000.
2. Robert Persons, *A Temperate Ward-word*, 1599, Downside Abbey Library, Somerset, DAL 47451, pp. 53–54.
3. Ibid, p. 128.
4. Scott R. Pilarz, *Robert Southwell and the Mission of Literature, 1561–1595: Writing Reconciliation* (Burlington, Vt., and Aldershot, 2004), p. 66.
5. Ibid., p. 69.
6. One of these priests, William Hartley, may have been an early influence on Shakespeare. Hartley was a remarkable character—a literary man whose first mission to England had been as Edmund Campion's chief printer and distributor of books, masterminding a number of daring escapades. He fled abroad after Campion's death but returned to continue the mission.
7. Philip Caraman, *Henry Garnet, 1555–1606, and the Gunpowder Plot* (London, 1964), p. 131.
8. Thomas Merriam, 'The Misunderstanding of Munday as Author of *Sir Thomas More*', *Review of English Studies*, New Series, vol. 51, no, 204 (2000), p. 562. The article traces Shakespeare's involvement with the company and with Lord Strange in great detail.
9. The name Bianca is used for another Catholic figure in *Othello*.
10. See Glossary, 'Revenge'.
11. Although Luther himself encouraged religious music, English Protestantism did not. Popular music was also attacked by Puritans.
12. Shakespeare repeatedly uses the differences between old and new funeral and wedding services as markers.
13. 'Precise' was almost synonymous with 'Puritan'.
14. See Glossary, 'Here I Stand'.
15. David Ewing Duncan, *The Calendar* (London, 1999), p. 307.
16. See 'Truth's Complaint over England' by Thomas Lodge in *An Anthology of Catholic Poetry*, ed. Shane Leslie (London, 1952).
17. See Glossary, 'Merchants'.

18. See Glossary, 'Well-Dealing'.
19. Garnet was dogged throughout his years in England by slanders from vindictive anti-Jesuit priests in Catholic colleges abroad. Father William Holt, who had returned to Flanders after working with Garnet, sneered that he was 'a little wretch of a man . . . who day and night thinks of nothing save the rack and gibbet' (Caraman, *Henry Garnet*, p. 207). Garnet also had to support the neurotic Father Thomas Lister, constantly on the verge of breakdown (ibid., p. 223). William Weston, the saintly Jesuit Superior who preceded Garnet as Superior before his arrest in 1586, became the focus of bitter wrangling among fellow priests at Wisbech prison and later attempted suicide during long years of solitary confinement in the Tower of London.
20. Luciana's servant is called Luce—another double 'Luke' marker.
21. Spenser puts his admiration of these men on record, though he buries it prudently towards the end of his *View of the State of Ireland*, lamenting the contrast between their self-denial and the lives of the self-seeking new clergy.
22. Luciana, new Catholicism, is balanced by Adriana, old Catholicism—her name recalls the only English Pope, Adrian IV, evoking England's pre-Reformation union with Christendom. Shakespeare uses the same reference in *Coriolanus*.
23. Like Southwell, in his *Epistle of Comfort*, the Abbess's solution to all errors is a life of virtue and self-discipline.
24. It is possible that Strange himself had a hand in this curious play. Unlike Shakespeare's, its style is lordly, discursive and—apart from the character of Parolles—humourless; nonetheless, its coded political treatment of the situation of England looks like a blueprint for much of Shakespeare's work and may well have been polished and retained in the canon for that reason.
25. *The Two Gentlemen of Verona* is a typical example of a play that depends for its success on awareness of the code. Even at the time, uninitiated spectators would have found it heavy going, apart from hilarious scenes (equally coded) between the servant Launce and his dog, Crab. A recent, refreshingly frank review of the play shows the result of our limited understanding of what Shakespeare was trying to do: 'It's only in Launce's observations on Crab that the unmistakeable voice of Shakespeare surfaces from the dross of a comedy that may well have been his first . . . hard to escape the feeling that the apprentice Bard was so bored with injecting a semblance of life into a stock tale of lovesick heroes and their ladies that . . . he allows a dog to upstage the lot of them' (Patrick Carnegy, *Spectator*, 11 December 2004).
26. Julia is a Roman name.
27. See Glossary, 'Shadow and Substance'.
28. Launce's departure reads like a parody of a histrionic contemporary account of the pious Edward Throgmorton's departure from England. See Pilarz, *Robert Southwell*, p. 140.
29. See Glossary, 'Faded Beauty'.
30. See Glossary, 'Sunburn'.
31. Persons, *Elizabethae*, quoted from a 1605 edition in Pilarz, *Robert Southwell*, p. 231.
32. For a detailed reading of the hidden level of this play, see Asquith, 'Oxford University and *Love's Labour's Lost*'.
33. Ben Jonson, in his preface to the First Folio of Shakespeare's works, 'To the memory of my Beloved, the Author, Mr. William Shakespeare: and what he hath left us'.

Chapter 5: Persecution, 1592–1594

1. David Cecil, *The Cecils of Hatfield House* (London, 1973), p. 117. The following portrait of Robert Cecil is drawn from David Cecil's account and from the *Dictionary of National Biography*.
2. Devlin, *Life of Southwell*, p. 288.
3. Traces of the cover story survive. Referring to the 'kingly' status of an unnamed patron, his contemporary, Sir John Davies, evidently believed that Shakespeare was rejected because he was a mere actor: 'Had'st thou not played a kingly part in jest / Thou hadst been a companion for a king' (E. K. Chambers, *William Shakespeare: A Study of Facts and Problems* [Oxford, 1930], vol. 2, p. 214). Strange's semi-royal status was often mentioned in panegyrics, for the earldom of Derby brought with it the title of King of the Isle of Man. Shakespeare himself encourages the impression that his elevation to intimacy with the nobility was a brief aberration. The decorative prologue to *The Taming of the Shrew* is a later addition and portrays a Stratford tinker who wakes from a drunken sleep in the clothes and rooms of an aristocrat—the victim of a practical joke perpetrated by a group of noblemen. One of them says laughingly, 'It would seem strange to him when he wak'd'; '[e]ven as a flattering dream', answers another (Induction, 1.1.41–42). Sonnet 87 uses identical language: 'Thus have I had thee as a dream doth flatter, / In sleep a King, but waking no such matter.' The estrangement and the humiliating cover story were clearly deeply hurtful and may lie behind a number of the sonnets of betrayal, making sense of the curious situations in Sonnets 34 and 36.
4. G.P.V. Akrigg, *Shakespeare and the Earl of Southampton* (Boston, 1968), p. 176.
5. Ibid., p. 180.
6. Oxford, Pembroke and Rutland were all urged by William Cecil to marry Protestant wives. Oxford reluctantly married Cecil's daughter, Anne. Pembroke, like Southampton, refused and married a Catholic.
7. 'Say shall we? Shall we? Wilt thou make the match?' (line 586) she pleads in matrimonial terms unusual for a goddess; and compares him, firmly locked in her arms, to a deer within the circuit of a park—an echo of a work Shakespeare is known to have studied, George Puttenham's influential '*Art of Poesie*', published in 1589, which describes Elizabeth's reign as a circular deer park, its subjects contained by oaths of loyalty.
8. See Glossary, 'Eyes'.
9. See Glossary, 'Eyes'. One of Elizabeth's favourites who became a victim of the regime was Southampton's cousin, Thomas Pounde, a much admired wit, masquer and dancer, whose open espousal of Catholicism led to life imprisonment. The image of eyes turning in their sockets to escape a vision of blasphemous savagery also occurs in the Jesuit play *Leo Arminus*, written in Latin by the celebrated English dramatist Joseph Simons (Shell, *Catholicism, Controversy and Imagination*, p. 209).
10. Elizabeth I, *Collected Works*, ed. Leah S. Marcus, Janet Mueller, and Mary Beth Rose (Chicago and London, 2000), p. 341.
11. Kilroy, *Edmund Campion*, pp. 59–88.
12. One of the two strongest earthquakes ever recorded in England occurred in the year 1580 in the south of England. Over a hundred contemporary reports survive of flooded seaports, disturbed birds and cattle and damaged buildings, particu-

larly in Oxford and London: the event occasioned a learned exchange of letters on the subject between Spenser and Gabriel Harvey, and is the source of frequent references to earthquakes in the writings of Shakespeare and others. The nurse says the earthquake happened 'eleven years' ago. Scholars concerned about the dating of the play have searched for alternative earthquakes or even landslides— but the 1580 earthquake was as memorable and unexpected an event as the English hurricane of 1987. Not surprisingly, such a dramatic natural event was seen as a portent; in this case, taken with other strange events recorded by Stow in the first edition of his *Annals*, but prudently omitted in the second (Persons, quoted in Caraman, *Other Face*, p. 112), it marked for Catholics the brief, momentous Jesuit mission that began in the summer of that year.

13. The year 1591, the year in which the nurse would be speaking if Juliet literally had been born thirteen years earlier, was a year in which Southampton would have been especially aware of the heroism of the English mission, for it was then that Swithin Wells, his tutor in Italian and rhetoric, was hanged opposite his own house in Gray's Inn along with priests and others who had been celebrating Mass there.

14. There are also echoes of Southwell's popular poem *St Peter's Complaint*, which associates Peter's betrayal, remorse and rehabilitation with the experiences of England's Catholics, who, like Peter, are portrayed as having broken their vow to Christ.

15. Charles Nicholl, *The Reckoning* (London, 1992), p. 55.

16. Ibid., p. 66.

17. Ibid., p. 55.

18. Some of his lewdly suggestive lines contain Marlowe's favourite turns of phrase: 'By her fine foot, straight leg and quivering thigh *And the demesnes that there adjacent lie*' (2.1.20) and so does the hint of rhythmic bombast—'soar with them above a common bound' (1.4.18). He plays obsessively with words, and his seamlessly witty, scurrilous manner resembles such parodies of Marlowe as Gabriel Harvey's *'Aretine and the Devil's Orator'*.

19. See Glossary, 'North'.

20. Cecil, *The Cecils*, p. 112. After Essex's death the crowds shouted at him, 'Robin with the bloody breast', and 'What are the Cecils? Are they better than pengents?' (p. 117).

21. Shakespeare finds ways to hint at the post-Reformation divide in this pre-Reformation context. Richard repeatedly employs an unusual oath, 'By St Paul', which associates him with the reformers, and is described, like the iconoclasts, as a 'foul defacer of God's handiwork' (4.4.51). Nemesis comes to his associate, Buckingham, on the day that symbolised the Reformation split—All Saints' Day, or Hallowmass. His opponents, like the opponents of the Tudor regime of Shakespeare's day, include a formidable soldier called Sir William Stanley; they gather under the banner of two doctrines outlawed by the English Reformation: 'the prayers of holy saints and wronged souls' (5.3.241).

22. Peter Holmes, *Resistance and Compromise: The Political Thought of Elizabethan Catholics* (Cambridge, 1982), p. 135.

23. This picture is recalled in one of the most famous speeches in the play, in which Richard declares, 'Not all the water in the rough rude sea / Can wash the balm off from an anointed king' (3.2.54–55). The speech ends with the arrogant belief in

divine support that led to his deposition: 'For every man that Bolingbroke hath pressed / To lift shrewd steel against our golden crown, / God for his Richard hath in heavenly pay / A glorious angel . . .' (3.2.58–61). An 'angel' was the name of an English coin at the time; but here Shakespeare was surely also thinking of the historical Richard's conception of the seraphim wearing his livery in the Wilton Diptych—a painting that embodies the glories of pre-reformation Christendom in which King, saints and angels and the Virgin are all part of the same divine company, but which also embodies the pride and presumption that led to its downfall. Recent cleaning has revealed another parallel between the picture and the play. At the top of a banner held by one angel is a roundel containing a symbol of England, a tiny map showing an island with a castle set in a sea of silver leaf—'a fortress built by Nature for herself . . . a precious stone set in a silver sea' (2.1.43–46).

24. Elizabeth I, *Works*, p. 341.
25. See the preface to *Venus and Adonis*.
26. See Glossary, 'Red and White'.
27. See Glossary, 'Troy'.
28. This standpoint is similar to that in the Jesuit play *Psyche and her Children*, in which Sleeping England is threatened by the quarrel between her children. See Chapter 2, note 12.
29. D. M. Palliser, 'Popular Reactions to the Reformation', in *The English Reformation Revised*, ed. Christopher Haigh (Cambridge, 1987), p. 102.
30. 'His beauty shall in these black lines be seen / And they shall live, and he in them still green . . .', Sonnet 63, lines 13–14.

Chapter 6: Rage, 1594

1. See Glossary, 'Rome'.
2. Michael A.R. Graves, *Burghley: William Cecil, Lord Burghley* (London, 1998). 'Old Saturnus, his nickname in some quarters, was not flattering' (p. 213).
3. According to Virgil's *Aenead*, Lavinia was the wife of Aeneas, who in legend fathered Brut, the founder of Britain. In the *Aenead* she, too, does not speak.
4. See Chapter 7, note 7 for a second version of the image of a dark-skinned child in *A Midsummer Night's Dream*.
5. The play lightly reinforces the dark-fair imagery with intriguing references to the panther and the hind—precisely the animals Dryden chose a century or so later to symbolise the Anglican compromise (the spotted panther) and victimised Catholicism (the white deer) in his poem *The Hind and the Panther*. Counter-Reformation iconography often used a spotted creature, such as a leopard or a panther, to represent heresy. A striking instance is the representation by the Spanish painter Francisco Ribalta (1565–1628) of St Francis treading a crowned panther underfoot as he embraces the crucified Christ (Museo de Bellas Artes, Valencia).
6. Shell (*Catholicism, Controversy and Imagination*) gives a full account of this ceremony in her study of sixteenth-century Catholic imagery, pp. 200–207.
7. Ibid., p. 204.
8. Ibid., p. 209. The language is strikingly similar.

9. Passages of coded, compressed chronologies like this recur throughout Shakespeare's work: examples include the opening scenes of *The Two Gentlemen of Verona*, Bassanio's casket scene in *The Merchant of Venice*, the quarrel in the woods in *A Midsummer Night's Dream*, King Lear's descent into madness. They represent the most ingenious aspects of his hidden work.

10. He has twenty-five children—an echo of the fifty children of Priam, King of Troy, drawing again on the myth of England as a 'second Troy'.

11. There is an echo here of the Hesketh Plot, in which Strange was tricked into betraying the innocent Richard Hesketh in a classic case of government entrapment.

12. Shakespeare's relatives, the Ardens and Somervilles, were particularly hard-hit in the notorious 'Somerville affair'. Michael Wood gives one of the best accounts of the purge of Catholics in and around Stratford in 1583. It was triggered by the arrest and death in prison of the deranged young John Somerville, a Shakespeare relative, who threatened to kill the queen, and culminated in the racking and execution of his father-in-law, Edward Arden, a respected Warwickshire landowner and head of Shakespeare's wife's family. See Wood, *In Search of Shakespeare* (London, 2003), pp. 88–96. Wood notes an overlooked tribute to Somerville in *Henry VI, Part 2*.

13. The word 'map' is used in the same odd context in the sonnets.

14. John Carey, *John Donne: Life, Mind and Art* (London, 1981), p. 21. Carey explores Donne's anguished religious position, torn between the old faith, which blighted his early life and led to his brother's death in prison in 1594 for sheltering a priest, and the new, which, he feared, predestined him to eternal damnation.

15. In this century, the poet David Jones begins his long poem on the Mass, *The Anathemata*, with a similar evocation of these ancient words: "Adscriptam, ratam, rationabilem . . . and by pre-application and for them, under modes and patterns altogether theirs, the holy and venerable hands lift up an efficacious sign' (Jones, *The Anathemata, fragments of an attempted writing*, [London, 1952]).

16. Gyles Isham, *Rushton Triangular Lodge* (London, 1986), p. 5.

17. Like the separated family, the image of England as a dismembered body longing for unity is a consistent image in recusant writings that also figures in many of Shakespeare's plays.

18. William Byrd, the recusant Catholic composer, emphasised the same hope of eventual rescue in his sacred music. See Joseph Kerman, 'Music and Politics: The Case of William Byrd (1540–1623)', *Proceedings of the American Philosophical Society* (September 2000).

19. The many epithets for the pit in Act 2, scene 3 are revealing. They include two allusions to elder trees. In *Love's Labour's Lost*, Shakespeare refers to the legend that the elder was the tree on which Judas hanged himself (5.2.609); and George Eliot, the man who betrayed Campion after attending his Mass, was known afterwards among the Catholic community as 'Judas'. It was also connected with the execution of criminals and was traditionally the tree on which Christ died. Geoffrey Grigson, *The Englishman's Flora* (London, 1987), p. 353.

Chapter 7: *Addressing the Queen, 1595–1599*

1. E.A.J. Honigmann, *Shakespeare: The 'Lost Years'* (Manchester, 1985); Merriam, 'The Misunderstanding of Munday'.
2. Ian Wilson, *Shakespeare: The Evidence: Unlocking the Mysteries of the Man and His Work* (London, 1993), p. 176.
3. See Merriam, 'The Misunderstanding of Munday', passim, for Munday's role in framing Strange's acting company.
4. An early passage wittily lamenting the divisions in England's religion under colour of the pains of love occurs in Act 1, scene 1, lines 31–149: it includes an allusion to the 'low' church ban on the 'high' image of the cross. The wordplay continues throughout the course of the lovers' quarrels: Hermia is twice described as a 'heresy' by Lysander (2.2.135–141).
5. In spite of the suggestively regal 'fairy queen' associations of Titania, commentators agree that one of Shakespeare's only direct references to Elizabeth occurs in this play and associates her with the moon—'the imperial votress . . . in maiden meditation, fancy-free'(2.1.164). She is thus portrayed as being serenely aloof from the sectarian squabbling.
6. See Glossary, 'Calendar'.
7. The image of the new religion as a fatherless child, adopted by the state, may have been a common one—in the seventeenth century, an Anglican clergyman, Edward Stephens, denounced the way the hard-line 1552 prayer book was 'hugged like a bastard child by a silly, abused husband' (MacCulloch, *Reformation*, p. 172).
8. 'Bottom' has similar bawdy overtones to 'Will', a name on which Shakespeare frequently puns in the sonnets.
9. Bottom's comically naive solution to the problems of 'love' parodies Shakespeare's own conciliatory line on the problems of religion. 'To say the truth, reason and love keep little company together now-a-days. The more the pity that some honest neighbours will not make them friends' (3.1.132–134).
10. Shell, *Catholicism, Controversy and Imagination*, p. 190.
11. Devlin, *Life of Southwell*, p. 212.
12. Caraman, *Other Face*, pp. 258–260. Plasden was arrested at the house of Southampton's tutor, Swithin Wells, a key member of the underground movement that assisted seminary priests. Mark Vickers, 'Saint Polydore Plasden', in *The Forty-Four* (Farnborough, 2000), pp. 27–29.
13. Peter Milward, *The Catholicism of Shakespeare's Plays* (Southampton, 1997), p. 14.
14. The Apocrypha includes the Book of Daniel and the Book of Tobit, both quoted in the text of the play.
15. Portia's opening speech evokes the Queen's difficulty in devising 'laws' for her hot-headed subjects with the aid of 'good counsel, the cripple'. The difficulty is primarily religious: 'If to do were as easy as to know what were good to do, chapels had been churches . . .' (1.2.10–24).
16. Elizabeth I, 'Her answer to the Commons' Petition that she should marry', *Works*, p. 59.
17. William Birch, from *A song between the Queen's Majesty and England*, 1564.
18. His study of the caskets is given a religious dimension; in accordance with Elizabeth's public stance, he rejects spurious ornament (3.2.77–81).
19. Persons highlighted the dangers of favouring Protestants over Catholics in

England: 'Who knoweth not, but that the bowels of England are so combined and linked together at this day in this point as hardly can the sword pass the one but it must also wound the other.' If toleration were not granted, he argued, the English would 'live in perpetual torment of hatred, suspicion, jealousies, aversions, detestations and deadly hostilities, the one with the other, a state more fit for hell than for any peaceable Christian commonwealth.' Besides, 'men grow desperate if all strings of hope are cut off' (*A Treatise Tending to Mitigation*, ed. D. M. Rogers 1607, [London, 1977], pp. 33–34).

20. Another echo of the Exultet: 'caligine peccatorum segregatos' (separated by the grime of sin).

21. Montague, *Instruction to my Daughter*, p. 148.

22. Sonnet 33 mourns a 'sun' that shone for 'one hour upon my brow'. The oddly truncated Sonnet 126, which can be read as a meditation on the moment of the boy's death, occurs at a central point in the sequence, employing the same imagery of reckoning as Ben Jonson's poem on the death of his son and ending with Hamlet's term for death—'quietus'.

23. Roland Whyte, in a letter to Sir Robert Sidney, governor of Flushing. Quoted in J. B. Black, *The Reign of Elizabeth* (Oxford, 1951), pp. 425–426.

24. Ibid., p. 139.

25. Ibid., p. 143.

26. Curtis Breight draws attention to the sympathetic commentary on the Northern Rebellion contained in Shakespeare's 'Henriad'. See his *Surveillance, Militarism and Drama in the Elizabethan Era* (New York, 1996).

27. Sonnet 101.

28. There may be a pun on the name of the writer Edward Dyer, who gained financially from his adoption of Protestantism. 'Eisell', which meant wormwood, recalls the variant spellings of Cecil.

Chapter 8: The Catholic Resistance, 1599–1600

1. Questier, *An English Catholic Community?* chap. 3, pp. 49–55.

2. Ibid., chaps. 4 and 5, gives a full picture of the Montague entourage, their vast social network, their various households and their often tacit, dissimulating patronage of a wide spectrum of Catholic dissidence. The change in their stance over the years is mirrored by developments in Shakespeare's own standpoint. Relatively relaxed under the 1st Viscount, the family became more oppositional in the mid-1590s under the 2nd Viscount; on James's accession, they did their utmost to persuade James to establish religious toleration. Questier calls the 2nd Viscount 'the thinking man's patron'.

3. Ibid., chaps. 4 and 5.

4. The theatre in Holywell was also close to a famous dissident household that would have offered books and contacts to subversive playwrights. Holywell was the London base of the earls of Rutland. The 5th Earl, Roger Manners (1576–1612) was a close friend of Southampton and like him had been a ward of William Cecil. He and his two brothers were supporters of Essex and were leading members of the Essex Conspiracy.

5. See Glossary, 'Rome'.

6. See Glossary, 'Thirty-Three'.
7. The poet and courtier Thomas Carew, writing in 1633, looks back on Shakespeare's time as an age of literary duplicity; he deplores 'the subtle cheat / Of sly exchanges and the juggling feat / Of two-edged words' ('Elegy upon the death of the Deane of Pauls, Dr. John Donne', *Penguin Book of Renaissance Verse*, ed. H. R. Woudhuysen (London and New York, 1993), p. 741.
8. The pains of banishment are a consistent theme in Shakespeare's work; they are lamented in *The Two Gentlemen of Verona, Richard II, Romeo and Juliet*, and *Cymbeline*. The most eloquent passage (*Richard II*, 1.3.153–172) dwells on the aspect that seems to have most impressed Shakespeare: the 'speechless death' of living among foreigners: 'The language I have learnt these forty years, / My native English, now I must forgo / And now my tongue's use is to me no more / Than an unstringed viol or a harp; / Or like a cunning instrument cas'd up'.
9. William Cecil to Sir Thomas Copley, 28 December 1574, cited in Caraman, *Other Face*, p. 141.
10. John Chamberlain to Dudley Carleton, cited in ibid., p. 101.
11. Ibid., p. 101.
12. Philip Caraman, *The Years of Seige: Catholic Life from James I to Cromwell* (London, 1966), p. 11.
13. Stanley's treachery became the subject of heated debate after Cardinal Allen published a defence of his actions in 1587 (*The Copy of a Letter . . . concerning the yielding up of the city of Daventry*). Allen justifies Stanley, using the same grounds the Free French did in justifying their actions when France was under occupation during World War II—indeed, there are parallels between the activist leaders of the sixteenth-century English exiles and Charles de Gaulle's London-based government in exile in the 1940s.
14. *As You Like It* closely parallels this poem by Lodge:
    'O happy truth, when as with sweet delight
    She laboured still for conscience not for fees'
    ('Truth's Complaint over England', lines 3–4).
    Compare:
    'O good old man, how well in thee appears
    The constant service of the antique world
    When service sweat for duty not for meed'
    (*As You Like It*, 2.3.56–58).
15. See Glossary, 'Rosalind', 'Gazer', 'Red Rose'.
16. Arden was also the name of Shakespeare's mother's family and the district of Warwickshire from which she came. Touchstone, whom scholars have associated with Shakespeare, could here be contrasting the hostile Ardennes with a more homely Arden: '. . . now am I in Arden; the more fool I; when I was at home I was in a better place' (2.4.13–14).
17. The four allusions are to the old religion: it was connected with 'better days'; generous hospitality; affective, emotional piety and poems; and church bells. The tolling of every kind of church bell was specifically banned in Archbishop Grindal's 1576 Visitation—'on Sundays or holy days'—except 'one bell in convenient time to be rung or tolled before the sermon'. Southwell's *Epistle of Comfort* contrasts Protestant frugality with the 'large hospitality in housekeeping' that proves 'the sincerity of our religion'. See Pilarz, *Robert Southwell*, p. 70.

18. The main branch of the Stanley family had the eagle and child as their crest; Sir William belonged to the Hooton Stanleys.
19. Patrick H. Martin and John Finnis, 'Thomas Thorpe, "W.S." and the Catholic Intelligencers', *English Literary Renaissance*, vol. 33, no. 1, (2003), p. 28.
20. Aubrey, *Brief Lives*, p. 253.
21. *Return from Parnassus*, Act 4, scene 3, quoted in *Norton Shakespeare*, p. 3327. The pun is suggested by E.A.J. Honigmann.
22. Introduction to *Every Man Out of His Humour*—a play that also contains a vivid vignette of 'narrow-eyed decypherers' in the audience, government spies sitting concealed with their notebooks out, attempting to read political meanings into Jonson's 'deniable' types (end of Act 2).
23. Lingard, *History of England*, vol. 6, p. 605n.

Chapter 9: Appeal to the Undecided, 1600

1. Andrew Willet, 'Synopsis Papismi', see the year 1590 in Taylor, *Chronology*.
2. *An Anthology of Catholic Poetry*, ed. Shane Leslie Burns Oates (1924), p. 186.
3. It was in this year—1600—that Southwell's *Humble Supplication*, was published in England. It refers to the 'most bitter corrosives' suffered by silent Catholic 'gentry or nobility . . . tender over their honours' who 'neither dare revenge their own quarrels for fear of a double offence, to God, and to your Highness, nor hope for redress by ordinary courses; so far hath disfavour excluded them from all needful remedies'.
4. 'Chorus Sacerdotum', *The New Oxford Book of English Verse, 1250–1590*, ed. Helen Gardner (Oxford, 1972), p. 118.
5. A. C. Hamilton, *Sir Philip Sidney: A Study of His Life and Works* (Cambridge, 1977), p. 111. The portrait of Sidney in the rest of this chapter is taken from the biography by Katharine Duncan-Jones, *Sir Philip Sidney, Courtier Poet* (London, 1991).
6. Duncan-Jones, *Sir Philip Sidney*, p. 126.
7. Ibid., p. 88.
8. According to the missionary priest John Gerard, who knew her well, she was only prevented from secretly converting to Catholicism by the angry intervention of her lover, Lord Mountjoy. John Gerard, *The Autobiography of an Elizabethan*, trans. and ed. Philip Caraman (London, 1951), pp. 34–36.
9. Duncan-Jones, *Sir Philip Sidney*, pp. 125–127.
10. Another identifying mark in this 'blazon' is the comparison of Hamlet's eyes to stars falling from their spheres. Sidney's alter ego in *Arcadia* and in court tournaments bore a pun on Sidney's own name: 'Philisides', or 'star lover'. It would be better to have fewer star-gazing sonnets to Stella, the ghost implies, and more of the militant porcupine, which traditionally shot quills at its enemy.
11. Duncan-Jones, *Sir Philip Sidney*, p. 260.
12. Aubrey, *Aubrey's Brief Lives*, p. 336. Hamlet's lines 'Yea, from the tablet of my memory / I'll wipe away all trivial fond records' (1.5.97) quote directly from Sidney's *Defence of Poesie*: 'let Aeneas be worn in the Tablet of your memory' (p. 21).
13. Duncan-Jones, *Sir Philip Sidney*, p. 152.
14. Ibid., p. 167.
15. Edmund Campion's comment, quoted in ibid., p. 126.

16. As so often, Shakespeare's choice of words points to the subtext: Gertrude once 'fed' on the mountain, the word 'fed' evoking the religious image of a flock, exploited by Spenser, among others, in his *Shepherd's Calendar*.

17. Scholars have noticed that the 'purgatory' described by the ghost resembles the purgatory imposed on Catholic prisoners in England. Southwell uses the term in a letter of 1590 to describe the most notorious of the London prisons. 'Almost all who are taken now may expect to taste of Bridewell, that place of shame; it is a slaughter-house where the cruelties inflicted are scarcely credible. The tasks imposed are continuous and beyond ordinary strength, and even the sick are driven to them under the lash. Food is not only of the scantiest, but so disfigured that it cannot be swallowed without retching . . . Bedding is straw matted with stinking ordure . . . It is the one Purgatory that all we Catholics dread, where Top-cliffe and Young, butchers, have complete licence to torture' (Devlin, *Life of Southwell*, p. 211). This was the situation Campion begged Sidney to redress.

18. It was at this nervous period that a law was passed forbidding satires, and the works of Thomas Nashe and Gabriel Harvey were burnt in the street.

19. Letter from Pibush to Garnet, dated 1600. See Caraman, *Henry Garnet*, p. 269.

20. Though William Cecil's son, Robert, is prudently omitted, Shakespeare was still sailing very close to the wind. A number of other surprisingly open attacks on the regime appeared at around this period. It was perhaps a measure of the confidence of the Essex faction at this point that such writers felt they could get away with it. Though Robert was the most powerful man in England, Essex unwisely underestimated his opponent, who was already planning his downfall.

21. Complimenting Laertes on his father's acumen, Claudius accidentally suggests that it is the throne that is indispensible to Polonius, rather than Polonius to the throne—exactly the parasitic relationship of which the Cecils were accused: 'The head is not more native to the heart, / The hand more instrumental to the mouth, / Than is the throne of Denmark to thy father' (1.2.47–49).

22. Polonius's role in urging Hamlet's suit to Ophelia after forbidding it not only mirrors Sidney's personal experience (the withdrawal of Ann Cecil was followed by the offer of a second 'establishment' bride, Frances Walsingham). It was allegorically precise. At this late stage, the Cecils began to promote a broad-church form of Protestantism, very like modern Anglicanism. It was based at Westminster Abbey and for decades remained no more than window-dressing for the regime, impressing foreign diplomats and gratifying the Queen, but rejected by most leading churchmen at the time. The figure of Ophelia represents this skin-deep synthesis of Catholic 'beauty' with Calvinism.

23. In his earliest version of *Arcadia*, Philip Sidney included his own allegory of the elusive Reformation ideal, in which his alter ego, Philisides, falls in love, not with the quarrelling goddesses representing the beauty of Rome and the chastity of Geneva but with their handmaid Mira, in whom 'beauty both and chasteness fully reign'. She vanishes, leaving him bereft. This passage was omitted in the darker *New Arcadia*. Fulke Greville, too, laments his abandonment by Myra, an embodiment of a lost spiritual beauty, nostalgically recalled in 'Myra', *The New Oxford Book of English Verse*, p. 118.

24. The so-called Bloody Question was put by government interrogators to test Catholic loyalty: it epitomized England's dilemma: 'If the Pope do by his Bull or sentence pronounce her majesty to be deprived, and no lawful Queen, and her

subjects to be discharged of their allegiance and obedience unto her; and after, the pope or any other by his appointment of authority, do invade this realm; which part would you take, or which part ought a good subject of England to take?'

25. Begun around 1610, it was eventually published after Greville's death in 1652.
26. Caraman, *Other Face*, p. 174.
27. See 'Grand Captain' (chap. 10), p. 62, of Questier, 'An English Catholic Community?' The question of burial is also raised by Hamlet's query 'hic et ubique?' (1.5.155) which comes from a Catholic prayer for those who '*here and elsewhere sleep in Christ.*' ("For those at rest in the Churchyard", *The Roman Missal*, London, 1960, p. 259*).

Chapter 10: Failure, 1601–1602

1. Lingard, *History of England*, vol. 6, p. 611.
2. Anne Somerset, *Elizabeth I* (London, 1991), p. 555.
3. Christopher Hibbert, *The Virgin Queen: Elizabeth I, Genius of the Golden Age* (London, 1991), p. 259.
4. Persons, *A Temperate Ward-word*, 1599, p. 128.
5. Somerset, *Elizabeth I*, p. 158.
6. Ibid., p. 158.
7. Chettle, reproaching Shakespeare for failing to mourn the dead Elizabeth, also associates her with Lucrece. Quoted in Honan, *Shakespeare*, p. 297.
8. The play repeatedly implies that there is something forced and unnatural about the 'dark' inheritance of Olivia, who is bound to preserve 'a brother's dead love' and whose household is run by a Puritan steward.
9. Antonia Fraser, *The Six Wives of Henry VIII* (London, 1993), p. 202.
10. 'Her majesty being our Queen is thereby also a mother . . . the Bishop of Rome to all Catholique men of the world is their spiritual father . . . But now our said two parents are fallen at debate . . .' (Persons, *Temperate Ward-word*, p. 128).
11. Missionaries to England called themselves 'lambs among wolves'.
12. Government propaganda encouraged those at home to view the exiles either as traitors in the pay of Spain or as cowards who had abandoned their country for an easier life abroad. The militant exiles, on the other hand, increasingly regarded the covert Catholics they had left behind as 'Appellant' collaborators. Their suspicions appeared to be confirmed with the news of the last-minute defection of leading Catholics from Essex's cause.
13. The play ends with an abusive speech by Pandarus to the audience, addressing them as 'traitors' and 'brethren and sisters of the hold-door trade'—beneath the vocabulary of prostitution, a hint at the Essex conspirators and their various jailors and minders (some were detained in private houses).
14. 'The world is like . . . unto a covetous and forgetful Host; who, if he see his old Guest come by his Inn in beggarly estate, all his money being spent, he maketh semblance not to know him: And if the Guest marvel thereat, and say, that hath come often that way, and spent much money in the house; the other answereth, it may be so, my friend, for there pass this way many, and we use not to keep account of all . . .'. Quoted in Pierre Janelle, *The Catholic Reformation* (London, 1971), p. 266.
15. Persons's *A Memorial of the Reformation of England* (unpublished ms., 1596, Down-

side Abbey Library, Somerset, DAL 26603) is an astonishingly thorough blueprint for the reconstruction of England after 'God in his mercy shall restore it to the Catholic faith', covering every aspect of public life. He presents the nation's current reduced state, 'after so long a storm of persecution', as an advantage, envisaging the future as 'gold coming out of the furnace, and a garden newly planted after the weeds and thorns are consumed by fire' (ff. 1–3). Its many practical proposals were examined by James II and studied by later political theorists after an edited version was published in 1690, with suitable Protestant disclaimers.

16. See Note 14 above, and Janelle, *Catholic Reformation*, p. 266.
17. Persons's *Memorial* addresses the problem, proposing that in the event of the return of Catholicism to England, a leasing arrangement might be put in place to accommodate the new landowners. (See Note 15 above.)
18. Caraman, *Henry Garnet*, p. 282.
19. On his release, Southampton almost incurred another jail sentence for his attack on Lord Grey, who cited lack of Catholic support as a reason for the failure of Essex's rebellion.
20. See Chapter 9, note 22.
21. Lingard, *History of England*, vol. 6, p. 324.
22. A dig, too, at Robert Cecil's secret dealings with Catholic Spain.
23. Kilroy, *Edmund Campion*, pp. 19–21.
24. Caraman, *Henry Garnet*, p. 304.

Chapter 11: The King's Man, 1603–1604

1. See the year 1603 in Taylor, *Shakespeare and Religion*.
2. Caraman, *Henry Garnet*, p. 305.
3. Ibid., p. 311. Garnet also noted, however, that the Queen had left no less than 'fifteen hundred rich gowns' and jewels worth £500,000.
4. Ibid., p. 309. Dr. Matthew Kellison, writing from Douai, dedicated his *Survey of the new Religion* to the King; the preface alleged that if the King adopted his mother's religion, he would be on the side of the majority of his subjects.
5. Lingard, *History of England*, vol. 7, p. 39n.
6. Ibid., p. 39.
7. Caraman, *Henry Garnet*, p. 308.
8. *Calendar of State Papers Venetian*, vol. 10, 1603–1607, ed. Horatio Brown (London, 1900), p. 87, Public Record Office, London.
9. Ibid., p. 87.
10. Alvin Kernan, *Shakespeare, the King's Playwright: Theater in the Stuart Court, 1603–1613* (New Haven, 1995), pp. 188ff.
11. Two sonnets in particular use topical references that indicate Shakespeare's reaction to James's accession. Sonnet 102 is a panegyric that refers to the death of the queen, 'the mortal moon', and welcomes the Stuart succession in the same terms as many others did at the time: 'peace proclaims olives of endless age'. Sonnet 125 is a fascinating discussion of Shakespeare's new role as James's court dramatist. It evokes the King's ceremonial entry into London when his procession passed through arches devised and constructed by the city's acting companies, decorated

with elaborately symbolic images of the 'eternal' and imperial Stuart line. The King was greeted en route by a series of learned speeches from Ben Jonson, among others. Records survive of the red livery issued to Shakespeare's company for this occasion, but though he 'bore the canopy' and honoured the 'outward' with 'my extern', Shakespeare denies that his own role in the new royal order implies compromise with Protestantism. The reference to the canopy relates the sonnet to the perennial debate among English Catholics about conformity. Gregory Martin's 1578 *Treatise of Schism* used scripture to prove that Catholic servants of the crown could attend Protestant services in order 'to bear the sword, the mace, the canopy, verge, train book etc'. (Peter Holmes, *Resistance and Compromise: The Political Thought of Elizabethan Catholics* [Cambridge, 1982], p. 92.) Contrary to appearances, Shakespeare asserts, the 'compound sweet' of the hybrid official religion is not for him. Unlike the 'pitiful thrivers' who have forsaken the 'gazing' old religion, he remains a 'true soul'.

12. The 2nd Viscount Montague was one. In 1603, he deputed Richard Smith, Lady Magdalen's chaplain, to join the 'tolerationist campaign to bend the Stuart King's ear'. Questier, *An English Catholic Community?* chap. 7, p. 44.

13. Antonia Fraser, *The Gunpowder Plot: Terror and Faith in 1605* (London, 1996), p. 78.

14. Ibid., chap. 5, 'Spanish Charity', passim; for the visit of the Spaniards to imprisoned Catholics, see p. 77.

15. The King's Men had already based an entire play on one of these incidents—*The Gowrie Conspiracy*, an attempt on his life that had been foiled, according to James, who enjoyed retelling the story, by his own courage and presence of mind. But the play had to be withdrawn, allegedly because it gave offence to one of the Queen's ladies-in-waiting, and the players were warned to avoid openly referring to contemporary events in future (see Chapter 12). James was also kidnapped by enemies at the age of sixteen and held prisoner for several months.

16. James signed himself I.R., Iacobus Rex.

17. Lancelot Gobbo in *The Merchant of Venice* argues with the fiend and his conscience, and the sonnets include a reflection on the 'two spirits', one fair and good, the other dark and evil, that haunt the speaker. The fullest development of the *psychomachia* occurs in *The Tempest*.

18. Cassio's name also contains a reference that typifies Shakespeare's 'witty' ingenuity. Iago's roundabout description of Cassio as 'an arithmetician' (1.1.19) associated with 'bookish theoric' of 'toga'd consuls' (1.1.24–25) connects him with the great champion of mathematics and time-reckoning, the fifth century consul and monk Cassiodorus, the aim of whose writings was to preserve the wisdom of men like Boethius from the coming Dark Ages. The allusion to Cassiodorus not only suggests man's highest faculties in contrast to Iago's animal nature but also acts as one of Shakespeare's 'calendar' markers, as Cassiodorus's book on the subject was widely used in the Middle Ages to calculate Easter; he believed that the *horologium*—an early form of clock—was the highest achievement of civilisation. Iago connects Cassio incontrovertibly with Cassiodorus with jibes about the equinox, and a unique Shakespearean word: 'He'll watch the *horologue* a double set' (2.3.122). Cassiodorus was also an authority on religious music and ancient wind instruments; Cassio is connected with 'clyster pipes' (2.1.178) and in an improbable scene, tries unsuccessfully to melt Othello's heart with the music of wind instruments— 'thereby hangs a tale', prompts the clown. See Duncan, *The Calendar*, p. 89. Yet

another name—that of Cassio's mistress, Bianca—indicates his Catholic following: 'Bianca', 'fair', is used for the same purpose in *The Taming of the Shrew*.

19. One of these engravings was addressed to James on his accession by Sir John Harington. See Gerard, *Autobiography of an Elizabethan*, pp. 96–107.

20. Jonson's comic Puritans in the *Alchemist* repeatedly refer to 'the holy cause', 'the sanctified cause', for which they will do anything, even a 'work of darkness': 'Good brother, we must bend unto all means / That may give furtherance to the holy cause'.

Chapter 12: The Powder Keg, 1605–1606

1. *Calendar of State Papers Venetian*, vol. 10, pp. 29–31.

2. Anothony Weldon, *The Court of King James* (London, 1650), p. 60.

3. Possibly a reference to Momford, a Jesuit, who in 1595 acted as an intermediary between the Spanish and the Irish. See Black, *Reign of Elizabeth*, p. 484.

4. 'Preface to Shakespeare and Selections from the Notes on the Plays', in *Johnson, Poetry and Prose*, edited by Mona Wilson (London, 1970), p. 593. Often mocked, Johnson's criticism of Shakespeare is frequently acute. He consistently draws attention to exactly those 'faults' that arise from the hidden level. In a trenchant paragraph (p. 500), he condemns Shakespeare's strange addiction to double meanings, speculating that they had 'some malignant power over his mind'; for their sake he 'lost the world, and was content to lose it'.

5. Pounde's grotesque treatment has gone largely unrecorded, but a manuscript account by Thomas Tresham describes the Star Chamber proceedings (Kilroy, *Edmund Campion*, pp. 100–101), one of Harington's epigrams refers to it, and in *The Judgement of a Catholic gentleman* in 1608 (p. 45), Robert Persons deplores 'the cruel sentence of cutting off the ears, of so ancient and venerable a gentleman as is M. Tho. Pound, that had lived above thirty years in sundry prisons only for being a Catholic, and now last in his old age, had that honour from God, as to be sentenced to lose his ears and stand on the pillory in divers markets for complaining of hard measure, and unjust execution, used against Catholics, contrary, (as he presumed) to his Majesty's intention'. There may be an echo of this notorious episode in Kent's 'low correction' in the stocks in *King Lear*.

6. Fraser, *Gunpowder Plot*, p. 189.

7. In March 1605, when the plot was already ten months underway, Cecil assured the Venetian Ambassador that 'a good Catholic must nurture in himself the firm resolve to be ready, for the preservation of his faith, to attack the life and government of his natural sovereign'. England was no longer at war with Catholic Europe, and there was no obvious terrorist threat, so the statement implies that Cecil was aware of the conspiracy from its very beginning, at least nine months before the projected explosion.

8. Here are some examples of the subtlety of Shakespeare's later code: 'hands' for executives; 'eyes' for leaders. The gunpowder plotters planned to blow up their own leaders along with the government.

9. This powerful image has been connected with Southwell's most famous poem, 'The Burning Babe', which Jonson said he would have destroyed many of his own to have written. Southwell's poem is an emblematic vision of Christ as a naked

child 'in the air', whose tears of pity contend with the fire of love, kindled by sin-ful man, which engulfs him.

10. A. C. Cawley, ed., *Everyman and Medieval Miracle Plays* (London, 1956), p. 176. The Centurion recounts in the York *Resurrection:* 'The sun for woe he waxed all wan, / The moon and stars of shining blan; / The earth trembled, and also man began to speak; / The stones, that never were stirred ere then, / Gan asunder to break; / And dead men rose, both great and small.' Note also the use of: 'eclipses', 'your veil rove in your kirk'.

11. Ibid., p. 165.

Chapter 13: The Post-Mortem, 1606–1608

1. Harold Bloom, *Shakespeare: The Invention of the Human* (London, 1999), p. 503.
2. These sonnets include numbers 127, 130, 134, 137, 138, 143, 144, 147, 149 and 152.
3. There is no space here to explore the contentious subject of Shakespeare's son-nets; however, an analysis of Sonnet 152 in the Appendix illustrates the way many of these poems, some of them deeply personal, can also be read on a coded level.
4. The question of the validity of mystical experience clearly preoccupied Shake-speare: the intensely meditative Sonnet 43 uses the imagery of shadow and reality to explore the question in a poetic form that predates Petrarch. For an introduc-tion to the tradition of mystical sonnets see Bernard O'Donoghue, *The Courtly Love Tradition* (Manchester, 1982), pp. 258–261.
5. See *Antony and Cleopatra*, ed. M. R. Ridley (London, 1965 [Arden Shakespeare]), p. xxxv.
6. Bloom, *Shakespeare*, p. 555.
7. Alan Haynes, *The Gunpowder Plot* (Stroud, 1994), p. 1.
8. See Glossary, 'Hercules'.
9. William Averell, *A Marvellous Combat of Contrarieties* (London, 1588).
10. William Camden's history of England, *Britannia*, quoted the tale of the belly as one of a number of 'Wise Speeches', and he gave it the same European context. According to Camden, the English Pope, Adrian IV, used the story to justify the right of the papacy, as centralised authority, to demand tribute from England. Shakespeare introduces a minor character named Adrian later in the play to strengthen the link; a similar play on the name occurs in *The Comedy of Errors*, where Adriana represents the pre-Reformation English church.
11. This was Lord Monteagle's view of Catesby. See Fraser, *Gunpowder Plot*, p. 91.
12. Throughout John Harington's heavily coded work *The Metamorphosis of Ajax*, he refers to certain noblemen as 'good freeholders, great housekeepers and builders'. They are glossed in marginalia as the Catholics Northumberland, Montague, Worcester and Lumley, all of whom underwent periods of confinement and who also patronised the construction of priest-holes by ingenious craftsmen such as Nicholas Owen. See Kilroy, *Edmund Campion*, pp. 89–120, for a study of the hid-den significance of *Ajax* and the rest of Harington's writings.
13. Ominously, Robert Catesby always dressed in red. This is one of the phrases that may have reminded spectators of this grim detail; another is 'his eye ['I'] / Red as 'twould burn Rome, and his injury / The goaler to his pity' (5.1.64–65).

14. The life of Timon of Athens was another familiar classical cautionary tale, which this time warned against improvidence. Timon is an open-handed patron who finds he has given away all his wealth. His friends abandon him, and he becomes a bitter misanthropist, living in the wild and cursing humanity, urging on the banished Alcibiades to return with an army to sack his native Athens. Shakespeare establishes a strong parallel between the early, prodigal Timon and King James, whose reckless generosity was legendary. He showered his favourites with lands, offices and jewels, granting over 800 knighthoods in his first year alone; under his slack direction, expenditure on the royal household rocketed. The play's unusually schematic format provides a skeletal version of Shakespeare's familiar persuasive technique. At first, the bait: a glamorised portrait of James in the Timon of the opening acts, a magnanimous, princely patron who enjoys philosophical debate, loves jewels, encourages poets and painters and masques, writes a little himself, feasts his friends and brushes aside the attempts of his steward to bring home to him the true state of his finances. And after the bait, the moral message— Timon falls. The hidden subject emerges as so often, in the third act. Shakespeare replaces Timon's hut in the original story with a cave, linking his ostracism to contemporary horror stories from Wales and the north of England, where noble families resorted to caves to avoid constant raids by pursuivants. The image of the embittered, dispossessed nobleman is accompanied by another recusant cameo: that of Alcibiades, banished for interceding on behalf of a disgraced friend.

15. Persons, *A Treatise tending to Mitigation*, p. 264.
16. Ibid., p. 33.
17. Kilroy, *Edmund Campion*, pp. 89–120.

Chapter 14: The Second Hope, 1608–1610

1. Susan Cole, *So Sweet a Star as Harry: A Consideration of Henry Frederick, Prince of Wales 1594–1612*, Royal Stuart Papers 39 (1992), p. 16.
2. Roy Strong, *Henry, Prince of Wales and England's Lost Renaissance* (London, 2000), p. 62.
3. Ibid.
4. Velma Bourgeois Richmond, *Shakespeare, Catholicism and Romance* (New York, 2000), p. 74.
5. Strong, *Henry*, p. 154.
6. John Hayward, *First Part of the Life and Reign of Henry IV*, 1599. Hayward was imprisoned in spite of an ingenious defence in the Star Chamber by Francis Bacon, who argued Hayward was guilty of theft, not treason, as so much of the text was lifted from Tacitus. Bacon's defence is echoed by Hamlet, who claimed that *The Mousetrap* was translated from an extant source, 'written in very choice Italian'. Many translations at the time contained a coded subtext: Thomas Watson's madrigals, for instance.
7. Strong, *Henry*, p. 93.
8. Shell, *Catholicism, Controversy and Imagination*, p. 206.
9. Shakespeare is meticulous in his use of dates. If the earthquake during which Marina is born refers back to 1580, then the final scene in the play, which takes place twenty-eight years later, brings the audience up to 1608 (Marina is fourteen

years old when she is captured by pirates, and is reunited fourteen years after that with her father). This extraordinary attention to detail is an indication of the care that went into his 'coded' subtext.

10. Shakespeare has already used the story of the retired abbess as an image of the survival of the old faith in *The Comedy of Errors*, also partly based on Gower's poem.

11. This is another instance of the paired and reciprocal truths of Protestantism and Catholicism. However quarrelsome at first, they are eventually united in Shakespeare's plays so far, and include the Antipholus twins; Julia and Silvia; the shrew and Bianca; Hermia and Helena; and the harmonious cousins, Celia and Rosalind. Here, however, they remain separated.

12. See Glossary, 'Miracle'.

13. *Johnson, Poetry and Prose*, p. 609.

14. Strong, *Henry*, p. 109.

15. A. L. Rowse, *The England of Elizabeth* (London, 1950), p. 64.

16. The snide, contentious atmosphere of the college evokes accounts of the 'stirs' in the English College at Rome that added fuel to the Appellant Controversy.

17. Another reduction of his 'noted weed' to its bare essentials occurs in Pericles: 'Did you not name a tempest, / A birth and death?' (5.3.33–34).

18. This was given spiritual application. Unbelievers 'lacked the head of faith . . . him who is the head of man, namely Christ' (Aponius, quoted in Karl Rahner, *Greek Myths and Christian Mystery* (New York, 1971), pp. 267ff.

19. Samuel Daniel also includes it in his Investiture masque, *Tethys*, calling it the 'Port of Union'.

Chapter 15: Silenced, 1610–1611

1. 'To My Muse', Epigrammes LXV, *Poems of Ben Jonson*, p. 31.

2. From Jonson's preface to the First Folio of Shakespeare's plays: 'To the Memory of my Beloved, the Author Mr. William Shakespeare', *Norton Shakespeare*, p. 3352.

3. Questier, *An English Catholic Community?*, p. 16.

4. See Appendix: Sonnet 152.

5. 'On Play-wright', Epigrammes LXVIII, *Poems of Ben Jonson*, p. 33.

6. 'Timber: or, Discoveries; Made upon Men and Matter', *Ben Jonson's Works*, ed. William Gifford (London, 1816), vol. 9, p. 175.

7. See Glossary, 'Caesar'.

8. Jonson changed these Italian names to non-Catholic English ones in his 1616 version of *Every Man in His Humour*.

9. Shakespeare's Sonnets 44 and 45. Pericles mentions the same human ingredients at Marina's birth: 'Thou hast as chiding a nativity / As fire, air, water, earth, and heaven can make' (3.2.32–33).

10. Another insight into the discrimination involved in Shakespeare's creativity occurs in *Rape of Lucrece*, as Lucrece sits down to write: 'What wit sets down is blotted straight with will / This is too curious-good, this blunt and ill; / Much like a press of people at a door, / Throng her inventions, which shall go before' (lines 1298–1302).

11. This key section, recalling his consistent standpoint, includes a hidden signature: 'The strong-based promontory / Have I made *shake*, and by the *spur*s plucked up / The pine and cedar' (5.1.47–48).

12. The year 1610 saw the completion of Henry's cherished project, the construction
of a spectacular ship, the *Prince Royal.* In that year, too, Henry became the patron
of a company set up to look for a north-west passage in the wake of Henry Hud-
son's voyages, an enterprise that appealed to his practical mind. Henry's instructions to the expedition that eventually set sail under Thomas Button in 1612 are
characteristic, advising him to keep strict records and to enforce moral discipline.
There was to be no drunkenness or lewdness or quarrelling, but 'let there be a
religious care throughout your shippes'. The play's 'royal, good and gallant ship',
the nautical terms, and the character of the boatswain whom Gonzago repeatedly
says is born to be hanged are all details that reflect Henry's obsession with the
navy and the intimate knowledge of ship-building that he owed to the shipwright
Phineas Pett. Pett became a close friend of the Prince, who successfully defended
him against a charge of corruption (of which he was, in fact, guilty). After the trial,
the Prince proclaimed that it was Pett's accusers who deserved hanging. Strong,
Henry, pp. 35–41.

Chapter 16: 'The Lost Man', 1611 and After

1. Epigrammes LVI, *Poems of Ben Jonson,* p. 27. The poet-ape at first gained a 'little
wealth and credit' by picking and gleaning from old plays. Now he 'takes up all,
makes each man's wit his own', and at the same time 'slights' his collaborators.
'Such crimes / The sluggish gaping auditor devours / He marks not whose 'twas
first: and after-times / May judge it to be his, as well as ours'.
2. C. H. Herford, ed., *The Two Noble Kinsmen, Fletcher and Shakespeare,* Temple edition (London, 1897), introduction, p. vii.
3. Ibid., p. vi.
4. *Norton Shakespeare,* p. 3113.
5. Samuel Johnson notes 'a subtle and covert censure of his other works' by the
writer, who, 'whoever he was', 'intended no great kindness to Shakespeare'. *Johnson, Poetry and Prose,* p. 587.
6. Along with Chapman and Beaumont, Jonson had in fact contributed a preface to
The Faithful Shepherdess—a commission that he adroitly used to record the fact
that its first performance was a dismal failure. Jonson was clearly riled by
Fletcher's presumption to be 'upmost on the muses' hill' after only 'one poor
flight'.
7. 'To My Muse', Epigramme LXV, *Poems of Ben Jonson,* p. 31.
8. The name Aeglamour suggests love of radiance or sunlight.
9. This portrait bears out the theory that Jonson staged Shakespeare as Virgil in his
1601 satire about literary London, *Poetaster,* in which he himself figured as the
poet Horace, castigating his critics, Dekker and Marston. Little is known of Virgil, except that he came from Mantua. Jonson's Virgil comes from the Campagna
(the countryside, or suburbs, around Rome), and in a detailed discussion in Act V,
he is given the characteristics Jonson attributes to Shakespeare in his preface to
the First Folio and in *The Sad Shepherd.* He has excellent judgement, a temperament 'refined / From all the tartarous moods of common men', and is as 'clear and
confident as Jove'. He is also self-critical to a fault, perpetually dissatisfied with
his own work. As in the First Folio preface, Jonson describes him as a timeless

genius. His work is not obviously learned, but 'direct and analytic', 'rammed with life', 'laboured and distilled' and so universally applicable that 'could a man remember but his lines' his own life would be governed by the same magnanimous spirit.

10. 'He was not a company keeper lived in Shoreditch, wouldn't be debauched, and if invited to writ he was in paine'. John Aubrey, quoted in Honan, *Shakespeare*, p. 122.

11. 'An elegy upon the death of John Donne', *Penguin Book of Renaissance Verse*, pp. 741–743.

12. The influence of this single passage by Fletcher has been immense. A. L. Rowse uses it as evidence that Elizabeth's reign was 'a long period of internal peace: that is the theme of the famous speech Shakespeare put into the mouth of Cranmer in *Henry VIII*: like Shakespeare's whole attitude on such matters it was representative, not exceptional' 'Queen Elizabeth and the Historians', in *Past Masters, the Best of History Today*, ed. Daniel Snowman [Stroud, 2001], p. 48. This is typical of the way misrepresented work by Shakespeare is still used as evidence of the country's peaceful acceptance of Elizabethan Protestantism.

Glossary

1. Samuel Daniel, 'Musophilus', *Poems and a Defence of Ryme*, ed. Arthur Colby Sprague (Chicago and London, 1965), lines 567–578, p. 85.

2. Christopher Marlowe, *The Massacre at Paris*, from *The Plays of Christopher Marlowe* (London, 1969), lines 1027–1028.

3. *The Mirror for Magistrates* includes the story of Nennius, a mythical British leader who resisted Caesar. The tale has an explicit moral: it 'encourageth all good subjects to defend their country from the power of foreign and usurping enemies'.

4. 'Timber', *Ben Jonson's Works*, vol. 9, p. 175. The literary parallel between imperial Rome and the Rome of the papacy was a familiar one, dating back at least as far as the works of Petrarch in the fourteenth century. Spenser and Edmund Campion both wrote poems relating the two Romes.

5. MacCulloch, *Reformation*, p. 550.

6. Letter from Southwell to Robert Cecil, 1593, quoted in Pilarz, *Robert Southwell*, p. 275.

7. Lawrence Manley, ed. *London in the Age of Shakespeare* (London, 1986). John Johnston called London the 'lightsome eye' in 1586 (p. 62), and in 1636, Wenceslas Clemens called it the 'eye and theatre of the world' (p. 69).

8. The English Jesuits were on bad terms with the English Benedictines, in spite of the monks' newly reformed identity.

9. See Shell, *Catholicism, Controversy and Imagination*, p. 175, on the tropos of 'Weeping England' in sixteenth-century English writing.

10. 'Miracles are ceased', *Henry V* (1.1.67); 'They say miracles are past', *All's Well That Ends Well*, (2.3.1).

11. 'The Hind and Panther', part 2, lines 497–510, in John Dryden (1631–1700), *The Poems and Fables of John Dryden*, ed. James Kinsley (Oxford, 1970). Dryden's magnificent poem is one of the most accessible entry points into the perennial English debate between Catholic and Protestant. Dryden seized the opportunity of a brief period of Catholic toleration to state the two opposing arguments in an animal

fable that picks up the same terms and images for the two religions that Shakespeare and his contemporaries deployed after the Reformation. In particular, his Catholic hind embodies the four 'marks' of the true church (one, true, holy and apostolic) that were such a bone of contention among sixteenth-century apologists (part 2, 525–638); these four marks are embodied in similar form by the allegorical figures in Shakespeare's plays who represent ideal Catholicism.

12. Lucy E.C. Wooding, *Rethinking Catholicism in Reformation England* (Oxford, 2000), p. 238.
13. Kilroy, *Edmund Campion*, pp. 39–58. Campion's poem on Rome is transcribed on pp. 49–194.
14. In *Love's Martyr*, the collection that includes Shakespeare's *Phoenix and Turtle*, published 1601.
15. John Leslie, *A Treatise of Treasons*, quoted in Gary D. Hamilton, 'Mocking Oldcastle', in *Shakespeare and the Culture of Christianity in Early Modern England*, ed. Dennis Taylor and David Beauregard (New York, 2003), p. 152.
16. See Shell, *Catholicism, Controversy and Imagination*, p. 188, for the various ways Catholic writers associated the imagery of water with their situation.

Index

PUBLICAFFAIRS is a publishing house founded in 1997. It is a tribute to the standards, values, and flair of three persons who have served as mentors to countless reporters, writers, editors, and book people of all kinds, including me.

I. F. STONE, proprietor of *I. F. Stone's Weekly,* combined a commitment to the First Amendment with entrepreneurial zeal and reporting skill and became one of the great independent journalists in American history. At the age of eighty, Izzy published *The Trial of Socrates,* which was a national bestseller. He wrote the book after he taught himself ancient Greek.

BENJAMIN C. BRADLEE was for nearly thirty years the charismatic editorial leader of *The Washington Post.* It was Ben who gave the *Post* the range and courage to pursue such historic issues as Watergate. He supported his reporters with a tenacity that made them fearless, and it is no accident that so many became authors of influential, best-selling books.

ROBERT L. BERNSTEIN, the chief executive of Random House for more than a quarter century, guided one of the nation's premier publishing houses. Bob was personally responsible for many books of political dissent and argument that challenged tyranny around the globe. He is also the founder and was the longtime chair of Human Rights Watch, one of the most respected human rights organizations in the world.

.   .   .

For fifty years, the banner of Public Affairs Press was carried by its owner Morris B. Schnapper, who published Gandhi, Nasser, Toynbee, Truman, and about 1,500 other authors. In 1983 Schnapper was described by *The Washington Post* as "a redoubtable gadfly." His legacy will endure in the books to come.

Peter Osnos, *Publisher*